The Logic of Automation and Writings in Economic and Political Sociology: Collected Essays

By L. Larry Liu

3

Table of Contents

7

Preface

Since the publication of *The Terminology of Bon Vivant Life and Other Sociological Insights: Collected Essays* (which chronicled my sociological insights during my time in the University of Oxford) two years ago, I have entered graduate school in Princeton University. Parallel to doing the coursework, doing quantitative assignments, writing an empirical paper, mulling over a dissertation topic, meeting with my adviser and professors, reading academic journals, attending academic conferences, submitting research papers to journals (no luck, thus far) and geeking out with fellow graduate students in the hallway, I have continued typing my blog posts, attempting to write at least two or three posts a month.[1]

Psychologically, I felt this was the only way to survive graduate school, because the tediousness of the research enterprise (the endless rounds of revision, the reading and reviewing of literature, the back and forth in the workshops and seminars, the cleaning of data etc.) contrasts sharply with the carelessness and stream-of-consciousness of writing blog posts, where I could develop my ideas freely without the constraints and high standards of the academic profession. Oftentimes the content in the blog was closely related to my academic passions, involving topics like the logic of automation of work, the universal basic income, the crisis and future of capitalism, but also broader topics like the rise of populism and authoritarianism, the political effects of extreme inequality, or simply country-specific histories to explain political events in Austria, Hungary, Zimbabwe or South Africa.

I also owe a great debt to my former mentor and undergraduate adviser, Randall Collins, whose thoughts on capitalism, violence, social stratification and emotional energy, which are also fleshed out in his own blog,[2] have spurred on my own ruminations. His macrosociology made me think about the crisis of capitalism and the logic of automation, while his microsociology made me pay attention to Theresa May's and Hillary Clinton's body language and the charisma of musicians like Elton John and Nile Rodgers.

In a world, where a lot of false advice and information circulates around the web, does it make sense to read and write blog posts? I insist that it absolutely makes sense. The victory of Donald Trump in

---

[1] Mr. Liu's Opinion, https://liamchingliu.wordpress.com
[2] Sociological Eye, http://sociological-eye.blogspot.com

the presidential elections implies that the belief and trust in existing institutions like the media or the political system have been undermined. At the same time, people have many more different potential sources for information, which has challenged the business model of mainstream TV stations and newspapers. In this confusing era, is it not all the more important to retain political and social commentary from the perspective of an academic? Despite facing the increasing market pressures of neoliberalism, the academic could choose to stand on the sideline and not address the pressing reality of worsening employment relations, toxic and authoritarian politics and climate change. But Noam Chomsky (1967) has been right to point out that intellectuals can choose between being court intellectuals, helping the powerful defend their imperialist policies, or critical intellectuals, who analyze and reveal the true intentions of their government. In other words, the academic cannot afford to remain silent, and must use his privilege to engage in public discourse.

Some readers may be dumbfounded by my chosen title, because there are only two posts that bear the title "Logic of Automation", which is the single-biggest thematic concern that I brought into my academic studies. Even though the posts deal with a great variety of topics, one of the biggest undercurrents is the social and economic theory developed by Karl Marx, namely that the dynamism of the capitalist economy comes from the gradual replacement of workers (the 'variable capital' in Marxian language) by technology (the 'constant capital'). My underlying argument is to reflect on the current political malaise, in which we produce economic growth that benefit the owners of capital and technology without allowing ordinary working people to benefit from this arrangement. In the absence of calls to nationalize the machines, capital taxes have to increase to fund the strengthening of the social safety net, such as a universal basic income. If we do not appropriately manage the ensuing automation wave, then a turn toward fascist politics and demeaning the Other (immigrants, minorities) could engulf the world into a destruction of the liberal order, which we have grown used to. The liberal order is already declining as we speak, because immigration laws in the west become tighter, populist leaders are intent on weakening courts, parliaments and the media, while free trade is undermined by the current US administration. Trade deals among the other great countries are still signed, but I doubt the global free trade sentiment will continue once the US isolates. Progress is not linear, but fragile.

The current batch of posts, which are chronologically ordered (there is no other way to organize it), range from September 2016 to June 2018, and cover a broad array of topics. If you, the reader, enjoy these op-eds and analyses I offer, and discuss it with friends, family and colleagues over coffee or tea, this collection will have been worthwhile publishing. Thank you for your support.

L. Larry Liu
July 2018
Princeton, NJ

Limits to Political Correctness
Posted on September 5, 2016

The University of Chicago made a big row over a letter that the dean sent to the incoming freshmen students by stating that the university does not support 'trigger warnings', disinviting speakers, whose views are opposed by many in the student body, and creating intellectual 'safe spaces', where people can retreat from views different from their own (Schaper 2016). For those, who are unfamiliar with the university jargon, a 'trigger warning' is when the professor warns the student before he brings up a controversial topic, which could hurt the feelings of the student, e.g. military combat, child abuse, incest and sexual violence. Many professors have reacted to the demand for trigger warnings by including the trigger warning in the class syllabus and before every new reading with the potential of requiring a trigger warning (Manne 2015).

Are there strong merits for implementing trigger warnings or does this heightened political correctness reflect the oversensitization of the modern student body? I would side with the latter case, but would actually find it more useful to reflect on the question of the origin of trigger warnings. One narrative we could spin is that the 1960s student struggle for inclusiveness and women's, gay, minority, civil and disability rights had been successful, and that after so many years of pushing for more inclusiveness and rights, trigger warnings are the final piece of inclusiveness. How can I feel included if my feelings are violated by offensive reading material?

While I strongly support the traditional struggle for inclusiveness coming from the 1960s, it is difficult to make the case that not reading offensive material or having to be warned about them fits in this inclusiveness discourse. I have substantially benefited from a liberal arts and humanities education, and would have found it troubling if I needed to be trigger warned about potentially disturbing reading material. It is part of growing up and learning to be confronted with mentally upsetting content, so I find no problem with having no trigger warnings.

But to focus on the struggles of the student movement would be an overly demand-side focused approach and neglect the supply-side, i.e. the college administrators, who have consented with the trigger warnings. If we reflect on the political economy of higher education, there is no doubt that the increasing college tuition (and top administrative salaries and staff, see critique in Ginsberg 2011) and the decreasing level of state funding (or 'neoliberalization of higher education') has transformed higher education from a place of learning to a place of meeting customer needs. The higher sticker prices for most colleges results in the increased desire of administrators to give their students an awesome experience, akin to a Disney World amusement park. Massive investments go toward creating nice gyms, football stadiums, recreation facilities and 'safe spaces'.

The formula is rather simple: no perks, no students, no money and vice versa. Of course, the administrator reckons, there are plenty of students who could care less about trigger warnings and political correctness, but the point is that even if a minority of students demanded that political correctness, it has to be granted because offending that group creates controversy, and controversy lowers the university's reputation. An unsensitive student is unlikely to not apply to a university with high political correctness standards, but a sensitive student is likely to not apply to a university with low political correctness standards (and potentially influence their less sensitive peers in their application decision as well). So better be safe with high standards. One might say that students desire to be safe from harmful intellectual exposure would not have come about without the neoliberalization of higher education.

Among the faculty, there seems to be a split opinion with regard to the trigger warnings and the heightened sense of political correctness. Many professors themselves come from the most left-leaning part of society, and they probably agree with the 'inclusiveness' agenda of the student body (the older professors now were in fact the forefront of the 1960s student movement). But there are some faculty, who recognize the limitation of heightened political correctness, but would have to go along because administrators and vocal student groups expect it of them.

Administrators, who rarely deal with students personally or academically, don't really care about the substance of the political correctness debate, but they do care about maximizing the customer satisfaction ratings that students and their parents give to the university. Given that there are so many universities, who compete for the education dollars of students, there is scarcely any administrator, who can afford to offend students. The University of Chicago might be a special case here, where the high reputation insulates them from customer fright. Try to replicate the dean's letter in a less well-known college.

My argument can be summarized as such: while trigger warnings and political correctness may be characterized as the final part of the 'inclusiveness' agenda, the neoliberalization of higher education is another crucial element to facilitate the growth of extreme political correctness. Countries that retained strong public funding for universities (central and northern Europe) have equally expanded political rights to previously excluded groups (women, minorities etc.), but have, thus far, restrained from the latest stage of political correctness. It might be that trigger warnings are coming to Europe as well, and I lack the data on it. But the customer-orientation of the university 'enterprise' (no pun intended) has not fully seeped in there yet, and will be unlikely to do so as long as the state's commitment to public higher education remains strong.

Endorsement for Hillary Clinton for the US Presidential Elections

Posted on October 7, 2016

Regular readers of my blog can follow the evolution of my views on the US presidential elections. I have been an ardent Bernie supporter (Liu 2016a), and then opted for abstention (Liu 2016c), then for any choice (Liu 2016e), and now a month before the general election, where people have to choose between Trump, Clinton, Johnson (Libertarian), Stein (Green) or abstain, I endorse Hillary Clinton for the US presidency. Let me justify in as clear terms as possible why I endorse Clinton rather than any other option.

Donald Trump is actually a horrendous choice for the American people. I had previously argued that while he may be a bad choice, he would shake up the system as an anti-establishment politician. But if we consider his positions carefully, Trump is more than willing to cut Social Security, give tax breaks to rich people like himself (he does not even pay any taxes, as reported leaks show), and harm the interest of the working class, whom he pretends to support. His pivot for the working class has been his stance on trade, which is to rip up trade agreements, and impose tariffs on foreign imports. But it is questionable how many jobs can be brought back, especially since automation has contributed mostly to a reduction in manufacturing employment. More important than trade (most jobs are in the non-tradable sector) are robust minimum-wage, public job creation and social insurance schemes (especially a universal basic income) to help working people, but he clearly has no support for these policies.

Trump is also a bigot, who is not afraid to bash another group of people that look different from him, whether it be minorities, immigrants or women. It is ironic that his most ardent supporters love him even more when he says outrageous things, because they take it to mean that he is authentic. But authentic about what? Authenticity is a rather neutral trait and can only mean something positive if the policies that he pursues will benefit the ordinary person. To be an authentic bigot is TV entertainment at best, and social discord at worst. This bigotry and throwing tantrums will then be the permanent sight when he is in the White House, which might be great for the ad revenues of the big TV stations, but bad news for people that are hungry for better economic policy.

Hillary Clinton has many progressive positions on her campaign plank. One of the reasons why Clinton has been counted to the establishment was because of Bernie Sanders running to her left. During the primary season, she counted herself as a moderate candidate, who would get "realistic" done things, which most progressive people understood to mean the preservation of the status quo. Given that the status quo is not helping people with significant college debt, medical bills and low-wage jobs, there is no reason why ordinary people should support Clinton. But when the primary was over, Clinton realized that she had to unify the Democratic Party by bringing the Bernie-populist wing into her camp for the November elections, so she has shifted on some political positions. On health care, she now supports a public option. On higher education, she would institute free college tuition for the bottom 83% of the income distribution. On the estate tax, she would bump up the top tax rate to 65%. Her social and economic plans will, therefore, bump up the weak welfare state, while paying for it with surtaxes on the wealthy.

Not even Bill Clinton would have gone this far. In an interview with Charlie Rose, he admitted that the Hillary platform is way to the left of the 1992 Democratic Leadership Conference platform on which Bill Clinton ran on. But political realities shift, and so do the Clintons.

Cynics might counter that there is no reason why Clinton would have to carry out a progressive agenda once she gets elected. We might think that all she cares about is to channel the Bernie-voters to turn out for her, and then return to the status quo once elected. When the progressive base is angry and disappointed, she will all blame it on a Republican opposition, which is still controlling Congress. Let us not forget that government gridlock tends to benefit the forces of the status quo, which includes the powerful lobbyists and the wealthy. That will serve the Democrats and Republicans very well. We know that Clinton receives enormous lobbying money from the banks and the corporations, and to assume that she is not influenced by this money is ridiculous.

That makes it all the more necessary for the progressive base to hold her accountable, but that is even beside the point here. Because in the presidential elections, we have a binary choice between Clinton and Trump, and all that matters is that the crazy candidate does not win. It is an existentially stupid choice to have, but the 2016 elections confine us to two non-optimal choices.

The challenge will naturally be how to convince the angry white working class that is backing Trump to shift their allegiance to Clinton. That is unlikely to happen. An interesting ethnography by

Arlie Hochschild (2016) reveals that Tea Party and Trump supporters have this strange ideology that the political establishment is betraying them, and that the government is to blame for helping out poor welfare recipients. Rather than blaming the whole political economy that rigs the economy in favor of the rich, the Trump supporters are more likely to blame Muslims, immigrants, welfare recipients and other marginal groups. They seem to be saying that they don't have much, but they don't want that little to be taken by these other marginal groups. To have to say that in the richest economy of the world is pathetic. One is reminded of the comic with the banker, the Tea Party supporter and the trade union member. The banker takes 19 of the 20 cookies and tells the Tea Party supporter that the union member wants to take away the last remaining cookie.

What is ultimately ironic is that the average Trump voter will be worse off with Trump at the helm. His vice presidential candidate is Mike Pence, one of those Republican governors, who when in Congress supported this awful Paul Ryan budget, which intended to savage the social programs. That is what Trump will be after as well, even though he cleverly blinds his followers with his insistence on trade policies.

Now, what about Johnson and Stein? Johnson is a libertarian, who wants to eliminate income and corporation taxes and replace it with a value-added tax, which is quite regressive. He wants coal and nuclear power plants, which is the energy policy of the past. He wants to repeal the Affordable Care Act and wants a "market" based health care system, whatever that means. These are all policies, which are going to increase income inequality, so he is not a good choice. Stein is a member of the Green Party, and pushes different progressive policies, like better social policies, a single-payer health care system, tuition-free colleges, a 15 dollar an hour minimum wage and many other positions that make sense. It would be natural for progressives to support Stein.

But the problem in this calculation is that unless over 50% of the people can be convinced to vote for Stein, she won't win the elections. There is tremendous inertia in the US political system, which makes it unlikely for her to win. Winning is really what matters. Stein has the potential to absorb a portion of the hardcore Bernie supporters, who would otherwise have backed Clinton. If there are enough progressives, who either stay home or vote for Stein, then Clinton could lose the elections, and Trump will win the elections. Bernie Sanders has made this point too in recent interviews.

The American people will make a momentous choice in November. There will be no guarantee that the policies will change when Hillary Clinton becomes president, but there is a shot for it if progressive pressure continues on her into the next years. There will be no shot at all for any progressive policies when Trump becomes the next president.

On Priests and Jesters
Posted on October 20, 2016

In the book that launched his career, Simone Polillo (2013) writes of the sociological conflict between so-called conservative and wildcat bankers. The conservative bankers ally themselves with government lawmakers to have strict laws on who is considered creditworthy. Their goal is to maintain the dominance over who gets to receive credit. These conservative bankers get challenged by wildcat bankers, who expand the realm of creditworthiness, and then force other financial institutions to also loosen their financial standards or they won't get the same share of the business. What is considered creditworthy is, thus, subject to historical change.

For us sociologists, the view of the binary conflict has substantial heuristic advantages, and very much defines the conflict sociological perspective. The classic thinker in conflict sociology is Karl Marx, who divided the social world in two classes, who are battling each other in the social economy: the feudal lords against the bourgeoisie, and the capitalists against the workers.

When the French Revolution happened, the political terms "left" and "right" were created. The left signified the people, who sat on the left of the podium in the national assembly and consisted of the Jacobins and the radicals. These were the people, who screamed for an end to the monarchy, the beginning of equality, freedom, justice, a new calendar, new science and the new republic. On the right sat people, who defended the status quo, the monarchy, the aristocracy, what is known and what is familiar. Edmund Burke (1790) had famously attacked the French Revolution for throwing overboard all the institutions, which retained stability in France. He pointed to the bloodshed, the devastation, the mass executions and the near civil war as the inevitable outcome of the revolution. Eventually, Napoleon Bonaparte took over and the masses were flocking to him, so as to re-embrace stability. But the radicals naturally deserve a fair hearing too: who would consider it just when a few people own much of the wealth of society while letting people, who do all of the labor, live in poverty?

The overall point in this contention is simply that there are binary social forces that signify social conflict and usually contain the element of change. The one force tends to be conservative and wants to preserve what is already there, and the other force is discontent with the status quo and wants to shake things up. In this post, I focus on the community that I know best: academia. Whenever I meet academics, I evaluate them based on their substantive research interests, their intellectual persona (which not everyone has, e.g. pure positivists, who "do science", but do not live and breathe it and retain curiosity in many aspects of life- and I do admit that my experience in Oxford has spoiled me in my views), and on whether they are academic priests or jesters.

This might sound like very harsh terminology to use to evaluate colleagues, but it became crystal-clear to me once I found myself on the 'jester' side of the fence. (Priests being more conservative can afford to be ignorant on this distinction, similar to whites not having to worry about race relations because they belong to the dominant racial group.) Let me begin by where this term comes from: the ardent Polish communist and anti-cleric, Leszek Kolakowski, eventually became an ardent anti-communist and cleric. What an intellectual biography! In his later years, he compared Marxism to a religion because of the eschatological element that all contradictions will result in a final resolution and that all human suffering will be dissolved in a final day of judgment.

Ardent Marxists become priests (conservative), who defend the catechism with rational and less rational arguments, and their critics become jesters (radicals), who reject any form of rigid thought and value a high degree of skepticism (Connelly 2013; think of Popper's (1963) principle of scientific falsifiability, which Marxism does not meet in his eyes). Within Christianity, we have 'priest' priests, who uphold the actual catechism, and the 'jester' Martin Luther types, who simply question the catechism (though sometimes becoming priests for the new religion themselves rather than perennial critics, like Noam Chomsky).

For academics in general, I consider a priest to be someone, who wants to maintain strict standards in his field and in his profession, and a jester is someone, who has a general sense of those standards, but might be critical of them and welcome alternative standards.

A priest might ask whether someone is asking legitimate research questions, citing the appropriate literature, applying the right method the right way. When they are at the journal referee, hiring and tenure evaluation side of things, they will be the most uncomfortable to deal with.

A jester is fine when all of these factors are somewhat fulfilled, but direct most of their energy to speak of their substantive interests in the research. When they are on the evaluation side, they are purposefully lenient, and probably have a good understanding that scholarly life is about the leisure of thought and independent inquiry rather than six top journal articles and the academic press book. Sure, devote your life to science, but don't forget to smell the flowers.

Now, some people may say that it is the academic institution, which forces us to become priests, even if we don't want to. Let's not forget that the academic standards for tenure have increased because the universities are minting too many graduates relative to the available tenure employment. And as a sociologist and institutionalist, I would be foolish to ignore these structural constraints, especially because it's by making this point that we see our field's value-added. But all of these forces don't matter at the *individual* level even if they matter at the *structural* level. We strangely still see both priest and jester types even as the academic competition has become harsher.

Another complication to the theory is that single individuals may be both priests and jesters but at different contexts. Think of a lenient grader for students and a harsh reviewer in academic journals or vice versa. This is true, but I am just dealing with Weberian ideal-types, and will not be able to make a comment on variations in all cases (though that is ultimately the goal of the ideal-type: to compare the real cases with the ideal-type).

We also need to qualify the theory for older vs. younger faculty, which I made in an earlier post (Liu 2016b). It is from my experience that the older faculty (jesters) tend to be more relaxed than the younger faculty (priests), and that could be the result of the fact that graduate training has become more rigorous for the younger cohort of teachers. It could be that coming fresh out of the methods training that one want to apply those standards as strictly as possible. It could be that the harsher tenure environment ups not only the standards of "good research" but also the general expectations of it. This is similar to the education credentialing phenomenon widely observed in sociology (Collins 1979). As more and more people get a college diploma, it is worth less in the labor market, and will be expected of all job applicants rather than make the degree holder stand out from the rest of the crowd. For whatever reason, the inclination of the older faculty is generally associated with more relaxed standards.

Let me use an example of an academic workshop that I attend. I am relatively new to this kind of academic format, where all the participants read one person's work, usually a dissertation chapter or a draft journal article, and criticize it. There is one discussant, who writes the critique up, and the rest just chime in with comments and verbal feedback. The research area is not particularly of interest to me, but the critical attitudes of the audience was. I distinguish between three types of people in the workshop: the senior professor, who is also the convener, or jester; the junior professors, or the priests; and the graduate students, some of whom becoming priests and others being loyal to jesters.

The senior professor would lean back in his chair and listen intently without ever raising any questions or criticism. He would nod along with interest, and laugh when everyone else does. It seems like he is just attending the meeting to learn something about the paper and the research. The junior professors pay close attention to the arrangement of the paper (footnotes vs. main body; topic sentences, paragraph structure, logic), the rhetorical impact, the citation of the 'proper' literature, the use of evidence. "We know how this academic game is played, so make sure you tick the right checkboxes."

With the graduate students there is not much of a clear pattern, and most line up between the extremes. I suspect that the younger graduate students retain their default jester position, because of their inexperience with critically evaluating arguments and papers. Given enough time and continued exposure to the comprehensive experience of academic life, they might adopt the same mentality as the junior professors. As of now, I consider myself a jester, because the structural flaws in the papers that I read are not so interesting or not so obvious as much as the content of the argument and whether it poses any substantive interest to me.

Conflict drives historical progress, as Hegel might have claimed. It is only when conservatives and radicals, priests and jesters clash that new truths are uncovered. The priests are the standard bearers of orthodoxy, while the jesters are trolling and questioning those standards. What the two sides have in common is that a conservative cannot live without the jester and that a jester cannot live without the priest, because without the critics, there is nothing that needs defense, and without a standard bearer there is no standard to be violated. One of my jester professors (on par with a bon vivant intellectual) said, "There are two types of people. Those who divide the world in two and those who don't." To perfectly contradict herself, I considered her to be part of the latter category (if we exempt the first sentence in the quote). She enjoyed social theory and considered all social science discipline as being related and one.

She likes to violate conceptual boundaries and occasionally pontificate on topics dear to her heart. And I think she also likes to smell the flowers.

Responding to Left-Criticism of UBI
Posted on October 23, 2016

I address a criticism of the universal basic income from the left (Roberts 2016).

Roberts claims that a UBI does nothing to alter the class power relations in society (technology owners will remain owners), and that the right-wing would support UBI only if it lowers the cost of labor. On the latter point, it will be a struggle to define a UBI that is sufficient for the necessities of life, while still enforcing strong wage claims on those still in employment. The counter-argument would be that UBI would raise the reservation wage, which suggests an upward rather than a downward pressure on wages. We'll just have to see where the chips fall.

On the first point, I would also question the current power structure, but being discontent with current ownership structures is NOT an invalidation of the UBI. We might say that under technology-nationalization the UBI becomes more independent of the political ruminations of the current private owners to willy-nilly refuse tax payments, which could undermine the financing of the UBI regime. But the second best option of retaining private property and have a technology tax finance the UBI is still technically feasible. But both objections are not substantive enough to undermine the benefits of UBI.

Roberts has a strong preference for work shortening and full employment, which suggests that a UBI would not be his immediate priority. But the libertarian inclination in me, which suggests that people are supposed to be have the freedom to reject an abusive or bad employer, would prioritize UBI, though I will never oppose full employment and work-shortening proposals. Either way, full employment and UBI would have to lower the current asset mountains of the 1%, which is indubitably contentious.

Presidential Body Language: A Microsociology

Posted on October 31, 2016

Both major presidential contenders, Hillary Clinton and Donald Trump, cannot miss out on the Alfred Smith dinner, which sells expensive dinners to business people and political leaders to fund Catholic charities "to support the neediest children of the Archdiocese in New York, regardless of race, creed, or color" (Wikipedia, "Alfred E. Smith Memorial Foundation Dinner"). In such a high-profile event, the charity tends to be able to raise more money, so they raked in 6 million dollars in one night. Clinton and Trump both attended the event and were strategically seated next to Cardinal Thomas Dolan.

Both of the presidential candidates deliberately look relaxed, as if they were enjoying the dinner. When Trump was called to do the speech, he had to go past Clinton to get on the podium and even tapped Clinton on the shoulder. The speeches themselves were entertaining to read, as they were knocking each other for their weaknesses. Trump called Clinton corrupt (Trump transcript),[3] and Clinton called Trump out for his bad temper and bigotry (Clinton transcript).[4] Clinton's speech reads more self-deprecating and self-critical than Donald Trump's, who even in a scripted speech displays greater level of boastfulness.

The more interesting part of the dinner was when the two shook hands, which is a simple gesture, which they tried to avoid during the presidential debate. It seems to be that the dinner was considered to be a more entertaining event, and they could let their guard down somewhat.

What is absolutely key is to observe the body language in this brief interaction. Clinton's body is positioned as far as possible away from Trump. She can make this possible by stretching her right arm as long as possible. She is not as tall as Trump and can afford to stretch her arms and still catch his hand. The upper arm is slightly tilted downward and the lower arm is parallel to the ground. Her face is only visible sideways, and her mouth appears to produce a smile, but upon closer look she is not smiling as much as feigning the smile.

---

[3] http://time.com/4539981/read-the-transcript-donald-trump-speech-al-smith-dinner/

[4] http://time.com/4539979/read-transcript-hillary-clinton-speech-al-smith-dinner/

One might interpret this fake smile with teeth clearly visible with the feeling of disgust or discomfort. This emotion fits well with why she would want to position her body as far away from Trump as possible. I interpret her body language to reveal her desire to end the interaction as quickly as possible. Clinton is known to have many spin doctors help her out with what to say, how to craft responses and how to behave, but, surprisingly, she is showing her emotions quite strongly in this direct interaction with her opponent.

Now let's look at Trump. Trump does not have any proximity issues. His upper arm is almost parallel to his body and orthogonal to the ground, and only his lower arm is stretched out, which suggests that he has no problem to reduce the physical distance with Clinton. Notice also that his body is leaning forward, which is in opposition to the stiff and straight Clinton posture. It is not clear whether Trump genuinely relishes the interaction, but he is certainly not afraid. This might be a reflection of a gender dominance pattern, and we have certainly heard much about Trump and his relationship with women. Trump's face has a rather neutral expression, so I can't read much emotion into the face. It should be noted, however, that he squints with his eyes, which might reveal a feeling of suspicion. Unlike Clinton, Trump does not even bother to fake a smile. Meeting an opponent for the highest office in the country is likely less pleasant than meeting one of the many Miss Universes he is used to hang out with.

What can't be read from the image is how tight the squeeze is during the handshake, but Clinton's female hands are clearly smaller than Trump's male hands, which allows him to surround her hand completely, while hers rests firmly in his palms. I don't know whether this is normal for cross-gender hand-shakes or whether there is a typical male-dominance pattern that is involved here.

The second photo with the handshake stands in stark contrast to the first photo, where the two candidates were sitting apart from each other and could enjoy their dinner physically separated. The distance allows them to hide their true emotions, and put in a big laugh after each joke. It is the handshake, which is the prototype of the direct confrontation, which reveals their true selves.

One should not think that because one of the two will occupy the highest office in the country that they have lost their humanity. They are still human beings, whose real feelings and sentiments get revealed in their micro-social interactions.

SEPTA on Strike: More Workers Deserve a Union
Posted on <u>November 1, 2016</u>

SEPTA, the Southeast Pennsylvania Transit Authority, which is one of the largest public transportation companies in this country had decided to go on strike, citing dissatisfaction with benefit and wage conditions proposed by management. Drivers complain about a lack of break time and limitations on pension benefits (which are uncapped for management) (Laughlin 2016). They have negotiated a contract for the last few weeks, hoping to avoid a strike. But there is a certain historical pattern to these strikes. It is the eleventh strike, the last one being in 2009, which also happened to be my first year in Philadelphia. I was also dependent on the buses to get me home. Growing up in Austria, industrial relations tend to be a lot less controversial, though more workers are covered in unions and labor laws and protections are overall stronger.

Wikipedia ("<u>Septa</u>") says that SEPTA has had more strikes than any other transport agency in the US. SEPTA is owned by the local county (Delaware Valley), serves 3.9 million residents, has 307 million trips per year, and has 5,700 drivers and operators. Some would say that 5,700 operators are holding a whole city hostage. Many people, who rely on SEPTA to go to school, work or to the doctor now have to scramble to find alternatives to get to where they need to go, such as carpooling, Uber, walking, or bicycling.

But what is strange to me is that the public discourse is so strongly opposed to the transit operator strike. How dare these people go on strike? Part of the reason why the opposition is so strong is because labor unions have become so weak that it is rather unlikely to see any strikes by any group of workers. It is the triumph of the management and the leaders of this country to have established an anti-union hegemony, which then also gets repeated by other working-class people.

The only way for the working class to press their interests against management is by showing solidarity with other workers. Given that there are only a limited number of drivers and their service is so vital for the community, they have so much power if they decided to band together. Imagine if all the 1 million Walmart workers could coordinate for a strike. They could double their pay overnight. Prices would go up a little, but profits will still be there, reflecting the high rent incomes for the Walmart owners. And these are important jobs too: imagine management consultants, lobbyists and lawyers going on strike: they earn a lot more money, but the country would not stop working without them.

What the SEPTA strike reveals to me may in the worst case situation be a last stand of the working class, but it could also reinvigorate a labor movement, because people do not forget that a strike is still the most effective way to redistribute income from management to the workers. It is wrong for other members of the working class to begrudge drivers for their decent incomes, which should spark emulation rather than envy via union organizing efforts.

The unfortunate reality is that there are only very few workers, who are as privileged as the SEPTA drivers. Most of the employment that communities have are in the low-wage service industry, in hotels, bars, restaurants, retail shops, in Uber taxis, but also in hospitals, schools and universities. It is the most proper to organize these workplaces. (Princeton graduate students are apparently interesting in forming a union, though the graduate student government declared itself to be "neutral" on this issue: seriously? A student government that is supposed to *represent* the student workers' interests?)

Some right-wing critics are running around with the meme that a higher minimum wage, unions and wage demands will accelerate the automation of service industry jobs. But those critics are making a wrong trade-off. Automation will happen regardless of whether there is any upward wage pressure. As soon as management receives new machines, which have the potential to offset labor costs and raise profits, they will install it *at any given wage*. For the workers it would be foolish to be afraid of automation and self-flagellate by refusing to make a better living and feed their families. Automation on such a large scale with tremendous effects on community life requires a smart government policy in response, which includes industrial policy for employment creation and/ or the universal basic income. The rational calculation of the workers, however, is to always demand higher wages.

The automation phenomenon is admittedly nothing to be scoffed at. Some SEPTA managers might subscribe to newsletters of tech magazines that promise that self-driving vehicles will soon come out. Managers are really looking forward to cash in when that time comes. Perhaps in a few years, self-driving buses and subways will completely remove the need for human operators. Some subways do not even use any human operators anymore. It is commonplace for many subways to have human operators, but they literally just sit and let the autopilot do the driving and operating the doors in the stations.

But as I said, these facts should not affect the tactical strategy of SEPTA driver union negotiators, who need to negotiate fair contracts for their members. It is the responsibility of public policy to ensure that all people can receive new jobs or a social safety net.

President Donald Trump: Why? What Next?
Posted on <u>November 10, 2016</u>

Most of the pundits and my liberal friends did not think that Donald Trump could become the president of the United States. One may say that he is even an illegitimately elected president, because he received about 2 million fewer votes than Hillary Clinton, which implies that she won her states with bigger margins than Trump won his, and the populous Clinton states had fewer Electoral College votes. But that does not matter, because our Electoral College system privileges the majority within the Electoral College. All the electoral votes in a state go to the candidate with the plurality of the votes in that state rather than proportionally according to the relative vote. But Clinton has already conceded defeat, and Trump gave his brief victory speech, where he did not outline any policy but merely promised to heal the "divided" nation, whatever that means.

There are two pertinent questions which arise: (1) why did Donald Trump win the election? and (2) what kind of policies and policy environment can we expect under a Trump administration?

Why Donald Trump Won the Election?
The first question is undoubtedly easier to answer than the second, but I shall venture on my guesses. Let's begin on the first. I will briefly say something about explanations, I don't find convincing: I reject the claim that third party voters spoiled the vote in favor of Trump, because the overall support for the third parties was rather negligible. I also don't think that misogyny kept Clinton from the White House, in the same manner that racism didn't keep out Obama in 2008. I will also reject the claim that half of Americans are racist. There is no doubt a sizable number of racists and secret racists in the country, and they have backed Trump, but not every Trump voter is a racist.

(a) Hillary Clinton represents the hated establishment, which many people don't like. During previous election cycles, few people would have cared whether the leading candidate belonged to the establishment. I have argued previously that screwing working people with stagnant wages, rising health care and education costs and growing economic insecurity will create electoral backlash. The establishment had no interest in the plight of those working people, and thought it was more convenient to do big fundraisers with the

1%. Clinton epitomizes the establishment, because she has been part of the national Democratic Party for 25 years if you count the time with her husband. She was mired in a cloud of scandals, which the news media fired up, and she lacked the charisma to communicate to people why they should support her (very much unlike her very charismatic husband). Because of her establishment connections, it didn't even matter that her policies were more to the left than her husband's 25 years ago (mainly due to the Bernie Sanders effect). What matters is the public perception of mistrust. It also did not help that the president and the previous presidents and other Republican establishment figures were backing her, because that lowered her credibility among establishment skeptics.

Trump was not part of the establishment, even though he was a businessman getting rich off that corrupt campaign finance system, which he even admitted in his rallies. He vowed to fix it, though not how, which suggests he has no serious policy ideas, but what matters are not the sanity of policy proposals, but the sentiment of the anti-establishment spirit, which he embodied. The media and the liberal public was chastising him for his sexism and bigotry, but that actually increased the appeal of Trump among his supporters. They felt the political incorrectness was a breath of fresh air. Political correctness for the Trump supporters is really a way to silence their grievances, which they think they have a right to air, and Trump was the figure, who was never shaken by any scandal directed against him. In fact, he deflected any scandal against him, and threw spoonful of allegations back against Clinton. That made him the decisive anti-establishment figure.

(b) The angry white working class around the rustbelt turned out in larger numbers. Clinton clearly won a vast majority of the black, Latino, Asian and female vote, so there wasn't much false consciousness among the different demographic groups that Trump derided. But their groups are still a minority and if their turnout is low, because of lack of enthusiasm for Clinton, then the very enthusiastic Trump supporters sway the elections. Michigan, Pennsylvania, Ohio, Wisconsin and Florida all went to Trump. With the exception of Florida, these are all rustbelt states, which heavily relied on steel, car and manufacturing plants for employment. They have been the losers of globalization, automation and the motions of capitalism. Opioid addiction, alcohol addiction, suicide, early death, unemployment are all problems there. Almost all of the income gains are concentrated in the top 1% of the population.

The Trump supporters are the most angry about the Clintons having sold them down the drain in the 1990s with the free trade agreements, which had bipartisan consensus. Even though Clinton later backtracked on the free trade agreements (for electoral reasons, because I think she would have negotiated the TPP once elected to "assert American interests", like Obama has) and her tax and job initiative policies would have helped the white working class men more than any shady initiative by Trump, it didn't help her. The optics were so much turned against her. Trump, however, championed these voters in the many well-attended rallies he had, because he promised them that jobs would come back when he rips up trade agreements and imposes tariff barriers on foreign imported goods. It was all a hoax because the tariffs won't bring the jobs back, and I don't think he will rip up the trade agreements because of his close ties to business people, but that didn't matter, it's the optics that mattered, and people need something to hold onto.

(c) The left-wing crowd was not enthusiastic about Clinton. This point does not need much elaboration. One of the reasons why Bernie supporters are correctly saying that he would have received more independent votes than Clinton is because the left and many in the center would have strongly supported his policy positions. He would have been competitive in some Republican states in a way that Clinton could never dream about. It is true that most Sanders backers swung around to vote for Clinton, but the enthusiasm gap for Clinton has cost her some votes, probably in the form of abstention. Another interesting detail was that the African American vote now was smaller than in 2008 and 2012, which would suggest that the Obama-boost, as first African-American president, cannot be completely denied. But a Trump-Sanders showdown would have been fantastic for the dynamics in US elections, because both do not represent the establishment and would have galvanized both of their bases, while the actual election galvanized the Trump voters but not the Clinton voters, who had the best advisers, campaign funding and canvassing strategy, but no general enthusiasm.

(d) Trump has charisma. Charisma, according to Max Weber, is a mythical, magical quality in a leader, which inspires followers to support this leader. His charisma is in part cultivated with his experience as TV host and as businessman, negotiating contracts and getting "good" deals. It does not even matter what the results are, because he had lost a lot of money in lawsuits and failed investments and his policy proposals are flimsy and superficial. Only experts can uncover Trump as a charlatan, but that is not what most people want to hear. I have people in my family and among some friends, who are devotionally inspired by the Trump campaign, because he blurts out what he thinks, even if what he says is not deep at all. Clinton desperately tried to hammer Trump on his sexism, racism and bigotry, and the low-point of the Trump campaign according to mainstream media and the politically correct sectors of the country (like Ivy League universities) was reached, when he made approving comments of grabbing women by their genitals. But that racism and sexism framework being bad (e.g. trigger warnings) only works in parts of the country.

The white working class turnout, which was decisive for his victory (ironically, a shrinking part of the electorate, which implies that future Republican candidates have to increase mobilization in this electorate even further if they want to be competitive in future elections), reflects not the direct approval of Trump's bigotry, but the liking of his authenticity. He says what he thinks, which is very much unlike the establishment, which has to formulate very sweet words. The more outrageous things that Trump said, the more authentic he became in the eyes of his ardent supporters. Trump by marking himself as against the establishment could take the liberty of pushing the boundaries of what can be said.

With Clinton the opposite impression is true. If you watched her during the debates you will see her very well thought-out and careful statements, every word having been spin-doctored and rehearsed. There wasn't any emotional touch that she could create with her audience. This outward appearance is not relevant to policy wonks like myself, who are only interested in what policies the candidates had to present. In fact, if policy content was the only thing that mattered, then Clinton would have won the elections. But the country does not consist of policy experts, so we need to have the charismatic leader. People need leaders, who can inspire them, even if the policy content is fake. If you consider the Republican primary debates, all of the candidates were actually very much alike on the policy content, but you could also see the wooden tone and the artificiality of the other politicians, who have experience as politicians. All that Trump had to do to gain more popularity was to show that he was outwardly different from them, that he was a businessman non-establishment candidate, who can shake things up from the outside.

What Policies Can We Expect from a Trump Administration?

What Trump's victory boils down to is massive discontent against the establishment, because it has not delivered on the needs of the working class, who were sold out by their leaders and the capitalist economy, which pumps profits for the bosses rather than take care of worker needs. If that is the case, then the question arises what it means for the country politically. Will Trump be able to deliver on his promises to (1) rip up the trade agreements, (2) revoke environmental and business regulations ("red tape"), (3) reform the tax code (i.e. give tax breaks to the rich), (4) build the wall with Mexico and deport illegal immigrants, (5) repeal Obamacare, (6) appoint conservative Supreme Court Justices?

On a policy-level all of these proposals are very concerning, and I have no doubt that the "little guy", who has put him into power, will not benefit from any of these policies. Trump is intent on doubling down on trickle-down economics, a slap in the face for his white working-class supporters. Trump is after all a member of the billionaire class, and he had a natural indifference to the people below him, which is evidenced by his refusal to pay of contractors and workers in his businesses. There is no reason to assume that simply because he called out the corruption and he is above the campaign-cash (which turned out not to be true: he got money from some rich people) that he will not serve the people of his own class.

The best predictor of his economic policy will be the kinds of people he will appoint to his cabinet. The Financial Times circulates the names of high-level Wall Street bankers and investors. Steve Mnuchin (former Goldman executive) and Wilbur Ross (distressed asset investor) as Treasury secretary. Other economic advisers include Lawrence Kudlow, former chief economist at Bear Stearns, and Steve Moore, conservative Heritage Foundation economist (Fleming and Donnan 2016). The entire anti-establishment sentiment is directed against Wall Street, but Wall Street will be the fox guarding the hen house.

The policy proposals are visible too: Trump will work closely with the Republican Congress to massively slash taxes on the rich, who are supposed to get an average tax deduction of 13% as opposed to 4% for the general public (Rubin 2016). Before people are jumping up and down for the lower taxes they now have to pay to the government, they should consider that people also rely on social programs like Medicare and Social Security, which are also on the chopping block on a Republican administration. The Republican Congress will likely also work together with Trump on reducing the power of the EPA, and perhaps even phasing it out. They will want to benefit the coal, gas and oil industry and accelerate climate change, which Trump considered to be a hoax. He does not care about any externalities to business activity, and we should race headlong into a warmer future without doing anything about it and defunding any scientists, who do serious climate research.

It is questionable whether Trump will deliver on his plans to build the wall, but what is for certain is that doubling down on deporting illegal immigrants is actually not such a great departure from the status quo. Obama had the double-faced policy of massively expanding deportations while protecting under-age undocumented residents in school from deportation. Trump wanted to give a huge boost to the prison and law enforcement agencies anyway, so deportations are a natural method of getting there. Being tough on immigration is politically one of the easiest things to do, because the frightened natives can quell their subjective fears while the veto power is relatively small, as non-citizens have no entitlement to vote and punish the current leaders.

Ripping up trade agreements will be much more complicated. He might derail the TPP or TTIP if he does not actively promote these agreements. Drift will result in policy failure. On the other hand, his commitment to destroy NAFTA, PNTR with China and CAFTA is more difficult to accomplish. It is easier to say no to what will come than to destroy what is already there and has vested interests in support. Trump prided himself to be independent from the lobbyists in the business community, but given that he will appoint people from the business community, he is signaling policy continuity to that business community, which does not want an end to the trade agreement. The Republican Congress is unlikely to back him on retreating on the previous trade agreements, because the entire party is owned by the business class. But the trade agreements are a centerpiece of Trump's campaign, though he will know how to sell himself and weasel his way out of it.

Repealing Obamacare is a genuine possibility and it is possible to attack the fragile law by upending cost-sharing (which subsidizes high-risk insurance plans, i.e. plans with many sick patients) or repealing the mandate, which would reduce the number of insurers on the exchange, because they are banking on everyone paying the penalty or signing up for their insurance plans, and repealing the mandate would remove such impetus. But the difficult calculation for Trump will be that if he repeals Obamacare, it will immediately remove 20 million people from health insurance, which could create a massive political backlash because it is easier to prevent new benefits than to remove benefits on which people already rely on. This might be a risk that Trump is willing to take given that he is not a natural politician and would treat one or two terms in power as equally satisfying.

The Supreme Court will become substantially more conservative. The Republicans have blocked the appointment of a new Justice for almost a year after the death of Antonin Scalia. Trump has signaled that he will appoint the anti-abortion, pro-corporate Justices, and there is no doubt that he will be successful here. Ruth Bader Ginsburg is 83, Stephen Breyer is 78 and Anthony Kennedy is 80, which means that within 10 years there will be three new Supreme Court Justices (unless they each live until 100). Ginsburg and Breyer were both liberal Clinton appointees, while Kennedy is considered a moderate conservative. If we add the three more conservative judges to that there could be six out of nine justices that are right-wing justices.

Conclusion

Does the Trump presidency offer any positive prospect for the country? Slavoj Zizek thinks that even as Trump is a horrendous candidate for power, he will move forward the dialectics. The reasoning here is rather simple: it has to get worse before it gets better. The German Communists were happy that the economy descended into chaos in the 1920s, because that would make it easier for the communists to succeed. But will that really happen? Hitler came first and imprisoned the communists. Communism succeeded in East Germany under the direction of the Soviet Union, but crumbled under its internal contradictions in 1990. But there is no genuine reason to believe that history will have such a dialectical movement. Where are the forces of revolution to emerge out of the carnage? And even if it were true, I find it ethically questionable to tolerate a deterioration of the current reality for people.

But, of course, I get it. Let us not forget that this was not a pro-Trump, but an anti-establishment election. The costs that are attached to a Clinton presidency would perhaps be economically smaller (Clinton would not have been as progressive as Sanders, but she was fairly close at that stage), but politically it would be bigger. Her win would have suggested that the elites can continue celebrating the party among themselves, and maybe hand just one or two extra crumbs to the crowds. Let us not forget that an essential part of the Clinton strategy was to give big speeches in the big banks, do fundraisers with Hollywood actors, cozy up with big industries and lobbyists, and hire the pollsters, the pundits, the campaign shenanigans. Her victory would have sanctioned the status quo, and none of the voters want that. The fact that we still have the institution of democracy means that people will resort to the protest vote until their situation gets objectively better, whether that's the Greek bailout referendum, the Dutch referendum on the EU-Ukraine association agreement, the Brexit referendum or the Trump victory. As it turns out, Trump is following his class instincts, and I expect him to change less about the status quo than his supporters would have hoped for, but that does not change his voters' views of Clinton.

What it all boils down to is that Trump is a marketing genius, who in his businessman manner was capable of selling his white working class a dream about a better economic situation, but has to sell them out in practice. We are in for some exciting times, though this is not meant in a positive way.

2016 Does Not Mean We Are All Doomed: Lessons for the Left

Posted on December 19, 2016

In one of John Oliver's shows[5] immediately after the Trump elections, he had a segment condemning 2016 and being happy that such a bad political year will be over soon. There is no denial that we have had a horrendous year behind us: Brexit and Trump. I will not re-litigate why they had been bad choices for their respective countries (see my posts: Liu 2016d; Liu, "President Donald Trump: Why? What Next?", this volume).

I will also not deny that the electoral choices clearly reveal the anti-establishment vote patterns that emerge from a national political class that is incapable to redress the economic and social grievances of a working class that is battered by international competition and growing automation, and the ethno-national uncertainty of a diversifying population. For that reason, any democratic vote in the immediate future will always be decided in direct opposition to what the establishment demands, since the voters rightly attribute their discontent to ignorance and helplessness of their own political class.

Democracy now mixes very uncomfortably with capitalism, because the latter pushes up inequality and the former cannot persist without sufficient equality. Something has to give and in the short term in Greece, for instance, democracy is losing, because electing a left-wing government means absolutely nothing. They can't even hike their pensions without Wolfgang Schauble's, the German finance minister's, permission. France will face an awful set of choices in 2017, as the socialists are discredited, and the conservative right-wing (Fillon: pro-neoliberal, cut civil service and welfare) battles with the extreme right-wing (LePen: protectionism, anti-immigrant and anti-Muslim campaigns).

There is also very little doubt that some of the directional gains of political liberalism may face reversals, and some clear indications of that can be seen in Poland, Turkey, Russia or China. It is becoming increasingly less comfortable to be a member of the press or the political opposition in these countries. In China, the government has developed the Orwellian idea to assign points to people's good behavior (e.g. visiting their parents) and deduct points

---

[5] https://www.youtube.com/watch?v=I--LtuTA7K8

for bad behavior (e.g. protest against government) such that everyone has an online profile and contribute to what the rulers regard to be a "good society". Turkey's Erdogan abuses the July 2016 coup against him to throw all of his political opponents either in jail or remove them from office.

We might as well bury our heads in the sand and never try to look out again, but my argument today is that not all is lost. Naturally, the default in a world of economic and political uncertainty is to have nationalist-protectionist and authoritarian sentiments prevail. But there are also signs for a positive turn in the global discourse.

First, notice the sharp negative global reaction to president-elect Trump's statement that he might rip up the Paris climate agreement. This agreement has the intention to limit the rise in global temperature to 2 degrees celsius, which is rather ambitious given that we are already 1.2 degrees on our way there, and even if we were to shut off all sources of CO_2 now, we would still experience more warming in the short-term given that it takes some time for the CO_2 to be absorbed by the oceans or exit the planetary atmosphere. The serious effects of climate change even in the short-run imply that the economic growth-CO_2 reduction tradeoff can no longer apply. It is when we face an immense and immediate planetary crisis that the world leaders are jolted to do something about it, even if they are intent only to save their own asses.

Second, wherever electoral opportunities arise, there are not only regretfully right-wing forces that arise, but also left-wing and progressive political forces. In Spain, a 2015 election catapulted the left-wing Podemos party to third place, which created a fractured political system and no government could be formed. A repeat election in 2016, increased the vote-share for the establishment Popular Party (Conservative), but Podemos was able to retain their seats. Popular Party has now formed a government but without a real mandate. The decimated socialists (PSOE) abstained, but Podemos now has the front row seats and can see the government's austerity program further unravel.

In the UK, Jeremy Corbyn faced a direct leadership challenge in the Labour Party led by Owen Smith, who made an about-face from being a Blairite (e.g. his support for private-finance initiatives and farming the NHS out to private providers) to a Corbynite. The only selling point he made was that Corbyn was not a credible candidate, and it would be better to have someone who appeared moderate to outside voters, but would also push the Labour Party left-wing agenda. It was evidently a poor selling-point and he lost the leadership challenge. The Blairites have to lick their wounds and they have likely lost control over the Labour Party for many years to come. Will the Labour Party be able to win any UK elections? It will be difficult given that the loss of the Scottish heartland to the SNP in 2015 meant a severe blow to the Labour Party. Without being able to reach out to rural English voters, who are staunch Tories, there is no possibility for shifting the political fortunes for Labour. It is theirs for the taking given that the Brexit will be poorly negotiated by an outgunned May administration.

In the US, everyone has been lamenting the loss of Bernie Sanders in the Democratic primaries (including the author), and the Sanderistas are already riding the I-told-you-so wave against the Clinton campaign, arguing that Sanders would have easily won against Trump. I would support that view, but understand that it does not make much sense now to litigate the past and dream up counterfactuals. But we should remember the historic moment by which a self-described democratic socialist received 46% of the primary vote in a major political party. When Sanders went out to give his hour-long political education lectures on inequality and lack of college and health care access, there were tens of thousands of people, who showed up and were willing to listen to the new message. Finally, someone who took the working man and woman seriously!

Sanders is really only the third part of the progressive political narrative: the first part begins with the 2008 financial crisis and the bailout for the banks. We can debate whether the government did the right thing with the bailouts, but what matters here is the optics: people experience that the banks were able to get rich, be declared so systemically important that taxpayers should bail out these big banks, while they pay their top bosses with bonuses. In the meantime, people, who took out mortgages that they could not service, were forced to surrender their houses, and were all of a sudden morally to be blamed for what really was the combined regulatory failure of the government and the banks, who only cared about the housing fees.

There had previously been already economic losers in the US, whether it is the factory workers of the Rust belt (who now voted for Trump in larger numbers than Clinton) or service workers trapped in low-wage jobs and other personal problems like drug or alcohol addiction. But the 2008 crisis made it plain to the entire middle class that their position was no longer safe. We are no longer talking about marginal groups that can get stiffed. People were working longer hours for lower wages, but someone had to still articulate their troubles.

The second stage of the progressive narrative was the Occupy Wall Street movement. Political scientists like Theda Skocpol and Vanessa Williamson (2016) make a big deal out of the Tea Party and they have become an entrenched political force in the US. They are bankrolled by the Koch brothers, while the popular front makes it appear as if they expressed an anger coming from middle America. There is some truth to that, as rural white voters tended to show the strongest support for a movement, which was disgusted by the bailouts, by the Washington establishment, and had the desire to "have the government hands off my Medicare".

But there was a left-wing antidote in the cities, which was the Occupy Wall Street movement, which began around September 2011 and ended about 2 months later. A democratic society usually tolerates public assemblies. In China, online regulators tend to be lenient on political criticism, but are notoriously harsh on cracking down on any kind of online activism that results in mass demonstrations or assemblies as that would directly undermine the political regime. But even in democratic societies rulers get really scared when people assemble over extended periods of time, because the extended socialization on public squares might create a larger movement that overthrows the neoliberal economic configuration, which serves the powerful so well.

The city and the police forces across the country coordinated rather well in getting rid of what they officially called the "public nuisance". That is what the Hong Kong protesters also had to listen to. Here governments all over the world are the same. They cite the blockage of roads, public squares, hindering traffic and commerce, the defecation and urination on the streets, the noise and the stench as a reason to get rid of the tents and the encampments. But what they were really after was to crush the spirit of the movement, which could radicalize as long as the encampments were there, but wither away without them, despite all the social network activism in the world.

So OWS is dead and nowhere to be seen, right? Wrong. What survived was the legitimation of the class-based discourse. The chant of the occupiers was that the 1% got richer at the expense of the 99%.

I occasionally read some academics, who have the desire to correct the simplifying statement of the 1% by focusing on the top 0.1% or top 5% or saying that these figures don't help much, but what really matters is that there is something inherently wrong when almost all gains flow to the top 1%.

But the question of 'what is to be done?' still hung above us after the failure of OWS, and here we fit Bernie Sanders into the narrative, who announced his presidential candidacy in the May of 2015. Would Sanders' message have resonated without the financial crisis and OWS? I doubt it. Now, we have to move to stage four and win elections.

It might very well be that a fascist wave will take over and engulf us in political darkness before any progressive leader can step in. But those on the left have no reason to be discouraged as long as we have the political resources to fight back. The world is ours for the taking.

Consumption as a Curse
Posted on <u>December 28, 2016</u>

In a recent video, I argued that economic growth is not always beneficial, because rising economic growth is associated with rising inequality, spiritual unhappiness via the Keeping-up-with-the-Joneses syndrome, and because the environmental effects of endless economic growth are becoming less and less tolerable as climate change advances.[6] Today, I want to focus on the second point to argue that consumption is a societal curse rather than a boon.

Our culture tells us that we have to consume as much as possible or else we are not worthwhile human beings. Naturally, because we are still a liberal democratic society, the powerful in the companies and the government can not force us outright to buy as much as we can. So Edward Bernays (1928) had made the argument in the 1920s that what liberal democratic societies needed was the submission of the mass of the population to the consumerist order, where people's opinions and habits are steered by the rulers of society. This submission is generated through relentless propaganda in the form of TV commercials, newspaper advertisement, public branding of firms, political campaigns, school instruction and news anchors telling us that we should buy Christmas gifts and shame on us if we waited until the very last minute to get a gift.

The latter example is really what had motivated me to write this post. My first association with Christmas, which I think is shared by many people, is an opportunity to meet relatives, to not be so stressed out about work for a few days and to enjoy longer sleep. These practices are implicit as part of the holidays, though it is used by more religious people to be reminded of the birth of Jesus Christ, a rather radical figure, who had the idea to spread the monotheist religion to Gentiles.

Unfortunately, I had the TV on, while being back home for a few days just to discover that the local TV station was reminding people of holiday shopping and showing the crowded shopping malls. Some of the TV presenters said in jest, "You really should feel guilty for pushing it up until the last minute to buy your Christmas presents". The newscasters, naturally, do not reflect on why they are imploring people to loosen their wallets, and it does not seem that they have to,

---

[6] https://www.youtube.com/watch?v=vXaYvakHZAM

because the crowded shopping malls clearly show that the newscasters are merely reinforcing what already exists in US culture.

On a more benign note, people might simply decide to shop for Christmas presents as an affirmation that they care for one another, and loving thy neighbor or loving thy family at the very least is clearly very spiritual and very Christian. But there isn't any obvious link to celebrating the founder of Christianity and gifts except the mythical story of the three wisemen gifting gold, frankincense and myrrh to infant Jesus. But why is the gift in the Jesus story linked with gift-giving in today's world? Capitalist interests, especially in the retail sector, live off exploiting the story of Jesus for their own benefit, and by convincing people with the help of the complicit media that the circle of gift-receivers should be as large as possible and the spending per gift should also be as extravagant as possible.

Gift-giving is nothing peculiar to consumer capitalist society, and also existed in ancient societies. In Malinowski's (1922) classic study of gift-exchange of the Trobriand islanders, gift-giving has a reciprocal element, i.e. gifts that were given out had to be returned with a gift of greater magnitude; the items that were traded were non-useful items like necklaces and armbands; the gift-giver had a higher social status than the gift-receiver; because most of the gift-items were under the possession of very few individuals in those communities, those same few owners had the most influence and power.

In today's capitalist society, this element of social hierarchy is reproduced with gift-giving, because it tends to be parents, who give their children presents rather than vice versa. (This is a principle that is strictly enforced in my family where my parents refuse to even entertain the idea to let me pay for anything when we go out together.) Though the fact that children upon earning their own income then also become normatively obliged to buy gifts for their parents and other siblings shows that the ancient forms of gift-hierarchies become muddier.

But what I am really trying to say here is that in consumer-oriented societies the social rank hierarchies may or may not get reproduced, but it is all secondary to the commodity structure that filters these gift-relations. Gift relations are retained only within the family or friendship network, but given that most people nowadays don't use their own mechanic skills to build a product from scratch, but instead buy the gift from the supermarket or online, there is priority for the commodity relationship. From the standpoint of the capitalist producer, he/she does not care whether the buyer or the gift-receiver consume the commodity as long as the buyer transfers the money to the capitalist.

Economic sociologists may be perfectly happy in just pointing out that money can be "earmarked" for specific purposes (see Zelizer 1994), or gift-items for that matter. But for me it is normatively not sufficient. The question, which I raise, is whether gift-giving is absolutely critical in the framework of Christianity? If we could say for sure that people's moods are uplifted with practical acts of kindness, then we should by all means stay with gift-giving. If people have treated me well or if I hope to be viewed favorably, I would use gifts as a means of appreciation. But in the case of Christmas, we are institutionally required to hand out gifts, which evidently has nothing to do with an act of kindness but fixed social expectations.

It would be difficult to establish the different levels of spiritual happiness effects of a gift received at random when the gift-giver thinks the receiver deserves it versus a gift received during Christmas, but I would hazard to assume that the former produces a greater level of happiness for the receiver because the gift is linked directly with the individual person rather than the institution.

The conclusion that I make can, therefore, neither be to abolish gift-giving nor Christmas, but to question whether gift-giving should be intrinsically linked with Christmas and should require the combined propaganda of corporations, retailers, schools and media to mobilize the largest amount of Christmas shoppers with the most willingness to loosen their wallets.

Let us consider the problems: It is problematic that the innocent act of Christmas gifts can produce anxiety among lower-class children, whose parents cannot afford the nicest gifts. It is problematic that the consumer propaganda makes people feel guilty for not intending to purchase gifts for others. It is problematic that so many people return the gifts the next day because they don't like them (which suggests to me that people might be better off with a gift card rather than gift items; I, for instance, only value books and only very few people would know the kind of books I would want to read, so I reward myself with "gifts" through online book orders). It is also problematic that gift-giving has been absorbed into the normal capitalist order.

Consumption that exceeds people's genuine needs and controlled wants become a curse to the extent that our spiritual happiness (defined as long-term contentment rather than joy for the moment, eudaimonia in ancient Greece) is not increased, but to the extent that we are trapped in the hedonic treadmill, where only added increments of material goods can increase pleasure further. For most people not born with a silver spoon in their mouths, that means more exertion, more work, more performance, more overtime, more promotions, more bonuses, more raises.

Cheerleaders of capitalism claim that more consumption and hard work is associated with human progress. In capitalism's creative destruction, there is, after all, a creative element in it. I am no opponent of progress, but I am an opponent of hedonistic consumerism, which shall not be confused with the desire to tinker and create new things, which make us very human and shall continue to exist under any social mode of life.

The stoics argued that contentment and satisfaction can only be received if our material demands on life are reduced to a minimum. We don't have to go that far, and may appreciate the benefits of what has been created. But we can heed some of their calls to attempt to live a more fulfilled life. I come from everything but a rich family, and one of the most important lessons I received from my family was the importance of being very frugal on my spending habits. Capitalist propagandists would condemn me as a miser, who refuses to benefit the economy and spur the creation of new jobs (or celebrate me as a hero for generating high savings for the country's investment, but we'll go with the first argument for now).

But the frugality has also allowed me to not have the desire to cheat on people, so that I can have a temporary pecuniary gain. It has allowed me to maximize my leisure preference, which may have come at the expense of "productive work" for society, but has allowed me to live a life of the mind (albeit imperfectly), read an inordinate amount of books, newspapers, journals, write numerous blogposts, watch movies and documentaries, and join long intellectual discussions with bon vivant friends. I can scarcely imagine any better life, yet consumerism blocks the path toward such a free and content life for most individuals.

Some critics might object that most people may intrinsically have a consumer-good rather than leisure preference and that my intellectual preferences are peculiar to few other individuals like me. But how can such critics know for sure that consumer-good preferences are autonomous decisions? The standard libertarian has to assume that people intrinsically choose how they can maximize their own levels of utility, but to ignore the externality of influence through the consumer propaganda machine is short-sighted. It is true that consumer culture has formed the standard common attitude toward consumer-good preference, but we would not really know what people's genuine preferences are unless there is a parallel universe or society where people are not exposed to the consumerist propaganda.

Ironically, it first requires leisure before people realize what they are really after and what really produces contentment in life. And in such case, there will be a much greater number, who will then voice their leisure preference, than what is the case today, while a few people nonetheless choose workaholism even when given the leisure, because work is the only thing that fulfills them. That would be fine too, because the work and consumer-preference would not result from coercion through manipulation (rather than coercion through force). We are ripe for the universal basic income to test the waters on people's true preferences.

(Not) Draining the Swamp
Posted on <u>December 29, 2016</u>

Donald Trump had promised his voters that he would drain the swamp, which means that he would ensure that lobbyists and other special interests would not prevail in his administration and that he would place the interests of the whole nation before that of the special interests. With only a few weeks to go before inauguration, it is time to call him out on what turned out to be a non-promise.

The Trump Cabinet

Let's start with a small selection of the people he had decided to appoint to his cabinet: Betsy DeVos, a billionaire, campaigning for the privatization of the public school system to use public dollars to benefit education investors like her and other buddies, became the secretary of education.

Steven Mnuchin, a high-level executive of the much detested Goldman Sachs bank, became the Secretary of Treasury, following in line with the tradition of appointing Goldman Sachs bankers to the manage the nation's finances (after Robert Rubin serving under Clinton, and Hank Paulson serving under Bush; the former advocating for Wall Street deregulation and the latter throwing tax money after Wall Street following the great crash).

Wilbur Ross, a leveraged-buyout investor and billionaire making a fortune from buying up bankrupting companies, loading them with debt and then selling at his own profit, is going to become the Secretary of Commerce, ensuring that similarly shady deals will be performed under a Trump administration.

Andrew Puzder, a chief executive of a fast food company, who railed against minimum wage laws and favored accelerated automation of jobs so that pesky workers can't bargain or strike for higher wages or better working conditions, becomes the Secretary of Labor.

Rex Tillerson, chief executive of Exxon Mobile, a giant oil corporation, who is very interested in making profitable business deals rather than maintaining balanced foreign policy, will be the Secretary of State.

Ryan Zinke, Montana Congressman, who voted for oil and gas drilling, will be Secretary of Interior, which is charged with overseeing federal land that might be tapped for oil and gas drilling despite the criticisms of environmentalists.

Scott Pruitt, Oklahoma attorney general who led lawsuits against the EPA for the Clean Power Plan (setting carbon limits for power plants) and Clean Water rule (limit pollution in the nation's rivers, lakes, streams and wetlands), will become the Administrator of the Environmental Protection Agency.

Tom Price, Georgia Congressman and critic of the Affordable Care Act, will become Secretary of Health and Human Services, which is tasked with overseeing the implementation of the Affordable Care Act, especially the smooth running of the exchange.

Carl Icahn, multibillionaire investor, will be Trump's special advisor to "cut red tape" and government regulations, which usually implies the same barriers that hinder investment profits, like worker safety or environmental standards. He advocates for a tax holiday for companies stashing their earnings overseas in the hope that the cash will be repatriated. (It is safe to assume that Icahn will benefit from such a move.)

Peter Navarro, a University of California Irvine economist raging against trade deals with China and the rest of the world for undermining US production and increasing US trade deficits, was selected as director of the National Trade Council.

Now, it turns out that Icahn and Ross were major Trump donors, and they helped him stave off bankruptcy in the 1990s, when his businesses were in trouble. He is repaying his wealthy friends by appointing them to the cabinet. Trump is as much beholden to the big donors as Clinton, Bush and all of the other establishment figures.

Evaluation

The pattern of Trump's appointment is that most of his appointments tend to be businesspeople, who will benefit themselves or their industries substantially by working directly for the government, or politicians, who have a vested interest in helping various businesses make more money. All of these efforts are likely to intensify the swamp. Remember that the reference to the swamp was about a broadside attack against a politicized (crony) capitalism, where the state helps lobbyists and special interests enrich themselves at the expense of taxpayers and the general public. But to appoint the very same special interests to become part of the cabinet is actually even worse than the current corrupt political culture of politicians currying favors with their donors. Cut out the middle man.

Taxpayer/ public-politician-business/ special interest
gets simplified to
Taxpayer/ public- business/ special interest

If your initial thought is that the Trump administration mean that the rich will get richer, and the working and middle classes that put Trump to power will be neglected again, there is strong reason to believe that this is exactly what will happen. Bernie Sanders and some other progressives are already calling for mass mobilization to ensure that social programs like Social Security and Medicare get defended (Fernholz 2016). Trump has not made it clear that he wants to slash entitlement programs, though he might ultimately not be opposed to it given that he did not invite any social policy academics or other left-wing representatives into his cabinet and staff of advisers.

"Speeches are in poetry, while governing is in prose", is one of the proverbial pieces of wisdom in Washington politics. What this means for us is that the people have appointed their shiny charismatic leader, who is a skilled con man and TV celebrity, but this leader cannot govern without his bureaucracy. The bureaucracy then turns out to be drawn from the military, the Republican political establishment and the elite business community. People's anger was targeted at the elites, but what they get back are the very elites, who can't care less whether working people have struggle to afford their rent. The next four years will be a hell of a ride.

The Politics of Populism: Technology and Inequality
Posted on January 18, 2017

The politics of populism is what marks the contemporary political period. In every single election, where the working class is given the opportunity to punish the establishment with a vote that goes against the ruling view, it happens. Brexit, Trump, the Italian referendum. There are elections in France and Germany this year. The authoritarian countries like Turkey, Russia or China are becoming more so. Directional liberalism becomes directional authoritarianism.

The contemporary capitalist period is marked by fragility. Global debts are bigger than before the crisis. High debts imply that means for refinancing become restricted, which can slow down investment and economic growth. Rising debt level also reflects the inequality between nations and the wealth gap between rich and poor. Oxfam says that rather than 62 people owning as much wealth as the bottom half of the world population (about 3.6 billion people), it is now only 8 people, in whose hands the wealth becomes concentrated. The rather high level of inequality predicts political instability, which then justifies some authoritarian and nationalist-protectionist sentiment on the political front.

Unemployment is stagnant at a rather elevated level, while the technological boom develops largely unhindered, eating into previously stable middle class professions. So far retail and low-skilled workers are most affected by automation, but advancements in artificial technology do not preclude that even bankers, lawyers or educators will be affected by automation. It is probably correct to make the objection that automation won't happen quite this fast, because the institutions of the labor market, political regulations and other social norms might slow down the adoption of technology, though I doubt it will hinder such adoption.

The technological effects on inequality should not be underestimated. Let us take the 8 rich faces and see what pattern emerges:

Bill Gates is the founder of Microsoft, a tech billionaire. Amancio Ortega, founder of the Spanish fashion and design company Zara. Warren Buffett, the CEO of a financial/ investment firm. Carlos Slim, the monopoly owner of Mexican telecom. Michael Bloomberg, is the founder of a media and financial data firm. Larry Elliot, the CEO of a technical firm, Oracle. Mark Zuckerberg, the founder of the tech social network Facebook. Jeff Bezos, the founder of the online tech retailer Amazon. 4 of the top 8 in the list are clearly part of the tech industry. Bloomberg should perhaps also be considered part of the tech giant industry, because providing financial data to clients is made possible through the internet and other computer data. Buffett is the only American on the list, who does not clearly belong to the tech industry, though he is in a supporting role as his company holds 11% of its shares in technology companies (otherwise, it has a bigger portfolio in finance, e.g. Wells Fargo, and general consumer items like Walmart, Coca Cola or Kraft Foods, see Nasdaq as of 9/30/2016). The Latino billionaires (Ortega and Slim) are also clearly not in the tech sector, but in retail and telecom, though political relations granting their monopoly status matters at least just as much as global market penetration.

The technological boom has created obvious winners. If we look at the most valuable companies here, the top five are all tech firms:

1. Apple ($appl): **$570.7 billion**
2. Alphabet ($goog): **$560B**
3. Microsoft ($msft): **$434B**
4. Amazon ($amzn): **$365B**
5. Facebook ($fb): **$354B**
6. Exxon Mobile ($xom): **$351B**

Source: Business Insider (2016)

Why would technology have the impact of increasing inequality? The answer is not too difficult. It takes massive investments and technological know-how in order to create and develop tech products. This is definitely the case for hardware producers like Apple and Microsoft and software producers like Oracle. For the internet companies (Amazon, Facebook, Alphabet or Google), there is a massive advantage in having a large centralized network, which makes it more difficult for smaller firms to offer their services. When the internet came out, the people were celebrating the possibility for an evening out in the market sphere. Lower costs imply lower entry barriers to participate in the market when using the internet. But that is only true for the provision of personal services. My brother, for instance, regularly orders pizza online using a central platform (which probably makes the most money from the pizza shops and advertisements), and more pizza shops now have the opportunity to offer their pizza.

But here there is a limitation to the pizza analogy (and other services like hair dressers, accountants and so forth), because the really big tech giants provide the platform and are guaranteed to make the most money. It is their service that we all collectively use. When we watch a video on Youtube, the money flows to Alphabet. When we do a google search, the money flows to Alphabet. The traditional argument in free market capitalism is that a competitive marketplace facilitates a dynamic market, but the opposite is true for these big networked tech firms. I have recently done searches on Yahoo and found the quality of the search results much worse than in Google. The reason why Google produces "better" search results is because they have developed a more refined way to search items. They have more ad money, better engineers, better algorithms, better variety of data etc.

Similarly, we would not want people to turn away from Facebook not despite but because of the more than a billion worldwide users. While I do not think that social relations have become better because of Facebook we have benefited from being able to stay in touch with friends that we otherwise had not been able to meet for a long time. The importance of face-to-face relations, which is the most natural form of social relations in human history, is not smaller than in the past, but to the extent that Facebook is a supplement of communication it is better than not having it.

But if we really do appreciate the control and domination of our tech overlords are we not also legitimating the current capitalist system that then benefits one of these faces that we see above? Absolutely. We are trapped in a conundrum, but only because we believe in the fallacy that accepting the services of tech giants means that we automatically accept the given level of income and wealth distribution. If we are interested in maintaining social stability and economic justice, it would be only fair to massively increase taxation on these giant tech firms or at least their owners.

The argument for social stability is not so difficult to present, because the ever-growing rift between rich and poor provides the fertile resource for populist politics. Aristotle (1988) himself had argued that only a broad and vast middle class can retain overall political stability, because the middle class can serve as citizens and rule as rulers and because everyone has a stake in society. In a society, where a few people own most of the wealth, the wealthy can only rule and the poor can only serve and lack any stake in society. They are then easily susceptible to demagogues of different forms, who themselves usually want to concentrate power in their own hands. Political uncertainty then undermines the free capitalist society itself. Relatively greater economic egalitarianism also provides the purchasing power, which feeds into economic growth.

The argument for economic justice is harder to understand in ideologically more capitalist countries. Defenders of tech billionaire wealth say that if the tech owner provides services that everyone wants to buy (e.g. Microsoft products), they deserve all of the wealth. But is that really the case? It is certainly true that Bill Gates is the pivotal figure in Microsoft, because without his will to put the firm together, it would not exist, though we could imagine that someone else would have done it if it were not him. What matters, however, is that any tech company can only hope to develop its products as a result of hundreds of years of innovative capacity of many different human beings. The government had massively invested into the defense-industrial complex, which created the early forms of the internet and the computer. These tech innovations were then gradually privatized as commercial applications became available. So if we are really concerned about "just deserts", we would have to pay off some of our dead ancestors, who developed the previous forms of innovation that served as the basis for today's innovation, and we have to pay off the government in the form of higher taxes. The former case is harder to make, but the latter case is much more justifiable.

We should also not underestimate the importance of the contributions of current tech workers, as a look at the revenue per employee of leading tech firms show. $2.1 million for Apple workers, $1.8 million for Netflix workers, $1.4 million for Facebook workers and $1.2 million for Alphabet/ Google workers.

In four of the top-listed tech companies, the revenue is more than a million dollars per year. Most people will say that because of the high productivity of these tech workers (which really reflects the higher sale value that is possible for tech products, e.g. a Youtube video can be downloaded millions of times), they receive higher than average wages anyway, which is true, and the sky-rocketing real estate prices in the Bay Area is clearly evidence of that (which pushes out low-income residents there). But I have never heard that an Apple engineer earns nearly 2 million dollars, even though productivity would justify it.

The revenues are not wages, because the company owners get to decide what happens with the revenue, so it is not surprising that the biggest beneficiaries of the revenues are the tech company owners. In a traditional Marxist account, the workers would not only get paid more than they currently do (which would make the handsome faces above much less wealthy than they currently are), but they would also control the company's surplus. But I would claim, that even such statement is besides the point. Even if an Apple worker were paid 2 million dollars, it would still be massive theft from downstream workers (like manufacturers of Apple products, who operate in a more competitive market and have much smaller margins of profit). That illustrates that we can't really solve the inequality problem by strengthening the case for a labor aristocracy, while the uneducated, untrained, underemployed and unemployed rabble can vote for Donald Trump and otherwise screw themselves.

The tech industry is at the heart of growing inequality, and it is inevitable that if we want to have a claim for social, political and economic justice it is necessary to renew the social contract. That would first require an expansion of social policy. The masses cannot merely be fed resentment against weaker groups that are not to be blamed for our social problems (i.e. women, minorities, immigrants etc.). They need to have social policy that actually helps them, which may include the expansion of traditional programs like a higher minimum wage, social insurance, universal health care, free higher education, free child care, generous family leave policies and higher pensions. There is a limitation to such an approach as well, because it does not do enough for people, who are pushed into unemployment. The old institutions insist on the laborist political economy, which centers on wage work as a primary means to survive. The new institutions have to sever the tie between wage work and survival. The universal basic income would help as well, but I doubt it will be enough.

Max Weber (1994: 16) gave us the brilliant insight that history can provide us with nothing more than struggle. There is no doubt that the immediate future will be rife with struggle despite all the economic abundance that could make our life quasi stress-free.

The Executive Reign of Terror
Posted on January 30, 2017

Critics of the imperial presidency are having their heyday. They would warn against the rule-making by fiat of a single powerful president. To some extent, the great presidential power might have been made necessary by the ineptitude of US Congress to pass more laws to address the challenges the country is facing: universal health care, free higher education, a moratorium on student debt, a massive job creation program, scaling down of the military and covert forms of military aggression (drone warfare, special ops), just to name a few. That was never going to happen under the Obama administration, which by its temperament was moderate in policy. And it certainly wasn't going to happen in a Republican Congress, which declared its goal to block passage of any meaningful legislation that could benefit the American people.

Yet, here we are. We have a deranged, narcissistic new US president, who has not been wasting any time to sign executive orders in the fulfillment of his campaign promises. I go through it in order, laying out the precise problems with each order, and then reflect on the institution of executive orders. Despite the deranged nature of the current president, I defend the importance of executive orders when Congress makes law-making so difficult, because (1) laws require both chambers' approval, (2) laws often need bipartisan consensus to pass, (3) the dynamic of wealthy people and corporations influencing the political process in Congress make any populist program a la Bernie Sanders unfeasible to pass.

The discussion of the Trump executive orders does not cover the presidential memoranda, which are also worth remarking on: Trump's memoranda approve two oil pipelines (Dakota Access and Keystone), falling in line with his love of oil companies (Rex Tillerson, Exxon Mobile CEO, was appointed secretary of state). This bodes ill for the environment and will accelerate the troubling effects of climate change. He banned the use of federal dollars for abortion-related counseling in poor foreign countries, which will have a negative impact on the health and well-being of women of childbearing age in those countries.

He withdrew from the TPP, which I think is so far the only positive policy. The Obama administration had sold the TPP as the US' ability to write the trade rule in the Pacific as opposed to China. But in this geopolitical game the administration was ignorant of the harm that a trade treaty imposes on people, because the TPP favors investors with an investor-dispute-settlement system. If people consider this "just", they should think twice because the trade settlement would override national jurisdictions via international tribunals that are run by corporate lawyers. It is like being a thief and have your criminal case be handled by your brother. Generally speaking, there is not much appetite for trade treaties in the developed world, because the mass of workers know they won't benefit from it. Xi Jinping had recently appeared in Davos to defend free trade, but he knows that the Chinese economy is still most likely to benefit from such trade the most. I don't support a high tariff policy for the US and generally favor free trade, but thus far the labor losses were concentrated in the high-wage locations.

On to the executive orders: On his first day in office (January 20), Trump signed an executive order (#13765) to declare his intent to repeal the Affordable Care Act, which currently provides health insurance to 20 million people. The order also prescribes that the health secretary has the right to block any provision, which would add costs to the states and to the people insofar as it does not subvert the law. But we can imagine how the order will subvert the law.

The ACA is a rather fragile law, which requires the full determination of the administration for it to work. If any funding for the subsidies were restricted or if the website on which the exchange operates did not work so smoothly, then people's health insurance access would become limited. That may increase the ire among the population and might make them, ironically, support an ACA repeal, but the bigger problem is that the Republican Party really has no intention to create a new health care plan. The dilemma is they can't really say they want to return to a status quo ante, where the denial of coverage for pre-existing conditions and a lifetime limitation on insurance reimbursement would come back. The only positive way out is a single-payer system, which is, however, not even being debated. In the meantime, the ACA is piecemeal dismantled without any more positive prospects. The Republicans don't have better ideas on health care, because the ACA comes from the Heritage Foundation and the Republicans themselves (Reich 2013).

The next executive order (#13766)[7] was signed on the 24th and intends to expedite the environmental review process for public

---

[7] https://www.whitehouse.gov/presidential-actions/executive-order-expediting-environmental-reviews-approvals-high-priority-infrastructure-

infrastructure projects. The process of approvals by the federal administration shall be limited to only 30 days. This might be considered a positive executive order, but one shall think carefully what the impact on the environment is going to be. The order does not say anything about increasing funding for the agency responsible for implementing the environmental reviews, and to the extent that administrators will now be forced to expedite the review process, they will be less likely to be careful in safeguarding the environment.

The next two executive orders (#13767; #13768)[8] on the 25th mandate an expedited process for the deportation of illegal or undocumented immigrants, especially those committing acts of violence or felony. Any federal funding for sanctuary cities (local jurisdictions that refuse cooperation with federal officials to identify undocumented immigrants) shall be "reviewed". 10,000 federal officials shall be added to enforce the expedition of deportations. The first order sets up the southern border wall with Mexico. The deportation of undocumented immigrants has the precedent in the Obama administration, but is unfortunately stepped up under the Trump administration. A more rational solution would be to create a path to citizenship for undocumented immigrants, who are easily scapegoated, because they currently do not have any voting rights (though their US-born children do, but they are too few and many of them still not voters).

The more troubling part is the Mexican border wall, which the Mexican administration has repeatedly refused to pay for, but has been part of Trump's campaign plank. The trouble is not only on the human level (e.g. the difficulty of reuniting separated families), but also on an international relations level. It is troubling that the US administration would risk to deteriorate economic and political relations with Mexico, the closest next-door neighbor, by building this inhumane wall. The administration had also suggested that Mexico will pay for the wall, and that shall happen via a 20% import tariff on Mexican goods. This may affect Mexican producers, but it will also affect US companies deciding to build their products in Mexico and bring it back to the US. More importantly, it will affect

---

projects/

[8] https://www.whitehouse.gov/presidential-actions/executive-order-border-security-immigration-enforcement-improvements/ and https://www.whitehouse.gov/presidential-actions/executive-order-enhancing-public-safety-interior-united-states/

US consumers through the higher prices they will pay in the market. These higher prices will more than offset any gains of protectionism, which might help only a few domestic producers.

On the 27th, Trump signed another executive order (#13769),[9] which banned his highest federal staffers from taking on any lobbying position for five years, but critics already say that this order is a weakening of ethics standards for federal officials because it strips a public disclosure requirement, which makes it difficult for the public to determine whether the stricter guidelines will be enforced (Gold 2017). They probably won't be. It is also hard to think that a cabinet of billionaires and lobbyists will be able to disassociate itself with any conflicts of interest. Trump's cabinet has more wealth than the bottom 1/3 of the US population combined (Calfas 2016), so much for "taking care of the forgotten men and women" and "draining the swamp".

In the newest executive order also signed on the 27th (#13780)[10], which has been the most controversial, the US suspends the refugee program for 120 days and bars nationals of six countries (Iraq, Iran, Libya, Somalia, Sudan, and Yemen) for 90 days and from Syria indefinitely, regardless of visa. Initially, the Department of Homeland Security (DHS) included current green card holders as well, which was just reversed earlier today. The ban does not affect dual nationals of those seven countries and the US, but does affect dual nationals of those seven countries and any other country. Trump must have thought that the Muslim ban would really work well with his white working class supporters, many of which have no sympathy with foreigners and refugees that they either perceive to take their jobs and benefits or simply don't know anything about.

But this time the country was no longer silent. People gathered around airports to carry out mass demonstrations against federal officials, who held hostage the affected people and denied their entry into the US. Don't forget that international airports tend to be located in the larger cities that overwhelmingly vote Democratic and oppose Trump vigorously. The cities are the base for anti-Trump resistance, which will be way more grassroots than the billionaire-funded Tea Party. Liberal Congress members, governors and mayors

---

[9] https://www.whitehouse.gov/presidential-actions/executive-order-ethics-commitments-executive-branch-appointees/

[10] https://www.whitehouse.gov/presidential-actions/executive-order-protecting-nation-foreign-terrorist-entry-united-states-2/

showed up at the airport to join the protests. Social media feeds are filled with a passionate condemnation of the new president's executive order. The ACLU and other civil rights organizations filed a lawsuit on the eve of the 27th. The next day, New York federal judge, Ann Donnelly, issued an order to release the held-up refugees (though DHS continues to insist on executing Trump's order).

The morality is easily stated: how fair is it in the name of "protecting against terrorists" to target innocent refugees fleeing from a civil war and other civilians (students, scholars, business people, workers), who have nothing to do with terrorism? How can the US claim it is the land of the free and the home of the brave, when it excludes people, who have been playing by the rule? (NB: it takes 2 years to receive US security clearance for refugees.) How much is the US guarding against terrorism, when rejected individuals return to their country, develop distrust against the US and might become receptive to the terrorist preachers?

The US administration is setting a dangerous precedent of excluding people based on their religious belief and their country of origin. For the latter case, we unfortunately know that there is a precedent with the Chinese exclusion act of 1882, which barred the entry of Chinese nationals into the US and was not loosened until the Magnuson Act of 1943. For the former case, I have not heard of any religious ban, even though for most of its history, the US did tend to favor immigrants from Christian-majority countries. For that reason, the Trump administration defended the order by saying that the ban had nothing to do with religion, but it was about ensuring national security procedures were in place before resuming the entry of such nationals (Schultheis 2017).

The administration can also claim that not all majority-Muslim country nationals (e.g. Turkey, Malaysia or Saudi Arabia) were banned from entering the US. What is interesting to note, however, is that those Muslim countries were exempted from the ban, which the Trump organization does business with (Painter and Eisen 2017). It shows that Trump is incapable of separating himself from his business interests, speaking of ethics standards. The Bush and Obama ethics lawyers (Painter and Eisen 2017) write, "It appears that immigrants from countries that can afford to do business with the Trump organization are free to come and go from the United States. Immigrants from countries that cannot afford such transactions may very well be detained at the airport and sent home, where some may perish."

There is no doubt that the administration is specifically targeting Muslims, because Trump noted his preference for Christian refugees (Schor and Kim 2017). He is making partially good on his campaign promise, which is driven by fear and hatred of Muslims and refugees. The bigotry is massively escalating under the new Trump administration that does not offer much social protection for what he had called "the forgotten men and women" (Killian 2017), but instead words of resentment against the outsiders, who are easy prey as they are not numerous or influential enough to defend themselves. To ban any Syrian refugees from entering the country is irresponsible insofar as American bombs and gun exports to Syria have contributed massively to the violence and civil war in the region (see the "Assad must go" line by Obama, Clinton and Kerry), and taking on even just some of the displaced civilians is the fair albeit insufficient compensation for the carnage that the US had helped to create in the Middle East.

Instead, the Europeans (who did their fair share of bombing) have been held responsible for accepting many of the refugees, while an even greater share ended up with Syria's immediate neighbors: Jordan, Lebanon and Turkey. I understand that the new administration is not responsible for the mess in Syria, but given that Trump had authorized continued bombings in Yemen (Ackerman 2017) there is a tremendous amount of policy continuity from the old administration. The US bombs the Middle East and takes no refugees, which is the most hypocritical foreign policy position of all countries.

What's the way forward? What makes me quite hopeful is that the enormous public pushback against the Trump administration galvanizes the pushback against the Trump administration in the coming months and years. Continuous mass mobilization might result in calls for impeachment or other forms of expression to prevent the negative excesses of the current administration. There is a natural danger and fear that not much will happen as time goes on, because Trump might hit the heavy targets early on in his administration, but then rule quietly. That could, in fact, be the best prospect for the country if that were to happen. I doubt it, though.

The most scary aspect to me is that while the media and the public will be so obsessed by the outrageous statements and actions of Trump, his billionaire cabinet and the Republican Congress can quietly work on their real objectives: to defund the last pillars of the New Deal social safety net and empower billionaires with more tax breaks and favorable policies. The rather dystopian vision for this country is that income inequality will become larger, while the common people are so distracted by either attacking a minority group or having to waste their energy to defending this group. Historically, only a civil war or a foreign war can mitigate this powder keg.

The question as it stands from a constitutional viewpoint is whether the president should have such latitude in executive power. I would still say yes, because the constitutionality of particular decisions would still have to pass the test of judges, virtually all of which had not been appointed by the Trump administration (which will change as time goes on). But given that most federal judges stay for a long time (there is no term or appointment limit), Trump will not be able revamp the entire judicial system all at once (there are over 3,200 federal judges). In addition, the country does have a need for a powerful president if legislating in Congress is made complicated by the three obstacles I had outlined, i.e (1) laws require both chambers' approval, (2) laws often need bipartisan consensus to pass, (3) the dynamic of wealthy people and corporations influencing the political process in Congress make any populist program a la Bernie Sanders unfeasible to pass.

I know there will be people, who will attack me for sponsoring a "benevolent dictator", when our dictator is everything but benevolent. In countries, where authoritarian rule is way more harmful for individual freedom, expression and dignity, the dictatorial powers are so bad that constitutional limitations on their power would make sense (though it would remain inefficacious if the norms and traditions of a country are stacked against a free and democratic order). But I should remind people of what the alternative is to weaken the powers of the president: to have a system that makes it really difficult to change the country for the positive. A Sanders presidency, for instance, could have changed the political dynamic massively even with a Republican Congress. While much of what Sanders campaigned on are spending programs that require Congressional approval, he could sign executive orders that tilt the balance in favor of working people without the xenophobia that we see with our current president. In that sense, the flaw is not exclusively to be found in a given institution, but in what individual is put into the position of responsibility.

We can see today all the negative implications of an imperial presidency with a leader, who questions the foundations of US values and norms like few previous presidents. But it is the immorality of the leader and not the institution that poses problems to us. The country can only hope to fight back when mass mobilizations don't abate. We have no other choices in these dark days ahead.

Review of Rodriguez-Franco: Internal Wars, Taxation and State Building

Posted on January 30, 2017

Rodríguez-Franco, Diana. "Internal Wars, Taxation, and State Building." *American Sociological Review* (2016), Vol.81 (1): 190-213.

I found a fantastic case study of internal wars resulting in state-building in Colombia. The author claims that a patriotic desire and fear for their security because of the danger of FARC rebels make the elites willing to support higher taxes (wealth tax) on them by the state, so it can finance the military to fight FARC. President Alvaro Uribe's (2002-2010) fight against the FARC apparently worked, as the security fears of the elites diminished. Some troubling aspects, however, deserve remarking on:

(1) the patriotic motives of elites were entirely self-reported and I doubt that many elites would be that patriotic if they could survive on their own private security.

(2) the abatement of non-state violence would reduce elite commitment to the state and would imply their desire to reduce taxation. In the Colombian case, rising tax obligations were associated with rising welfare expenditures, but state taxation has also increased on all levels, not just wealth taxes but also the broader income tax.

(3) What follows is also the premise that it requires elite willingness and permission for the state to raise wealth taxes, suggesting that it is hard to keep up wealth taxes if they oppose it. Austria's post WW II settlement, for instance, retained the wealth tax until the 1990s, which coincided with a period of austerity and budget consolidation on social programs. The US estate tax is slated for abolition under billionaire president Trump and his billionaire cabinet, while Trump has also surrendered any pretense to maintain Social Security and other welfare programs post-election. Short of a new civil war, there won't be any elite commitment to wealth taxes, and any mass mobilization tends to obscure the link between wealth taxes and welfare state spending. In the words of our commander-in-chief: Sad!!!

Donald Trump Is Neither a Kantian Nor a Normal Politician
Posted on February 2, 2017

The title of the post may be really obvious to many observers of daily political life in America, but it is still worthwhile to flesh out how the election of Trump ushers in an era of illiberal democracy (Zakaria 1997), where "alternative facts" (or lies in the words of reasonable people not caught up in Orwell's *1984* [1949]) rule.

In reference to conflict of interest among politicians, I distinguish between a Kantian politician (very idealized, very rare to find), a normal politician and a Trumpian politician. These three brands of politicians can be distinguished based on the ideal they hold, the public statements about themselves they make and their real actions.

We do have a record of Trump saying that "[t]he law's totally on my side, *the president can't have a conflict of interest*" (Arnsdorf 2016). A conflict of interest would be if the president used his presidential office to enrich himself or his family. Trump's claim may be considered a statement, but it appeared to me that he was equating the law with what is ideal. Here Trump was referring to his many businesses that he refused to put into a blind trust to ensure that he could not continue making deals and enriching himself while being president.

The fact that presidential enrichment can happen is shown by the fact that the Argentinians had been holding up a building permit for a Trump Tower in Buenos Aires until Trump was elected president after which it was approved. At that point, the government of Argentina realized that it was inopportune for Argentina to offend the president of the United States by refusing a building permit to his organization (Stahl 2016). Even if his children are running the business, the fact that he is working closely together with his family means that business interests will still remain front-and-center while Trump runs the federal administration. In addition, the fact that foreign dignitaries prefer to stay in a Trump hotel enriches the president, while the guests hope they can curry favor with the US administration. Trump can claim that they prefer to stay in a Trump hotel because they like the quality of the hotel, but the fact that so many dignitaries now choose the Trump hotel cannot be considered a coincidence, for if they liked the Trump hotels so much why would they not sign up to it before he was elected president? (Carroll 2017)

As far as his statements are concerned, he noted in his press conference that he could have taken advantage of a very profitable deal but did not take the deal, even though, as he said, he could have, because the law did not prescribe anything. Don't forget that as president, he now has the political clout to demand laws to close the Trump loophole by tightening up legislation on presidential conflicts of interest, but out of self-interest he will not demand such legislation such that it can be presumed that, according to Trump, the current conflict-of-interest law is ideal and shall not be changed. In the press conference, Trump stated,

Over the weekend, I was offered $2 billion to do a deal in Dubai with a very, very, very amazing man, a great, great developer from the Middle East, Hussein Damack, a friend of mine, great guy. And I was offered $2 billion to do a deal in Dubai — a number of deals and I turned it down.

I didn't have to turn it down, because as you know, I have a no-conflict situation because I'm president, which is — I didn't know about that until about three months ago, but it's a nice thing to have. But I don't want to take advantage of something.

Source: New York Times (Jan. 11, 2017)[11]

As far as action is concerned, it is evident that Trump is engaged in conflicts of interest. We now have enough information to fill a table of the three types of politicians and interpret it.

Table 1: Conflicts of interest and the three types of politicians

Politician	Ideal	Statement	Action
Kantian	"Conflicts-of-interest are unacceptable."	"I don't engage in conflicts of interest."	Does not engage in conflict of interest
Normal	"Conflicts-of-interest are unacceptable."	"I don't engage in conflicts of interest."	Engages in conflict of interest

---

[11] https://www.nytimes.com/2017/01/11/us/politics/trump-press-conference-transcript.html

Trumpian	"President can't have conflicts of interest."	"But I don't want to take advantage of something [i.e. conflicts of interest]."	Engages in conflict of interest

The Kantian politician will consider refraining from conflicts of interest as most ideal, will say that in public statements and act accordingly. A normal politician will also find conflicts of interest unacceptable, will make public statements to that effect, but unlike the Kantian politician, the normal politician preaches water and drinks wine. His/her action is driven by conflicts of interest. The list of politicians falling in that framework are too numerous to list, which is why I had called that group the "normal" politician.

As I stated before, Trump's ideal may not be to explicitly endorse the statement that "conflicts of interest are acceptable" but implicitly he endorses it, because he accepts the current legal framework in which the law does not prescribe that the president has to divest from all his businesses, even though that has been the historic tradition of previous presidents. His statement of not wanting to "take advantage of something" (i.e. conflict of interest) is equivalent to that of the other two politician types, which means that he says of himself that he does not engage in conflicts of interest. His actions (foreign dignitaries staying in Trump hotels; foreign countries approving Trump projects; accepting donations from foreign governments or organizations etc.) indicate that he is engaged in conflict of interest, just like most other politicians.

(NB: One may think of a fourth type of politician, who finds conflicts of interest acceptable on all counts, even for statements. Perhaps there are mafia bosses, who say that conflicts of interest are okay, and that would be as far away from Kantian ethics as possible, or one could say it lines up the most neatly because of the consistency. I have trouble to think of the implications of such a fourth type.)

To state it even more simply, I evaluate the ethics of the three types of politicians. The premise hereby is that conflicts of interest are unethical and no conflicts of interest is ethical:

Table 2: Ethics of the three types of politicians

Politician	Ideal	Statement	Action
Kantian	Ethical	Ethical	Ethical
Normal	Ethical	Ethical	Not ethical
Trumpian	Not ethical	Ethical	Not ethical

Only the statements makes all three politicians the same, which should tell us that we should automatically be wary about anything any politician tells us even if there are a few Kantians among them. The normal politician is what we have come to expect. Great political power translates into great economic power as well. More troublesome in our age is that with Trump rejecting the ideal of the ethical he is getting away with the worst of all lies: "A president is legally allowed to have conflicts of interest, but because I am such a nice guy, I won't partake in it, but, of course, I will really be engaged in conflicts of interest when the camera is not watching." With that line of reasoning he is building himself a higher defense wall than he deserves. A normal politician would only be in a position to maintain an ethical stance for the statements, but not on the ideal.

The implication for the public that has the greatest interest in the least amount of conflict of interest and corruption among high officials is that it should challenge the unethical ideals and actions with all might. But with what Trump had denounced as "fake news" it would be difficult to accomplish. Not that I agree with Trump's Orwellian reversion of the truth, but I do think that journalists (especially on cable news) have treated politics as if it were a soap opera rather than about issues that affect the real lives of people. There are some alternative sources of news media that hold the leaders accountable even during our transition to an administration run by a pathological liar and narcissist, and who can't wait to diminish any role and influence of the fourth estate.

Steve Adler, the editor in chief of the Reuters news agency, informed his staff that given the anti-press sentiment of the new US administration, reporters should treat the Trump administration as if it were an authoritarian government.

"Get out into the country and learn more about how people live, what they think, what helps and hurts them, and how the government and its actions appear to them, not to us."

The letter encouraged reporters to "never be intimidated" by the administration.

Source: Edwards (2017)

In very Orwellian times, when what is right is wrong and what is wrong is right, it matters more than ever for journalists to stick to what is right and demand politicians to idealize, speak and act more Kantian.

Schwarzenegger vs. Trump: A Styrian Oak Resisting The Donald

Posted on February 6, 2017

The big news of the week was that James Robart, a Washington federal judge, lifted the travel ban for seven Muslim countries, whose nationals are now allowed to re-enter the US with their visa and green cards. It was a major victory for the rule of law, though it won't do much to change the shock and awe type policy orientation which marks Trump policy for the next few years.

On a more entertaining note, Trump had ridiculed Arnold Schwarzenegger, former governor of California, bodybuilder, movie actor and entertainer on his Celebrity Apprentice show for his low ratings compared to what Trump himself was able to accomplish.[12] Schwarzenegger, himself a person without a small ego, lashed back against the President by proposing in a videotape to switch roles between him and Trump.[13] Trump knows the TV entertainment world so well, while President Schwarzenegger would allow people to "sleep comfortably again". Who is this bodybuilder/movie star/real-estate investor/governor/entertainer?

I had read Schwarzenegger's (2013) autobiography in parts and watched a few of his old bodybuilding videos explaining what bodybuilding was, while endlessly promoting it. His strong Austrian accent betrays his heritage, which he always sought to escape. Having also spent most of my childhood in Austria, I may be able to speak about an important personality characteristic that lifts him above the average Austrian and make him have such a strong ego that gets engaged in public conflicts, as is the case with Trump.

Schwarzenegger was born and raised in Thal, near Graz in Austria, in 1947. His father worked for the local police in postwar Austria. At that time, the British had occupied the southeastern part of Austria (it was divided in 4 between 1945 and 1955 under allied occupation, which ended with the state neutrality treaty- the most crucial founding story of the second Austrian republic). The war had just ended. The country was destroyed. Most people had rather meager incomes, as did his parents. His mother administered the family income, which was exclusively earned by his father. His father wanted him to become a police officer like himself, and his mother

---

[12] https://www.youtube.com/watch?v=XXg74qdfBuo
[13] https://www.youtube.com/watch?v=4Xo-Nn2Jz1w

wanted him to go to trade school, though he was satisfied with none of it.

Showing an early entrepreneurial talent he would work part-time besides school at a young age, so he could buy the equipment for bodybuilding. He was first inspired to take up bodybuilding after visiting a gym. He had also watched a movie about the US, which had big highways, bridges, buildings and roads. He was so mesmerized by the large size of objects in the US that he really wanted to live there, while everything else in Austria became too small for his taste. He began bodybuilding at age 14 and realized that it would get him the entrance ticket to immigrate to the US, which happened promptly at age 21 shortly after he won the Mr. Universe. A talent scout in the US became interested in Schwarzenegger and invited him to train and compete in a US championship (very instructive is a recent 2016 interview with Schwarzenegger, where he laid out his dream to immigrate to the US[14]).

Schwarzenegger's immigrant dreams are most clearly expressed via his undiminished praise for America. Consider, for instance, this recent interview in his own Schwarzenegger Institute at the University of Southern California, where Schwarzenegger said that the US was going through challenges (i.e. a Trump administration) but he was optimistic it could get out of the bind, because America was the promised nation. That is where immigrants want to go to, not China, Russia or the Middle East.[15] In some sense, being a naturalized American he is more obsessively American than native-born Americans themselves. One can glean it from his passion and desire to make a better life than what was possible in Austria. The kinds of cultural, social and economic gains he made were unique to his US immigrant experience and would not be possible in Austria. In Austria, very few people cared about bodybuilding, movie-making (there is a small domestic movie industry, but it's entirely local and irrelevant internationally) or entertainment (entirely self-referential and local). There is a political life in Austria, but it is also heavily focused on domestic policy, because the country is too small to have much political weight. Austria hosts the UN, claiming its status as a neutral country, but Schwarzenegger's feet were too big for the small shoes that Austria offered him.

---

[14] https://www.youtube.com/watch?v=wFiNHn8sZ-A

[15] https://www.youtube.com/watch?v=nPDZfN4iXF8

There was also a political element in Austria that Schwarzenegger had deeply disliked. Consider his 2004 speech at the Republican National Convention, where he passionately explained why he became a Republican:

I finally arrived here in 1968. What a special day it was. I remember I arrived here with empty pockets but full of dreams, full of determination, full of desire. The presidential campaign was in full swing. I remember watching the Nixon–Humphrey presidential race on TV. A friend of mine who spoke German and English translated for me. I heard Humphrey saying things that sounded like socialism, which I had just left.

But then I heard Nixon speak. He was talking about free enterprise, getting the government off your back, lowering the taxes and strengthening the military. Listening to Nixon speak sounded more like a breath of fresh air. I said to my friend, I said, "What party is he?" My friend said, "He's a Republican." I said, "Then I am a Republican." And I have been a Republican ever since.

Source: Wikipedia ("Arnold Schwarzenegger # Early Politics")

Austria was "socialist" in the eyes of Schwarzenegger. I find the comparison somewhat facile given that even the most progressive Democrats are still somewhat more conservative than conservative Austrians. But the point hit home for the cheering American audience. Austrians would never understand why the state does not take the responsibility to address social problems, while US discourse would legitimate more private sector involvement even if that meant not enough poverty reduction or fulfilling other social goals like universal health care. What Schwarzenegger was looking for was an outlet to make money and to make it big, and it is true that the US would provide him an outlet, which he would have been denied in Austria.

In Austria, there is this concept of the "Neidgesellschaft" or society of envy. If you worked harder than a colleague and gained a promotion, it would be looked down on and be part of gossip among coworkers. In that context, there is not much individual advancement. US culture cannot be accused of envy. From my own experience, I was academically a quite reasonable student in Austria, but did not make much out of it. The teachers gave me high marks, though their main attention was on the "problem students" with low marks, and the other students didn't care or labeled me a 'nerd'. When I came to the US, the teachers in high school all the way to university had recognized my academic talent and nominated me for all kinds of class best awards and scholarships. By the time I got to UPenn that honor went to other gifted students, who were even more accomplished on visible performance criteria than me. In any case, the recognition for success in US society is unique enough to have the most excellent performers be recognized. (Needless to say, the disadvantage in US culture is the massive tolerance for inequality, which has become so counter-productive that it led to the election of a crazy right-wing billionaire for president.)

In addition, Austria has what is called an "Obrigkeitsstaat" or hierarchical state, which enforced strict division between the emperor, the aristocracy, the bourgeoisie and the working class. The boundaries are not as strictly enforced as the Indian caste system, but a class system remains a class system. Careful observers of Austria will now object that we no longer have a monarch in Austria, but remember Crown Prince Otto's death in 2011, where the entire political establishment attended his funeral, even though they were supposed to not have ruled for almost 100 years at that point. There is plenty of Obrigkeitsstaat-mentality left in the Austrian society. Another example would be the Austrian use of titles and education qualifications that are attached to one's name in every correspondence both written and spoken. No such entrenched formality exists in US culture, where people of all ages are addressed with their first name. That facilitates social mobility at least on a cultural level (if not economic level) much more than in European societies. I would often recognize returning home from travel in Europe, when random strangers would start talking with me in the airport in the US. In Europe, it doesn't happen that often because of the clearer status differences, which increases suspicion to interact with strangers.

Back to Schwarzenegger: at age 21, he got to the US and continued on his stellar bodybuilding career. What is notable is his enormous stamina and willpower to train and work hard every day to grow his muscles and compete in tournaments. He used his bodybuilding and mail-order business revenues to finance real estate. The rental properties (both business and private housing) made him a millionaire. The real success, however, happened when he switched from bodybuilding to acting in movies. He got the role of Conan the Barbarian, apparently a great role for him, because his English was still heavily accented, he didn't have to speak much and it required a muscular person swinging around the sword. He had long expressed his desire for acting, which was a clever move given that a bodybuilding career has physical age limitations (he retired in 1975 and made a brief comeback in 1980 to win the Mr. Olympia). Schwarzenegger's most successful movie series was Terminator, where he seemed to have immortalized himself with his famous line, "I'll be back." As a clever self-promoter, similar to Trump, who slapped his name onto all kinds of buildings as a branding effort, Schwarzenegger would make sure that he could recycle his famous movie lines in other movies, public interviews or other presentations (see this Youtube compilation[16]).

Whatever movie profits he made, Schwarzenegger kept on reinvesting them into real estate, stocks, bonds and other financial products, thus ensuring that he would have a solid cashflow under any circumstances. If the American Dream meant making a lot of money, he certainly achieved it with different estimates of his net worth ranging from 200 to 800 million dollars. Such a fortune is not impossible in Austria, but unrealistic given that he came from a family with modest financial background. Notice in the list of the super-rich in Austria that all of them made their money from a big corporation they have founded and directed (or inherited). There is no movie actor or bodybuilder or any kind of one-man shows among it. You can earn a decent salary as an Austrian actor, but they usually don't tend to become super-rich as Hollywood stars.

Making movies, being famous wasn't enough for Schwarzenegger. While being in the US, he married Maria Shriver, the daughter of Eunice and Sargent Shriver, who were members of the Kennedy clan, at one point the most powerful political family in the US. Schwarzenegger said he was very inspired by his in-laws' spirit for public service and giving back, which is what ultimately also motivated him to run for governor of California. Looking back it is hard to ultimately prove whether it was only his dedication to public service that had sparked his political interest. Given his big ego and desire for advancement (remember the 12 year old child in Graz imbibing the glitzy images of New York's huge buildings and streets during a movie screening?), he must have also been seeking for a new outlet to realize his passions, his need for attention and domination, an alpha-male characteristic that reminds us of Trump. Wendy Leigh, a biographer of Schwarzenegger, quotes his obsession for power,

---

[16] https://www.youtube.com/watch?v=-YEG9DgRHhA

"I wanted to be part of the small percentage of people who were leaders, not the large mass of followers. I think it is because I saw leaders use 100% of their potential... I was always fascinated by people in control of other people."

Source: Borger and Campbell (2003)

Schwarzenegger, typical for his show-biz orientation, decided to announce his candidacy for governor of California during an interview with Jay Leno in August 2003. The state's electricity and budget crisis opened the political opportunity for Schwarzenegger to run for governor. There wasn't any doubt that he would win the election. Yes, there were political opponents, who tried to bring him down for his sexual molestation of women, another similarity with his nemesis Trump. In a profoundly Puritan US, a sexual molestation charge is quite serious and damaging to a political career. But the governor at that time was also highly unpopular, and Schwarzenegger had a name recognition like no one else given his background as a Hollywood actor. Despite lacking any formal political experience, Schwarzenegger was elected governor in the recall election of 2003.

It wasn't the case that he was able to solve California's chronic budget problem better than his predecessors, especially as he had to manage a great recession which reduced tax revenues. The political system in California made tax increases difficult, requiring a two-thirds supermajority to approve them. The income tax is progressive but limited to a few very wealthy individuals, which suggests more space for untapped revenues. Schwarzenegger oversaw the 2008-9 recession, where he massively pushed for spending cuts while the opposition Democrats wanted tax increases, so not much got done and he left office in 2011 with a low approval rating.

The one area of success as governor was his environmental initiative, which he signed in 2006 under heavy opposition of the oil lobby. He lowered the permissible carbon emissions in factories and prohibited contracting with companies that refused to submit to these carbon rules. Schwarzenegger's major cause is to fight climate change, which is an issue that many people can get behind. It isn't something that Trump or most other mainstream Republicans receiving checks from the oil lobby would sign up for.

The one area of controversy in his governorship for Austrians was when he signed the death penalty order for a prison inmate (Stanley Williams) in 2005. Typical of most other Republicans, Schwarzenegger wanted to show that he was tough on crime, but

Austria had long ago removed the death penalty, which the EU also sees as a requirement for entry. Peter Pilz, a Green politician in the Austrian parliament, lobbied parliament to revoke his Austrian nationality for "damaging the reputation" of the Republic of Austria. It didn't go anywhere. I think the judges were more than happy to have such a powerful exponent of their country hold such a powerful political position in the US. Another controversy emerged when people of Graz (his hometown) began protesting the continued naming of the local football stadium after Schwarzenegger. It was a newly built stadium in 1995, which local officials had named after Schwarzenegger, but when the death penalty was decided on during Schwarzenegger's tenure as governor, local protesters wanted to have his name removed. Schwarzenegger heard of the criticism in his former home town and he sent a letter to the city government in Graz, prohibiting the use of his name for the stadium, thus resolving the controversy. His name was removed from the stadium shortly thereafter.

The Austrians are hereby taking the moral high ground. Of course, the death penalty is wrong, though I doubt that such extreme reactions were warranted. But, clearly, there is a moral dark side to US crime policy, which manages to incarcerate more people than China despite its four times larger population and way more authoritarian government.

After Schwarzenegger's tenure as governor, he immediately headed back to his movie career, continuing to shoot movies, even though the age wrinkles were clearly visible in his face. He is turning 70 this year. There are still speculations about his political ambitions. He was interested in running for the US presidency, and he would have a good chance given that his foreign background and his celebrity status would make him an establishment outsider, which is what Americans are craving for so desperately. But that was the real problem, because the US constitution prohibited a foreign-born president. Speculations about a legal challenge were quickly quashed in 2013. Would he have been better than President Trump? No doubts can exist.

But Schwarzenegger had virtually accomplished all his goals, making a steep rise from his youth in Austria. But one could sense the restlessness in many of his actions. Success becomes like a drug. Once you have something, you want more because the old dosage is no longer sufficient. Schwarzenegger is no Stoic. Consider, for instance, his 3 minute video advertisement of the Celebrity

Apprentice, the iconic TV show initiated by Donald Trump, where famous people compete for the favor of the show host. In this video, Schwarzenegger proudly recounted his career milestones, and it made it seem as if a TV host entertainer was simply the next highest goal to aim towards.[17]

But how did he get to the Celebrity Apprentice? Schwarzenegger eagerly looked forward to a new entertainment venue beyond what he was used to. Schwarzenegger enjoyed watching the Apprentice. Once he found out that Trump was running for the presidency, his agent contacted Trump's and said that Schwarzenegger could fill Trump's role, which Trump passionately agreed with. One would think that Schwarzenegger was the perfect fit. He even had his own line. Not "you're fired", but "you're terminated". No one can steal this line from him with credibility!

One would think that being a US president would keep Trump so busy that he can no longer worry about his former entertainment life. But Donald remains Donald. He lambasted Schwarzenegger for the lower TV ratings, and Schwarzenegger had to hit back. The Donald against the Styrian Oak (or Austrian Oak in the US). Two people with large egos rubbing their shoulders to the great amusement of an amusement-seeking mass audience (and to the terror of seriously-minded people worried about the fate of the country). Schwarzenegger's suggestion to switch jobs was brilliant even if meant in a joke. But the irony is quite strong here: Trump makes himself ridiculous by wasting his precious attention as commander-in-chief in commenting on a silly entertainment business, while Schwarzenegger's reaction was comedic on the one hand, but made him more presidential than the president on the other hand. Meanwhile the charge against Schwarzenegger that he wasted his time with a social media war with Trump did not apply. After all, Schwarzenegger acts first and foremost as an entertainer, and he is entitled to engage in silly discourse, because that is what the definition of an entertainer is. Politics is for serious people, entertainment exists for the masses.

It is all the more ironic that the statesmanship then comes from a current entertainer and the entertainment comes from a supposed statesman. In that sense, the close similarity between Trump and Schwarzenegger disappears. Yes, the two men have their large egos in common. Yes, the two of them have shifted from entertainment to

---

[17] https://www.youtube.com/watch?v=cvqNed_XSuA

politics like chameleons. Yes, they have a strong sense for getting attention, power and control. But while Schwarzenegger is not a narcissist, Trump is. Schwarzenegger has the ego to climb to the top, but that desire does not distort his compassion, composure and dignity, especially when he focuses on public policy. His recent ten-year commemoration speech of the environmental law he signed as governor was on point and had none of the mocking, erratic tone that you would find in any Trump speech.[18]

It appears to be that the semi-entertainer and semi-politician Schwarzenegger, a fellow Austrian emigre, taking on Trump is the next best hope or at least source of entertainment that we have in these deeply troubling times.

---

[18] https://www.youtube.com/watch?v=q00ZcCcIdjI&feature=youtu.be&t=34m

The Political Establishment is Wrong (Yet Again)
Posted on March 27, 2017

The Dutch elections resulted in elation among the political establishment. The reaction is very reminiscent to Alexander Van Der Bellen's win in the Austrian presidential elections, having defeated the far-right Norbert Hofer. In the Netherlands, Geert Wilders PVV, the right-wing party, only came in second place with 13% of the vote, while incumbent prime minister Mark Rutte's VVD got 21% of the vote, thus receiving another mandate to rule, very likely without the PVV.

The political establishment consists of people like Angela Merkel, the German chancellor, and for many the leader of the "free" world, because Donald Trump is not establishment enough to be such a leader (though in many ways he is quite a conventional politician given that he has no strong political ideology on his side). Merkel spoke of the victory of the pro-European forces and that the Dutch people had made a reasonable choice (Chambers 2017). Italian Foreign Minister Paolo Gentiloni tweeted his approval: "The anti-EU right has lost the election in the Netherlands. All together for change and revive the (European) Union." The French Foreign Minister Jean-Marc Ayrault tweeted, "Congratulations to the Dutch for preventing the rise of the far right". (Said-Moorhouse and Jones 2017) The implication hereby is that the defeat of the far-right gives some breathing room for the political establishment to continue on their current policies of austerity and growing precarization of labor. I argue here that this is a miscalculation by the political establishment.

Does the political establishment have sufficient reason to rejoice? Let's look at the results in some more detail. While the liberal VVD is still number one, they have lost 5 points, which is 20% of their voter base from the last elections. That is quite a voter punishment. It is true that PVV has not gained as much as they might have in the past (their peak was 15% in 2010, when they also served in government), but they have restored some of their losses to rank in second place. The splintering of the political party system allows the PVV to be ranked second even with only 13% of the vote. The GreenLeft has been the biggest beneficiary of the election, which shows that progressive forces can also benefit politically, but the most astounding result is the collapse of the Labor Party (PvdA), which lost 19 points or 80% of their voter base. PvdA is practically no longer a political force and they have to be happy that they were able to hold on to any seats at all. Historically, PvdA held 1/4 of the parliamentary seats throughout the post-war period, but they are now a spent force.

Some people would say that Social Democrats can no longer retain their vote share because they were too successful. The welfare state which made the people vote left has already been established, it remains vigorously strong, and thus people want to vote for environmentalist parties like the Greens. The standard of living in the Netherlands is rather high, but the erosion process of the Social Democrats cannot merely come from the success of the pro-welfare state agenda. People in formerly Social Democratic counties are quite upset about (1) austerity budgets from the government, (2) the rise of precarious labor especially part-time work (women were dragged into the workforce only since the 1980s and only under the condition of part-time work, which affects 80% of women, Economist 2015), (3) decline in median wealth (from 50,000 euros to 29,000 euros between 2008 and 2011, see Oxfam 2013), (4) the rise of the unemployment rate (at 7% compared to less than 4% before 2008) (5) the diversification of neighborhoods, mainly from Suriname, Morocco and Turkey, but also Iraq, Somalia and Afghanistan. It can never be a happy mixture when economic insecurity is mixed with ethnic diversification, because the local population will blame their economic plight and the decreased subjective sense of physical security on foreigners and immigrants.

That's exactly what Geert Wilders promised his voters: ban the Quran, shut down all mosques, withdrawal from the EU, assimilation of all immigrants, stop to immigration from Muslim countries (Donald Trump, anyone?), police officers can't wear veils, repatriate Antilleans (with Dutch nationality) and foreign nationals with a criminal background etc. No surprises here. Wilders does not have good reasons to defend why anti-Muslim and anti-immigrant sentiment will make his voters any better off, but they are hooked, because people feel that he is the only one speaking for the little guy. Politics is about emotions and the populists control emotions really well, while the political establishment that takes the form of Jeroen Dijsselbloem (from the decimated PvdA) can only promise harsh austerity because "there is no alternative" and tell Greeks they shouldn't waste the bailout money on women and booze (Harrison 2017).

There really is no reason for rejoicing by the political establishment. What they were able to say with contempt for the grievances of the public is that they can do the same policies that they had been doing (bailout for banks, austerity and precarity for the masses), and then hope things won't blow up in the next round.

Europe faces two more elections in major countries, while they are negotiating the Brexit with the British. There are French presidential elections in April and German parliamentary elections in September. Let's begin with the French. Below you can see the poll values for each candidate.

The figure to worry about is the Front National leader Marine LePen, who has kept her vote share about even. She is another political figure to assail the pro-EU and pro-immigration course, and one would think that she would have more support given the recent terrorist attacks that have kept the French on the headlines since 2015. The socialist government under Francois Hollande used the terror attacks to impose a state of emergency, which has been continuously extended even until today. Has that calmed the moods? LePen would lose even though she would almost surely make it to the second round. In the first round, she would get about 25% of the vote, and in the second round, she would only bump up to 30 or 35%, which suggests that she is a polarizing figure. Those that vote for her like her very much, and those that do not vote for her, would never consider voting for her. Such fate would make her similar to her father in 2002, who made it to the second round but failed abjectly in the second round, because cordon sanitaire held (i.e. left-wing voters holding their nose to vote for the conservative Chirac). That would create the impression that France might dodge the right-wing bullet, but since Brexit and Trump we perhaps should be more careful about such predictions.

The frontrunner on the right had been Francois Fillon from the conservative party, who prevailed against the oldtimer, Alain Juppe. Fillon campaigns on balancing the budget and bringing in neoliberal reforms, whereby the French workers tend to be the most resistant to labor deregulation. But his polls had been dropping the last two months since his coronation, because he is involved in a scandal, where he hired his family for political work, even though they didn't do anything for him. That is an example of nepotism, which is regarded as very negatively in France.

Interestingly, promiscuous sexual relations that are frowned upon in the US, are perfectly acceptable in France. The new frontrunner to displace Fillon is the young Emmanuel Macron, who had served as the economy minister under Valls and Hollande. So what about Macron and sex? His wife is Brigitte Trogneux, his former high school teacher 24 years his senior. Trogneux spoke lovingly of Macron, who was her favorite student, as she regularly read his poetry out loud in class. He was the teacher's pet. Macron's parents frowned upon the intimacy between teacher and student and sent their son away to another town. Macron spoke with Trogneux about the decision, and she advised him to do what his parents told him. Macron then said to her that they will stay together and when Macron returns they would get married. Indeed, as soon as Macron graduated at 18, Trogneux divorced her husband with whom she already had 3 children and moved in with her young lover Macron. 11 years later the two were married (see Gee 2017).

Politically, Macron promises voters to bring fresh wind into the old structures of French politics. En marche (forward, on the move) is what he called his new political movement. He is a progressive, who wants to "transcend left and right". He favors the free market (read: neoliberalism, labor deregulation, more profit incentive for capitalists) and reducing the public budget deficit (read: austerity). He scores political points by condemning French imperialism, as was the case during the colonization of Algeria. He favors more EU integration, especially in the form of a common EU finance minister with more authority and budget (which in the current configuration strengthens neoliberal power, because of the preference for liberalization and opposition to an integrated social policy). He favors the acceptance of many refugees, and thus runs counter to the right-wing populists.

Macron is the dream come true for the political establishment, and his lead in the polls is again suggesting that the establishment seems to have done everything correctly. He follows along the trails of Justin Trudeau, the Canadian prime minister, who shows his teary face when welcoming Syrian refugees into Canada, greeting people celebrating different ethnic and religious holidays, while signing oil contracts with Texas billionaires to exploit the shale gas in Canada without regard for climate change, proliferating low-wage jobs and offering cheap foreign workers indefinite staying rights. It's neoliberalism with a human face (Walkom 2016), and that is what Macron can offer his voters. I doubt that most French voters will vote based on some rational calculus, but based on the feel-good atmosphere that Macron vibrates. "En marche". Let's march. Let's do something. Let's be active. Let's make France great again! Of course, Macron is not going to tell his voters the social implications of his agenda, but all he has to do is to say that he presents the young, fresh face to end the political gridlock in the country, which has kept unemployment so high. The strategy seems to pay off in part, as he leads the polls and is replacing LePen as frontrunner.

The real tragedy is that there are two big left-wing candidates. The communists field Jean-Luc Melenchon, and the socialists field Benoit Hamon, a left-wing critic of his party colleagues Valls and Hollande. Hamon has campaigned on a universal basic income and more generous social policy, and Melenchon isn't that far apart from Hamon. The tragedy is that they are two candidates each with about 12-13% approval rating, which combined would put them up ahead with a chance to snatch the presidency. But no, the left is internally divided, stealing votes from each other and not even having the appearance of a chance to win the presidency. The media makes fun of these two candidates, especially Hamon, who represents the governing party that is so despised by the voters. Hollande promised he would not run for re-election if he could not substantially reduce the unemployment rate, and he wasn't able to, so he didn't even bother to run. People seem to equate Hamon with Hollande, even though their political positions are quite different. No matter, the real left-wing alternative is blocked, and French voters are seriously contemplating a neoliberal, presenting himself as a "fresh" face (but same content), and a right-wing extremist. No wonder that old democracies are now becoming the farce!

Germany is considered to be the key anchor of European stability. That has partly to do with their sheer economic strength and also with the surplus-producing function of the German export economy, which lends the Germans the power of the purse that had been used against other southern European economies that cannot remain competitiveness with Germany given the strength of the euro currency controlled by Germany. Germany has been rather peculiar in pushing down the unemployment rate even during the crisis, and they have balanced their budget. Some problems persist like the growth of low-wage work following the draconian social welfare legislation of the earlier Social Democratic government, which now struggles with permanently lowered popular support the last decade or so (holding about 1/4 of the vote).

Until Martin Schulz came along. When I wrote my German politics paper during my undergraduate years in the spring of 2015, I genuinely thought that Merkel would sit in office until she died or decided to retire. Merkel certainly did not decide to retire and announced her candidacy for a fourth term. She is the center of political stability, having been the CDU (conservative party) chair since 2000 and chancellor since 2005. Only Helmut Kohl had been in power longer than her. It is his record that she can break if she can hold onto the chancellorship.

But then the refugee crisis broke out, and people began blaming the CDU for the inundating of the country. Over a million refugees were absorbed into Germany in 2015 and into 2016 until the pathway was blocked, when the EU struck a deal with Turkey to withhold the refugees and prevent them from entering the EU. An apparent success for Merkel, who was subsequently able to consolidate her poll figures (and also led to the decline of the rising star of the right-wing AfD). She did not have to hold the 42% of votes she got in the last elections, but she only had to have more votes than the second-ranked SPD to continue on a grand coalition under her leadership.

The SPD having been part of the Merkel government for the second term now had a problematic optic: in order to beat Merkel, they had to sell themselves as anti-establishment, but as members of the governing coalition they were part of the establishment. On top of that, the SPD had an unenthusiastic leader, Sigmar Gabriel, who loved his SPD chairmanship, but hated the idea of running for the chancellor, which he turned down twice when offered to him: once in 2009, when Frank-Walter Steinmeier became the frontrunner, and a second time in 2013, when Peer Steinbruck did the same. Gabriel apparently hated competitive elections, and not being the leading candidate allowed him to stay on as party chairman and ultimately vice chancellor. The problem is that the lack of charisma and second fiddling does not win elections.

Martin Schulz, the EU parliament president, who had only experienced EU politics and no German domestic politics, was called upon to take the SPD chairmanship. Schulz is not showing his political ambitions for the first time. In 2014, the EU established for the first time competitive elections with figure heads for the EU commission president (which were previously appointed by the EU council). The conservatives (EPP) fielded Jean-Claude Juncker from Luxembourg and the Social Democrats (S&D) fielded Martin Schulz. The TV debates were held in English, French and German, languages that both candidates were all fluent in (Schulz can also speak Italian and Dutch, and Juncker Luxembourgish). But the election was entirely comical, because they both understood each other well, and there wasn't much of a political contrast. There wasn't much fervor in the EU parliament elections, because the real power was in the EU council which consists of the prime ministers of the EU countries and also in the national governments themselves that controlled most of the budgets.

Now that Schulz was demoted in Brussels (against the will of Juncker, the commission president, who liked cooperating with Schulz, as EU parliament president), he was seeking for a new political outlet, and so he was given the chancellor candidacy. Now the CDU and SPD are neck on neck, and the SPD has a genuine chance to regain the chancellorship and unseat Merkel. Some commentators already predict the new axis of Macron and Schulz, which will revive the Franco-German axis and deal with the Brexit and any future integration of the EU. Schulz sells himself as a pro-EU, having served in its highest positions. He also brands himself with a more left-wing rhetoric, which is a demarcation from Macron's neoliberalism. But if we scratch away the surface, we find that Schulz isn't all that much different from the rest of the political establishment. There are some progressive ideas for Schulz policy. He wants to close the gender pay gap, curb executive compensation and invest the budget surplus in education and infrastructure. But the Hartz agenda, which had earlier brought down his party, shall not be fundamentally changed given that it is partly responsible for the export surplus of Germany (another major part being the euro). He condemned left-wing calls for an abolition of benefit sanctions for welfare recipients not meeting the work requirement.

No matter where we look in Europe, democracies are showing public discontent, but so long as the moderate parties can win the elections, there will be plenty of discontent that the political parties cannot transform into positive energy for more sustainable political-economic solutions. The malaise of economic crisis, investment crisis, inequality, poverty, low-wage work and ethnic diversification cannot be resolved by the political status quo, yet that is all that we are served today. Without a new positive vision, we are doomed.

Book Review: How Will Capitalism End?
Posted on April 8, 2017

Symptoms of Morbidity in Late-Capitalism

If we read Wolfgang Streeck's (2016) most recent analysis, we might be inclined to think that the capitalist economy is about to collapse. The multiplicity of morbidity symptoms are too numerous to enumerate, but are well worth restating:

(1) declining economic growth

(2) rising inequality in income and wealth (as well as life chances)

(3) increases in money supply without much precedent from the central banks

(4) financial and economic breakdown as we had seen in 2008, and as becomes the norm with rising levels of overall debt

(5) decline of social democracy, i.e. collective state and trade union institutions to ensure economic opportunity to the masses, and the commensurate rise of the oligarchy, the power of the moneyed elites

(6) the rising commodification of labor, nature and money beyond what either nature or humans can tolerate

(7) corruption and associated winner-take-all rent-seeking

(8) declining public infrastructure, privatization and commoditization of public goods

(9) U.S. not providing the hegemonic world order, which creates geopolitical instability and economic uncertainty (p.15)

Post-Democratic Malaise

More depressingly, Streeck also notes that we lack the practical collective resources to mount a fightback against the current malaise (see p.20):

(1) Historically, the underdog workers would be able to **strike** against their employer to gain a wage increase, which was true until the mid-1970s, when the turn toward anti-inflation policies as well as capital and labor deregulation shifted the economic and political power back to the elites.

(2) The political struggle then moved from the economic to the political arena, because the European welfare state shouldered the larger social costs of international competitiveness and the growth of precarious employment (in the US, some share of the burden is carried by the criminal justice system but also a limited welfare

state). People **voted** for politicians, who would preserve the welfare state. Good old, power-resource theory (Shalev 1980; Korpi 1985). But public budget consolidation since the mid-1990s, coming on the heels of realizing rapid demographic aging, mounting public debt, joining of the European Union (and the European Monetary Union) with the cognitive turn to austerity, reduced the scope for welfare state expansion, which justifies the entire literature on retrenching the welfare state, which is still bigger than in the past, but no more growing at high rates.

(3) The rise of private indebtedness in many western countries as evidenced by rising student, car, house and general credit card loans has created substantial economic insecurity for the masses, who find themselves having to negotiate with the bank over the "fair" terms of lending, though the struggle is very much individualized and the ability for people to press their demands is substantially reduced compared to strikes and voting. That is also the time when you see some vague attempts of **general public protest**, but struggles are interestingly quite local, while the locus of power is diffusely international.

(4) The latest phase of the struggle cannot even be defined as a struggle, namely with **central banks**. Can individuals struggle against central banks, when ordinary people have a scant understanding of what their own governments are doing, let alone their central banks? Central banks since 2008 have temporarily supplanted national governments, who were just quick to throw tax money after failing banks. Central banks did just the same, but they had way more leverage as they controlled the money supply and could endlessly expand their balance sheets via asset purchases. This so-called quantitative easing has the intent to expand lending in the real economy, as interest rates are also kept close to zero and in some cases are even negative. Savers are losing out under that model, and it is quite interesting that despite repeated calls by Janet Yellen to raise interest rate, it is still at 1%, having only been raised since late-2016. To me it seems like high debts overall make it difficult to raise interest rates, which make defaults increase, thus undermining trust in the financial system which could result in financial chaos.

I think Streeck is somewhat overdoing his emphasis on the financial overlords in the central banks, though their decision was doubtless influential in shifting a greater share of capital wealth onto the global oligarchy, who- in the minds of our wise leaders- are never supposed to lose their savings with a debt haircut. Instead, the cheap money flows shall enable them to further boost real estate speculation to line their pockets, while houses in prime real estate locations become unaffordable to the masses.

But his sentiment of the post-democratic malaise of globalized capital, who can undermine national taxation and regulation regimes, weak labor/ low wages, low growth and high profits in the monopoly sectors of industry (p.22) are absolutely correct. Specifically, the European Union is an entity that allows the unrestrained rule of the central bank and the European council, which consists of the heads of state of the countries that send them, in favor of empowering corporate interests, while neglecting a social policy agenda (p.56; p.158). Nation-states are powerless against international creditors, who demand budget consolidation on the backs of the working and middle class, even though the same creditors were partly fed by the trough of public bailout money, otherwise there will be a rise of the interest rate (p.93). A sad example is Greece, which is getting smashed with endless bailout-cum-austerity demands to pay off loans that everyone pretends to fully repay. Ironically, austerity hurts the capitalists themselves, because a lowering of social spending undermines the public legitimacy for the capitalist order and a lowering of public investment lowers long-run growth potential for the capitalists (p.137).

US

One might critique that Streeck focuses too much on the European example, but it would be simple to expand his crisis perspective to other countries that are also suffering from an unfavorable climate of economic growth. The Trump phenomenon derives from the dissatisfaction of the masses with a political system that is unresponsive to their needs. There is a veritable crisis of legitimation for the current economic order. It is the US, which also harbors most of the millionaires and billionaires in the world, largely because the US has become the international center of finance as well as high-tech, with the few oil magnates strewn in between. The massive ramp-up in the national fiscal deficit and debt creates the perennial call for austerity, which is made worse by the Republican agenda that illogically attempts to lower taxes on the rich, cut spending and balance the budget. Something will have to give, and I suspect that with small spending cuts (in the arts, sciences, humanities, foreign aid, environmental protection, housing and urban development etc.) and large raises in the military budget and a strong priority for tax cuts for the rich, the balancing budget agenda is out of the question, thus promoting imminent political struggles that either say to US, Chinese and other creditors that they either have to take a haircut, the US wealthy and corporations have to pay more taxes (instead of lending money to the government), or the people continue to bite into the sour apple.

The US is also unique in having the weakest collective buffers against economic insecurity for the masses, having drastically slashed the welfare program for the poorest during the conversion of AFDC to the more stringent TANF program; not indexed the national minimum wage to inflation (let alone national productivity); allowed lax regulation for financial institutions to raid businesses, lay off workers and strip their assets on behalf of a shareholder value maximization agenda; make the unionization of workers rather difficult; incarcerate a substantial portion of the poor (especially black) population; entrap countless millions of people under medical, education, consumer and mortgage debt, which even European countries are still somewhat reluctant to fully adopt.

Japan

In Japan, there is a unique combination of unfavorable demographic circumstances (declining population, rapid aging, high life expectancy, low fertility, low migration) on top of the economic and debt crisis that is engulfing the country. The Japanese have an unusually strong sense of national identity, which attributes characteristic traits to a certain group of people tied together by kinship and ethnicity (Lie 2004). The nationalist sentiment translates to a government policy that substantially restricts migration, which is unusual for a wealthy capitalist country that tends to develop labor shortage during early phases of rapid economic development. The labor shortage is apparently, in part, bridged by the overall high skills development in the Japanese labor force, which is then used to promote the export of high value-added goods like consumer electronics and manufacturing, which suggests a lesser need for lesser skilled laborers. Another peculiar feature is that the female labor force is only marginally attached to the workforce, thus allowing employers to draw on a pool of women as reserve labor.

The geographic feature of Japan being an island nation may also help the government to carry out isolationist migration policies, as migrants would have a hard time swimming across the sea to get to Japan. Of course, there are people that are flying in, but the lack of secure legal status, long-term history of immigration and good welfare benefits, there aren't that many migrants. There are some Brazilian nationals in Japan, but most of them are of Japanese descent. There are some Southeast Asians, like Filipinos, who work as hospital nurses. The largest immigrant group are Koreans, which is a legacy from the Japanese empire, which ruled over Korea. Ethnic Koreans in Japan have not taken up Japanese nationality in large numbers and they receive employment discrimination, which suggests that there is a refusal to ensure the full integration even of immigrants that are culturally similar to Japan.

The foreclosure of the migration route increases the burden to accelerate economic development via increased birth rates, but the fertility rate has been below the replacement rate since the mid-1970s and has reached an all-time low of 1.26 in 2005, having stabilized to 1.41 in 2014 (World Bank).[19] The expectation that women are supposed to be homemakers and raise the children cannot hold up in a world, where many men cannot secure the full-time, permanent jobs (sararaimen or salarymen) that allow comfortable, middle-class family life. Even worse, the disappearance of the Japanese salarymen is associated with a decline of marriage, household formation and childbearing, as women are unwilling to mate a man that does not bring home the bacon at a stable and high income (Piotrowski and Kalleberg 2015).

The result is rapid demographic aging, which creates practical fears for the extinction of the Japanese people. But before that happens, they will have to face constraining social and economic choices. The economic growth rate is structurally lower because of the demographic component. The Abe administration promised comprehensive economic reform, which involves further labor deregulation, fiscal stimulus (on overbuilt infrastructure) and monetary easing (very low interest rates). But there are limitations to fiscal expansion, because debt to GDP had reached 250% in 2016, though it has leveled off the last few years. There is some austerity that the government enforces via the increase in sales tax, which was hiked from 5 to 8% in 2014, which they had planned to raise to 10% in 2016, but was delayed now to 2019 because of "weakness in the economy". It is difficult to bring the Japanese to spend more money

---

[19] http://data.worldbank.org/indicator/SP.DYN.TFRT.IN?locations=JP

on consumer items, as they already consume much of what people need, and the choices for greater consumption is limited already by the limited availability of good-paying jobs. But to raise the sales tax further will drag down growth even further.

How about the Emerging Markets?

It is usually much harder to prove the case that emerging markets like BRICS (Brazil, Russia, India, China, South Africa) suffer from a systemic economic crisis, because their growth rates are higher, they are catching up with the west, benefiting from the demographic dividend (many young workers and few old), and receive foreign capital with their cheap labor force. But it would be erroneous to assume that emerging markets are buffered from a systemic growth crisis in the west. Let us not forget that the most successful economies are all dependent on the international flows of capital and investment.

China is the engine of much of global growth, and that was made possible by the export to western countries, especially the US. The US hegemon is no longer capable of importing all of the surplus cheap goods, as the minotaur is exhausted (Varoufakis 2013). That brings the Chinese growth model in trouble, which partially gets compensated by raising up ghost cities and overinvesting in fixed assets, which is enforced by the low wages, capital controls and high bank capital that administratively directs funds to state-owned enterprises and local governments to build different kinds of infrastructure projects, even at diminishing marginal returns. The rising debt of the local governments indicates a limitation to endless expansion, and the mounting oversupply of basic inputs like steel or coal already forces a cutback in investment and some limits to further credit expansion. China is, as of yet, in no position to displace the US as global hegemon, playing the second fiddle as the biggest hoarder of US treasury bonds (Hung 2017).

South Africa, Brazil and Australia are examples of countries that are highly dependent on Chinese import demand for copper, zinc, rare earth metals, soybeans, food stuffs etc. The political crisis in Brazil, where a right-wing leader displaced the ruling president, Dilma Rousseff, amid massive lack of popularity is a case in point for the economic dilemma plaguing South America. The official discourse revolves around the corruption scandal of Petrobras, the state oil company, but corruption usually is not an issue during good economic times, when everyone gets at least some bread crumbs from the generously decorated table.

Russia is also in no position to celebrate as their entire wealth is built on rising oil prices, which was capable of papering over the endemic corruption of the political class and the oligarchs that divided among each other the valuable state property in the post-Soviet era, while leaving scraps for common people. Russia is one of the few countries where male life expectancy faced reversals. People had it somewhat better under president Putin, but only because of the high oil prices. Then came the plunging oil prices, the covert wars in the Ukraine and Syria, the western sanctions and the big economic crash. Putin seems to think that military confrontation can buy continued political support, similar to what Bush had achieved at the beginning of his presidency fighting two major wars. Even the most successful emerging market economies cannot insulate themselves from what is happening in the core capitalist countries.

Conclusion: Schumpeterian Pessimism and Gramsci's Dilemma

So what's the conclusion? Can we expect a terminal decline of capitalism? A Schumpeterian interpretation of capitalist development allows both conclusions (Schumpeter 1942). Schumpeterian optimists would claim that the creative destruction of capitalism would imply that we will have new innovation, which will allow a productivity revolution, and the mass replacement of workers by robots might point us in that direction. There is naturally a limitation to such optimism, because a mass replacement of workers would reduce consumption, which feeds capitalist growth. And productivity data would suggest that the computer revolution has only briefly resulted in an increase in productivity, but this increase is fizzling off, because most businesses already have computers. Another pernicious insight is that mass labor displacement shifts the labor wage equilibrium downward, such that a growing pool of low-wage laborers successfully compete with expensive machines. If labor remains cheap because of abundance it slows down the adoption of new technology.

Schumpeterian pessimism looks more defensible to me. Schumpeter himself was quite a pessimist, because he believed that the long-term development of capitalism would be declining innovation as larger, bureaucratic businesses come to dominate the economy. In the pharmaceutical industry, it does not tend to be the big firms that are at the forefront of innovation but the smaller ones, who sell their patent to the big company that can scale production.

To return to Streeck's discussion, he never really answers the ominous question in his title (how capitalism will end?), and that would certainly go beyond what can be expected of historical sociologists. We can predict the present malaise based on past patterns, but can't really say much about the future. Marxism is often taken to be a faith, because there is this idea that not only is capitalism a historically-specific mode of production, but it will also end with the revolutionary takeover of the working class that will get rid of universal alienation and exploitation of man by man. Streeck is not a Marxist, but he agrees with Marxists on the decline of capitalism. Unlike Marxists, he believes that "no revolutionary alternative is required, and certainly no master plan of a better society displacing capitalism" (p.13). The ruling class is confused about what to do: printing money to generate growth in the real economy; attempt to restore inflation with negative interest rates; the weakness of the US as a global hegemon (p.35), thus entrapping us in a Gramscian dilemma, where the old is dying but the new is not born.

Having been able to read Arne Kalleberg's (2018) draft for his new book, one actually becomes even more pessimist, because he documents the rise of precarious labor. Stronger working class organization might keep this trend in check. But he does not even think that the energy for working class organization will come from within the working class, but instead comes as a result of a coalition with mass social justice movements, the street protesters and the ballot box. The foreclosure of a fight at the point of production shows that labor is structurally outmaneuvered, even though we will continue to see local insurgency on behalf of worker organizers in different parts of the world at different level of success. Michael Schwartz, another historical sociologist, told me that "the revolution is not going to happen in my own lifetime".

I am very inclined to agree with Streeck that capitalism might implode before something new arises, because there aren't any strong social forces that point to alternatives. History is a concatenation of improvising, muddling through, figuring things out as they come along, applying bandaids to cascading cancer and severe illness. It is the intellectual class that might recognize the dysfunctionality of the current order, but is least likely to be aligned with practical forces for social change, while the elites and the masses don't know what they have to strive for. Bourdieu (1993), taking the cue from Weber, made us aware that history is about a series of endless struggles within the fields that we collectively create. Capitalism and its associated twin, rationalization (the growing means-ends calculation, profit orientation and bureaucratization of life), slot individuals into different ranks, and we have to live with the morbid outcomes as long as we allow it to happen and lack the vision and willpower for a different kind of future.

Streeck himself emphasized that we must not abandon concepts like socialism or communism.

"What other concept is there in any case for the more communal, more other-regarding and more collectively responsible way of life that we today seem to need more urgently than ever, a life with much less license to externalize the costs of private pleasure-seeking to the rest of the world? And how are we to name a social organization with much more shared control over the collective fate and with a strong collective capacity to avoid the unanticipated consequences of freely expanding market relations-consequences that unendingly mystify us today when as individuals we cause effects that we cannot possibly want, not just as a society but also as individuals?" (p.234)

Herrmann's Thoughts on Capitalism
Posted on May 11, 2017

Herrmann (2015) discusses (in German) the history and trajectory of capitalism: capitalism is about the use of technology to augment labor productivity to accumulate capital, not the hoarding of money wealth.[20] It began 250 years ago in Britain. The depressing insight is that there is no guarantee that really poor countries can catch up with the high productivity wealthy countries. The impetus behind economic growth is not low wages, but high wages, because that would encourage labor-saving innovation. A universal basic income could extend the growth model via higher reservation wages (wage below which workers don't work). But there are still constraints to further economic growth: (1) demographic aging, (2) ecological limits and climate change, (3) monopoly of firms, (4) concentration of income at the top.

The technological primacy in the development of capitalism reveals its strength and its very vulnerability: because augmenting labor productivity pushes people from machine-intensive into labor-intensive, low-productivity, low-wage sectors, innovation, broadly shared gains and economic growth all decrease.

---

[20] https://www.youtube.com/watch?v=MKFsrlDxPI4

The Ideal Academic Adviser
Posted on <u>May 22, 2017</u>

For those of us, who are trapped in the academic treadmill and just getting our feet wet in the world of research, it can be quite a nerve-wrecking process to just get familiar with our area of research and write papers, let alone develop the good relationships with academic advisers that are crucial for our success. As a sociologist myself and leaning on my grand teacher in undergrad, Randall Collins, I can say with full assurance that one's academic success depends not only on one's independent intellectual interests, but also the network support that comes from a helpful academic adviser. This network has to be face to face and contains a charismatic element.

Collins says,

Ancient philosophers and mathematicians had to meet face to face. You had to be there in Athens or wherever in order to have that network connection. But as printing came in, the network patterns didn't change. Jean Paul Sartre could have dealt with people in South America by mail, but meetings in cafes were still at the core. The networks around Steve Jobs and Bill Gates were still face to face networks. Even when long-distance media exist, the advantage is in dealing with key people face to face. It is faster as well more intuitive and emotional.

Creative people put a lot of emotional force into their ideas. [Steve] Jobs is a terrific example of that. Einstein and other intellectual heroes tend to be emotionally overpowering and you can't get that just by reading their writing.

Margonelli (2017). Also see Collins (1998)

Here are three features of the ideal-type academic adviser. And just to be clear we are in the Max Weber world of ideal-types, which is about the analytical categories that are an approximation to reality, while they are not necessarily found in the real world; in other words, we might not find such an academic adviser in the real world and will have to do without or with only 1 or 2 of these features fulfilled:

1. Mentor

It goes almost without saying that the first precondition for being guided in the right direction is to have a professor who is concerned about *your* success. This tends to be easier with more senior professors, whose status and tenure allow them to scope for talent that they find worthwhile supporting. I like to call mentors 'talent-spotters', i.e. graduate students are like college basketball players to be spotted by the NBA talent scouts (and are supported intensely upon hire). Mentors are generally interested not merely in your ideas, but also where you might be able to have your work published, where job openings might be, and what you might want to do with yourself. They must also have an interest that you develop your skills as a researcher and put you in touch with the right contacts that help you in your research project. They will write your reference letter, and informally put out a good word about you in front of other scholars. They will want to write a paper together with you, knowing not only your talent but also the usefulness to your academic career path.

2. Technically competent

In a sense, it is insufficient to have an adviser, who is not so different from a personal career adviser. The adviser also has to be technically competent in the positivistic or humanistic enterprise in the natural and social sciences and the humanities. They have to be well-read in their subfield, and share specific readings that are helpful for you to think through your project. They have to know the methods (quantitative, qualitative?) that help you answer your research questions. They have to provide detailed or general comments on your paper drafts to make them better polished. They will tell you which journals or academic presses take your article/book. They will evidently leave the grunt work of your own research to you, but they will share their insights that help you in the process.

3. Bon vivant (big thinker)

The French bon vivant denotes a very well-nourished person, who enjoys good food and wine. It would be nice to have an academic adviser like that, but that is naturally not often feasible… But what I mean by the bon vivant is someone, who doesn't only know the methods and the literature very well and apply it with great rigor to get published to survive in the academic enterprise. The academic rat-race with the lack of tenure-track positions and increasing methodological sophistication is scary enough. We want to have an adviser, who also enjoys discussing big ideas that tend to get shoved into first-year graduate theory courses in the social sciences and never to be pulled out again.

Whether it's hearing anecdotes of Charles Darwin's sources of his theory of evolution or exploring the differences between Aristotelianism and Confucianism or the value of Diamond's Guns, Germs and Steel thesis, what's wrong with discussing those big ideas? What's the point of being part of the academic enterprise if we can't have fun engaging in the big ideas? By only having technically competent mentors as advisers, we are merely technicians, and for that there are other professions that pay a lot more to be like that. The adviser meeting has to be more than just another dentist appointment. We want to *live* and not merely *survive* in the academic enterprise. The renewal and regeneration of emotional energy, in Collins' (2004) framework, or what I would call 'intellectual energy', has to happen within the context of interacting with big thinkers, who then also help us to think differently or have new insights within the context of our own research. Great ideas come from great thinkers (within networks!), while bad ideas come from... you know how to complete the sentence.

To illustrate the big thinker, I want to bring up the example of Barrington Moore, the towering figure, who has single-handedly defined the field of historical sociology (having influenced scholars like Theda Skocpol and Charles Tilly). Moore was of aristocratic background, but his research interest was about how various forms of class struggle create modern political configurations (dictatorship, democracy). He also took some of his graduate students at Harvard to his boathouse and on a little boat ride to talk historical sociology and whatever his students wished to talk about. (This story was told to me by one of his students, the late Ivar Berg, when he was 85 years old!) What can be more bon vivant than that?

It won't be easy to find the right adviser, but it's good to know what it means to have a good adviser, and perhaps it encourages some of us as future scholars and advisers to aspire to be like that. In Confucius' own words,

When you see a good person, think of becoming like her/him. When you see someone not so good, reflect on your own weak points. (Wikiquote)[21]

---

[21] https://en.wikiquote.org/wiki/Confucius

British Election Tragedy (?)
Posted on <u>June 5, 2017</u>

Theresa May had set an election on June 8, and the polls indicate that it could very well backfire for her. When she had announced the election in April and had the parliament vote for it on April 19, the Tories were leading by 20-25 points. Now the polls narrowed to 5-10 points, and some polling agencies would go as far as predicting a hung parliament. The gap had narrowed as the electorate is searching for a political alternative amid the turbulent Brexit negotiations. It still takes some time for people to link their political dissatisfaction with the Tory policies of austerity, especially for local, social and health services. In this article, I claim that the British people are better off voting for Labour and have them negotiate the Brexit than the Conservatives.

Needless to say, it would be a tragedy for the Conservatives to win re-election (and they might given that polls tend to skew Labour, while election results favor Conservative), but there is now mounting evidence that May had miscalculated and that the expected expansion of a Tory majority was too ambitious. May had thought she could wing the elections and be guaranteed more support in the current leadership, so she "can negotiate a good deal for Britain" amid Brexit. Part of the challenge for her comes from the poor handling of the conservative campaign. Because she thought that she would win by a landslide, she refused to participate in a leadership debate, which to her is not as useful as "being quizzed by the British people", even as she cancels the last interviews right before the election. May is clearly not a seasoned politician, as she excels better sitting behind closed chambers as opposed to performing in public and debating with an opponent that has better arguments than her.

Her second mistake was that her smug attitude had emboldened her party to put forward a draconian social agenda, which revolves around reducing social care and pensions spending, both areas hitting the core Tory voters (senior citizens) really hard. Will her loyal voters call out the Tories for their stupid austerity? The conservatives backtracked on these cuts, but who will believe them?

Relatedly, the third problem is a matter of credibility. It was the Conservatives, who called for the EU referendum, hoping to undercut the EU-skeptic Tories and the UKIP, which had much more support back then (now no longer, because the independence desires of the Independence Party are realized by the Brexit, so what's the point of voting for them now?). Blaming EU migrants was also a convenient way to cover up the folly of austerity. ("You lose your pension because of the benefits for EU migrants and the EU contributions." No, because of Tory austerity!) Then they (both David Cameron, then-prime minister, and Theresa May) had campaigned for remain, but now that the narrow Brexit vote was realized, Cameron retreated and May announced to carry out the Brexit, even as she was opposed to it.

How are people going to trust the Tories when they are so unreliable, and with the full extent of the Brexit might have caused the greatest economic calamity in recent British history? Also, why does May first say she does not want to vote until 2020, and now says that this is what she will do? Her reasoning was that there are some people in her own party and in the opposition that want to undermine her political position (and she really trusted the polls to get the landslide).

The political weakness and lack of credibility of the May administration is counter-balanced by the growing popularity of her nemesis, Jeremy Corbyn's Labour Party. Having been shouted down by the Blairite centrists, who are only different from conservative policy in that they support moderately greater social spending, but otherwise support the same neoliberal initiatives, Corbyn had risen to the Labour leadership since the last parliamentary elections two years ago to return to a more classic social democratic agenda. Corbyn is not a charismatic figure, as his speeches appeal mainly to more intellectual audiences, who rightfully attack austerity policies.

The Blairites were in the Parliamentary Labour Party (PLP) and fought back against Corbyn by pushing for a second leadership election after the Brexit referendum. The Blairites were represented by Owen Smith, who ironically supported a similarly populist agenda to Corbyn, claiming that he would be taken more seriously by the mainstream media, i.e. he will fake left (for the public) and act right (for the media and the powerful), the oldest trick in the hat. Corbyn's party supporters were not fooled and mobilized for a second time to re-affirm Corbyn at the party leadership, but this time all of the attempted caesar-murderers in the PLP resigned their positions, and Corbyn had to fill the shadow cabinet positions with younger and less experienced allies.

Corbyn is not only opposed by his own party but also by the entire business community and the powerful media conglomerates, who control the political discourse in Britain (some newspapers like

Independent and Guardian have exceptionally pro-Corbyn coverage). No wonder that Corbyn had been viewed so negatively by the public. But the election campaign changes the picture, as Labour more successfully mobilizes in their campaign trips. The young voters are overwhelmingly favoring Corbyn, though they are not voting in the same numbers. Now the older voters will have to recognize their self-interest and give their vote for the Labour Party, which could create a political upset. Further, the higher the vote participation rate the better for Labour.

On the other hand, the overall strategic position for the Labour Party is less favorable than for the Tories, because the Tories rely on the English heartland, which has the most amount of seats. Labour is fighting off Plaid Cymru in Wales and, more importantly, was literally wiped off the map in Scotland after the SNP had won most of the Scottish seats. It would be big if Labour could even receive some more seats and thus undermine a possible new Conservative administration.

There is a genuine choice for the British electorate, though I am not so sure whether the short amount of time that is given to the campaign (less than two months) will give people enough time to think about their choices. To some extent, that is what the Tories think will directly benefit them. The short campaign will lower the public exposure that the destructive Tory agenda will receive and time for the public to recognize the utter incompetence of the May administration. Also, Labour benefits from a high voter participation, while the Tories want a lower voter participation, because in that case it tend to be the older Tory voters, whose vote carry the biggest weight.

More importantly, the May administration justifies the short campaign with the 2 year time frame that Britain has to negotiate a Brexit deal with the EU. Article 50 was triggered in March, so March 2019 is the deadline for the Brexit negotiations. May argues that she needs to have a big majority, so she can negotiate the Brexit and have it be rubber-stamped by the parliament. But why is she the person and the party that should have the majority? Further, what can the UK expect from a Brexit?

The downside risk is substantial, because losing access to the single market will force the British to potentially pay tariffs for exports and reduce overall trade as parts and goods that seamlessly cross the channel are now subject to border checks. The UK government prefers access to the single market, but knows that it probably won't work without guaranteeing the right of all EU nationals to stay, live and work in Britain. May can't bring herself to sell it to the voters given that the sentiment for Brexit derives from the angst and anger against EU migrants taking British jobs. The fear has no basis in reality, and, in fact, by making it harder for qualified EU migrant workers to enter Britain, the health or transportation service will face shortages that can't be filled by British nationals.

Within the EU there is not much of an appetite to be lenient on the British, given that the Eastern Europeans have sent a large contingent of their people to Britain, and the Poles are not really keen to welcome all of their compatriots back given that they have more opportunities and income in Britain. Poland is thus unlikely to back a weakening of the free movement of people within the EU. But even other EU countries are unwilling to grant a generous Brexit deal, given that they all belong to the pro-EU political establishment and are unwilling to have more countries leave, thus resulting in a full implosion of the EU. That's where we would be had Marine LePen won the French presidential elections.

The European leaders, who want to maintain the EU, therefore, have every interest to make it as difficult as possible for the British to leave the EU to discourage more countries from taking that step. But that is really a reflection of the failure of the EU at the present moment. The EU used to inspire people based on the idea of peace and unity, but they have now gotten to a stage to have to defend a construct by the barrel of a gun. "We are bad, but the alternative is worse." If the EU leaders can't come up with better ways to address dissatisfaction (e.g. by easing on austerity, promoting eurobonds, and a new Marshall plan), the EU will fall apart in a matter of a decade or two.

British nationalists will latch onto the apparent crisis of legitimacy of the EU, and merely state that they are about to end a project on which they had always been quite lukewarm. But the death of the EU is a long-term process of decline, while the immediate pain to the British population is acute and might not be worth the sacrifice. To be quite frank, I thought the worst thing that would happen with Brexit was that Britain would become another Switzerland or Norway. Naturally, given the relative size of the British economy (second largest behind Germany), they would get some nice deal, such as perhaps a British negotiator working in "consultation" with EU negotiators for international trade deals, but the four freedoms would remain untouched (including access to the single market and free movement of people). But that's not the intention of the May administration.

"No deal is better than a bad deal", says Theresa May over and over again with little regard for the negative repercussions for Britain. May has no basis on which to walk out from negotiations given that its economic fate is so closely linked to what happens across the channel. And how is Britain going to negotiate the over 700 trade treaties that the EU currently has across the world? It is another empty bluff, or let's call it a lie.

Now the relevant question for the British electorate (given that the EU-internal issues can't be solved in the next few days) is whether prime minister Corbyn would produce better results for Britain in a Brexit negotiation? Corbyn clearly backs the Brexit, having himself only lukewarmly endorsed the remain campaign. Corbyn's reservation is similar to my own position, which is that EU workers rights do make sense, but that when it comes to the essential topics of public interest the EU is incompetent at best (no common social policy) and harmful at worst (permanent austerity and pro-business "competition" policy).

We can't know whether Corbyn will be a skillful politician, and I suspect that a left-wing leader leading the Brexit negotiations is in no more of a desirable position than Syriza when it won elections the first time in 2015 and having to negotiate with hyenas at the IMF and the EU without pity or economic foresight. The only thing that would endear a Corbyn premiership to the electorate is that he would argue for a soft Brexit, which would be in line with what I had proposed. The Tories will put him up as a sell-out, and any residual dips in the economy in the form of a recession will be blamed on him, yet the Tories would have to account for a counterfactual of even more economic deterioration under a hard Brexit.

A soft Brexit may also allow the Corbyn administration to promote a greater investment agenda, higher taxes on corporations and high-income earners, and a needed shoring up of university and health care funding. That in turn will make the British people more relaxed, and I subsequently wish the Labour Party the best in the general elections.

On a final note, will the three recent terrorist attacks (two in London and one in Manchester) swing the vote either way? One might think a terrorist attack helps the governing party, but one does not get the feeling in the polls, which means that either voters are more concerned about other issues or that voters realize the gross incompetence of the Tory government, which has slashed public security and police spending amid these terrorist attacks.

Is Neoliberalism a Useful Word?
Posted on June 8, 2017

In one of the many heated Facebook debates I have had with friends the major question arises whether it makes any sense to use the word "neoliberalism" to describe anything. It is naturally important to define in each case what we mean by neoliberalism and if it is clear in the mind of the readers and discussants what is meant by neoliberalism in each case, we can make an authoritative statement about whether we should use the terminology.

But first to directly answer the question: 'yes', for me personally, and 'it depends' for whether it is generally useful. The usefulness of the term neoliberalism depends entirely on the political perspective of the person. People, who hate neoliberalism, use the word all the time (just do a Google Scholar search and get 253,000 results), while people, who like neoliberalism, hate the word. Thus, we have an interesting distinction between the word, the meaning and political perspective.

A normal word has a close association to its meaning and ideology often plays no role. If I say 'table' and assuming your knowledge of the English language, you will likely think of an object made out of wood, plastic or metal with a flat surface and one or a few legs to hold it up. We can have a different viewpoint around how many legs an ideal table should have or what the best material is, but we would not politically contest the basic definition I have given here. But in neoliberalism there is a clear distinction between word, personal ideology and meaning. Liking the ideology reduces one's liking for the term, while hating the ideology increases one's liking for the term.

Is neoliberalism a scientific term? People with a more natural scientific inclination would frown and dispute that a term that is so laden with personal feelings and ideological background can have any usefulness in science. If the theory of relativity were not $E=mc2$, implying E=Energy, m=mass and c=speed of light in a vacuum, because we have different political ideologies, then we don't have a useful concept. Observations in nature that follow a particular rule have to be summarized in a theory that makes sense to all individuals and by replication of experiments can be repeated precisely.

Clearly, another important scientific domain- where we need to have full agreement over the content regardless of political ideology- is climate change. Here it is superbly difficult given that there is an extreme political faction in the United States that denies the existence of climate change, claiming that there is a political ploy to reduce US competitiveness (see President Trump and the Republican Party). The lack of deference to climate scientists, who have devoted their careers to study these very questions, creates the dilemma that we are ineffectively doing things to tackle and counteract climate change.

But let me just make the statement here that neoliberalism can be used as a term in the social sciences regardless of the diversity in views on its usage. My argument here is that we are naturally not applying the standard of the hard sciences, which says that all people regardless of political ideology have to agree on its meaning. For neoliberalism to be made social scientifically useful, all we have to do is to *find a definition in a given article that can describe social phenomena of interest and is clearly communicated to the reader.* In the most ideal case, this means that at least among the neoliberalism-haters or anti-neoliberals, mostly on the political left, who are throwing around the term like we regularly gulp down water to quench our daily thirst, we all agree on what it means. This does not necessarily happen, so the only way how we can keep the term in our daily discourse without losing scientific credibility is if we rigorously define it in the context that we are using it.

So after beating around the bush, I have arrived at the hard question at the heart of the matter. What is neoliberalism? It may be described as

- a political ideology (the glorification of markets, the individual, the private entrepreneur, the investor, the capitalist; the detestation of government regulation of business and the welfare state; the penetration of the market logic/ consumerism in all elements of life, such as family, religion and social relations) and

- an economic practice (promotion of free trade, deregulation of firms and financial institutions, privatization of public goods, tax cuts for the affluent, the creation of winner-take-all markets, the growth of technological forces favoring the capitalists, the shift of risk from the society, government and firm to the individual, the weakening of social welfare services, the precarization and insecurity of employment relationships in the labor market, the growth of income and wealth inequality and the degradation of the natural environment, especially in the form of climate change).

Also see Harvey (2005); Saad Filho and Johnston (2005); Dumenil and Levy (2011); Centeno and Cohen (2012)

Naturally, neoliberalism-concept-supporters or neoliberals (who are neoliberalism-word-haters) will focus on the political ideology, which like the belief in any religion revolves around some desirable features that have to be taken on faith (i.e. ideology), while discussions on economic practice remain by nature fragmented. Surely, free trade and privatization sound good, but precarization of the workforce and concentrating wealth at the top are undesirable, so they either remain silent on it or claim that neoliberalism or obsession with 'free' markets favoring the capitalist class have nothing to do with these undesirable social developments. Or they might acknowledge these social developments but accept it as a cost of an "innovative" society.

Conversely, neoliberalism-concept-haters or anti-neoliberals (who are neoliberalism-word-supporters) will focus on the economic practice, especially where the evidence for socially nefarious consequences is the strongest. But even where the neoliberals think they have a strong hand, there is criticism from the anti-neoliberals, e.g. free trade is criticized as not as desirable as 'fair' trade, or privatization benefiting a few big owners is not as desirable as state or worker-owned enterprises. Politically moderate anti-neoliberals (e.g. of the Keynesian social-democratic variety) might be inclined to be silent on the political ideology element, and good examples here is the Third Way of the 1990s led by people like Blair, Jospin and Schroder. "We are not against the market, and we are for labor market activation and an inclusive economic policy" etc. Left-wingers will attack both economic practice and political ideology at the same time, as a more communitarian, solidaristic ideology is incompatible with the principles of neoliberalism.

We may conclude that the social sciences are deeply political and that our own personal viewpoints pierce through every element that we analyze. For those, who have been socialized in Marxist thinking, this is the nature of the game. Social science is the analysis of social phenomena at the same time as it is the advocacy of social change based on underlying moral-political desiderata. For those, who want to hold onto the Weberian ethics of value-free science, we are still salvaged by my definition rule, i.e. define the word neoliberalism in the context of the argument/ article in which it is used to give readers a clear idea of what it means. It is only for natural science standards, which wants to eradicate all ambiguity in meaning and political intention, that neoliberalism cannot hold up to strict scrutiny. Too bad.

May's Sad Face, Corbyn's Happy Face
Posted on June 9, 2017

The SNP and Conservatives are losing seats, Labour is winning seats. The Tories will likely form a coalition government with DUP from Northern Ireland, but May will go into Brexit negotiations weakened. I am waiting for the overthrowers in the Tory ranks, though I suspect they have not nurtured a real political talent in their own ranks (Boris Johnson, seriously?). With 29 seat gains, the Labour backbenchers will have a hard time unseating Corbyn and I suspect a longer campaign would have given him an outright majority given May's unpopularity and disastrous campaign.

But politics is after all also about emotions. Collins (2017a) analyzed campaign photos of Donald Trump on the election night. Everyone in his family and political circle is visibly elated and looking forward to the presidency, except Trump. Trump was looking serious, and actually was sad for leaving behind his business empire. He visibly had fun while giving his half-sentences and audience-irritating statements on the campaign rallies, but was sad that he now had to take the reins of a very powerful political office, where he could no longer keep things as secret as in his business empire.

For the seasoned politician Theresa May the insight is precisely the opposite. She was banking on snap elections to increase her majority in the House, and the polls were telling her a 20-25 point landslide against the Labour Party, which she hoped was thoroughly discredited by a left-wing leader, who did not fit the ruling opinion of Rupert Murdoch and his media empire. Naturally, the strategy did not work out for her, and her own personal incompetence at the campaign brought about her downfall based on: (1) disingenuity about cuts to the social care and pension budget (hitting her old voter base), (2) disingenuity with a hard Brexit being better for Britain ("no deal is better than a bad deal"), (3) refusal to participate in the leader TV debate, (4) the repetition of empty platitude without positive messaging (in contrast, to the social justice plank of Jeremy Corbyn).

If we only read May's press statements, she says that she wants to have a period of political stability in Britain and that would require a coalition government with the DUP (unionists in Northern Ireland), many of which favored terror campaigns against Irish nationalists in the past. That is not really a harbinger of stability. Given the Tories lost more seats than the DUP has in total, the governing majority for May is also less than it is pre-election. This is everything but stability, which shows again that we can't trust anything that comes out of her mouth.

So let's turn to her face.

The first remark is that May is not a very good actor, and she does not hide her feeling of sadness. She looks down. Her mouth is pulled down on the sides. There is perhaps some embarrassment. She is not pleased about the election result, having clearly failed in her gamble to generate a bigger majority in parliament. Not even the pro-Conservative right-wing papers deny it, and say it as is.

In the next photo, May is looking up, but the expression is very grave. Examining other photos of her, she usually does not have a double chin, and this suggests that her head is tilted forward permanently on that election night, at least in front of the cameras. Again the lips are together and tilted downward on the sides. Even though she has enough votes to form another government, what matters in politics are also the overall impressions or the optics, and they look bad for her. She might continue to govern but with a lack of credibility. Whatever Brexit deal she will want to put together, what will haunt her is the lack of legitimacy that she has, having gone to the voters and not receiving a majority for her party.

May's sadness stands in contrast to Corbyn's relief and happiness. In the next photo, he is posing next to another Labour candidate, he pointing at her and she pointing at him.

In this photo, he is smiling, and facing a cheering audience. The smile is genuine, because the eyelid is folding as well. He is quite exhilarated after gaining 29 seats for his party.

What is remarkable is that the overall power constellation is not really changing, as May remains PM, while Corbyn will likely remain opposition leader. There is still a 57 seat margin between Conservative and Labour, and so Conservative has the best claim to power. After people no longer have reason to support UKIP after Brexit, the LDP (the only pro-EU party) not having recovered from their coalition experience with the Tories, and the SNP losing seats after continued insistence on a new independence referendum (which scared many Scots people), the vote share for Conservative and Labour has increased to old levels, suggesting a consolidation of the established party system.

What matters above all else is not just the facts on the ground but the optics. May wanted the increase in seats, but was not able to get it. The Labour leadership suggests that the hung parliament creates an opportunity for the Labour Party to run the government and replace the Conservative government, though if the DUP backs the Conservatives, then this constellation is very unlikely. An anti-Tory block in parliament would have to consist of all the other political parties, including Greens, SNP, Plaid Cymru and LibDems, which will be very difficult.

Book Review, Yanis Varoufakis, Adults in the Room (London: Penguin, 2017)

Posted on <u>June 15, 2017</u>

On May 4, 2015, I had argued (Liu 2015a) that Yanis Varoufakis was the best finance minister in Europe, as he was one of the few people in political power that knew that continuous extend and pretend policies of the troika (European Central Bank, European Commission and IMF, along with the powerful Eurogroup) would wreck Greece further while ensuring that the creditors would never get their money back. I had argued that it was a mistake that prime minister Tsipras had on April 27, 2015 decided to sideline the only person in the cabinet who was so committed to the ending this extend and pretend, hoping that by being somewhat more conciliatory to the troika he would be able to get a better deal. It was all for naught. What I wrote back then, is as true as ever, having now read Varoufakis 500 page memoir, recounting his experiences as Greek's finance minister from January to July 2015. On the back of the book, Jeffrey Sachs, one of Varoufakis key foreign advisers, had called him the "Thucydides of our Times".

Just a comment on the style of his writing: Varoufakis writes in a very unpretentious style, explaining the complex economic relations between his bankrupt state and the intransigent negotiators at the troika such that even people without a PhD in economics can grasp the fundamentals. He includes rather entertaining episodes of personal encounters he had with European and international officials, revealing how the powerful were very reasonable and made intelligent comments about the Greek debt crisis, while in public statements they would shoot down any proposal that Varoufakis and his team had put forward.

Unlike normal political autobiographies which are self-congratulating acts of self-vindication, Varoufakis does not have the pretentiousness of a typical politician, and has retained the honesty of an academic, who wants to debate ideas and defend views as he sees fit. He also tells very little about his personal life or some other Oedipus complex that normal politicians suffer from, but focuses entirely on the fate of his country's economic and political situation. That makes his memoir infinitely more valuable than what can be expected from a normal politician's memoir.

The book read like a political thriller and ultimately like a Shakespearean tragedy with enough hints at foreshadowing of a bad ending. It unfortunately is not a novel, though it took such style, but the very sad reality of Greek and ultimately European political economy of the last 2 years, and a reflection of the last 20 (at least since the euro was introduced). His witty analogies range from John Steinbeck to Aesop to George Orwell, and his political economic insights are lucid with no obfuscation.

As Varoufakis himself portrays it, the tragedy comes precisely from the fact that all the actors that were putting stones on his way and wanted to force the Greek government into capitulation were at the same time quite reasonable in personal dialog with the finance minister. There were always some people that really wanted to be hard on the Greeks and force them to accept the bailout-cum-austerity (extend and pretend), while there were other people, who probably would have relented, but thought that they could not speak up for fear of being shot down by the other actors.

There is a really deep web of individuals that were in positions of power, which made it impossible for Varoufakis and his government to get the debt restructuring he thought that his country needed. Before naming names (which is the heart and the meat of the tragedy/ memoir) and how each of these actors within the troika interacted with Varoufakis (only told from his point of view, obviously) to produce the sorry outcomes, the reader will likely benefit from a brief summary of how Greece ended up being boxed up by the troika, how Syriza got to power and how they were defeated.

How the Greek Crisis Started

It all began with Greek membership in the eurozone in 1999. Hitherto Greece had a weak export economy, which was reflected in a weak currency and repeated rounds of drachma devaluation to restore competitiveness. Greece really wanted to be part of the eurozone, but Germany would only agree to a common currency if all member states bring their public budget deficits and debt down. Greece was not capable to do it in such a short period and instead took advantage of the Italian and, of all cases, German accounting strategy to shift the deficit off the books into the future. Greece was subsequently included into the eurozone, even as it did not fulfill the financial convergence criteria.

What followed was about 10 years of increasing capital imports, which Greece had never experienced before. The export-strong Germans had their products made more competitive by the euro that was weaker than the D-mark and could sell many more products into Greece and other parts of the peripheral eurozone countries clustered in the Mediterranean. The swelling profits among German manufacturers (and to smaller extent French) was converted into loans of German and French banks given to the Greek government (to some extent Italy and Portugal, and the private real estate market in Ireland and Spain). Greece could now consume above its means (while Germany kept wage rises in check, which was made simpler by cheap East German labor and the Hartz IV reforms), and wages could be inflated by the expansive fiscal policy made possible by the greater loans from northern Europe.

The party came to an end in 2008 when Lehman Brothers went bust. The German and French banks were facing financial abyss as they were sitting on toxic (non-performing) loans, so their governments generously bailed them out. The ripple effect on Greece was that the northern European banks called in their loans, while demand in the economy and national income was shrinking amid the recession. The Greek government could not pay up, and the northern European banks were facing an abyss again.

But instead of agreeing to a second direct bank bailout, German chancellor Merkel and French president Sarkozy convinced the IMF and the EU to organize a bailout of Greece, selling it to the public as a solidaristic bailout for their Greek brethren. It was a sham operation because the IMF got involved when Dominique Strauss-Kahn, a potential French presidential contender, wanted to bail out Greece, even as a bailout to a bankrupt country without restructuring violated the IMF statute. Greece at that point was clearly bankrupt, and so were the exposed French and German banks, but Merkel and Sarkozy wanted to save the latter, so that all states paying into the IMF (most countries in the world) and the eurozone (27% stake for Germany, 20% for France, and smaller stakes for other countries) had to come up with the first bailout for Greece in 2010. Germany and France were able to force smaller eurozone economies (like Slovakia and Latvia) plus world economies via the IMF to pay for a Greek bailout out of which almost the entire proceeds went to bailout the German and French banks! By 2015, the private creditor (non-troika) share of Greek government debt was lowered to 15%, and the German and French banks with the biggest debt exposure were basically of the hook.

Bailing out a bankrupt country now created a follow-up problem of how Greece can manage their new debt to the troika creditors.

What is worse is that the troika demanded rapid privatization of Greek public goods (at firesale prices!), massive cuts to social programs such as pensions and health care, layoff of civil servants, VAT tax rises and greater efforts toward tax compliance (which most Greek governments and later even the troika ignored!). We'll give you a bailout, but only if you perform austerity and continue paying us back the loans. But the government saving money during an economic crisis, when the private actors are pulling back on spending merely exacerbates the public debt problem.

The principle of why austerity is self-defeating can easily be illustrated by an example: imagine a country with a debt of 60 dollars and a national income of 100, which creates a debt-to-GDP ratio of 60%. We also assume that 50% of the national income comes from government spending, which is not an unreasonable assumption in most European economies. Now, imagine you force down austerity, which would slash government spending in half. Government spending is reduced from 50 to 25, total national income decreases from 100 to 75, thus the debt-to-GDP ratio has gone from 60/100 to 60/75 or from 60 to 80%. The debt load here has not increased (unrealistic assumption given the expected interest payments that accumulate as the country is incapable of paying even just the interest on the debt), but the debt burden has increased as income decreases.

Soon enough the Greeks after having been on the verge of default in 2010 nearly defaulted again in 2012. By that time, the German and French banks were already off the hook, but after having committed the first crime, the EU leaders had to come up with a second crime to cover up the first crime: pass a second bailout, not out of solidarity but to allow the Greeks to repay the old loans, and tie them down with even more austerity. Varoufakis claimed, rightly, that the extend-and-pretend loans kept the Greeks in a debtors' prison, and it was time to leave this prison.

At the same time, many southern European economies could not allow relenting on the Greeks and give them a much needed debt restructuring because it could empower the political left in Spain, Italy or Portugal, who can overthrow their political leaders by accusing them of having sold out to the troika while the Greeks have gotten a nice deal for themselves. France was cautiously interested in debt restructuring, but could not offend the Germans, whose cooperation was needed to support the French banking system (p.519, F11). The Germans simply did not want to own up to the fact that they were bailing out their banks, and Angela Merkel also refused a Grexit option, which would have gone along with debt restructuring (while Schauble was notably open to Grexit). Only the IMF noted in internal reports and discussions (including Poul Thomsen, see pp.482-3) that debt restructuring in Greece was unavoidable, but in practical discussions always deferred to the Eurogroup. Strange political calculations were thus blocking good economic solutions.

While the political situation did not favor debt restructuring, Syriza led by Alexis Tsipras won the election on 25 January, 2015. This was the first time that a party of the left, consisting of socialists, social democrats and communists, won the plurality of the vote. PASOK (social democratic) and ND (conservative) had been in power for most of the post-dictatorship democracy since 1974. But PASOK destroyed itself with the acceptance of the first bailout-cum-austerity in 2010, and ND was demolished after first campaigning against the first bailout and then accepting the second bailout with the associated austerity. Had there been an earlier opportunity for elections, Syriza would have won big beforehand, though they blew their first real chance in 2012.

Varoufakis had attacked Syriza at the beginning for their lack of economic competence. He had been advising Syriza's economic policy during the 2012 elections and saw them essentially ignore his disciplined message to negotiate for a debt restructuring with the EU partners. Instead Syriza had campaigned on expanding popular social programs that the incumbent government had savagely cut.

But in January 2015, it became serious. Tsipras and his team were capable of convincing Varoufakis to become finance minister in the case that Syriza got elected (as the polls suggested), and Varoufakis had accepted the offer but only when he could run for a parliament seat himself. He was invited to run for a parliament seat and won it with the biggest vote for an MP.

Some cynics abroad claim that Greece had been on an economic recovery trajectory before Syriza got elected and their daring negotiation stance had threatened such recovery. But the small increase in GDP was hiding the fact that prices were shrinking faster than nominal incomes such that the economy did not recover. The lower prices did not help the Greeks given that the debt repayments continued to suck income from the Greeks. The other counterargument is that austerity pushes down labor unit costs and makes Greek exports more competitive, and with a positive foreign trade balance they could pay off the debt. However, while labor costs were coming down, it was not exports that increased but imports that decreased.

The Home Front

Alexis Tsipras became prime minister. Yannis Dragasakis, became deputy prime minister. Minister of state was Tsipras confidante Nikos Pappas. Influential was also the cabinet secretary Spyros Sagias, and Varoufakis chief ally Euclid Tsakalotos, who became deputy foreign minister for economic relations. Stathakis became economy minister, and George Chouliarakis became chair of the Council of Economic Advisers. All these people formed the inner circle of the "war cabinet", which met daily to discuss the next step forward in the economic negotiations with the troika.

This war cabinet, if we are to believe Varoufakis narrative, was initially nearly united in their negotiation stance. On their first day in office, Varoufakis had visited Tsipras, who told his inaugurated finance minister. "Listen! Don't get comfortable in here. Don't learn to love the trappings of office. These offices, these chairs, are not for us. Our place is out there, on the streets, in the squares, with the people. We got in to get a job done on their behalf. Never forget that this is why we are here. For no other reason. And be ready. If the bastards find a way to stop us from delivering what we promised, you and I must be ready to hand back the keys and get out on the streets again, to plan the next demonstration." (pp.147-8)

The determination at the beginning was huge, especially among Tsipras, Pappas and Tsakalotos. Dragasakis, the deputy was wary of supporting a too aggressive stance against the quasi bankrupt Greek banks, which is the approach that Varoufakis would have favored. Chouliarakis, the economic adviser, was the most concessionary and had been temporarily removed by Varoufakis only to be restored at the end of April at the behest of the troika. Chouliarakis agreed with the unrealistic growth targets that the IMF and the troika had proposed, thus giving a blank cheque to the bailout-cum-austerity packages.

Varoufakis went to the European capitals to negotiate debt restructuring for Greece, but as the situation became more and more hopeless and the pressure against the Greek government increased substantially, Syriza's high leaders gradually gave up. Tsipras, Pappas and Sagias backed Dragasakis and Chouliarakis in demanding a full-scale surrender to the bailout demand (the third one). Varoufakis still believed in getting a debt restructuring deal, and if threatened by the shutdown of the Greek banks (by the ECB refusing to release euros to the Greek banks) he would have liked to activate a parallel payment system, which works like an IOU for the duration of the bank shutdown. He would have also demanded the non-payment of the SMP (Securities Market Program) loan to the ECB. With such a tough negotiating stance he was hoping to avert a Grexit and get debt restructuring, though Grexit was still better than the Memorandum of Understanding (MoU, i.e. continue bailout-cum-austerity).

But as the political pressure on the Greek cabinet continued, Tsipras and his colleagues sidelined Varoufakis in favor of Tsakalotos to the relief of the Eurozone partners around April 27. (Ironically, Tsakalotos was the only major cabinet member to side with Varoufakis on policy, though he rarely spoke out in cabinet meetings and when he became finance minister he faithfully did his party's bidding of surrender.) The final gamble happened as the Greek cabinet agreed to a bailout referendum to be put in front of the Greek people in July 5. The ECB, thus, shut down the banking system as the loans became due and as a political warning to the electorate that they should vote 'yes' to the referendum. The political leadership was fairly restrained (likely hoping to "lose" the referendum, i.e. a yes vote), though Varoufakis campaigned on a no vote. The voters voted no with 61.5% of the vote, thus defying the troika once again despite having gone through a week of closed banks.

Varoufakis pressed for the implementation of the parallel currency and cutting the ECB loans, but Syriza leaders would have none of it.

Tsipras and his inner circle panicked and decided to ignore the referendum results and sign the bailout agreement regardless. What a sham to call the referendum, when Tsipras did not care about the result except if he had "lost" it with a yes vote, which would have been easier on his conscience. But given that voters rejected the extend and pretend, the Syriza government was now in a position to openly have to betray the electorate that had put their trust in them. Tsipras noted in a conversation with Varoufakis that he was scared of a coup d'etat (p.469). But the more likely explanation (and here Varoufakis offers no more than speculation given that he can't look into the mind of his boss) is that Tsipras and the inner circle were simply tired of half a year of bad news from the overpowerful troika, which seemed to hold all the cards in their hand. Better to capitulate and not face pressure from an intransigent troika and hope that the voters will put them back to power given that the political alternatives are even worse. Varoufakis compares his Syriza colleagues to Orwell's 1984 character, who came to love Big Brother regardless of how oppressive he is (p.461).

Tsipras reasoning is quite bad because a Greek pensioner, who had seen his pension cut by 40%, will not care whether it is a Syriza or ND or PASOK or technocratic government which had imposed these cuts. It's all equally bad. Unbelievably, when Tsipras called out snap elections in September 2015, his party was returned to power with the loss of merely 4 seats. There just wasn't any alternative, but they had 300,000 fewer voters, which reflects a voter turnout that was 7 points lower (56%) than in January (63%).

Furthermore, Tsipras had offered Varoufakis another cabinet position (while pushing him out of the finance ministry), which Varoufakis rejected as he was no longer interested in participating in a government that would agree to extend and pretend, violating the original mandate of why voters would support Syriza. This is the final reasoning for Tsipras' U-turn. While at the beginning he was skeptical about power, after having sat long enough in the prime minister chair he was beginning to become comfortable in power and did not want to leave. I doubt that if the elections were to happen again, he could rely on such broad electoral support. With the removal of Varoufakis, the prison rebellion was over.

Varoufakis has bitter memories of his Syriza colleagues, largely welcoming the hatred of the European establishment, but not easily accepting the self-undermining disunity of his own government. Martin Luther King said, "The ultimate measure of a man is not where he stands in moments of comfort and convenience, but where he stands at times of challenge and controversy." We are all left-wing revolutionaries in our dream, but when David is fighting Goliath, will David hold onto his dream or surrender in the face of adversity?

The Foreign Front

Varoufakis at the beginning had the thankless task to negotiate with the Eurogroup finance ministers and the troika to get debt restructuring. Thanks to his rich account (again, very one-sided by definition as it is a memoir), we can paint the colors, i.e. who plays an important role in the negotiations and how could the troika view prevail?

I begin with Varoufakis' allies, who used to work for the other side, and were thus steeled in their negotiation strategy: Elena Panariti, a former World Bank economist, who opposed the bailout and had experience in imposing austerity on other countries, thus being especially resistant to the ways of the troika (p.119). Natasha Arvaniti, a Greek civil servant and EU technocrat, who also gathered experience with the devastating troika policies. Glenn Kim was a banker, who was involved in the bond deals between Greece and the eurozone (p.120). The French investment bank Lazard led by Daniel Cohen and Matthieu Pigasse, who had charged the Greek state enormous sums for consulting on the second bailout, had a guilty conscience and lent a helping hand to Varoufakis (p.121).

Other useful friends were the former UK conservative Chancellor of the Exchequer, Lord Norman Lamont; Columbia University economist and World Bank economist in the 1990s when pushing for rapid privatization in Russia, Jeffrey Sachs; Thomas Mayer from the Deutsche Bank (one of the big beneficiaries of the bailout); former US treasury secretary and economic adviser, Larry Summers; US senator from Vermont, Bernie Sanders (who wrote letters to Fed chair Janet Yellen to demand an easing on austerity); and Texas economist and friend, Jamie Galbraith. Sachs accompanied Varoufakis to many meetings with high officials, and so did Galbraith. In addition, Galbraith also helped Varoufakis draft a parallel currency program, which ultimately was not activated.

There is another peripheral actor that is worthy to mention:

Emmanuel Macron, France's economic minister, now president of France, made a very positive impression on Varoufakis, understanding the Greek plight and similarly advocating for an investment program that could help Greece and Europe end the financial crisis, regretting that he was the economy minister as opposed to the finance minister, where he could have done more to help Greece (p.191). In another important intervention in June 28, Macron wanted to travel to Athens to consult with Varoufakis and his government directly, and also tried to get president Hollande to intervene on behalf of Greece to avoid the bank shutdown. Hollande and other higher circles shut him down and cancelled his planned trip.

At a summit meeting he had argued that the troika deal with Greece was a "treaty of Versailles", which resulted in Merkel calling on Hollande to neutralize Macron (pp. 453-4). Macron subsequently resigned from the socialist government in 2016, decided to run for president himself, won the election this year, and is slated to gain a landslide from the French parliamentary elections. Now, being on par with Merkel, it is questionable whether he can pursue such an aggressively pro-investment, anti-austerity agenda, especially given that his agenda is about slashing public employment, loosening labor protections.

Now for the opponents among the troika (even as individuals within them were sympathetic to the Greek position):

The first part of the troika Greece faced was the **International Monetary Fund**:

Christine Lagarde, leader of the IMF, former French finance minister, succeeded the disgraced Dominique Strauss-Kahn (at the IMF), who fell after a sex scandal. Lagarde had some sympathies for Varoufakis and Greece during their meeting, but was shot down by Thomsen. She was personally quite skeptical about the Greek ability for meeting its financial obligations and paying off the debt, falling in line with many IMF internal assessments that said the same. But, more importantly, during the negotiations, she deferred to the Eurogroup and the ECB. There is also incongruence in the IMF, namely that internal reports criticize bailout-cum-austerity while the IMF staffers on the ground promote it insistently. Lagarde only wants "adults in the room", i.e. sign the MoU, give up, Yanis.

Poul Thomsen, director of IMF's Europe department, was very strict in the personal conversations with Varoufakis and Lagarde, but in their first encounter, he was surprisingly open to lower primary surplus targets (which would make it easier for Greece to budget). He also favored debt cancellation and targeting tax evasion (pp.183-5). Though this never came through in the decision-making. He was responsible for creating unrealistic economic projections, which assumed high growth rates and thus make harsh austerity technically feasible. According to Wikileaks tapes, Thomsen has admitted to other staffers that the third bailout is not economically sustainable, and that the IMF's economic projections were fallacious.

The second group included the **Eurogroup**, consisting mainly of finance ministers of the eurozone countries

Thomas Wieser is the president of the Eurogroup Working Group. The Eurogroup Working Group is an advisory body to the Eurogroup finance ministers and is very influential in formulating policies. Wieser is an Austrian Social Democrat, but having worked in the banking sector most of his life has developed quite a favorable view toward repaying loans to the creditors in full. One exchange between Wieser and Varoufakis is noteworthy: Merkel had dispatched Wieser to chat with the Greek officials in Athens. Varoufakis noted that without EU funding, Greece would have to default on debt repayment, to which Wieser replied that Greece could last longer by plundering the reserves of pension funds, universities, utility companies and local authorities. Thus, more austerity please.

Jeroen Dijsselbloem is the president of Eurogroup finance ministers and Dutch finance minister. He has become well known for his encounter in February 2015 with Varoufakis in Athens. Dijsselbloem thought that he could bring the newly elected Syriza government to immediately cave in and accept the Memorandum of Understanding. "The current program must be completed or there is nothing else." (p.162) During the press conference, Dijsselbloem insisted on the current program, while Varoufakis insisted on renegotiating the deal. Dijsselbloem then took of his translation device, leaned over and whispered in Varoufakis ear, "You just killed the troika." (p.170)

Wolfgang Schauble, the German finance minister, is the most powerful finance minister in Europe. He is from the conservative CDU and the southwest German province of Baden-Wurttemberg, where Merkel's famous and proverbial Swabian housewife lives and saves diligently. He is a lawyer rather than an economist and enjoys being the bad cop (p.210). The Eurogroup meetings are dominated by Schauble, who disciplines Greece and other peripheral Eurozone countries to keep their deficit in line and enforce austerity. His natural allies are the Austrians, Dutch, Maltesians, Belgians, Luxembourgians, Finns, Latvians, Estonians, Lithuanians, Slovakians, Slovenians and Portuguese who agree with Schauble on all policy statements. The recipients of discontent are the Irish, Italians, Spanish, Greek, Cypriots and to a smaller extent the French. The latter group, however, rarely dared to speak up for Varoufakis, because they feared rebuke from Schauble and were also concerned that if the Greeks got a debt restructuring the left in their own country would throw them out of office for not having gotten such a debt restructuring themselves.

Varoufakis writes,

While some, including the Lithuanian, Slovakian and Slovenian finance ministers, clearly believed Schauble's pronouncements on economic policy to be sound and self-evident, it became apparent that even those who disagreed with the economics of austerity would support him- in the case of Italy, Spain and Ireland out of fear that upstart Greece might escape having to do what they had been forced to do already, in which case their own people might demand to know why they had not resisted austerity too- and in the case of a small but significant group, with France at its centre, out of fear that Schauble would force austerity upon them in the future if they undermined him. (p.237)

I quote Varoufakis on the seating arrangements in the Eurogroup meetings:

At one end, to my left, sat the Eurogroup president, Jeroen Dijsselbloem. On his right was Thomas Wieser, the Eurogroup Working Group president and the real power at that end of the table; on his left were the IMF representatives, Christine Lagarde and Poul Thomsen. At the other end of the table was Valdis Dombrovskis, commissioner for the euro and social dialogue, whose real job was to supervise (on behalf of Wolfgang Schauble) Pierre Moscovici, the economic and financial affairs commissioner, who sat on the Latvian's left. On Dombrovskis's right, meanwhile, sat Benoit Coeure and beyond him Mario Draghi representing the ECB.

At the same corner of the table as Draghi, but on the longer side at at right angles to him, sat Wolfgang Schauble. Their proximity would on occasion give rise to intense heat, though never any actual light. Along the same side as Schauble were what I came to see as his cheerleaders: the Finnish, Slovakian, Austrian, Portuguese, Slovenian, Latvian, Lithuanian, and Maltese finance ministers. My seat was almost diagonally opposite Schauble's, alongside the other profligates, nicely lined up together: to my left was Ireland's Michael Noonan, to my right Spain's Luis de Guindos, and next to de Guindos was Italy's Pier Carlo Padoan. France's Michel Sapin also sat on our side, next to Padoan. (p.232)

When Varoufakis proposed the debt swap agreements to lighten the Greek debt, Schauble did not even consider this proposal deferring to the "institutions" (troika). Schauble in a personal meeting with Varoufakis, however, noted his preference to solve the Eurozone crisis and end the extend and pretend primarily via a Grexit. Varoufakis opposed Grexit because the reintroduction of the drachma would be like announcing a currency devaluation a year before it happens, giving Greeks enough time to withdraw all their euros and keep them in a northern European bank account.

The chaotic shift of currency would require the Greek government to impose stringent capital controls, which would create a painful short-term economic uncertainty. Though he also thought it was better than the alternative of continuing extend and pretend. Schauble would have favored a little break for the Greeks, leave the currency for a while, get their household finances in order and then return back to the euro at a later point. When Merkel had heard of Schauble's plans she immediately rejected it. Schauble, thus, had his hands tied and ultimately pressed Varoufakis for the signing of the MoU. In a notable exchange between Schauble and Varoufakis the latter asked whether Schauble would have signed the MoU as Greek finance minister. "As a patriot, no. It's bad for your people." (p.413)

Michel Sapin, the French finance minister, was ideologically siding with Greece, but only behind closed doors. In a personal meeting with Varoufakis, Sapin confided, "Your government's success will be our success. It is important that we change Europe together; that we replace this fixation with austerity with a pro-growth agenda. Greece needs it. France needs it. Europe needs it." (p.188). But when Sapin and Varoufakis appeared for the press conference, Sapin's tone changed and he admonished Greece for not being earnest enough in applying austerity. Varoufakis was shocked. Sapin did not want to cross the Germans by being too helpful to the Greeks.

Sapin also confessed to Varoufakis that he did not know much about economics and wrote his postgraduate thesis on the "numismatic history of Aegina" (coins in ancient Greece). During Varoufakis' first Eurogroup meeting, Sapin briefly defended the Greek proposals, but then was shut down by Schauble, who replied, "Elections cannot be allowed to change economic policy." (p.237)

Angela Merkel, the federal chancellor of Germany, is not a member of the Eurogroup and is hereby listed as the only head of government in Europe, because of her influence and power. The Eurogroup finance minister meetings are led by her colleague Wolfgang Schauble, but given that the two disagree on the handling of Greece, she deserves a special mention. It was her intervention that ensured a February 20 agreement to extend the Greek loans (which would otherwise have resulted in bank closures in February as opposed to July) and blocked Schauble's Grexit proposal, as she was more concerned about holding the currency union together at all political/ economic costs, even if it meant more bailout-cum-austerity. Varoufakis claims that Tsipras became too over-reliant on Merkel's help, though it can ultimately not be established what happened in the interactions between Tsipras and Merkel, as he only had personal dealings with Schauble. Even today, with Varoufakis gone and replaced by Tsakalotos the same pattern emerges: Tsipras intervenes personally to get Merkel to make concessions to Greece while she defers to her finance minister (Spiegel 2017).

The second part of the troika consist of the **European Central Bank**:

Mario Draghi, chairman of the ECB, former Goldman Sachs banker and chairman of the Bank of Italy, presented himself as a technocrat, who was not making political decisions which would be left to the Eurogroup, when in fact his decision to launch the QE bond-buying program and the refusal to extend liquidity to Greek banks, which forced the shutdown of their banks, due to the unwillingness of Varoufakis to sign the MoU, are deeply political interventions. Draghi had no interest in debt swaps, and when pressured deferred to the ECB Governing Council which tied his hands in making decisions.

While going out for dinner with two German officials, Varoufakis received a phone call from Draghi. "Hello Mario, what can I do for you?"

"I wanted to let you know, Yanis, before you learn it from the media, that as I foreshadowed this morning, the Governing Council voted to withdraw your banks' waiver [which foreshadowed a bank run]. But this does not mean much since your banks will continue to be supported by your central bank via emergency liquidity assistance, " Draghi reported on the phone (p.207). The waiver was restored after the February 20 agreement, which continued liquidity and continued financing until the July shutdown of the Greek banks.

Benoit Coeure, is the French member of the ECB executive board, and in private meetings was very "mild and agreeable" (p.185). He also entertained the debt swap proposal that Varoufakis put forward in a private meeting (p.186). During the meeting with the ECB board, Coeure also lobbied Draghi to take seriously the debt swap proposal, which Draghi ignored by changing the subject (p.204). In another personal encounter, Varoufakis told Coeure that he would activate the parallel payment system in case of the ECB denying liquidity to the Greek central bank, and Coeure thanked him for telling him this and promised to ask the EU council to push for more favorable monetary action to give the Greek government more breathing room (pp.382-3). It went nowhere because even as the Greek banks were denied liquidity, the Syriza government refused to entertain the parallel payment system and instead capitulated to the demands of the troika.

In the decisive Eurogroup meeting on 18 June, Draghi and Coeure both conspired to worsen the bank run that was building up in Greece.

Nothing speeds up a bank run more effectively than a central banker [Draghi] reciting its progress while his deputy [Coeure] signals their intention not to intervene except perhaps by closing the banks in three days' time. (p.430)

A minor set of actors were the **EU commissioners**, as they had very little practical input in policymaking, and their conciliatory tone with Greece was overruled by the more powerful Eurogroup (p.262). (Ironically, the EU commission is counted as third part of the troika, though in Varoufakis' account it is the Eurogroup which holds the practical power.)

Jean-Claude Juncker, the president of the European Commission, was personally very sympathetic to Syriza's cause, having issued a draft communique, which read that "the economic and social impact of the crisis on Greece and its citizens has been immense" and that "there is a need to move to a new relationship based on a mutually beneficial agreement for Greece and for Europe as a whole" (p.257). Juncker's message also demanded a restoration of liquidity for the Greek banks and an end to troika officials unilaterally imposing humiliating policies as if Greece were a minor colony. In late June, right before the bailout referendum and the bank shutdown, Juncker issued another communique, which approved of the Greek debt swap proposal, but that was shelved either by the Eurogroup or by the Greek government ministers willing to capitulate (pp. 452-3).

Pierre Moscovici: The Frenchman is the EU commissioner for Economy and Finance, and has also been sympathetic to the Greek cause, endorsing the Juncker communique. Varoufakis was gleeful, but soon realized that without Dijsselbloem's and especially Schauble's support the communique is as valuable as a white paper in an obscure academic journal. Moscovici and Varoufakis took the communique into Dijsselbloem's office, who had no interest to entertain the commission communique and instead submitted the

MoU proposal to Varoufakis. The following scene is best quoted in full,

Turning to Pierre [Moscovici], who was already looking downcast, I asked what was going on. "You just showed me a draft communique that I was happy to sign on the spot. You are the EU's commissioner for economic affairs. I am the finance minister of a stricken EU member state. Can I please have some clarity from the only person in this room that has official status to represent the EU."

Without looking at me, Pierre turned to Jeroen and made his first and last attempt to salvage the European Commission's dignity. "Can we combine some of the phrases in your draft and this?" he implored in a broken voice, pointing at the draft he was holding in his right hand.

"No!" Jeroen cut him down with what could only be described as controlled aggression. "Everything that could be taken from the draft has been taken", he stated categorically.

...

"Pierre", I asked, "are you just going to submit to the enforcement of this totally one-sided communique against the commission's views and the draft that you prepared?"

Avoiding eye contact and in a voice that quavered with dejection, Pierre responded with a phrase that might one day feature in the European Union's tombstone: "Whatever the Eurogroup president says." pp.260-1

Moscovici also assured Varoufakis to speak with Coeure to find a more conciliatory position on ECB liquidity, which resulted in a phone call between Coeure and Varoufakis, promising potentially some higher intervention favoring Greece (p.382). Varoufakis ultimately compared Moscovici with Sapin: sympathetic but helpless and without ideas themselves (p.404).

Declan Costello: EU commission mission chief for Greece did not figure prominently in Varoufakis' account, but was described as a hardliner on indebted countries. He was in charge of drafting the Memorandum of Understanding, or the pretend and extend list.

Conclusion

Varoufakis' memoir is a true tragedy, as many political actors, especially the French ones (Lagarde, Sapin, Moscovici, Macron, Coeure) were rather favorable to the negotiation position of his government, which was made abundantly clear in tete-a-tete exchanges behind closed doors. But none of these actors could dare to go against the overarching logic of the troika, and the politically short-sighted logic that ending the bailout scam could reveal the stupid criminality of officials, who had decided to save their banks and cover it up from their own taxpayers. Ending the austerity scam could have also exposed countries that have undergone harsh austerity or might face it in the future as too weak to resist the unreasonable demands of the troika. In a true tragedy, the outcome is not only bad, but the actors in it know the consequences of their actions, but still can't depart from the already reached consensus.

If there is to be any realistic hope to resolve the Greek debt crisis the leaders will be forced to accept a different paradigm, revolving around either a painful Grexit or debt restructuring. We might hope that another political faction rises up in Greece to replace Syriza, which is rather unlikely, and the Greek suffering had increased in the meantime such that it will be harder to face another period of financial uncertainty for pensioners, workers and unemployed Greeks that had lost so much. The uncertainty in Greece, which the bailout-cum-austerity agenda enforces, is also applicable for the Eurozone taxpayers, as Greece will be expected to request a fourth bailout with which to repay the loans from the third bailout that they were in no better position to afford back then.

Varoufakis has gone on to help found his own left-wing political party (DiEM25), which is designed as a pan-European movement to demand an end to austerity, debt restructuring in the weak economies, a new investment agenda, better social and workers' rights, higher taxes on companies and the wealthy and, most importantly, democratic accountability and transparency for the ruling political class. With this book Varoufakis has made a contribution to the latter demand to an extent that is unusual for a person who had been in power. He also shows that it is possible for a political outsider to be in a position in power, even though the actual policy changes are not there. While participation in the levers of power for the good has to be lauded and encouraged, Varoufakis ultimate political failure rests from the inability of the political left to mobilize on a united front to challenge the European technocrats, who have made a sham out of democracy, and made the Brexit decision even somewhat plausible. One can only wish the best to DiEM25.

As my book report has taken on mostly positive tones (as I don't hide my left-wing sympathies), I have to address an important and valid objection: how can one make valid conclusions about the actors in the Eurozone tragedy when these descriptions all come from one person's account? To make valid statements for scholarship or even investigative journalism one has to corroborate these accounts by reading all the accounts, including from people that were described by Varoufakis and may appear in a very negative light. That would certainly be a worthy project and would require me probably to devote an entire career to study the Eurozone crisis as opposed to reading a book in a few days. I certainly don't deny that the Varoufakis story has to be read with a grain of salt.

But to be fair there are not many comprehensive accounts of the Eurozone crisis. What we have instead are the purely academic perspectives that are focused on broader political economy patterns (as opposed to the daily minutiae of actors making political decisions) or are only relevant in econometric, economic and finance journals, or the journalistic encounters with meaningless statements of political leaders made in rehearsed press conference settings. In the absence of having a ubiquity of smart people within the circles of power narrating how the architecture of power works (think of John Perkins *Confessions of an Economic Hit Man*, 2005) while eschewing the unreasonableness of a conspiracy theory, Varoufakis' account remains an important contribution to the public understanding of the Eurozone crisis.

In a telling encounter, Larry Summers told Varoufakis that he better choose whether he wants to remain a political outsider, where he can say whatever he wants but does not get heard by people in power, or a political insider, who will get heard by the powerful and might be able to change the outcomes, but cannot tell on insiders or criticize them behind their back. For six months of his life Varoufakis accomplished the rare feat of being a political insider while having been a political outsider all along. Government insiders are trying all they can to squash any attempt to inform the masses about what's happening inside the circles of power, see the continuing prosecution of Wikileaks founder Julian Assange. As Congressman Charles Binderup (1937) said in a paraphrase of Henry Ford, "It is perhaps well enough that the people of the Nation do not know or understand our banking and monetary system, for if they did I believe there would be a revolution before tomorrow morning."

Assange and Varoufakis are radicals to the extent that their efforts are reducing the distance between the rulers and the ruled, thus making the distinction between the political insiders and outsiders less relevant (for how could there be insiders if governance is made transparent to the public). That is a threat to any ruling class. We owe individuals like Varoufakis or Assange a great deal of gratitude for insisting on leaders to be accountable to a public that has confided in its leaders to watch over it.

How Brain Cancer Saved the Lives of Millions of Americans
Posted on July 28, 2017

At this point the US political system has become so absurd and so much dominated by oligarchic politics that only fortune's strike on a Republican senator, John McCain, led to the demise of the disastrous health care bill brought before the Senate. I am not celebrating McCain's brain disease and personally wish him the best in his recovery efforts, but do find it ironic that he became the crucial vote to avert the Republican health care bill. Was his brain cancer making him have the sympathy for the more than 20 million Americans that were immediately going to have their insurance coverage terminated (and their lives endangered) upon passage of the Republican health care bill after realizing that he got great insurance coverage from the government to have his brain cancer treated? We cannot know for sure, because we lack the counterfactual of how McCain would have voted without illness.

We should first discuss what the Republican bill (American Health Care Act or AHCA) contains. From what we know of the bill that passed the House, it forms a repeal of the Affordable Care Act (ACA), which contains several important pillars. (1) Repeal of the individual mandate, which removes fines on individuals not obtaining health insurance, which could destabilize the existing insurance markets, where many loss-making insurers had already decided to withdraw leaving individuals purchasing their plans on the exchange not able to obtain any insurance. (2) Insurance companies are still prohibited from charging customers more for pre-existing conditions but only if insurance had not "lapsed" for more than 30 days in a year. (3) Eliminate income-based subsidies and replace them with the far less generous age based insurance subsidies ($2000 for young people and $4000 for older people, considering that medical bills are way higher than that). (4) Repeal all taxes associated with the ACA, including tax surcharges on high-income earners amounting to nearly 600 billion dollars in tax savings (i.e. redistribution of income back to the upper 1% of earners). (5) Introduce state waivers, i.e. allow states to repeal any provision of the ACA as they see fit. (6) Convert Medicaid into a block-grant program. Thus, instead of guaranteeing a certain percentage of a state's Medicaid costs to be funded by the federal government, the federal government would instead pay a fixed amount proportionate to the number of residents to the state's

Medicaid program, which would result in substantial cost savings for the federal government. But this also means either substantial cost burdens for states or for Medicaid recipients, who are left holding the bag after allocated Medicaid funds run out.

While all these provisions in the AHCA sound very complex the intention is very simple: (1) cut more than 20 million people with current insurance from the rolls, (2) increase the cost burden on individuals and families to obtain their own insurance coverage and cover their medical expenses even if they can't afford it, (3) massively slash taxes on the wealthy, whose lifestyle will not change an iota after adding these tax benefits to their cozy bank accounts.

It is no surprise that most American people are opposed to the AHCA, and so are most of the greedy insurance providers, but also doctors and health care providers. Who would thus favor such a draconian social policy reversal? We should not underestimate the role of the Koch brothers and other wealthy donors, who want to repeal every social legislation and transfer these public program funds into the coffers of the billionaire class that cannot care less about rising political instability resulting from their endless greed.

It has become common knowledge that this billionaire class controls virtually the entire political class (except some odd figures like the widely popular Bernie Sanders from Vermont), which includes Democrats and Republicans. But there are some notable partisan differences. The Democrats are an internally split party that want to please the big donors on Wall Street, Silicon Valley, Big Pharma and law firms at the same time as they want to win the support of the little guy but without exploding the public budget deficit. How does that become feasible? Via identity politics. Hillary Clinton's campaign generated the lackluster support among some segments of the urban, middle class voter base by appealing to LGBT, minority and women's rights. These are certainly worthy causes, but they don't replace the bread-and-butter issues that Sanders was consistently stronger on than Clinton.

With the Republican agenda, it is hard to discern any sympathy for the little guy. There used to be a time when Republicans would make the effort to involve the little guy, and the Tea Party was such a faint attempt, closely mobilizing diffuse anger against political and economic elites mixed with racial hatred against the first black president. But these days, serious Republican presidential contenders and candidates for Senate and House races have become the employees (or paid shills) of the powerful Koch brother network of donors, as they have to pitch their crazy right-wing ideas in the Koch fundraising events.

Republicans tended to dominate the electoral map since 2010 mainly by evading political arousal and mass mobilization. They did that largely by actively suppressing the vote via voter ID requirements (that do nothing to stop fake voting, but do stop Democratic-leaning poorer and minority constituencies less likely to own government IDs from voting), redrawing the political districts in a way to maximize their number of seats, also known as gerrymandering, and keeping all political details of their agenda behind closed doors with as few hearings and public inquiries as possible. More recently, the Republicans are proposing to defund the Congressional Budget Office, which assesses the economic implications of government policies and pointed out the number of people that would lose health insurance as a result of repealing the ACA. If people don't know how much they are harmed, how should they complain about it?

It is, therefore, not surprising that there will scarcely be anybody who would want to vote for the Republicans unless, of course, it was for the tradition of always voting Republican. But then Donald Trump came along and changed the game of US politics. Hitherto the establishment Queen Hillary thought that she had a safe passageway to the presidency. It wasn't so much that Trump had any better ideas than the other Republican candidates. In fact, some of these plans were even worse and made no sense, such as building a wall across the US-Mexican border when the net migration of Mexicans had actually become negative or canceling trade agreements on which the US economy depended. It shall be no surprise that the crazy parts of his agenda had not been carried out, as his fellow plutocrats also opposed these measures.

Trump successfully appealed to the white working class that had been left in the gutter by politicians in both parties. They were sold on Trump because he spoke differently and more "honestly" than other politicians, who spin doctored their oratory on every campaign trail event, while Trump spoke off-the-cuff, incoherently and with repetitive, simple language to the entertainment of the masses, who were intent to vote against the establishment as opposed to the fluffy "hope" and "change" that Obama did not deliver 8 year prior. However, Trump is mostly show with very little political substance. That is also clear in the current health care debate where he angrily tweets against anybody opposing the health care bill even as he does not actually know what is in it. As long as there is a health care bill on his desk he will sign it, no matter how many people it will hurt.

And that makes Trump as nefarious if not more so than the other Republican politicians, who are intent to "deconstruct the administrative state" as per Steve Bannon, Trump's White House adviser. This is a code word for plundering the state assets to benefit the rich and harm everyone else. With an outwardly respectable politician like Jeb Bush or John Kasich, the political discourse might have revolved more around the policy content, which could actually hinder the passage of the nefarious agenda as people wake up to the negative implications on their lives and resist it. But with the erratic and narcissist Trump the corporate media becomes obsessed with any nonsense that comes out of the president's mouth, while the Republican donors and their employees called elected representatives in Congress are working overtime to carry out their right-wing agenda behind closed doors.

Methods of public resistance against the Trump administration largely remain ineffective, especially in the absence of another major economic crisis. The last major anti-establishment convulsion happened with the Occupy Wall Street movement, which was a direct response to the outgrowth of many years of neoliberal policy which combines the growth of low-wage and insecure work with rising private debt (home purchase, health care and student loans), growing wealth and income inequality and government transfer policies benefiting the very rich and the financial sector. But it was also made possible by the outrage against the Wall Street bailout and the major financial crisis. It is the apparent improvement in the labor market, which seems to quiet overall dissent, even as people are not much safer economically as the underlying economic challenges persist.

Now, what about the health care bill process? The House had passed the AHCA back in May with the aforementioned provisions. The Republican Senate leadership under Mitch McConnell wanted to copy and paste the House resolution to bring forward a vote. The Republicans have 52 senators to 48 for Democrats, but 2 Republicans, Lisa Murkowski and Susan Collins, oppose the AHCA because they did not want to face the electoral backlash for ripping health insurance from their constituents. All Democrats oppose the AHCA (subsequently called American Health Care Freedom Act), so the vote to get a vote scheduled passed narrowly with 51-50, with Vice President Mike Pence casting the tie-break. But from then on,

Republican efforts to pass their bill went downhill. The house bill had been opposed by 7 more Republican senators, which was thus killed with 43-57.

The Republican leadership then brought forward a second "skinny" bill, which would only repeal the individual and employer mandate while defunding Planned Parenthood and allowing states to opt out of ACA provisions. Taxes and subsidies and other provisions in the insurance market would remain in place, but repealing the mandate will undermine the insurance market, because healthy people will opt out of insurance and not bear the burden of paying for the sicker population, the precise point of obtaining insurance. The skinny bill brought some of the Republican senators back to the support side, but Murkowski, Collins and all Democrats would still oppose the skinny bill. But McCain also did not switch sides. In his speech, he pushed for bipartisan cooperation to get a health care bill passed. On his left eye brow, you can see the surgery cut as he is still recovering from an unfolding brain cancer treatment. Whether he would have voted the other way if he were healthy, we cannot say for sure, but on that day the disastrous AHCA was killed 49-51, but the Republicans might still find a way to pass it later.

There is no doubt that the AHCA is disastrous, but so is the ACA. The ACA is merely an improvement to the previous health care system, where patients' treatment could have their insurance claims denied because they have preexisting conditions. But the key weakness of the ACA is now becoming apparent, especially as the current administration attacks its pillars by signaling that they refuse to subsidize loss-making insurance providers, who take on a sicker population.

Free market fundamentalists argue that we have to introduce more market elements into the health insurance system in order to bring costs down, but these people fail to mention that such a free market produces perverse outcomes. A so-called free market would firstly create unequal access to health care, whereby poor and sick populations would regularly be priced out of the market. Secondly, the inevitable creation of multiple tier insurance pools would segregate healthy and younger populations from sicker and older populations, as the former cluster in low premium, high deductible plans and the latter in high premium, low deductible plans. The lack of healthy people in the latter pool would drive up costs, such that premiums would continue increasing, which pushes even more healthy people out of the sick insurance pool. This death spiral of the insurance pool will push up the uninsured rate, which is known as adverse selection.

The way how you solve this problem is by a single-payer health care system, which would combine the entire population in the same insurance pool, thus allowing the government to charge all people the same proportion of their income to fund the common health care system. Single-payer would also eliminate the inefficient and profit-hungry insurance system, and limit health provider and drug costs through central bargaining of medical prices.

People think that America is incapable of providing common insurance to all people, yet Medicaid and Medicare that has existed for more than 50 years now already provides the government infrastructure upon which any single-payer system would be based. The problem is of a political nature, as most people would benefit from a single-payer system, but are unlikely to all be activists for reform, while the sick might want to be activists but are too few and probably too concerned about their disease to demand political reform. The prime culprits and beneficiaries of the system (insurance, hospitals and pharmaceuticals) have the most resources to influence the system, but don't want any changes. The only thing that makes me hopeful is the dialectic process, by which as things get worse and problems can no longer be denied, some change will eventually happen.

North Korean Woes and the US
Posted on <u>August 23, 2017</u>

It is not so much that Kim Jong-un and his North Korean regime stand at the precipice of deploying their nuclear weapons that cause heightened anxiety among people all over the world, but the fact that the US has the brain of a toddler in the highest political office. Donald Trump's rash impulsiveness had catapulted him into political office, as his supporters were thinking that he would finally deliver on political changes that the spin-doctored rival candidates would not even dare to think about.

But in foreign policy such rash impulsiveness could be enormously dangerous, as when Trump responded to the nuclear test in North Korea by promising "fire and fury" to rain down on the paranoid regime in Pyongyang. This was in response to Kim's announcement to want to strike US territory at Guam, where the US has a military base.

Luckily the conflict could be contained, primarily thanks to China's intervention. China being the only reliable ally left for North Korea has declared that if North Korea were to strike the US first, and the US retaliated, China would not intervene to help North Korea as it did during the hot phase of the Korean War in the 1950s. Only if the US struck first would China respond with intervention. In that case, World War III would rain down on us and we could be wiped off the face of the earth.

Kim, as crazy as he might appear, could read the signs and called off the threats of confrontation. The reason why North Korea had now dissipated from the headlines is because we have had a new string of terrorist attacks in Europe, then the racist attacker in Charlottesville, Virginia, and all of a sudden our news focus shifted to Trump supporting white supremacists, a concerning yet unsurprising trend by itself.

But where are we really going with North Korea? Is there a possibility that we could get into another war with this country? Trump recently rolled out his Afghanistan strategy, which is basically an increase in US troop size, thus tying the country further down in the Middle Eastern morass. There is no political stability in Afghanistan whatsoever, as the Islamic State and various Taliban groups continue to control large parts of the country, thus nullifying any efforts of so-called "liberation" by the US since 2001. Afghanistan could mean that attention is diverted from North Korea.

But given the mental instability of Kim as well as Trump, as exemplified by their duel of words, we might be back onto war path, which is rather concerning to say the least. For Collins (2017b) the solution lies in integrating North Korea into the western consumption model, which would require western investments in the country as well as flooding it with cheap mass consumer goods. Some people would say that capitalism requires wars, but the opposite is just as true, namely that greater economic integration makes wars much less palatable, for businesspeople relying on commerce need peace. The mass consumer goods could dilute the heightened tension by transforming the politically brainwashed masses (Kim family over all!) into economically brainwashed masses (the I-Phone 8 will finally make me happy!). The continued political and economic isolation of North Korea, however, create the Stockholm syndrome, whereby the masses get whipped up by the leader, who promises strength and unity against the foreign hostility.

China is by no means a politically liberal regime, but the economic opening has resulted in a rise in overall living standards as well as an overarching lack of appetite for warfare. Among a certain segment of the Chinese population there is a great desire to learn English and study in the US or another western university. For these individuals, a military conflict with the US is undesired. But given that there are barely any North Koreans living abroad (if we count out the defectors that live in South Korea or China), there is no such emotional barrier to supporting a war-hungry leader to fight the US.

In any case, this economic integration strategy of North Korea would probably take some time to realize, but the very short term requires a return to the negotiating table, and that would require some minimal trust among the top leaders in the US and North Korea. One would wonder how different the world would be if there would be more capable people running foreign relations in both countries. We all remember the photo where Mao Zedong and Richard Nixon encountered each other to begin bilateral relations between China and the US, but the real impetus behind the Sino-US relations was the work of Henry Kissinger and Zhou Enlai. We need such capable people in the current period.

The Austrian Electoral Map
Posted on August 30, 2017

With the ascendancy of Sebastian Kurz to chairman of the Austrian People's Party (OVP) the political calculation in the Alpine Republic shifted in favor of the OVP, which had languished in the polls in the third place behind the SPO and the FPO. One would think that the perennial cost of being the junior partner in the coalition government is to be relegated to a remote place in the polls, but why does Kurz make such a big difference in the polls, now pushing down the FPO, which became big with the frustration over the lack of alternatives in the grand coalition?

The first observation would be that appointing a new party chairman generally will result in a bump in the polls. In May 2016, Werner Faymann, SPO chancellor, stepped down and was replaced by Christian Kern, and this resulted in the SPO bump in the polls and set back the OVP further. It was clear that the OVP chairman and vice chancellor Reinhold Mitterlehner could not lead the party himself into the elections, so he wisely stepped down in May 2017. He was then replaced by Sebastian Kurz, the 30 year old foreign minister, the youngest party chairman so far.

If he does not make any major mistakes, he will end up with about a third of the electorate support and become the next chancellor. The most likely coalition partner is the FPO, while the SPO might return back into the opposition. Back in 2000, when the OVP entered a coalition government with the Haider-led FPO it resulted in political sanctions against Austria, but today right wing parties are more powerful than in the past, even in the other European countries, such that sanctions are unlikely this time.

But what is the secret behind Kurz' popularity? It surely can't simply be his youth and his vigor, though he is selling himself as a new leader with new powers to control the party list and appoint many people, who have never run for the OVP ticket, thus standing for innovation, which many voters might support. It also can't be his political promises, which on most issues are quite conventional, such as the intention to reduce spending on administrative staff, tax cuts for the wealthy and big companies and reductions in social spending. In fact, these promises are quite unpopular in Austria and would provoke much resistance and protest if he were to carry out these promises.

No, Kurz' success story comes from his pandering to the right-wing, which partly explains the decline of electoral support for the FPO. When Kern became chancellor, the added SPO support came mostly from the NEOs and the Greens, which tend to be more liberal and left-wing on policies, but the FPO remained quite stable, but with Kurz as OVP chairman, the FPO is losing electoral support to the OVP. Pandering to the right-wing primarily means that Kurz sells himself as a more respectable bourgeois version of an anti-immigrant, anti-refugee leader, thus mobilizing a significant share of the domestic voter base, who blame their economic uncertainty on immigrants.

Kurz had a very promising political career, having dropped out of his legal studies at university and concentrating on politics. He was the chairman of the JVP, the youth wing of the OVP, relatively the least influential of all the associations that make up the OVP. But this position had allowed him to get elected to the Viennese municipal council in 2010. A year later, the federal government had negotiated the creation of the integration state secretary in the hope that a new ministry could help immigrants adjust to new life in Austria, which was urgently necessary as the foreign born population hit 15% and integration of immigrants became an ever-bigger concern in a country that was used to much less migration and most of it from culturally close countries like those from the former Habsburg empire.

In this new role, Kurz discovered that by being rhetorically tough on immigrants, placing high standards such as the fast acquisition of German skills or the attraction of high-skill immigrants, he could become a popular politician, while at the same time being able to funnel votes from the FPO to the OVP. The FPO had become the biggest party in the polls, so it was urgently necessary to do something about the "foreigner problem", and it would best be dealt with by adopting some of the language of the right-wing FPO. Kurz would never go overboard, and emphasize the possibility of integration, but the larger burden would be on the immigrants, which would be in line with what many FPO voters wanted.

But as long as someone else led the party, the OVP could not attract any more voters. The 2013 election saw another grand coalition government and created a vacancy in the foreign ministry, which was handed over to Kurz, who became the youngest foreign minister in the world at age 27. Austria is a lightweight in foreign affairs, so it wasn't a particularly influential post, but Kurz was able to keep a high profile in domestic politics as integration minister as well, where he continued to take a sharper tone against immigrants, some of whom apparently refused to integrate into Austrian society.

The real game changer was the refugee wave into Europe, which became the most intense in 2015, where 90,000 refugees entered Austria. In most years, Austria accepted about 10,000 refugees, which was still more than most other countries of comparable size, but was still quite manageable. But that year, the Syrian refugees in the camps of Turkey and Lebanon saw their chance to stream across to Greece and the Balkan route to enter central Europe, the most desirable destinations. While the refugee crisis was the straw that break chancellor Faymann's back (even his own party comrades booed him out during the May 1 parade), Kurz could ensure his continued popularity by arguing in favor of closing the Balkan route, which would stop the Syrian refugee wave. In addition to Syrian refugees, there were many Somalis, Pakistanis and Afghans as well, who saw the opportunity to get to Europe too. As there were so many countries that could send their surplus populations abroad, the absorption capacity of Austria was exceeded, and something needed to be done to end the flow of refugees.

The Austrian people saw in Kurz someone, who could talk sense. Without being a neo-Nazi he would confirm the anti-immigrant, anti-refugee and chauvinist impulses of the Austrian people, which became more urgent after what many perceived to be the mishandling of the refugee crisis, where many political leaders had become too permissive after opening the land borders.

Some countries that are in outlying regions like Greece or Italy are in the unenviable position to have to receive hundreds of thousands of refugees by boat, and it would be unacceptable to let the refugees drown in the Mediterranean. But Kurz also advocated the position to increase funds to strengthen the outlying EU borders to prevent a further flow of refugees. Refugees in Turkey shall also receive direct financial assistance to deter them from moving onto Europe.

Over the long term there is no reason to believe that the refugee wave will stop. There are three very undesirable developments to which no politician in the world has an effective response: (1) war, convulsion, retaliation, violence in the Islamic Middle East, (2) climate change, which makes much of the Middle East and Africa even less desirable to live in (e.g. droughts destroy food crops and make drinking water scarce), (3) continued population growth especially in sub-Saharan Africa, putting pressure on the food supply and encouraging further out-migration. It is entirely laughable for any politician to claim to solve these problems.

But in the meantime, Kurz is able to capitalize on the security needs of the Austrian population and steals crucial voters from the hitherto strongest party, the right-wing FPO. If the electoral map does not change fundamentally due to a mistake on either side, Kurz will definitely become chancellor. (The Silberstein affair in the SPO certainly did not help their electoral fortune. Silberstein was an SPO campaign advisor, who was imprisoned by Israeli authorities for graft and corruption charges. He was subsequently fired by the SPO, but the scandal still sticks around the party.)

People are willing to listen to a fresh voice, but with the exception of the anti-immigrant, security rhetoric I doubt that Kurz is a strong, innovative leader. His speeches are not very captivating, and his TV interview performances don't distinguish him from other politicians, who are used to give evasive answers to avoid the strict scrutiny of the journalists.

The innovation in the political spectrum in the next election is that Team Stronach is getting dissolved, as their leader Robert Lugar switches side to join his former party FPO. These are protest voters that get dispersed to other parties or stop voting altogether. The Greens have switched their party chair. Eva Glawischnig resigned and was replaced by Ingrid Felipe as party chair and Ulrike Lunacek as leading candidate. Felipe is the deputy governor of the province of Tyrol and Lunacek has been vice president of the EU parliament. As such she is not well known within Austria, and lacks the charisma to appeal to a larger voter base. On the contrary, they are losing voters to a former Green parliamentarian, Peter Pilz, who founded his own party. The Greens have to blame themselves as they wanted to force Pilz into retirement after over 30 years of serving in the Austrian parliament. Pilz still wanted to serve in office, leading his Eurofighter investigative commission to point out graft and corruption in Austrian politics, so he founded his own party to run in the next elections.

In the polls, Pilz takes about 5% of voters, while the Greens are down to 7% from over 10% they had in the last election. There is a liberal-left voter base in Austria, but it is no more than 35-40% of the voter base, which leaves a comfortable majority for OVP, FPO. It is also so splintered as SPO and Green tend toward social- economic equality, while NEOs are more classical liberal. Pilz is sympathetic to the Green position except on security and immigration, where he is also sympathetic to the right-wing.

In any case, the fragmented left creates a situation, where only three parties are likely to have a shot at government: SPO, OVP, FPO, whereby FPO is the kingmaker in the two combinations with either the SPO or OVP. The SPO has greater internal resistance against a coalition with the FPO, though there are party wings such as in Burgenland that have an active governing coalition with the FPO. Vienna's SPO opposes the coalition with the FPO, but SPO party chair and chancellor Kern is somewhere in the middle and finds preserving political power more important than blind adherence to principle. In any case, OVP-FPO coalition is made more likely by the similarity on security issues as well as economic policy, while the SPO welfare state agenda is likely opposed by the other parties.

There is still a chance that SPO and OVP will continue the grand coalition, but given that the OVP will likely have more votes, the OVP will regain the chancellorship. But it would be rather weird. The political impasse is that since 2006, the country has had three elections and each time emerged another grand coalition government. It would, however, be discredited. The irony is that any other party in power would mean the same-old system, which suggests that major issues like demographic aging, lower economic growth, higher unemployment, more precarious employment and rising immigrant population are trends that no government can genuinely solve. Durchwusteln (muddle through) is what the Austrians can do best.

India and China: A Conflict Defused, A Special Relationship

Posted on September 3, 2017

We cannot know for sure whether India and China have finally ended their conflict over the fragile land border in Doklam/ Donglang. The most recent announcement on the 28th of August is that the border dispute between China and Bhutan, with the latter being backed up by India, had been resolved and the Chinese and Indian troops on the border would be withdrawn. How did this conflict begin?

On June 16, 2017 Chinese troops began to build a road southward in Doklam, a territory both claimed by Bhutan and China. Bhutan saw this move as a provocation and requested Indian support to halt the road building. 2 days later 270 Indian troops with weapons and bulldozers entered Doklam, thus halting Chinese roadbuilding efforts.

China says that Doklam belongs to China because the 1890 Convention of Calcutta between China and Britain states that Mount Gipmochi is the tri-junction point between Bhutan, India and China, thus China would be entitled to occupy Doklam, which was to the northeast of Mount Gipmochi, including Zompelri ridge. Bhutan, however, insists that the tri-junction point is further up north at Batang La, which is where the actual locus of political and territorial control is prior to the present border conflict. China had built a road from Sinchela into the Doka La (Doklam) pass in 2005, which had not created diplomatic row even as it was built on disputed territory. But a further planned southward extension this year had sparked the conflict.

Because of the history of disputed territories, Bhutan had signed a treaty with India, handing over military and diplomatic affairs to the more powerful neighbor to the south, as the Chinese made large claims on Bhutan's territory. Multiple rounds of diplomatic talks from 1984 onward tried to resolve outstanding boundary issues, and there were agreements in 1988 and 1998 to the effect of mandating each side to pursue peaceful means to resolve border disputes.

India did not claim Doklam, but supports Bhutan's territorial claims. On June 29, Bhutan protested to the Chinese government about the road construction. Subsequently, the Chinese foreign ministry insisted on the 1890 Convention of Calcutta and published a map to buttress the claim of China and asserting that Indian troops were violating Chinese sovereignty by stepping into Doklam.

A day later, the Indian foreign ministry released the statement that China was violating the 2012 understanding of the governments to not change the status quo of territorial control. The next weeks throughout the summer saw repeated verbal exchanges between the Indian and Chinese administrations, though most of the commentary came from China, and can be read on the respective Wikipedia article ("2017 China India Border Standoff") for reference. Only on August 28, was the dispute finally resolved. China and India both agreed to withdraw their troops to the territory of control prior to the road-building effort and China ceased its plan to build the road. It certainly was not worth it to risk a war over this piece of land.

A further investigation of the history of bilateral relations between India and China reveals that this is not the first time that the two countries had clashed. They are two behemoths by population size and are separated by the Himalayas, the tallest mountain range in the world. It is not surprising, therefore, that two very different civilizations had emerged on each side of the Himalayas with different language, culture and even skin tone. For more details on the history of bilateral relations, I recommend the Wikipedia article on China-India relations ("China-India relations"). After having three major border clashes (1962, 1967, 1987), both sides still dispute Aksai Chin and Arunachal Pradesh.

But despite these political, natural and cultural barriers, there are still historically strong links between the two countries. An interesting quote cements this long-term history of bilateral relations:

India conquered and dominated China culturally for 20 centuries without ever having to send a single soldier across her border.

—Hu Shih, quoted in Consolation of Mind (2004). by H. K. Suhas, p. 111

What this quote implies is the spread of Buddhism, astronomy, mathematics, medicine, alchemy, music, incense clock, chess from India to China. Trade relations began to appear from the 2nd century BCE onward within the context of the Silk Road. Thus it is fair to say that Chinese civilization had benefited substantially from Indian influence. The older and more mature civilization was in India, though it is all the more ironic that currently it is China's economic development and human development that proceeds at a faster pace than in India, where political institutions are less effective and fragmentation is larger. This is evident in the language diversity, which exist on both sides of the Himalayas, but the Chinese central government had been more successful in promoting a national dialect. The one-child policy in China also proves the ability of its central administration to dictate population policy in a way that is not feasible in India.

Another point of mutual contact was migration. There are currently over 15,000 Indian nationals in China, though some would say it is as much as 48,000. Many are students, traders and professionals in MNCs, Indian companies and banks. Many Indians had also moved to Macao and Hong Kong due to their colonial past and the use of the English and Portuguese language in these areas. (English recruited Indian laborers to Hong Kong.)

But the flow in the other direction is also quite substantial, at least historically. There are an estimated 4,000 Chinese Indians in 2014 (ethnic Chinese with Indian nationality) and 5-7,000 Chinese expatriates. But in the past there were over 20,000. The first recorded Chinese settler in India was Tong Achew, a trader in the 1780s. He brought along with him a few Chinese workers to build a sugar factory south of Calcutta in Achipur. When he died soon thereafter the workers had moved to Calcutta to find jobs there in what was then already a British colony (since 1772). Amazingly, some Chinese still go to Achipur to pay homage to Achew at his grave.[22] Another recorded Chinese in Calcutta was Yang Tai Chow, who had arrived in 1778.

According to Ellen Oxfeld's (1993) study of the Hakka Chinese in Calcutta, there were three primary groups of Chinese, who had left to migrate to Calcutta: the Hubeinese dentists, the Cantonese carpenters and the Hakka tannery owners. Thus, there was a division of labor in the Calcutta economy. My family is among the Hakka tannery owners. Leather production was an interesting industry, because even though it was in high demand, the upper-case Hindus refused to lead these companies (too dirty, not respectable enough), while lower caste Indians could work there, but not lead the companies, so the profit-oriented Chinese became the tannery owners.

There might still be photos of my uncle somewhere wearing a soiled white shirt after having worked the raw hide. Before tanning, the hide is unhaired, degreased, desalted (removing any remaining flesh and fat) and soaked in water for up to two days. Tanning uses

---

[22] https://www.flickr.com/photos/rangan-datta/4375115335

tannin, an acidic chemical compound, which is needed to make the leather durable and stretched. The problem emerges when the chemicals are dumped into the groundwater, which then affects all of the water supply in the region as the dirty and carcinogenic chemicals are distributed via the river.

Environmental concerns resulted in the Calcutta government declaring leather tanneries to be illegal in the current vicinity and they had to pack up and move to a new location further away. As I hear from family stories, my uncle had been forced to move his tannery to the new location and was not compensated for it, though a report indicates that the "state government is providing financial incentives to tanneries that are relocating and ...will start production at Calcutta Leather Complex. The incentives include capital investment subsidy, employment generation subsidy, remission of stamp-duty and registration fees" (WBIDC 2010). As of 2014, residents continued to complain about the air and water pollution caused by the tanneries (Das 2014). More than one billion gallons of raw sewage and industrial effluent enter the river Ganges everyday. With 500 tanneries, Calcutta handles about a quarter of the nation's tanning and more than half of the country's leather export, and thus continues to be an important local employer and generator of economic value.

Another group of Chinese were convicts from the Straits settlements (Malaysia and Singapore), who were sent to the prison in Madras. The British colonial masters had done something similar to their own criminal convicts, who were sent to Australia. Among the Chinese convicts in Madras, there were reported cases of prisoner escapes/ Those who were released from jail continued to live in India, became farmers and settled in the Nilgiri Mountains where they married Tamil women, as there were no Chinese women along with them, thus producing mixed Chinese-Tamil offspring. Another group involved Chinese migrants to Assam, which is physically the closest to China. The Chinese men again took Indian women as wives and produced offspring, which could hardly be deemed Chinese, when the government rounded them up after the Sino-Indian War of 1962.

Political upheaval in China (Opium Wars, Sino-Japanese War and Boxer Rebellion) and largely unlimited immigration ensured a continued stream of Chinese immigrants. But the 1962 Sino-Indian War ended the tolerant policy. The Indian government had passed the Defence of India Act after the war, which resulted in the apprehension and detention of people suspected of "hostile origin", i.e. ethnic Chinese. 10,000 Chinese were detained and imprisoned in Rajasthan province, far away from their homes in Calcutta and other parts of India. The government had suspected these Chinese were spies for the enemy, even though there never was due process or evidence for these allegations. In 1964, many internees were deported, breaking up many families. Others were released in 1965 as costs for imprisonment mounted even as the Chinese were forced to find ways to feed themselves. The last internees were released in 1967. The Chinese were still considered enemies and had their movement restricted. They had to report to police stations once a month and had to apply for special travel permits until the mid-1990s. In 1998, the Indian government finally granted naturalized Indian citizenship to the ethnic Chinese.

Not surprisingly, most Chinese had left and see no future for themselves in India. Oxfeld noted in her research that a large number of Indian Chinese had moved to Toronto, Canada, and this is the location where 80% of my known relatives live. There are very few relatives left in India, some have gone to Taiwan, Australia, Austria, Sweden and the US, but most have gone to Canada, which has the most permissive immigration laws. Often it is sufficient to have one person in the family immigrate, who can then sponsor all the other relatives to migrate as well.

Despite the long history of bilateral conflict among the two most populous countries in the world, India and China also had an extensive history of exchange of ideas, beliefs, practices, material goods and people. The relative weight of both countries will continue to force both countries to cooperate with each other and prevent mutual conflicts. The price of failure is high. The fate and well-being of the remaining Chinese in India and the many Indians in China will also depend on the political calculations of the governments on each side.

Nigeria: A Country Profile
Posted on <u>September 10, 2017</u>

The media reports that Nigeria's economy suffers from weak economic development, growing at 2.5% in 2017 instead of the 6% that it averaged until 2014, after which the global economic slowdown dragged down growth in Nigeria as well (Cotterill and Pilling 2017). The lack of diversity of exports (95% oil, mostly crude oil, while it has to import 187,400 barrels of refined petroleum a day[23]) , associated fall in oil prices, corruption, mismanagement of public resources, lack of infrastructure (out of 193,200 km roads only 28,980 km are paved), ineffective judicial system, insecure private property, lack of public investments, infectious diseases (HIV/AIDS most prominently, but also hepatitis, typhoid, malaria etc.), low literacy rate (59.6%), inadequate sanitation and drinking water facility, low life expectancy (53.4 years), a rapidly expanding population (2.4% in 2017; 186 million people in 2016, expected to grow to 392 million in 2050; already largest population in Africa, far ahead of 102 million in Ethiopia) all make economic development rather difficult. What follows is a country profile, which may be relevant for contemporary analysis. The review shows that Nigeria's colonial history, regional economic inequality, inequality in vegetation, climate and natural resources, a rapidly increasing population, the weak and corrupt political institutions all play a role in preventing or slowing down national development.

Political History
Nigeria (and current-day Cameroon) is the origin of Bantu civilization, which spread over much of central and southern Africa in migratory waves since 2,000 BCE. Other major African populations include the Pygmy and the Khoisan. The Bantus reached the Great Lakes of East Africa in 1000 BCE and South Africa by 300 AD. The distinguishing feature of the Bantus was not only their language, but also their herding and farming practice, which came to displace previous Neolithic hunting and foraging people. The Bantus also interacted with Arab people, whose influence still exists with Arabic loan-words in today's Swahili language.

---

[23] https://www.cia.gov/library/publications/the-world-factbook/geos/ni.html

Nigeria is formed from many kingdoms and tribal states. The oldest known civilization is the Nok civilization in Northern Nigeria (500 BC to 200 AD), which currently is mostly dry and arid land, which suggests a different climate in the past. The next kingdom was that of the NRI of the Igbo people, which ruled from the 10th century until it surrendered sovereignty to Britain in 1911. The Yoruba people had the kingdoms of Ife and Oye in southwestern Nigeria, which rule from the 12th to 14th centuries. Edo's Benin Empire controlled southwestern Nigeria from 15th to 19th centuries. At the beginning of the 19th century, a jihad that was led by Usman dan Fodio created the Fulani Empire, or Sokoto Caliphate.

The consolidation of empires also facilitated trade with other cities, especially in North Africa. The 16th century saw the Spanish and Portuguese conquerors land on the shores of Nigeria to carry out the Atlantic slave trade. This slave trade would not have been possible without the active cooperation of the Oyo Empire in the southwest of Nigeria, the Aro Confederacy in the southeast and the Sokoto Caliphate in the north. The British ultimately were responsible for ending slavery due to economic considerations (no longer as profitable with the disappearance of the US as part of the British colony Jamaica and Barbados slave-fueled sugar production declined; the industrial revolution increased demand for free labor) as well as moral condemnation from the public. The British subsequently stopped ships on ports that were loaded up with slaves, and transported these slaves to Freetown instead. In 1851, the British bombarded Lagos to replace the ruler with someone that was friendlier to the British, which began the formal colonization of the British via the moving inland from the coast. British colonial claims were confirmed by the other European powers during the 1885 Berlin Conference. In 1901, Nigeria was formally included as British protectorate in the British Empire.

Nigeria was merged over the course of the 19th century under British Colonial rule. An important pattern that emerged, however, was that Nigeria contained a division between Northern and Southern Protectorates as well as Lagos Colony. People in the south were on the coast and as such had enjoyed interactions with the west, much more so than the inland people in the north. For instance, some southern elite families sent their children to attend British universities. In terms of contemporary economic development, it is the southern, coastal provinces that are more developed than the north.

As opposed to direct rule (more common in French colonies), the British favored indirect rule using traditional chiefdoms as ally. Such indirect rule also consolidated the religious cleavage in Nigeria, as the British validated the pre-existing Islamic culture, while the more western-oriented southern provinces had many people convert to Christianity. Post WWII, an exhausted Britain withdrew while Nigerian nationalism forced the hands of the British. Along with many other African states, Nigeria became an independent country in 1960.

But independence meant civil war, which raged from 1967 to 1970. This was due to internal disunity, and is reminiscent to the disunity in India after the British departure in 1947, which resulted in the split between India (Hindu), Pakistan and what later became Bangladesh (both Muslim). Wherever the colonial masters ruled, they kept the peace via divide and conquer strategies and, if necessary, the brute force of the British military. But British departure implied a power vacuum, as it is not clear which faction shall take the reins of the central government. Had there been no colonial power, there would have been no amalgamation of multiple tribes in the same national entity. But the existence of Nigeria and other post-colonial states could not be wished away, and the local elites had every interest to become national elites to milk as much national resources for their own benefit. Though to be fair, in Nigeria rulers have come from different tribes, and even when a northerner ruled the presidency, it has not enriched the north or allowed it to catch up economically with the richer south (which suggests that corruption at the top is more important than tribalism in affecting social outcomes).

In Nigeria, three major factions had emerged: the Nigerian People's Congress (northern Islamists, Hausa), the National Council of Nigeria and the Cameroons (Christian, Igbo, southeast), and the Action Group (Yoruba, southwest). When a referendum resulted in the split of territory to Cameroon, the northern faction now became larger and stronger than the south. The resulting political tensions and perceived corruption induced Igbo (south) soldiers led by Emmanuel Ifeajuna and Chukwuma Kaduna Nzeogwu to carry out a coup d'état, which killed the prime minister and the premier of the northern and western regions. A counter-coup in 1966 organized by Northern military officers overthrew the first military dictatorship. Igbos in the north faced persecution and fled to the east of the country, which then declared independence under the name

Republic of Biafra. Nigeria then declared war on Biafra to reverse the secession. The Civil War had resulted in many deaths following warfare, disease and starvation. The British and Soviet Union backed Nigeria, while France backed Biafra. Biafra was ultimately defeated and national unity preserved.

The oil boom of the 1970s, corresponding to the oil price hikes in developed countries, and the discovery of massive oil reserves (earliest in the 1950s) made Nigeria an oil-dependent economy. The massive scale of corruption among government leaders (estimated to be 400 billion USD from 1960 to 2012) ensured that the standard of living of the population failed to improve, businesses could not succeed and public infrastructure was neglected. The failure of development subsequently consolidated the role of the federal government to distribute oil revenues generated by sale of oil abroad. Irresponsible government policy, declining oil prices as well as a permissive international loan environment created mounting international debt by the 1980s, which resulted in the IMF stipulating a Structural Adjustment program (SAP). Some economists claim that SAP has merely weakened the purchasing power of the domestic currency, thus lowering the domestic standard of living, while the encouragement of new bank creation has proliferated speculation instead of production and development. The lack of development means that the country cannot generate surplus revenues with which to reduce the budget deficit and debt. But the nation's leaders don't accept SAP because it could improve their economy, but rather to embezzle IMF loans and allow the country to further deteriorate (Ogbimi n.d.). The vast majority of Nigerian survey respondents had opposed the SAP policies of the mid-1980s (Nwagbara 2011). Only in 2006 did the country pay off its debt.

Since the Civil War there had been a short period of democratic governance (1979-1983), while the rest of the period was marked by military dictatorships. A democratic election, such as the one in 1979, generated discontent among military leaders, who would then come to overthrow this government and install the chief general as president. Examples of such military dictators include Ibrahim Babangida and Sani Abacha. Democracy was not consolidated until 1999, after which the quality of the institutions improved, yet elections were still unfair. The first fair elections happened in 2011 with the election of Goodluck Jonathan, a southern Christian from the Ijaw ethnic group. Region, ethnicity and religion are salient to the extent that Christians live in the south, being subdivided into various tribes, while the north is Islamic, which includes the application of sharia law. The 2015 election was won by Muhammadu Buhari (northern Muslim from the Fulani tribe, the largest in Nigeria), who had ruled the country in the 1980s after a military coup (and was himself overthrown only 2 years later), but has since become a believer in democracy. To the extent, that democratic consolidation is rather recent and the political leadership consists of many former military generals, we cannot claim that Nigeria's democratic institutions are stable.

Ethnic Groups

The three largest ethnicities are the Hausa, Igbo and the Yoruba, but there are over 500 ethnic groups, which means that Nigeria is a multinational state, which is kept together by the colonial language: English. The most flourishing economy is in the south-west in Yorubaland, which contains the former capital city Lagos.

Religion

A further cleavage emerges from religion. The northern half of the country is Muslim and the southern half is Christian. Among non-animist religions, Christianity and Islam are the most influential in Africa, whereby the cleavage runs from the Islamic north and the east Africa to Christian southern portion of western Africa, central and South Africa. The northeast had suffered from sectarian violence via Boko Haram, which has killed thousands of people and injured many others. In 2014, 276 schoolgirls were kidnapped in the Chibok kidnapping, and in April 2016, Fulani herdsmen murdered 500 individuals from the Christian village of Agatu. Among the various tribes, there are tendencies as well, because the Hausa ethnic group is 95% Muslim and 5% Christian, while the Igbos and Ijaws in the south and east are 98% Christian and 2% practicing traditional religions. Yoruba have a large Anglican population, while Igboland is mostly Roman Catholic and Edoss are Pentecostals. Most Nigerian Muslims are Sunnis.

Sharia law is in effect in most provinces of northern Nigeria, which contains the Muslim population. Its penal code involves harsh sentences like amputation, lashing, stoning or long prison terms for offenses like alcohol consumption, homosexuality, infidelity and theft. Tribal religions facilitate other cruel practices such as branding children as witches resulting in their abandonment and abuse on the streets.

Topography, Geography, Climate

Nigeria's topography: noteworthy is the Niger river basin, which provides much of the fertile soil at the center of the country; the south faces the ocean and has had more contact with the west and seafaring nations, while the north is drier and landlocked; the densest population concentration is to be found along the coast

Precipitation of Nigeria: the south is the wettest, while the northeast is the driest area.

Vegetation: the very southern end of the country is wet and contains swamps and rain forests, while the center contains the drier savanna and the very northeast contains the driest sahel savanna.

After having examined the social cleavages in Nigeria, it is also useful to consider its geography, which similarly involves a north-south division: The south is marked by the tropical rainforest with extensive rainfall. At the very south one can find a "salt water swamp", to the north of it a "fresh water swamp" and to the north of that the rainforest. The Niger and Benue river valleys, which cut right across most of the country forms the basis of West African civilization, as the river supplies the crucial water for planting crops and supporting the vastly expansive population in Nigeria. The region between the far north and far south is the savannah, which contains more limited rainfall. The Sahel region in the very north has very little rain and contains some elements of the Sahara Desert. Among the driest section in the country is the northeast, which also has the most active Boko Haram forces that plot terrorist attacks across the country.

Population

Another factor to consider in Nigeria is the swelling population. Most people live in the major cities including Lagos, Abram-bra and Kano. The population is supposed to increase from 186 million in 2015 to 392 million in 2050 and perhaps even as much as more than 750 million by 2100, though one should be careful about population projections that go this far ahead, as the assumptions become less certain. If the current fertility rate is 5.6 in Nigeria in 2015, it is safe to assume to have a similar value in 2016, but not so much in 2100. The overall population trends are influenced by the mortality, birth and net migration rate. Evidently, the mortality rate is declining and the fertility rate stays high, though somewhat decreasing now. But this decrease in the fertility rate will only work to reduce population growth over the long term, while over the short term the large base of young men and women (especially women) ensures a steady growth of population.

Why is this population growth trend salient aside from the fact that Nigeria is already the most populous country in Africa? One may use the Malthusian trap claim, which posits that population growth outstrips food supply, resulting in mass starvation. Climate change is certainly putting pressure on the availability of fertile land, especially in countries like Nigeria. But in the present day, it is feasible to use food imports to make up for any gap in food supply. Indeed, the second largest Nigerian import it wheat accounting for 2.76% of all import expenditures. Thus, starvation is not the immediate sorrow, but the poor provision of a growing population certainly is. For people with aspiration it would be wise to move to Lagos, where much of the dynamic economic enterprises are, but it already has 21 million inhabitants, which make it among the biggest metropolis in the world with the attendant problems of infrastructure provision. And the movement toward urbanization is rather slow, as 78% of the people still engage in farming and out of the farming population only 15% are engaged in commercial farming, 35% in subsistence farming and the remaining half in a mixture of the two (NOI Polls 2016). Another route to escape the crowdedness of unwisely used resources (given rampant graft and corruption in the official sector) is to migrate abroad, producing a net emigration of 300,000 people, hardly enough to make a substantial dent in overall population figures. Nigeria does not have to fear mass immigration anytime soon.

Some people might say for ideological reasons that a growing population should be considered an asset. It is certainly true that the most advanced industrialized countries would do anything to increase the birth rate in their country, but such a thing cannot be legislated, especially because the fall in the birth rate has to do with social changes that are inextricably linked with modernity. The two most important ones are the rise in the overall standard of living, which increase the educational expectations and investments of parents, and the rising independent status of women, which makes them less interested in child-rearing and more in self-fulfillment. These are hardly social advances that any government would want to reverse. But these economic gains for the population and for women are hardly available in Nigeria. And what matters for a country's success is not merely the large population, but also the effectiveness of the central administration to provide functioning services and infrastructure. India and China have about equivalent population but the latter has lifted six times more people out of poverty than the former, so when human resources and overall economic conditions are still too basic, there just aren't enough economic opportunities to take care of such a huge population, let alone produce the required social progress to reduce the birth level.

Africa is the least urbanized continent, but has increased its share of urbanization over time. In West Africa urbanization has increased from 30 to 44% from 1990 to 2014, while in Nigeria it increased from 30 to 47%. Similar figures for 2014 in Europe are 73%, 80% in Latin America and 81% in North America (United Nations 2014). The gradual urbanization of Nigeria could mean improved access to services, but the overall weak quality of political and social institutions could also imply continued squalor in the city, which would give credence to political extremism. To evaluate where Nigeria stands in development questions, I examine its economic output.

Nigeria's Economy

Nigeria's employment profile indicates that the country is still very rural and agricultural, but there is a marked trend of declining employment in agriculture, which suggests that there is economic transformation favoring the service sector. The country also employs fewer manufacturing workers. This might not mean deindustrialization necessarily as many western countries employ fewer workers but more machinery, which maintains the high value-added in manufacturing output. Yet, Nigeria's manufacturing contribution as share of GDP had peaked as early as 1982 after which there was deindustrialization. Given that almost the entire exports are crude petroleum, and many imports are machinery, we can assume that Nigeria isn't producing a lot of manufacturing goods by itself. A few industries like beverages, textiles, cement and tobacco still remain, and they are concentrated in Lagos, Kano and Kaduna (Proshare 2015).

The country's overall infrastructure is still poorly set up with express roads still being rather short, making the connections among the cities difficult. It stands to reason that the conflict potential and the diversity of languages and cultural traditions are reinforced by weak transport infrastructure.

Industries, as in many other countries, are concentrated in some areas, such as tin mines at the center and coal mines in the southeast. With regard to agriculture, the north contains peanut and cotton farms, while the south produces cocoa and palm oil.

The economic divide between north and south is evident in the agricultural crop production, which tends to be concentrated in the south of the country.

Since oil makes up 95% of all exports, it is paramount to analyze where the oil fields are. All the oil fields are in the south coast, which also produces a bad environment and health problems because of the damage from oil spills. Should the country ever break apart, the northern provinces could be even worse off than they are now. One reason for the insufficient economic development in Nigeria is the over-reliance on oil exports, which don't help them at times of low oil prices.

The scale of industrial production has a bearing on the overall economic output in various regions. Even though the entire country is poor by developed country standards, the southern provinces along the cost are relatively the wealthiest, and this especially applies to Lagos ($4,333 in 2014). The northern, landlocked areas remain rather poor. The North is also the hotbed of Boko Haram's terror attacks. Money does not count for everything, and in this case misguided religious ideology plays a role too, but there is a correlation between the GDP of poor areas and the frequency of terror attacks. There are some fiscal transfers from the south to the north to mitigate social discontent, yet corruption also prevents funds from going through. In the meantime, Boko Haram attacks slow down production in an already struggling region, resulting in food prices to increase (Caulderwood 2014).

Education and Health

Regional economic inequality is also reflected in important social indicators like vaccination, which is more thorough in the more developed south than the north. Another indicator for social progress is the female literacy rate, which is the highest in the south and west, somewhat lower at the center and the east and the lowest in the northern areas.

Conclusion

I conclude that Nigeria's colonial history, regional economic inequality, inequality in vegetation, climate and natural resources, a rapidly increasing population, the weak and corrupt political institutions all play a role in preventing or slowing down national development, as well as aiding the cause of terrorists.

Book Review: The Great Leveler by Walter Scheidel (Princeton: Princeton University Press, 2017)

Posted on <u>September 17, 2017</u>

In this magnificent piece of historical sociology, the Austrian Stanford historian, Walter Scheidel, answers the question under what circumstances income and wealth inequality decline. His fascinating answer is that only so-called violent shocks in the form of (1) mass mobilization warfare, (2) political revolution, (3) state failure, and (4) lethal pandemics can effectively reduce inequality (p.6), while peaceful mechanisms like (1) economic growth, (2) democracy and (3) limited land reform have done nothing or little to reduce income inequality (p.9).

The historical basis for the growth of inequality are threefold: (1) surplus extraction from defensible resources (which presupposes a beyond-subsistence economy, i.e. agriculture or industry based, but also includes elements of coercion, debt peonage, extortive taxation, land confiscation, privatization of wealth), (2) transfer of that surplus to one's descendants, (3) a regime in which private property claims become legitimate. That part of his analysis shall not be so controversial, yet the four violent shocks or "horsemen" (from Albrecht Durer) are more controversial and deserve greater scrutiny.

Before we discuss the political implications of his findings it might be worthwhile explaining why these four horsemen can reduce inequality.

War

War costs a lot of money, destroys a lot of property and elevates the political power of the popular (poor) masses as they serve in the military assembly lines as well as fighting in the war. All of that tends to reduce both the political as well as the economic power of the very rich. War is a time period, when the country has to mobilize substantial resources to carry out the war, which comes at the expense of the private civilian economy. States then raise taxation on the wealthy, as it becomes difficult to raise taxes on the beleaguered middle class and impossible to draw more taxes from the poor. It is possible to also borrow money from rich people, and that can make some rich people even richer, as has been the case with the Rothschild banker family, which made its first fortune in the Napoleonic Wars. But this is quite exceptional.

The destruction of property comes at the expense of those who have the most to lose, i.e. the rich. Especially in the past, most of measurable wealth was not tied up in the stock market (which would tank anyway if companies are invested in the civilian sector as more resources get drafted for the war effort), but in real estate and land, and to the extent that such property can get harmed by bombing raids or enemy invasion will also contribute to the diminution of the wealth of the rich, and thus result in declining wealth inequality.

Finally, the popular masses are drafted into the war, and when they come back, they do expect certain benefits to come their way, whether it be Japanese samurais or Roman legions who received land, or US veterans getting the GI bill after World War II. One could scarcely imagine what would happen to the legitimacy of the government if these warriors would not be given handouts. There is no doubt that such enforced redistribution of wealth can also lower inequality.

Scheidel uses the example of post-war Japan from 1945 as an example for massive changes to the political economy after its humiliating defeat. The emperor Hirohito narrowly escaped punishment and kept the throne, albeit no longer as absolute but as constitutional monarch. But as far as social structures are concerned everything was fair game for the American occupiers. Their rationale was that in order to prevent a fascist military regime from rising up again, the central landholding among a few feudal lords had to end, thus the post-war constitution included a provision to parcel out the land to small farmers.

Any peacetime Japanese government would never have contemplated such an extreme step, but given that the Americans had full control over national policymaking, there was nobody that could hinder them. Ironically, the US would never have contemplated such a land reform in their own country, though they have hiked the taxes on the rich to pay for their own war effort. In addition, the Americans pushed for legislation that would strengthen organized labor, such that Japan developed labor unions, when it hitherto had none. There were also early elements of social legislation. Each of these measures worked to reduce income and wealth inequality, which albeit higher today is still below what can be found in many other industrialized countries.

On the other side, the absence of war and mass mobilization as was the case in Latin America (Centeno 2002) can prevent the build-up of progressive taxation and a strong welfare state. Latin America experienced noticeable decline in inequality only after the 1990s upon the conclusion of various military dictatorships. Though the rise of left-wing governments has played a positive role in reducing inequality, which suggests that democratic development can mitigate inequality.

Revolution

This is an easy one and Scheidel only devotes 44 pages to it. Essentially, communist revolutions are about the eradication of private property, the collectivization of the means of production and the forced leveling of economic resources, which has been the experience in the Soviet Union, China and other communist sphere countries. Scheidel does point to the enormous destruction of livestock that went along with Soviet collectivization of agriculture and much unneeded suffering.

State Collapse

If the state collapses, then social organization is hurled back to a less complex and more primitive state. There is less division of labor, less civilization and less cultural output. Such a development hurts the rich more than the poor, because the rich depend on revenue streams that become legitimated via the government. The government has the levers to redistribute income from the popular classes to the rich. Libertarians will now claim that if we had no government, then the rich would no longer be able to derive income via crony capitalism, but would have to work for it. Yet in a more primitive society without provisions for private property, it is not so clear how one could become rich. Most capitalist enterprises require strict provisions for private property, public security (i.e. no war), an educated and healthy workforce, and a public infrastructure, and these resources need to be mobilized by the state.

Scheidel uses the example of Somalia to show that the descent into anarchy after the toppling of the dictator was associated with a reduction in inequality, because there no longer were any corrupt elites who could appropriate national resources for their own benefit. That people had to suffer from a lack of development is another cost that had to be borne by the population, but it seems to be that the poor do not have much to lose regardless under which regime they live in.

Lethal Pandemics

A huge disease, which wipes out a substantial share of the population can reduce inequality in two ways: (1) the death of the old elite creates vacancies that can be filled by survivors resulting in upward social mobility; (2) the death of many more poor people results in a labor shortage, which raises the cost of maintaining serfs or laborers. Many more lords are facing ever fewer serfs. A lord is not a God-given title, but merely reflects the existing power balance in society. To the extent that serfs are fewer in number, they can easily switch their lord, and to keep the serfs on the land the lord had to lower rent or raise payment, each of which reduced the profit of the lord. This process results in less inequality. The key example is the Bubonic Plague in the 1350s, which some say has created the conditions by which the Enlightenment era and the Renaissance began. In any case, inequality was sharply reduced after the Plague and has crept back up again until the war-related upheavals of the 20th century.

While the Malthusian trap has been much maligned among some circles, it contains some validity, as a rising population is associated with more people being crowded in limited space, which then empowers the landlords, who tend to be few in number and can keep a tight leash on the toiling masses, who barely have enough land to sustain themselves. The Qing empire oversaw substantial population increases amid scarce land, such that people did not see any real wage gains even as more and more Chinese trekked overseas (including my ancestors) to escape the crowded conditions at home.

It should be noted that Europe still had regional variation in the relative power of the serfs. Western Europe generally granted more freedom to serfs to move around and find a better place to live, while Eastern Europe used force and suppression to ensure that serfs could not move, and under those circumstances inequality was not reduced.

Implications

So why is inequality increasing today? Scheidel does not offer unique answers in his conclusion except to restate the argument among economists. The most important claim comes from Thomas Piketty, who along with colleagues has been using cross-national tax data to show the extent to which income inequality has been rising over the last 150 years, and in most western countries since the 1970s. The 1940s were an exceptional period immediately after the end of World War II, where the aforementioned social and political forces leveled the income distribution with the creation of a permanent welfare state financed by progressive income taxes.

But the exceptional period has been ending with the rise of neoliberalism, which is essentially about allowing what Piketty considers to be the natural forces of capitalism to take hold and increase inequality. The natural forces of capitalism are summarized in the formula that $r>g$, where r is the rate of return on capital and g is economic growth. The postwar period is exceptional to the extent that economic growth was larger than the return on capital, which was undergirded by Keynesian investment policy, progressive taxation, labor-friendly policies, the expansion of the welfare state, national capital controls and stringent financial regulation. Neoliberalism is about removing these barriers to capital, thus returning us to the world of $r>g$.

To some extent, this rather clinical formula obscures the social relationship that Piketty undoubtedly intended to convey. r is controlled by the capital owners, i.e. the rich, while g is a diffuse force, but has the potential to benefit everybody especially in the form of employment creation, rising wages and social benefits. Thus, if $r>g$ then income and wealth inequality are bound to increase.

This is certainly a strike against the liberal dream enunciated by Simon Kuznets, whose Kuznets curve conveys the S-shaped movement from low inequality- low development to high inequality-high development to low inequality-high development. The first move is explained by the lack of political institutions to address inequality as development takes off. Think of Deng Xiaoping's "let some get rich first" statement. Specifically, rural people move into the cities and work in factories enabled by greater technological inputs. Labor competition pushes down wages and guarantees higher profits for the owners. The second move follows as democratic capitalism matures and institutionalizes ways in which wealth gets more evenly distributed. This can happen via the welfare state or via the economists' beloved market forces: more people accumulate human capital via education and can earn overall higher incomes, which compresses the income distribution.

The Kuznets curve has been soundly refuted, because Piketty notes that Kuznets made his pronouncements on inequality in the 1950s, precisely the moment when inequality in the most developed world had been lowered via changes in regulatory policy. The erroneous assumption is that the 1950s form the end of history.

Secondly, Kuznets data analysis was overly focused on Latin America as opposed to other parts of the world, thus reducing the validity of his findings across different contexts. (For the cited literature on criticisms of the Kuznets curve read Wikipedia, "Kuznets curve # Criticisms").

With respect to education, reducing inequality via the provision of more education is the economists' pipe dream, which the historian Scheidel does not miss out on pointing out. "[T]he strong rise in top incomes is particularly hard to explain with reference to education." Moreover, if education were so important and people are not getting enough of it, we should have an under-educated population. Instead, there is "a growing mismatch in the United States between education and employment in that workers are increasingly overqualified for the work they do" (p.413). Yet education is the panacea that some economists and many politicians tout as if it would make a dent in inequality. As if education would right the wrong-headed ship of lower corporate and top income taxes, labor deregulation, automation and outsourcing of work, lower economic growth and quantitative easing for the banks.

The reason why education is touted as a solution to inequality is that such promotion transfers the responsibility of reducing inequality from the state to the individual, which is more strongly the case in the Anglican countries that addressed deindustrialization of the labor force with rising college attendance and student debt, while countries like Germany or Sweden still stick to the collectivization of education investments in the young generation. But education also does not require larger scale state interventions to mitigate the scale of inequality and retains the myth that meritocracy only breeds success as opposed to plain inheritance and the exploitation of the laboring class.

Returning back to Scheidel: does he have a credible case for the Four Horsemen? I think he has and the implications of that are rather disturbing. Bourgeois reformers will insist, however, that democratic elections and more economic development will ultimately mitigate inequality. But there is no strong evidence for this claim. The major point of neoliberalism, a term that is admittedly overused by its critics and not acknowledged by its supporters (e.g. Dunn 2016), is that it does not matter really which political party is in power as there is only one game in town, which has been especially depressing for the center-left, social democratic parties, who drew clientele from the beneficiaries of the expansive welfare state and the working class. They pass the same neoliberal policies that exacerbate inequality, each time with the reference to some outside force like globalization, technology or international competition that is tying their hands. Why would we want to tax the rich, who have their wealth in tax-shelter islands when they can escape us so easily (aside from the fact that these small island nations can easily be forced to submit tax records to other countries)?

In the very developed world, further economic growth becomes more and more difficult. China is still the world's most dynamic economy, which can still accommodate many workers with substantial wage gains, yet the accelerated pace and pressure to complete the foreign infrastructure projects (One Belt, One Road) to export capital abroad, the diminishing returns on domestic infrastructure projects, the build-up of debt in local and provincial governments, as well as mounting political crackdowns on internal opposition shows that even China will have to recognize limits to its growth model. In the US, a growth that is made possible by the automation of work ensures that productivity gains are absorbed by Silicon Valley and its distant cousin on Wall Street (think of non-American equivalents in other parts of the world).

In developed countries the major concern is no longer how to generate additional economic growth, but how to find ways to redistribute these gains more broadly (while for instance countries in Africa need substantial economic growth simply because their populations are growing so rapidly). Our tech overlords, including Mark Zuckerberg and Elon Musk, think that there will have to be a basic income, and we cannot dismiss their views as naive. Countless hours of productive labor have been shifted onto the social media platform, which generates billions and billions of dollars in real revenues for the social media platform without returning any material compensation for the users. We get to have social validation via likes and comments on the stupid cat videos we post, and that would suffice to motivate us to continue posting on the site, yet it does not mitigate the injustice of having one platform monopolize our time and monetize our action for their own benefit.

Tesla's self-driving cars are not only targeting the driving industry (taxi, bus, rail, truck), but also the manufacturing of cars, which is the most robot intensive industry. The potential benefit of cheaper cars may be more than offset by the lack of employment creation in other sectors of the economy.

One area that is fabulously proliferating are the contract-based temp jobs, which are made feasible by the online marketplace (Uber, Airbnb, Mechanical Turk etc.). Given that there are so many workers looking for employment and that it is so easy to find some kind of work online, wages are kept continuously low, and politicians still feel little pressure to expand protective legislation on these online workers. Even if they found it worthwhile to improve the protection for these workers, in the absence of some major revolution I doubt that inequality can be tackled.

And that raises the final question: If we are to believe Scheidel in that we need a catastrophic event to sharply reduce inequality, should we hope for a war or pandemic to break out, for a genuine political revolution to happen (not of the Bernie Sanders type) to overthrow and reinvent the institutions of the state? Scheidel wisely does not answer this question, and he reserves his conclusion section to discuss common sense middle of the road economic policy (e.g. progressive taxation, expansion of the welfare state). He does acknowledge, however, that "[r]eforms at the margins are unlikely to have a significant effect on current trends in the distribution of market income and wealth" (p.436). He then goes on to also refute the notion that we can have mass mobilization warfare, as advanced technology, especially nuclear weapons, deter mutually assured destruction, and the proliferating use of drones in warfare make personnel mobilization less desirable. But without mass mobilization there is no reason for leaders to involve their population and level the wealth distribution.

He also thinks that revolutions are unlikely to happen and state collapse is restricted to sub-Saharan Africa and some countries in the Middle East (e.g. Syria). Pandemics will only affect the less developed nations as the more developed nations will quickly work to isolate disease. In each case (no war, no disease, no revolution, no state failure), our life can remain relatively unperturbed by violent shocks, yet we are bound to see more headlines of increasing income and wealth inequality. I remember reading the first Oxfam study a few years ago, when 400 individuals own as much as half the world population, and now we are down to 8 people. There no longer is any shock effect with these numbers, but we know that wealth is getting more concentrated. The poorest people may not necessarily be getting worse off, but the wealthy are just making most of the gains, and there just aren't any global institutions that can halt this trend.

It is this psychological pessimism and not the empirical accuracy which forms the greatest weakness in Scheidel's work. I have previously reviewed works by Wolfgang Streeck (Liu 2014b; Liu, "Book Review: How Will Capitalism End?", this volume) and Claus Offe (Liu 2015b), each of them brilliant welfare state/ capitalism/ political economy scholars in their own right. What the Germanic writers (Scheidel is Austrian) all seem to have in common is their Hegelian vision of the totality and the structuralist vision in their analyses. The captivating part about reading Karl Marx Capital was not the many British factory reports that he quoted, which demonstrated the plight of the working class toiling in the factories in the mid 19th century, but the exposition of the logic of the capitalist system as a whole.

While Scheidel's scope of work is not nearly as ambitious as that of the other German theorists, he does attempt to answer big questions pertaining to inquiry in historical sociology and historically-grounded political economy. But as a Germanic structuralist, the activist reader feels like he/she has no agency and cannot do much to mitigate inequality. Even the moderate policy prescriptions that Scheidel advocates for may be considered tinkering around the margins. Inequality cannot be resolved easily, but the irony is that such condition justifies the advocacy of socialism, because there is no need for socialism in a very egalitarian society.

The Defeat of the Governing Parties in Germany
Posted on September 24, 2017

For many months German and international media have insisted that Merkel would be the pillar of strength, which will halt the rise of right-wing populism. The narrative of the cosmopolitan elite was that Brexit, Trump and Syriza are crazy aberrations and what western democracy urgently needed was a return to normalcy, and that normalcy is Angela Merkel, the leader of Germany, the most powerful country in Europe, and therefore the right person to lead the West in openness, tolerance, cosmopolitanism, respect and human rights.

There never was any doubt that her CDU would win the election as all polls suggested she would have a wide leading margin against the social democrats, who had hoped that Martin Schulz, the former EU parliament president and not tainted by German domestic politics, would be able to challenge the chancellor. But the Schulz effect lasted for about a month and faded around April and May. The voters were not fooled as Schulz did not really promise a genuine alternative to what the SPD had previously been offering. The decisive moment of surrender in the SPD did not begin with Martin Schulz, but with Gerhard Schroder, who had campaigned on expanding the welfare state in 1998, won the elections and promptly promoted his welfare cut agenda in the form of Hartz IV and the Agenda 2010, which was rolled out immediately after his re-election in 2002. The only genuine "social democrat", who refused to accept the right-ward drift in social policy was Oskar Lafontaine, who resigned the finance ministry in 1999 and co-founded the WASG, which later merged with the East German Die Linke to campaign for the 2005 Bundestag elections.

The discrediting of the SPD was continued in every election, in which Angela Merkel was the leader of the CDU, because the party was led by technocrats, who had no vision for a different Germany except some slight changes around the margins like the introduction of the minimum wage in the 2013 coalition negotiations. Schulz tried to give nice speeches in favor of social justice and equality, but it is noteworthy that he had not denounced the basic contours of Hartz IV, which should be kept in place, because it would not make any sense to let scroungers take advantage of the welfare state instead of working to benefit the community (needless to say, the many jobs that were added come in the part-time, low-wage sector, which require tax subsidies to allow these workers to survive).

The result is that the SPD lost more than 5 points dropping to about 20.4% in the elections. But if the social democrats can be written off, can the CDU/CSU count as winner? Yes, but only if you are concerned about relative power balances. The CDU landed on top, but has lost an astounding 8.7 points to go down to 32.8%. It might not sound surprising that governing parties tend to be punished and this has clearly happened with both the CDU and SPD, which had served in government together for the last four years. To some extent, Merkel also made a clever move to coalesce with the SPD for a second time (first time between 2005 and 2009), because the punishment for the SPD means that the CDU is cemented as the largest power, which can pick its coalition partner and remain in government.

Merkel will certainly want to form a new coalition government and has excluded the AfD, a right-wing extremist party, which contains some racists, homophobes, anti-refugee, anti-immigrant traditionalists elements. Their win is the most astounding, as Germany did not have a right-wing party in parliament since its founding, partly because of the sensitive Nazi history. The AfD was originally founded by disappointed CDU officials, who did not support Germany's support for the Greek bailouts. It was a party led by the economist Bernd Lucke. But Lucke was ousted in 2015 by the national-conservative Frauke Petry, who exploited the incoming massive refugee wave from Syria and the Middle East to elevate her own position within the party. It was only since the refugee crisis that the AfD was taken seriously by ever more voters, many of which were upset about the unacceptably high standards of political correctness surrounding the refugee discourse. In their view, the mostly left-leaning media is sympathetic to the plight of refugees, while the AfD painted the media as "Lugenpresse", i.e. lying press, who ignored the fear of the domestic population of the many refugees that create an ethnically diverse country, where German-blooded people can no longer feel at home.

Ironically, the economic competition argument against immigrants could not be used in the context of Germany, because under Merkel's chancellorship the export economy and the Mittelstand continued to thrive (certainly aided by the effective control over European monetary policy, which mixes traditionally strong currency countries like Germany with weak currency countries like Spain and Greece, thus lowering the cost of German exports to say US or China), thus unemployment could be kept low. The number of employees dependent on government wage subsidies declined from 1.3 million to 1.2 million from 2013 to 2017 (Die Zeit 2017). Instead, the AfD concentrated on the immigrant and foreigner question in the context of cultural fear and rejection of the "other".

While elements of the AfD base and leadership might espouse conservative, homophobic, racist and anti-refugee views, one of their leading candidates, Alice Weidel, is a lesbian in a domestic partnership with an Indian descent woman and two sons with Syrian refugees as household help. It is quite astounding how Weidel can reconcile these contradictions, and one way seems to be to be silent on her homosexuality and personal life, while focusing her energy on the anti-refugee agenda. With her own household helpers she even finds the excuse that they are Christian Syrians, who are worthwhile protecting, suggesting that Muslim Syrians and other Muslims are not.

The other leading candidate is the former CDU veteran Alexander Gauland, who had made headlines by saying that he admired the footballer Jerome Boateng, a German national player with African roots, but no "real" German would want to have him as neighbor.

With the election of the right-wing nationalist AfD Germany's post-war era has now come to an end, as it becomes a "normal" European country with its share of right-wing populists. Critics of such a harsh depiction would counter that the AfD has been excluded by the other political parties, which has gained much support from non-voters and especially former CDU voters, who had no alternative on the right-wing. But the AfD exclusion is at most temporary, because if the AfD can durably increase its vote share continuously, then sooner or later it will serve in government, which is what we might expect after the Austrian elections in October with the FPO in power.

Merkel's other option is to form another coalition with the SPD, but Schulz declared that the SPD would definitely go into opposition, because they understand that the voters have punished them and they have to lick their wounds in opposition and hope to do better next time. The lack of a progressive political vision a la Corbyn or Sanders makes that all the harder. Merkel also refuses to speak with the Linke (9%), which probably reminds her too much of the ugly communist past, even though the Linke is the only party to be strong on the welfare state.

The FDP, which missed the 5% mark after the last election before which it was in coalition with the CDU, now makes it back to the Bundestag with about 10% support and the fourth-largest party. The FDP is a traditional coalition partner with the CDU. Their agenda is dominated by deregulation and lower taxes for businesses, which has some parallels to the CDU agenda. The FDP said that it wanted to claim the powerful finance ministry to direct economic and social policy, but the CDU will likely want to keep the post. In the last administration they held the health, justice, development, economy and foreign affairs portfolio, each of which can likely be conceded by the CDU. But they can't form a majority government, so they would have to take the Green Party, which wants a strong environmental portfolio and might even be interested in the social affairs ministry. The so-called Jamaica coalition (black, yellow, green) would get the majority of the parliament. In this coalition, each party will likely get portfolios that are proportionate to the number of votes: 3/5 for the CDU, 1/5 FDP and 1/5 Greens.

While the representation of the Greens in power might indicate some balance to the right-wing economic policy, one should consider that the current party leadership of the Greens are so-called pragmatists, which means they don't have a big vision and just want to serve in government. That suggests that with the exception of their environmental portfolio (lower kerosene usage in cars, climate protection, CO_2 reduction), they will not push for many other policies, and this may well be a cost that the business-friendly CDU and FDP will be willing to bear to be accommodated to power.

Most importantly for Angela Merkel, the announcement of the SPD to go into opposition will cement her claim to a fourth chancellorship. If she serves the entire term, she will be able to match her political predecessor Helmut Kohl, the unity chancellor of 16 years. I doubt that Kohl would have survived this long if it wasn't for German unity, which transformed East Germany from socialist SED to conservative CDU land. That was in the 1990s, now the picture is more heterogeneous, with the Linke and SPD also quite influential.

Some people would argue that Merkel is without alternative, but she will have to step down if not for political then for health reasons. The pundits had been speaking about the maintenance of the status quo, but I think that it is shaken by the loss of the two major parties. Next stop in Austria.

A Right-Wing Majority in Austria
Posted on <u>October 15, 2017</u>

The difference between 2000 and 2017 in Austria is that this time around right-wing populism has been normalized. Back in 2000, the second and the third largest party, OVP and FPO negotiated a coalition government, in which the third-ranked OVP was able to get the chancellory after convincing the FPO to cede the highest post. Party leader Jorg Haider subsequently retreated to his little empire in Carinthia, which he ran as the state governor. That was the beginning of the end of the Haider-FPO.

First, Carinthia became involved in the Hypo Alpe Adria scandal, the provincial bank, which had been most exposed to international speculation in real estate, which resulted in bank bailouts in 2008 and the nationalization of the bank in 2009 (re-privatization in 2015). The blame went straight to the Haider administration. Second, without Haider at the helm of the national party there no longer was a charismatic leader among the ranks of the FPO, who could agitate the masses for his party. Third, the FPO turned out to be a mere junior partner to the OVP. The one measure that they were really proud of was the stricter enforcement of immigration restriction legislation. The voters realized the fraud of the FPO government and switched their support to the OVP in 2002, which became the clear winner in the elections. Lastly, after internal quarrels, Haider had assembled his close allies to form the BZO, a new political party, which temporarily split the nationalist camp until Haider's car crash death in 2008.

When the OVP-FPO government formed in 2000 the great dismay of the EU-leaders resulted in nominal sanctions against Austria, which were lifted a few months after the inauguration. But 17 years later there are good chances that OVP and FPO will agree on a coalition government, thus returning the FPO back to power, but this time without sanctions. The OVP had been continuously serving in government since 1986, mostly as a junior partner to the OVP, as it had been difficult to become number 1, and yet in each leading position the OVP would enter in a coalition government with the FPO. The Vranitzky doctrine according to which the SPO would not enter a coalition government with the nationalist FPO kept the options continuously open for the OVP to remain in power.

The current parliamentary elections catapulted Sebastian Kurz OVP to the first-ranked position, which had long been anticipated, essentially since he became the party chairman. The OVP had received more than 31% of the vote, and will almost certainly receive the commission to form a government. Observers will recall that the principal reason for the OVP's electoral success lies not just in the perception of youth and renewal that Kurz represents. I think Austrian voters are cynical enough to not be fazed by it. They were instead directly responding to Kurz right-wing pandering, as he became more and more intent on problematizing the vast number of refugees as contributing to the inability to integrate them and burdening the welfare system. By using nicer words than the FPO, but responding to the same primal fears of the public, Kurz was able to draw votes to what otherwise would go to the right-wing.

But one cannot merely state that the votes come from the right, because the FPO itself gained nearly 7 points to reach 27%, historically the best result for the FPO. The FPO is clearly a winner in these parliamentary elections. In part, their better performance comes from the fact that the smaller parties are pushed to the side. The Greens catastrophically lost nearly 10 points (and might not make it to parliament), Stronach no longer runs and is thus losing 5 points, while the BZO also is virtually suspended, as it still had about 3% support in 2013. A new party with immediate gains is Peter Pilz list, which promptly gained 4%. Pilz is a former Green parliamentarian and thus has diverted some support from them. He also distinguished himself by speaking out tough on criminal refugees.

Noteworthy is also that despite the anti-immigrant and anti-refugee position, which dominates the FPO agenda, its leader Heinz-Christian Strache has toned down his rather aggressive rhetoric (in his first ever campaign as leader for the 2005 Vienna elections, he had campaigned actively against Islam), thus presenting his party as an acceptable party to plan governing coalitions. And here comes, therefore, the main reason that the OVP and FPO coalition appears most likely: both parties agree on harsh anti-refugee policies, reducing the inflow of many more migrants. Both also agree on economic and social policy, which is about tax cuts for businesses and wealthy individuals financed by drastic cuts in social spending. The latter part is not explicitly admitted on either side, and they instead dodge that bullet by demanding cuts to the "bloated administration", i.e. the vast army of civil servants that has been going back to the days of Maria Theresia.

The alternative to social spending cuts would have been more support for the SPO, which was just about holding even at 27% of the vote, being possibly second or third-ranked (remaining letter votes still have to be counted until next week). The incumbent governing party under chancellor Christian Kern faced several difficulties. First, by being the senior governing partner since 2007, the SPO is a used up force, and the voters indicate their desire for change. Second, while Austrian workers do suffer from the consequences of neoliberalism (shorter, more unstable work contracts, more uncertain work life), the perception of urgency has shifted from economic policy to migration, which the SPO refuses to capitalize on given their voting clientele, which includes many migrants.

Third, while leader Kern appears to be technically competent, he does not have the emotional appeal that his younger opponent Kurz had. What was noteworthy in their last common TV debate was that Kern had the greater technical competence, even going so far as denouncing Kurz for being corrupt by taking campaign donations from the rich and then writing a pro-rich campaign agenda, for which Kurz had no counterpoint. While the SPO had long ago proposed a political platform ("Plan A"), the OVP kept most of its plans secret until the middle of September, a month before the elections. But technical competence and debating skills are not sufficient to convince the masses, who decide the elections. Fourth, the SPO has been suffering from the Silberstein affair, a former party campaign manager, who was imprisoned for embezzlement in his home country in Israel. It then turned out that Silberstein was an expert in dirty campaigning, which the other parties then exploited to hammer the SPO on. Whether Kern was aware of Silberstein's dealings is unclear, yet it was a clear embarrassment to his party to have to deal with Silberstein allegations, which sows doubt among voters that the SPO is a trustworthy party.

Lastly, social democracy is under attack across Europe. Some scholars think that this is because the social democrats were too successful. Their raison d'etre was the creation of the welfare state, but now that the welfare state stands, there is no reason to support social democrats and people can vote for other parties. But I would argue precisely the opposite. The failure of the social democrats comes from their lack of defense of the welfare state. It certainly becomes hard to enforce retrenchment, but given the lack of huge economic growth the main engine to finance the welfare state is in trouble. The much missed Keynesian consensus depended on a unique class compromise among capitalists and workers, who share the abundant surplus among each other.

Social democrats thus become tolerated among capitalists, and welcomed by the workers, who no longer dream of revolution (if they ever did...). But these abundant surpluses are absent in today's world of anemic growth despite record-low rates of interest and high levels of public and private debt. A peculiar form of social democracy arose in the 1990s, as these parties resigned to the power of finance, which came to support the welfare state in return for its deregulation. There are now countless studies that show how finance reinforces inequality (Lin and Tomaskevic-Devey 2013), not good news for social democrats. Further bad news is that finance-driven economic growth is inherently unstable, which became evident with the financial crisis in 2008. Whether the finance minister was social democratic or not, there was a strange optic when the government unloads the debts of private banks and then pays for this burden via austerity measures. In that case, as social democrats side with the bankers to save the capitalist and financial system as opposed to the working class, they shall not be surprised that they get less support.

PASOK, the Greek social democrats, have virtually been wiped out and are no longer a political force there. PASOK had been the first party to manage the fallout of the Greek debt crisis and to the extent that Greece began its long trip on the knife of the EU austerity regime, voters had no reason to sustain them. Now the Greek political landscape is limited to the socialist left and the conservatives, but they agree on the austerity-cum-bailout regime, thus invalidating democracy in Greece.

There is some hope for social democratic revival in Portugal and the UK. In Portugal, the moderate Socialist Party went into a minority government under Antonio Costa, while being propped up by a left party, a communist party and the green party. Their course had been to stop new austerity, privatization, worker-right diminution measures from Brussels, though the struggle is defensive, it is an advancement to the previous administration.

In the UK, the election of Jeremy Corbyn as party leader was the game changer, as the former backbencher insisted on scrapping Tory austerity and increasing social spending. He was scoffed at by Blairite colleagues in the Labour Party, warning that Labour would never serve in government with a left-wing lunatic in charge. Except that the bungled Brexit negotiations revealed the ineptitude of the Tory government under Theresa May and voters were willing to embrace a more left-wing alternative, which destroyed the Tory majority in the last parliamentary elections over the summer. May converted a Tory majority to a minority government propped up by the Northern Irish DUP, which restricted its support for the government on some key areas like Brexit and national security but not on austerity decisions like not raising the pay for NHS workers.

Back to Austria: It is technically possible for the SPO to continue the grand coalition, but they would have to enter as junior partners. There would, however, be a lack of credibility for continuing a coalition government, which is not only discredited in the eyes of the voters, but also in the eyes of the two parties themselves. Why would they call snap elections (a year before due date) if it was not to end the grand coalition? The two parties have sufficient disagreements that such cooperation probably makes no more sense. The other option would be for the SPO to cooperate with the FPO. These are two almost equally strong parties, but the disagreements on economic, social and migration policy are bigger between these two parties than for OVP and FPO. So the latter combination is still the most likely.

The vote pattern suggests stronger right-wing forces, yet again. What is to be done about automation in the workplace? What is to be done about the precarious workforce? What is to be done about the growing wealth gap between the rich and the poor? What is to be done about multinational companies that pay less taxes than small business people? What is to be done to create a more harmonious life between indigenous and foreign-descent Austrians? These questions will not be well addressed in the immediate future, but which government has ever done so?

Can Workers Resist Automation?
Posted on November 23, 2017

There has been a long history of workers, who have resisted the oncoming wave of automation. For supporters of capital, these workers are throwing sand into the wheels of progress, and how dare these workers speak up? They are labeled as Luddites, which are workers, who destroyed the machines that were built and replaced the workers. Luddites protested the wave of technological unemployment, which has usually not been a problem in most developed countries, because we have thus far been able to shift workers into new industries. Should we thus side with the Luddites? I argue we should not. Workers should not so much resist automation by preventing it, but resist it by demanding a fair shake from capital.

Formerly, most people were employed in the agricultural sector as farmers, but the mechanization of agricultural production increased productivity per man hour, and as the entire population could be fed with fewer people involved, displaced farmers shifted onto different sectors. Further technological advancement meant that manufacturing goods would be produced, which from the nineteenth century onward also became a major source of employment. In some countries, like Germany 20% of the workforce is still employed in manufacturing, although it used to be 40% in 1970. The overarching trend, which became clear at least since the 1950s was that mechanization increasingly claimed jobs in manufacturing as well, and since then jobs have shifted onto the service sector.

This last transformation did not happen without friction, which may be expressed in the lack of power of organized labor in the service sector. Labor unions played no role in agricultural economies (perhaps occasionally an agricultural collective or commune), but they arose from industrial struggles of the emergent working class, a dynamic that is still captured in Karl Marx Communist Manifesto (not so much in his later writings on political economy). Marx beautifully pointed out that unlike previous slave-holding or serf-based societies on dispersed soil, an economy based on workers that become physically concentrated in tight urban spaces and factories, and in which capital continuously put the squeeze on workers would generate a substantial counter-reaction of the workers in the form of agitating for labor unions and collective bargaining rights. The issue has been that service-sector workers, especially in private industry, have been more fragmented and less capable to organize and strike for better rights, though their unionization rates are now higher than in manufacturing (Schmitt 2009).

But it turns out that historically capital (and their owners) is a much more versatile object than labor. Firstly, while capital can set up shop anywhere in the world, where it finds natural resources and exploitable labor, and in the form of finance capital find borrowers, workers are usually tied to the location in which they live. Naturally, there is the option of labor migration, but even that has certain limitations as no more than 3% of the world population permanently leaves their country of origin. Language barriers, lower socio-economic status and the maintenance of personal networks (friends, family) are great barriers to movement. The threat of capital removal without implementation might already scare enough workers to prevent them from carrying out strikes, which could threaten capital. Secondly, the sustained threat to profitability by continuously rising labor costs and labor action motivates the capitalist class to make more investments in mechanization to replace sufficient labor to lower labor costs both by a reduction in new hiring and in the greater competition among laid-off workers, which holds future wage claims in check.

Therefore, only in exceptional economic time periods can workers ever hope to gain a bigger share of the pie without facing the threat of a capital strike. Notably, the government has to institutionally support organized labor in the form of Keynesian, social democratic policies, including pro-union labor laws and institutions, a growing welfare state (which socializes the cost of caring for surplus labor, old/ sick/ disabled people etc.), counter-cyclical investment policy to maintain full employment, and national policies to regulate the flow of capital and encourage domestic investment.

However, even the best social-democratic policies (think of Sweden or Denmark) are limited by the subservience of labor movements and progressive governments to the needs of capital accumulation. Insufficient capital accumulation in a Keynesian context motivates firms to hike prices on consumers. Strong labor unions in the so-called "monopoly" sectors protect their workers through high wage claims, which produced a wage-price spiral and the high inflation of the 1970s, which was not tamed until the Volcker Shock (Volcker was the US Federal Reserve chair from 1979-

87) in the late-1970s (i.e. high interest rates induced a recession; a higher unemployment rate weakened the power of organized labor, thus putting a stop to inflation). In addition, the removal of pro-labor legislation and constraints on government investment policies in public works projects and the welfare state, diminished the pillars of institutional support for the working class.

This set of so-called 'neoliberal' policies revolves around the removal of limitations to capital mobility and capital decisionmaking by the capitalist class, and its 'success' gets measured in the increasing gap between the rich and the poor both with respect to income and wealth. As Karl Polanyi (1944) had pointed out, early phases of liberalism are self-undermining to the extent that workers are not perfect commodities that can easily be discarded like a cell phone. To limit the extent of commodification, workers tend to organize and erect barriers to the free decisionmaking of the capitalists. But this so-called double movement can also become undermined by innovative ways of capital to circumvent borders, i.e. via outsourcing and automation.

With the threat of mass strikes and organized labor having disappeared, workers in the developed world might have an interest to take out their sledgehammers and quickly smash the machines, because as Branko Milanovic' (2016) "elephant" graph shows, they have been the only losers of neoliberal globalization, while the middle class in the emerging countries (chiefly China and everyone else trading heavily with the Chinese) are gaining ground, and the oligarchs all over the world are multiplying their fortunes by leaps and bounds. But in a historical analysis of the Great Depression era discourse on technological unemployment, Amy Sue Bix (2001) points out that workers have generally fought a rather defensive struggle against the collective forces of capital. The best deal that workers can get for themselves is limited to automation agreements that individual unions negotiate with their individual employer. These may be temporary worker retraining benefits, longer unemployment compensation, transfer within the firm or slower adoption of technology. In no case, however, have unions been able to halt the forces of technological displacement.

But even if we miraculously dream up a social situation where workers become strong enough to smash all the machines that exist, and thus force capital to stick it out with labor, would this halt of technological innovation be desirable? No, because under capitalism, where the means of production are privately held and those private actors seek capital accumulation, barriers to capital in the form of strong labor organization will impede capital investment, and will create new avenues by which the newly established social contract with the workers gets revoked. Even aside from the logic of capital, would we want to toil away with dull jobs that can be automated with given engineering advancements? The Luddite success would damn humanity to endless labor, which I would not enjoy even if the workers owned all of the means of production and distributed the spoils of society's resources in an egalitarian fashion.

Another ethical problem is that the differential distribution of the spoils of globalization, where the western workers lose out and the other workers gain, make it patently unfair for western workers to determine to halt capital decisions that had lifted workers in developing countries into middle-income countries and out of poverty. On the other hand, the jubilation of the Chinese working class is tempered by the realization that upward-rising labor cost pressures induce Chinese capitalists to also contemplate outsourcing and automation. The record number of robots are ordered in China, not in the West (IFR 2017).

We are long overdue for another Polanyian double movement swinging back to favor the workers and the popular masses, but in a truly globalized world economy it would require that workers surrender their focus on localism and themselves embrace globalism via cross-national solidarity campaigns with workers in other countries. Progressive thinkers have long advocated for the industry-wide organization of labor unions across countries as opposed to national-level or national industrial unions. But even in a world of the internet, local network ties and affiliations by far dominate and structure our daily interactions and actions. But an international labor organization is becoming more and not less important in the context of automation and greater job anxieties.

Ironically, it may be a market mechanism which by itself could limit the scale of automation, which critics of fast automation do not tire to point out (e.g. Mishel and Shierholz 2017). Critics of automation and massive job displacement argue that if automation were a serious threat to employment it should be reflected in higher investment and productivity figures, which is not the case. Gordon (2014) goes as far as asserting that the computer is not as important as say electricity or other early forms of technological progress for productivity rises. Another way to look at it is that initially fast automation in some sectors may push people into "stagnant" productivity sectors that are not automating, and are unlikely to automate given the cheapened wages as desperate workers put up with any working conditions (Storm 2017). The rise of the so-called gig economy (Katz and Krueger 2016) which reflects the servile conditions of highly flexible labor that are mediated on internet platforms partly reflects the new labor market opportunities for desperate workers (Scholz 2016).

A useful case study is the retail industry, where department stores have on net lost 448,000 jobs from 2002 to 2016, while net gains are registered in e-commerce (178,000) and warehouses (841,000) (Gebeloff and Russell 2017). By raising the convenience and lowering logistics costs, Amazon has created an e-commerce bonanza for customers, which provides new opportunities to warehouse workers and transport workers via Amazon Flex. Unlike with the department store retail sector, however, the specter of automation is constantly hovering over the massive Amazon workforce, as productivity rises and optimization happen unilaterally via the introduction of warehouse and transportation robots.

Responding to the critics of automation's impact, Brynjolfsson et al. (2017) counter that the modest productivity growth is associated with the lag effects of innovation, i.e. it takes time before robot diffusion will be reflected in the productivity statistics. Robots also affect local labor markets, because areas with more robots have fewer jobs and lower wages (Acemoglu and Restrepo 2017). However, the fact that robots are clustered in manufacturing production tells an important part of the story of deindustrialization. The robot nightmare scenario of mass unemployment only becomes realized once the high-demand service jobs are under threat (e.g. self-driving trucks and cars on the transportation industry; medical apps and robot surgeons on the medical industry; legal software on the legal industry; investment and trading algorithms in the financial industry etc.).

The outflow from the labor force has already been observed by men, whereby the labor force participation rate has been reduced by 10 percentage points to 88% over the last 60 years (Black et al. 2016). Might that be linked to the opioid addiction crisis that raised the mortality rate among working class white men (Case and Deaton 2017), or pushed them into video game addiction in their parents' basement (Aguiar et al. 2017)?

Workers should not so much resist automation by preventing it, but resist it by demanding a fair shake from capital, which may take the form of employee stock ownership, progressive taxes with welfare redistribution or a universal basic income, which severs the link between a job and income. As giant tech companies increasingly monopolize revenues (Facebook for example having 1/7th of humanity as a customer base), new innovations are pushing workers out of secure jobs, and financial companies are pre-emptively guaranteed perpetual bailouts for risky lending policies, each of which hoarding opportunities at the top while growing the gap between the very rich and everyone else, the case for an out-of-market economic solution to unemployment and underemployment become more important than ever.

For now, the regressive political and economic agenda (i.e. Trump, Brexit, Macron) seem to prevail. Trump's fake populism-having gained on the national sentiment against immigrants and in favor of protecting a few coal jobs by scrapping NAFTA- is revealed as fake with the imposition of trillions of dollars in tax cuts for the richest 1%, whether it is in the form of abolishing the inheritance tax or lowering the corporate tax rate (Wolf 2017). If there is anything positive that will emerge from the plutocratic agenda of the Trump administration it is that the counter-mobilization against his bigotry and elitism will provide opportunities for general upheaval.

The Logic of Automation

Posted on <u>November 24, 2017</u>

We hear with great trepidation about Frey and Osborne's (2013) study, which claims that 47% of jobs in the United States are going to be replaced by the rise of robots. But the really interesting question is not how many jobs might be displaced by robots based on job tasks that economists themselves determine, but whether capitalists want to invest in a given robot or not. Naturally, in a market-based economy it is rather difficult to assess the precise equilibrium outcomes of rising automation, and- in the absence of good data- philosophers and futurists (Bostrom 2016; Ford 2016) are trying to prime us on a future without work, when the robots have displaced most human workers.

Some economists have now ventured to make empirical investigations into how robots will affect productivity growth (Graetz and Michaels 2015) and overall employment figures (Acemoglu and Restrepo 2017). There is no doubt that we need more of these empirical investigations.

What I will do in this post is to theoretically lay out the logic of automation, which is summarized in the following graph:

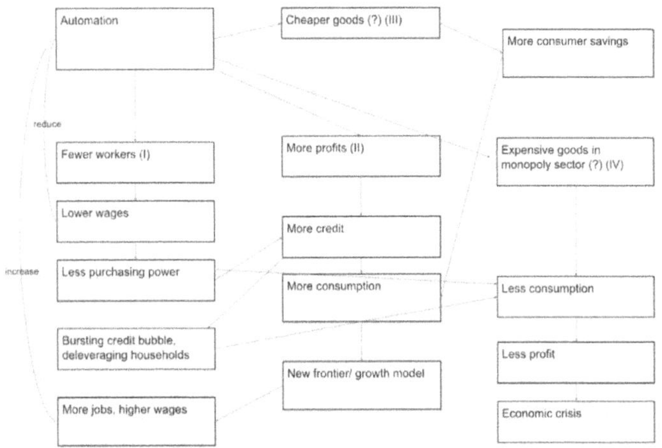

In this model, the foundational assumption is that automation is already happening. The first effect is on the side of the employment channel, namely that it reduces the number of workers. Historically, we might argue that automation actually creates jobs, and in some modern tech sectors there is evidence of continuous automation among software engineers leading to more innovation and thus new job creation in that sector (Shestakofsky 2017). In the case of the retail sector the displacement of department store workers has thus far been offset by the growth in e-commerce, which creates jobs in warehouses and transport logistics.

But in my model, the potential growth of jobs is captured in the automation effects on the consumer channel. Lower prices of goods will increase savings of consumers, which can be channeled into increasing consumption in the same industry or in other areas of the economy. But we might also assume the opposite, namely that automation reinforces the monopoly sector's profits (Google, Amazon and associates) and thus retains the high cost of living despite rising automation. Continued high product prices in the absence of competition implies less consumer purchasing power. Lowered consumer purchasing power also happens via the channel of displaced labor (as mentioned in the beginning), which has to compete for jobs in other areas of the labor market, which lowers the organizational clout and wage claims of workers.

The rescue for beleaguered consumer-workers happens via the consumer finance channel, as rising profits are deposited in financial institutions, who have to aggressively market those accumulated savings in the form of credit. Credit expansion in turn is made possible by lax government regulations, but it crucially buys time for the capitalists because they combine rising profits with declining wages but rising consumption. The problem with the consumer finance route is that it is inherently unstable as the lack of rising income among the masses means a high risk of default and financial crisis. Deleveraging households thus create the third way in which consumption is lowered. Lower consumption in turn predicts less profits, less investments and an economic crisis.

Automation decisions themselves are endogenous to wage trends. In the case that automation displaces workers, increases competition in the labor market, thus reduce worker bargaining power and lower wages, the pressure to automate might actually decrease, as cheaper workers compete with expensive robots. Developing countries upper middle class can still afford human butlers, which is the preserve of the upper class in the developed countries given the high cost of human labor. In the contrary case, a new consumer bonanza will allow workers to gain higher wages, which will increase the pressure to automate. This theoretical prediction has some empirical evidence as the Europeans have a higher robot penetration on average than the US, while the former also have better labor-protective legislation and higher wage costs with more generous social contributions to finance the pensions and other social welfare spending. In addition, China is the hottest market for robot imports, partly because of the manufacturing dependence of the country and partly because of the massively rising wages in the export-intensive manufacturing sectors.

Can we, thus, formulate a summarizing statement about the logic of automation? I would say, perhaps not, because the arrows are pointing to two possible outcomes: (1) a higher economic equilibrium with more productivity growth and economic growth with rising wages and more jobs, and (2) economic crisis, a depletion of middle class employment options, an entrenchment of monopoly capitalism and a further concentration of wealth in the hands of the few. For whatever reason, the more pessimistic perspective takes overhand in our contemporary experience with automation.

The National Oligarchy Prevails… For Now
Posted on December 7, 2017

Introduction

When David Koch ran on the ticket of the Libertarian Party as vice presidential candidate in the 1980 US presidential elections, he barely got 1% of the vote. Their platform was to drastically shrink the size of the state through massive reductions in social spending programs, the elimination of public education, the dismantling of environmental protection, the abolition of the IRS and the income tax, and on the side they were also quite liberal on social issues like LGBT rights or prostitution legalization (Sanders n.d.). However, it was evident that the two-party system could not so simply be undermined by the attraction of electoral votes for these libertarian principles. It simply wasn't true that the vast majority of the American people would willingly vote for this libertarian agenda, which was about the massive transfer of wealth from the working and middle class to the rich. Instead of endlessly repeating the election bonanza, the Koch brothers turned to funding right-wing think tanks and Republican politicians (Skocpol and Hertel-Fernandez 2016). In this way, they ensured that they could expand their wealth and make it very hard for the popular masses to reclaim some of that oligarchic income via a genuinely populist electoral platform. Now, the passage of the Republican tax bill will further entrench the wealth and power of the oligarch class.

Two Party Oligarchy

In the 2016 elections, Gary Johnson had run on the libertarian ticket, and received 3% of the vote. By this point, David and his politically activist brother Charles Koch had abandoned direct electoral campaigns on their own party platform. There just wasn't any likelihood of succeeding with the libertarian party platform. The more successful strategy of the business community has been to infiltrate the Republican Party and to some extent the Democratic Party. It was clear, however, that the mega-donors tended to side with the Republicans in more cases, because of the weird coalition of big oil, big finance, big real estate on the one hand (i.e. the oligarchs), with evangelical Christians and the white working class (i.e. the popular class) on the other. The former group would deliver the campaign cash, and the latter group would deliver the votes. The popular class does not materially benefit much from the economic policies of the Republican Party, but as part of the conservative tradition they tend not to vocally or openly resist the leadership (Frank 2005). Donald Trump seemed to upset that established order, but it turns out that he is a skilled showman, who doubles down on behalf of the oligarchs, to which he belongs. More on that later.

The Democratic Party, on the contrary, also has to contend with two major factions, which were personified by the Clinton and Sanders campaign in 2016. Hillary Clinton represented the establishment, which includes the big law firms, big tech firms, big Wall Street/ finance firms, big pharma and similar industries (some of which clearly overlap with the Republican Party as part of the donor base). Her popular base consisted of white and older voters, the latter feature of which was important for her to clinch the nomination. Among older Democratic voters, there was a strain of thinking that also tended to favor the establishment. Bernie Sanders was the only meaningful presidential candidate, who dared to run a campaign without any direct financial support from parts of the oligarchy. He ran a purely popular campaign financed by small donations and could get the entire progressive grassroots of the Democratic Party on his side (Sanders 2016). The party machine, which supported Clinton, ensured that Sanders ballots are miscounted in some states. In addition, it took time for his message to spread around the country, and there wasn't enough for him to win the nomination.

When Clinton clashed against Trump in the general elections, there were several features that disadvantaged the Clinton campaign: (1) the Democratic Party was the incumbent ruling party and Clinton explicitly ran on continuity with the Obama administration, which some liberal voters took as justifiable betrayal to abstain from voting, which would not have happened with Sanders. (2) The mainstream media kept on receiving and airing Clinton's email leaks, which many in the Democratic Party had traced back to Russia and Vladimir Putin, which publicly tarnished Clinton's reputation (which is also her favored account of why she had lost the elections). (3) Clinton had been in the national spotlight for nearly 25 years. The public dislike against her and the system that she represents created so much anger that some people preferred the bully billionaire on the other side, who had promised to blow up the political system.

Trump Electoral Campaign

The Trump campaign created some electoral momentum in the states, which Clinton's campaign had deemed "safe", i.e. Pennsylvania, Michigan and Wisconsin. In each of these deindustrializing states, the mass mobilization of rural, working class white voters proved crucial and more than compensated for the few urban clusters (e.g. Philadelphia) that solidly vote Democratic (and were rather unenthused by the Clinton campaign). Trump's promises included building a wall to Mexico (unrealized), tearing up the trade agreements (unrealized), and a nebulous attack against the corruption that had pervaded the oligarchic political economy of the country: "drain the swamp" (the opposite happened with the greatest swamp ever). It appears to be that the popular base bought the argument, even as the Republican donors and the establishment politicians were less than convinced that these promises made any sense, financially nor politically. Was there also the fear that draining the swamp could unravel the cozy crony capitalist arrangements they had so much gained from?

In any case, there was no chance for the Republican establishment politicians to do well with Trump making brazen promises, while the establishment had to stick with conventional promises of general tax cuts and "strengthening the private sector" (understandably not an emotional connection to generate votes). The social mobilization agenda via the evangelical voters also became a spent force, because that voter base is now much smaller than under Reagan and Bush sr. and jr (Jones 2014). Rick Santorum could Biblethump the whole day against the practically agnostic (nominally Christian) Trump, but it wasn't resonating. In fact, evangelical voters might even be inclined to support Trump (Smith and Martinez 2016) because while he doesn't share their religious values, he at least formed credible mass support, which might also help beleaguered evangelicals.

It is not true that racial minorities are better off than whites on average because of affirmative action or President Obama, but it is certainly true that the working class white Trump voter is hurting really badly. It is a rare feat for an industrialized country to regress on basic social indicators like the spread of the hookworm disease (McKenna 2017), opioid addiction deaths (Rudd et al. 2016) or life expectancy (Case and Deaton 2017). Blacks in America are still worse off on many social indicators and experiences than whites, e.g. the high imprisonment rate of blacks (NAACP, n.d.; Pettit and Western

2004), but it is the perception and experience of deterioration among the white working class, which encourages their search for scapegoats. Trump exploited the atmosphere of anxiety by whipping up the hate among the crowds, which became evident in his campaign rallies, where he incited violence against his protesters. He hired the right-wing media strategist Steve Bannon to run his public messaging. Academics like to think that in a democracy rational people vote for candidates that promote their best interest (Meltzer and Richard 1981), but that is not true. Simply because some of us can read the New York Times hours on end and make informed political judgments does not mean that the average person will do so. Politics, at least from the perspective of the masses, is about raw emotions, and strong emotions whether it is hope, fear or anger are each strongly mobilizing forces.

Oligarchic Cabinet

To return to the donor class, it is rather strange how the candidate they did not initially support turned out to be just fine for their interests. When the Republican nomination came up, the donors finally backed Trump. The Koch brothers said they wanted to support down-ballot Republican candidates, but they were not as terrified of Trump as they would have been of Sanders. Trump made clear that he expected the full financial backing of the oligarchs now that he was the party-bearer. Upon his election, the public held its breath on Trump's cabinet appointments, which were all either part of the oligarchic elite (oil executive Rex Tillerson became secretary of state, former Goldman Sachs banker Steven Mnuchin became secretary of treasury, heiress Betsy DeVos became secretary of education etc.), standard Republican politicians of the conservative (i.e. pro-oligarchic) variety (senator Jeff Sessions as attorney general; Congressman Mike Mulvaney as budget chairman etc.), or retired generals (chief of staff John Kelly, defense secretary Jim Mattis etc.). Only the generals did not clearly represent the oligarchic elite, though they were part of the military-industrial complex, one of the few departments that were beefed up with the Trump budget.

Pierre Bourdieu had distinguished between the nurturing left hand of the state (social security administration, education, health care, social services etc.) and the punishing right hand of the state (finance, treasury, justice, military, internal security) (in Droit and Ferenczi 1992), and it is quite evidently only the right hand that is prevailing under the Trump administration. This makes Trump one of the most regressive US presidents, thus standing in line with policies that battered the popular classes since at least Ronald Reagan.

By appointing wealthy heirs like Betsy DeVos or businesspeople like Wilbur Ross, Trump's cabinet became by far the wealthiest cabinet in US history. This cabinet is a big change from historical precedent, where the oligarchs control politicians (mostly lawyers by training) indirectly via the financing of elections. But in the current cabinet, the middlemen have been partly displaced by the oligarchs themselves, most obvious of which is the real estate mogul Trump himself. Ironically, it is precisely Trump's wealth, which had allowed his message of "draining the swamp" to resonate given that he genuinely could afford to not care about the views of his fellow oligarchs. But he was nothing more than a wolf in sheep's clothing.

The problem of politics, as had been noticed by Max Weber (1978) long ago, is that even the most populist of all leaders still has to rely on an army of bureaucrats to run the country. The disruptive cultural effect of the Mongolian conquest of the Chinese empire was tempered by the Chinese literati that formed the bureaucratic class, which continued to run the empire as before at least in rural areas (in the big cities, there was a substitution for Central Asian and European officials). With the exception of Trump's own family (his three children and son-in-law Jared Kushner), Trump does not really trust anyone else that closely, and as real estate mogul it wasn't necessary to trust many more people, but the federal government is a giant bureaucracy which needs to be re-staffed whenever a new president enters office (Collins 2016).

Failing Trump Administration?

In very important ways, the Trump administration had appeared to be a failure: the Muslim travel ban was halted in courts, though most recently the Supreme Court has granted the ban. The coal miners, who were promised a restoration of jobs, cannot hope to return to employment when natural gas is displacing coal use. The much feared wall on the Mexican border, which "Mexico will pay for", turns out to be rather modest in scope, and quite nonsensical given that there are not as many Mexicans coming across the border as in the past.

The biggest failure appeared to be in health care, where 3 Republican senators proved the crucial vote to sink the Obamacare repeal in the Senate. But Obamacare is not out of the woods, because the tax bill will pull the plug on the mandate and the financial penalty for not carrying health insurance, which could sky-rocket insurance premiums. Many insurance companies had already pulled out of the insurance market. The Trump administration had carried out administrative measures, which already weakened pillars of Obamacare. It, for instance, shortened the time period of the open enrollment, which is limited to a little over a month every year, which is a peculiar arrangement given that other insurance policies (life, car, home etc.) don't have such an open enrollment window. The administration also reduced advertising expenses, such that fewer new people are reached to sign up for insurance. The essential weakness of Obamacare is that it is fragile to political attacks by an unfavorable administration, and it builds on the dysfunction of the existing health insurance system, which is largely built on administrative waste and greed. It takes enlightened leaders unencumbered by oligarchic lobbying interests to promote policies that are more durable, such as a single-payer Medicare for all system.

The repeal of the Dodd-Frank financial policy had long been announced by Trump, which he alleged to prevent job creation via the limitation on reckless bank lending procedures. While the policy remains largely intact, Republican legislators are pushing for its repeal, which could accelerate another round of speculation.

Oligarchic Regulatory Success

On another front, Trump has been a splendid success: by appointing an EPA (Environmental Protection Agency) administrator, who was the former attorney general of Oklahoma (Scott Pruitt) and has sued the EPA on behalf of oil, gas and coal companies to diminish government regulation on CO_2 emissions or environmental protection measures, the fossil fuel interests have come to prevail, as environmental regulation is continuously removed, even when it comes at the price of polluted groundwater and increased sickness in the population (Worland 2017).

Organized labor, which has been on a downward trajectory since the 1950s, as deindustrialization, automation, outsourcing, the displacement of labor and pro-business government policy have combined to exert pressure on labor unions, got another shellacking by the new administration, which appointed two new members to the NLRB (National Labor Relations Board), thus tilting the balance to 3 Republicans and 2 Democrats. The business community demands a deregulation of franchisors (like McDonalds), who were previously ordered to maintain decent working conditions to the employees in the franchises, the repeal of so-called micro-unions and a slowing down of union election procedures (Wheeler 2017). In August 2016, the NLRB had given graduate students at universities the right to organize in a union, because research and teaching assistants provided necessary labor to their universities. Universities are capable of keeping a low-cost and docile workforce by maintaining the legal fiction that a stipend is not really a wage payment, and thus graduate student activity is not really work. Subsequently, some university students jumped on the bandwagon and filed petitions for a unionization vote and certification of student labor unions, which succeeded in some cases. But the time window had been rather narrow, as the new Trump appointments to the NLRB suggest that the NLRB will be less favorable to unions, and the university administration is hoping to drag their feet to effectively prevent unionization (Flaherty 2017). The same fate might await home health aides, airport staff and other workers in the service sector that had campaigned on unionization. As the government sides with big business, oligarchic interests prevail.

Another deregulation example is the Federal Communication Commission, which is led by Ajit Pai (former legal counselor to Verizon), who wants to repeal the net neutrality rule, which has prevented Verizon and Comcast from charging higher rates or slowing speed for different users using different websites (Fung 2017). Given the quasi-monopoly power of the major internet providers, the profits will almost certainly increase while the quality of consumer services will decrease, at least for people with less resources.

Oligarchic Tax Bill

The latest sign of the success of the oligarchic agenda is the passage of two versions of the tax bill in the House and the Senate, which somewhat differ in their scope, but both have in common their intent to shift a substantial amount of economic resources from the bottom and the middle of the income distribution to the top. Reported here are some of the provisions in the Senate plan, which are slightly less regressive than the House given the much smaller positive margin of Republican votes there.

(1) The corporate tax rate will be reduced from 35 to 20%, which is permanent in the tax code, i.e. does not require re-authorization by Congress in the future. This is by itself a staggering provision and is

justified by the Republican leaders as encouraging the repatriation of foreign capital, which will magically result in job growth, even as some honest corporate leaders claim that this will not really happen. It is also remarkable that the Republican Party has a zeal to reduce the nominal tax rate, when the effective corporate tax rate is rather low in international average (13%). The long-term trend has been that the US government became less and less dependent on corporate tax revenues, and here they are gifted with even more presents to hand out to top shareholders and executives. Another corporate provision is to allow a complete tax write-off for investments in buildings for the next five years.

(2) The top income tax rate will drop from 39.6% to 38.5%. The Senate plan keeps the seven current tax brackets, but shifts up the thresholds. The top tax threshold will shift from 470,000 to 1 million dollars

(3) The estate tax threshold is doubled to 11 million dollars for individuals and 22 million dollars for couples, which reduces the overall take from this revenue source, which only affects the richest people.

(4) The state and local tax deduction, which has a greater benefit to high tax states along the coasts and mostly Democratic, is completely scrapped.

(5) The personal deduction of 4,050 dollars will be scrapped and replaced by an increase in standard deduction (12,000 for individuals, 24,000 for married couples).

(6) The individual health insurance mandate will be scrapped, which will undermine a key pillar of Obamacare. (Long 2017)

The first part of the Republican agenda is to ensure that the donors get what they want. House Republican Chris Collins said that he could either vote to pass the tax bill or not bother to call his rich donors ever again (Scott 2017). This will inevitably drive up the fiscal deficit, as 1.4 trillion dollars are added to the debt in 10 years, which comes on top of the already projected debt increase without any legal change (Carney 2017). The second part of the agenda is to blame the deficit in the federal budget on Social Security, Medicare and other programs, which will then receive cuts, a point that Senator Marco Rubio admitted to (Hiltzik 2017). In a heated exchange in the senate between Bernie Sanders and Pat Toomey, the former pressed Toomey on whether he would cut the entitlement programs in the future, and Toomey gave the evasive answer that *current* beneficiaries would experience no cuts to their benefits, which

Sanders called out on as suggesting that future recipients will experience enormous cutbacks. Toomey claimed that if the Republicans wanted to slash entitlement spending, they could have packed it in the current legislation. But that is disingenuous, because there is nothing that will prevent Republican politicians in the future from cutting these programs given the enlarged deficit following their tax policy.

Conclusion

The ascendancy of the Trump presidency has given the faint hope to the working class base that Trump will have the charismatic ability to shift the balance of the political forces on their behalf. The reality, however, is that his election reinforces the power and influence of the oligarchic elite, in large part because Trump himself belongs to the ruling elite. David Koch may have been a peripheral figure 37 years ago on the ticket of the Libertarian Party, but their success is best achieved behind closed doors. Domhoff (1967) maintains that within the corporate elite there is a moderate and an ultra-conservative faction with the former being okay with some Keynesian investment policies, while the latter want to massively slash taxes and otherwise reduce government spending. To the extent that the latter succeeds, there is no corresponding pressure to balance the books by immediately slashing spending, which is, in fact, increasing with regard to military expenditures, which reminds us of the functionalist Neo-Marxist account that rising state expenditures that are associated with the social costs and infrastructure requirements created by capitalism will generate a fiscal crisis of the state (O'Connor 1973).

However, the tax cut agenda for the rich will provide no temporary economic stimulation, because rising corporate profits and shareholder returns to the wealthy in the past have not contributed to a jobs boom (Lazonick 2014). A jobs boom can at best happen if the lower and the middle class receive higher incomes given their low propensity to save, which stimulates the economy. The Republicans claim that they are providing a tax cut agenda for the lower and middle classes too, though these rate cuts are sunset at 2026, and for even lower income people various cuts in tax deductibility will ultimately eat up the small gains they have made via the tax cuts.

It is hard to imagine how the political economy effects of the tax cut can drive an even more regressive agenda. The leaders of the tech and finance companies have already raked massive profits, and the Trump deregulatory agenda will pile up more short-term gains for big oil, fossil fuels and real estate developers. The ever more extreme oligarchic demands placed on the state will further sap resources that could be used to retrain the workforce or invest in their education. Structural factors like technological change and the unrestrained mobility of capital will further enhance inequality and contribute to less stable and more precarious employment relationships.

The only realistic hope for the masses is some external force that will shift the balance of power in their favor. Scheidel (2017) argues that only four interventions can realistically reduce extreme levels of inequality that have built up as a result of the path-dependence of allowing private property to accumulate: war, social revolution, state breakdown and pandemics. He does not believe that democracy can dent the level of inequality, as the rich continue to control the political institutions that make up the democracy. It will take some time before progressive counter-mobilization can oppose the normalized path toward oligarchy.

Chinese Migrant Workers' Displacement and the New Stage of Development

Posted on <u>December 10, 2017</u>

When a few weeks ago, fire broke out in a two-story building in Beijing, 19 people died, most of them migrant workers from the countryside (Tan 2017). Migrant workers could only afford to live in certain neighborhoods in Beijing, and now the Beijing city government used the fire as a pretext to evict migrant workers for "safety" reasons giving only a few days of notice. Never mind that the city could have taken some responsibility in improving safety precautions for the migrant worker residences. But the real objective of the city government was not to provide decent housing or safety for the millions of migrant workers in the city, but to fulfill their objective of removing "low-end" population from the city perimeter (Huang 2017).

It is the objective of the city government to limit their population to 23 million people by 2020, while it is already near 22 million at the moment. The enormous population growth in the recent past reflects the country's trend toward urbanization, a process that is intimately linked with capitalist development. The factories and service industries are mostly concentrated in the large cities, which then also creates the purchasing power among a local middle class, which can then afford to hire cheap workers that are recruited from the countryside. Important services are in the delivery of food and other items, and staff for shops and restaurants.

It is the historic lack of regulation of migrant worker movement, which facilitated their en masse movement into the big cities and fueled its growth and development. The enormous convenience of deliveries in the cities is based on the low cost of labor: When I was in Beijing, I ordered low-cost drinking water shipments, which was handled by one man along with his wife and two children, who would sit at the motor vehicle downstairs, loading and unloading the vehicle.

In addition to the classic story of capitalist exploitation of low-cost labor, which sought to escape the poor and uneconomic circumstances in the farm at home, the Chinese local governments have maintained the hukou, the household registration system, which works like an internal passport. While any Chinese citizen is free to live anywhere they desired, their access to education, health care and social services was determined by the possession of a local hukou. Since living in the large city was preferred by most people, the city hukou became the highest coveted good, especially in the four major metropolis: Beijing, Shanghai, Guangzhou and Shenzhen. Only under exceptional circumstances are outsiders capable of acquiring a local hukou in the large city, such as with marriage to a local resident or working for the city government or an industry/ field the government regarded as high-skill/ strategic. But each of these outcomes were rather unlikely for rural migrant workers without strong social connections to people in higher classes.

The consequence of classic capitalist exploitation as well as hukou-based government/ institutional discrimination was the subsidization of the urban middle class as well as the ruling class consisting of the Communist Party cadre and the capitalist business owners via the rural migrant workers. While rapid economic development has provided many opportunities for most Chinese people (with over 700 million people lifted out of poverty since the economic opening reforms in the late 1970s), the class segmentation described above created one of the largest gaps between the rich and the poor. The Gini coefficient, an index of inequality, had increased from 0.30 to 0.55 between 1980 and 2012 (Wikipedia, "Income Inequality in China").

In the meantime, the Beijing city government hopes to attract more high-skilled migrants, who will contribute more taxes to the treasury, but even with more high-skilled workers, there are certain low-skilled jobs that are not yet automated, and these positions still need to be filled, but regardless, the low-end population has to leave from the perspective of the government.

What happens with the migrant workers? Some of the migrant workers are forced to return to their hometown and search for employment opportunities that are a lot worse than what they find in Beijing. There is a way out for some of the migrant workers. JD.com, which is a major delivery company, had announced it would provide housing for its workers, who were affected by the demolition (Huang 2017). It is quite understandable why these service delivery companies are quite interested in helping out their workers. There is already some evidence that the evictions are exacerbating the trend toward labor shortages, which could be interpreted as a threat to the business model of these delivery companies (Yang and Liu 2017).

This raises the important question of what the next stage of Chinese development will look like given the contradiction between the government objective of limiting the population and the drain on city resources provided by endless expansion, and the capitalist objective of expanding the population to cheaply service the ever-growing consumer market and provide profitable outlets.

The Communist Party is really forced to walk a fine line between promoting their capitalist enterprises, maintaining ecological sustainability within the city and protecting what they deem the "low-end" population. But we also know that accomplishing all of these objectives becomes more and more difficult. Aside from the migrant removal, the party is becoming increasingly aggressive in cracking down on massive environmental polluters that have made breathing very difficult in most coastal cities. If China is quick and effective enough in shifting to alternative energy, then the effects on economic growth might not be noticeable, but given the complication and length of transition time, the economy will inevitably be negatively impacted. In addition, government regulators are increasingly cracking down on housing investments, a preferred tool of speculation by affluent households, thus pushing down house values and removing one area of domestic investment growth.

Another factor that will restrain the capitalists is the slow going demographic transformation via an aging population and a declining labor force. This demographic shift will lift worker wages, and might explain the recently strong wage gains of manufacturing production workers, even as nominal labor unions are found under the tight leash of the Communist Party (Friedman 2014; Estlund 2017). On a more positive note for the capitalists, rising wages will promote the growth of a middle class, which will fuel a virtuous cycle of rising consumption and rising wages.

It is to some extent the overwhelming strength of the party government, which has fueled past development and it will do so in the immediate future. But as the economic growth rate inevitably declines with every new attempt of less and less effective investment strategies- either in export, domestic investment or foreign investment- certain social and distributional struggles are bound to increase. Workers might take it upon their own hands to establish an independent union, as the state union is not perceived as giving them fair benefits. NGOs might be more inclined to point out official human rights abuses. Environmental groups might want more regulation of polluters and so forth.

The coronation of Xi Jinping for a second presidential term, which has also been accompanied by his anointment as a high leader similar to Mao Zedong, the party founder, and the lack of appointment of an obvious successor to his own rule, marks the apparent stabilization of the political regime, and reflects the international breeze of authoritarianism, which has been felt from the Philippines, Russia and the United States- of all places. Xi's political stabilization is precisely about pre-empting potential social unrest when economic growth inevitably declines. For Xi there have been two principal challenges: (1) removing potential opponents from the ranks of CCP leadership, and (2) retaining political legitimacy in the eyes of the Chinese people.

The beginning of his rule in 2012 involved the fulfillment of these objectives via continued credit-driven infrastructure-based growth financed by the numerous shadow banks and implemented by the local governments. That strategy is now increasingly facing limits as leverage on the debt rises and make it harder to repay, thus the greater focus on foreign investments via One Belt One Road, which creates another can of worms of how to protect foreign-bound investments.

Another linchpin to Xi's strategy of power consolidation was the corruption crackdown, targeting other high officials, most importantly the popular former mayor of Chongqing, Bo Xilai. One can naturally take Xi by his word, and claim that the corruption crackdown was genuinely about removing bad apples and restoring popular faith in the party, but if some powerful internal opponents are removed along the way, all the better.

But the anti-corruption efforts are not enough over the long term to please a restive middle class that demands other things like democratization, free speech and the protection of human and social rights, the latter of which being violated by the example of the migrant worker expulsion. Xi's rule also meant more persecution, arrests, prohibition of public gatherings, monitoring of social media activity, social media censorship and other forms of punishment, surveillance and control. The agony to regime critics and NGOs in the form of direct punishment or self-censorship are tremendous, and contrast sharply with the largely open atmosphere in the pre-Xi era. In a recent example, a Chinese man texted to his friends a joke about an extramarital affair of a senior government official, which was tracked by the government and resulted in his arrest, interrogation and a few days of jail time (Dou 2017).

The government's surveillance capacity has substantially increased, as Chinese people increasingly rely on data and online services to conduct much of their transactions and social interactions. In order to remain within the law, internet giants like Alibaba or Tencent have to cooperate closely with the government, which includes handing over data to the government so they can censor messages or prosecute individuals posting information they don't like. I have seen no confirmation on this, but I would not be surprised that censorship and prosecution can increasingly be done via algorithmic tracking tools without having a human sifting through all of the billions of messages that get exchanged daily all over the country.

Jeremy Bentham (1843) had long ago described the panopticon as a prison, where prisoners think they are permanently observed such that they self-regulate their behavior to pre-empt punishment. A worse version is George Orwell's (1949) depiction of the surveillance state in *1984*, where the protagonist ultimately surrenders to the power of Big Brother: "But it was all right, everything was all right, the struggle was finished. He had won the victory over himself. He loved Big Brother."

If the total surveillance state shall succeed, it would begin in China, where the government is already setting up a social credit system (by 2020) to allocate points to individuals based on their behavior, e.g. how filial are they in their duties to their parents? The trustworthiness index which is created is publicly visible and will determine whether you can get a mortgage, a job, education, date or take the airplane (Botsman 2017). The Chinese society is already quite used to test scores and assessments in their education system, which determines high school, college attendance and ultimately socio-economic success. But the social credit score takes it to another level, and if introduced successfully will put people on an eternal treadmill of mutual comparisons and competition (and will ironically decrease trust).

But even the most repressive regime has certain limitations, because Mencius' principle of the Mandate of Heaven (Nuyen 2013), which prioritizes on regime stability emanating from popular legitimacy, has never been deactivated, neither in China nor elsewhere. As for the migrant workers, can their forceful removal from the big cities be considered a vehicle for social change in this new phase of capitalist development?

The Misrule of Zimbabwe with Uncertain Outcomes
Posted on December 19, 2017

With Robert Mugabe's handover of power last month, his 37-year rule over Zimbabwe came to an end. The streets of Zimbabwe were filled by celebrations, as a much disliked and incompetent government was finally removed from power. But it would be difficult for regular Zimbabweans to rejoice given that the post-Mugabe era is still mired with uncertainty. I begin this blogpost with a biography of Mugabe, a description of political events that immediately resulted in the ouster of Mugabe, and then evaluate the economic history of Zimbabwe, which gives good clues to the general reader why he was ousted.

Robert Mugabe was born in 1924 and grew up as a son of working class parents in southern Rhodesia, which was to become Zimbabwe. His father was a carpenter and his mother was a Catholic teacher. In his early years, he was not very politically active, but because he excelled academically he gained a scholarship to study at a University in South Africa, where he became a member of the African National Congress, learning about the nascent independence movement in sub-Saharan Africa. He then lived in Northern Rhodesia, which was to become Zambia, working as a teacher, while reading Marxist and anti-colonial literature.

In 1960 he returned to Southern Rhodesia, and witnessed the arrest of National Democratic Party (pro-independence) activists, which encouraged him to join the revolutionary struggle to overthrow colonialism. The anti-colonial parties split into two after internal disputes: the ZANU (Zimbabwe African National Union), to which Mugabe belonged, and ZAPU (Zimbabwe African People's Union). Mugabe was imprisoned for his activism in 1963 and was not released until 1975. From 1964 to 1979, the country was run as Rhodesia, which was de facto independent from British colonial rule. The prime minister was Ian Smith, a Rhodesian-born British, which was still regarded as illegitimate by the majority black population, who wanted to transfer power and influence to the black majority. More on that later.

Under greater political pressure to end white dominance, Mugabe was released from prison, and promptly joined guerrilla warfare, giving speeches and disseminating radio broadcasts. Mugabe had called for the overthrow of the white Rhodesia government, the expropriation of white-owned land and the transformation of Rhodesia into a Marxist one party state. White rule came to an end as even the white government of South Africa and the UK government had pressured the Smith administration to give up white rule. In 1979, Smith first ceded the premiership after parliamentary elections, which handed power to Abel Muzorewa, a politically moderate black bishop.

Another general election in 1980 delivered most popular votes to Mugabe's ZANU-PF, which promptly made him prime minister in the newly founded Zimbabwe. He gradually built up his power structure and clientele such that by 1987 he was powerful enough to change the constitution to increase his power by merging the presidency with the premiership with him becoming the president. He also purged all remaining white parliamentarians, who were leading the formal opposition against his rule.

One might say that the dictatorial takeover of the first black leader in Zimbabwe and the lack of institutional constraints on Mugabe allowed his rule to last for so long and prevent his downfall. But surely no one would have cared if Mugabe was a good policymaker and decided to stay for so many years. Why would you overthrow a regime that ruled so well?

What immediately brought down Mugabe was his fateful decision to push out his vice president, Emmerson Mnangagwa, who had attempted to replace his boss as far back as 2005. What made Mnangagwa's position so precarious was a feud with Mugabe's wife Grace, who herself was jockeying for the top job upon her husband's death. This feuding of wives reminds me of Jiang Qing, Mao Zedong's scheming wife, who was aiming for political power, but was imprisoned after Mao's death when she turned against his chosen successor Hua Guofeng.

Grace Mugabe then convinced her husband to sack Mnangagwa, who disappeared into exile in South Africa. But Mnangagwa had powerful allies in the military, chiefly Constantino Chiwenga, the chief of the Zimbabwe Defence Forces, which hated Grace Mugabe more than anyone else. The military then held Mugabe under house arrest, forcing him to resign, which Mugabe initially refused. Now the suppressed parliamentarians of his own ZANU-PF party rose up to pass a motion for impeachment, but before the vote was formally held, Mugabe tendered his resignation, which led to the installation of Mnangagwa as the new president. But Mnangagwa is also part of the ZANU-PF, and we can't say much yet about how much he wants to change a political system that had brought much discontent to Zimbabwe.

Now to the question of what created the political discontent that led to the ouster of Mugabe as president. At the heart of it is economic mismanagement. Since the British formally colonized Rhodesia in 1890 under Cecil Rhodes (conveniently, the country was named after him), most of the valuable land was apportioned to the British and other white settlers. But while the white settlers were certainly keeping the spoils of wealth away from the black majority residents, who felt they should gain a fair share in what is after all their land, it was also the white settlers, who brought in the knowledge and cultural capital to use the land to the best advantage to produce cash crops like tobacco or sugar. Blacks were forced to live in so-called tribal areas, which happens to be the land that the white colonizers deemed unworthy for plant cultivation. The poor quality of tribal land soil and the associated overcrowding and lack of resources there forced many blacks to move to white settlements and work as their servants, reminding blacks of their inferior social status.

The political tensions resulted in strong yearnings for a black administration, because white rule will never result in a voluntary surrender of the control of the most important economic resource, i.e. land. Foreign and domestic pressure resulted in the end to white government in 1980, and Mugabe was supposed to fulfill the aspirations of the black majority for economic justice. But Mugabe was less inclined toward violence and more toward reconciliation upon becoming elected to the government. He realized that it made no sense to alienate the white landowners, as a mass exodus of whites would result in the economic destabilization of Zimbabwe.

In addition, there were external incentives for Mugabe to not expropriate white farm land, as the UK government in the Lancaster Agreement had agreed to grant full independence to Zimbabwe and help the gradual, voluntary transfer of land from whites to blacks using foreign aid and subsidies to the Zimbabwean state to ensure this transfer. But for the UK, the key was the voluntary consent, i.e. Zimbabwe could not simply expropriate white farmland.

But the exodus of whites started as far back as the early-1980s. The black population regarded the transfer process as being too slow (as white farmers were unwilling to give up their only property), and a bigger problem was the corruption that was endemic to this land transfer scheme. In other words, even if the state acquired land, it was preferably given to high-level generals, friends and family of Mugabe and other high officials.

Over the course of the 1990s, the perceived lack of progress had convinced the Mugabe administration that it became necessary to increasingly use force to transfer land to blacks, which forced whites to take up arms in their own defense and accelerated the white exodus to mostly western countries. In 1997, the new Labour government in the UK pointed to the violation of the spirit of the Lancaster House Agreement and suspended any more payments to the Zimbabwe government. Other donors in the World Bank and the IMF also reduced financial help, and all of a sudden Zimbabwe was driven to the wall.

While the economic situation was deteriorating, Mugabe still scraped together funds to engage in a war in the Congo Civil War, supporting president Kabila. When the soldiers returned as veterans their pensions contributed to another drain on the national budget. Mugabe also distracted the public from the economy by increasing attacks on the LGBT community, branding them as immoral elements to society. Despite these distractions, the constitutional referendum (another power increase for Mugabe) ended in defeat, and parliamentary elections in 2000 resulted in the loss of the two-third majority of Mugabe's ZANU-PF.

For Mugabe, it was the straw that broke the camel's back: instead of selectively expropriating white farmers, they now had to be systematically expropriated. From 2000 to 2013, all of the remaining white-owned farmland had been expropriated, providing over 230,000 Zimbabwean households with access to land. The mechanism through which the expropriation campaign was conducted was extreme: mostly young people were instructed to march on white-owned farmlands, initially with drums, song and dance, but then also with guns and bare hands. They drove out the white owners and their black workers, who then faced unemployment.

The expropriation campaign proved to be an economic disaster, as economic production declined substantially. The former bread basket of southern Africa turned into a malnourished country, where 45% of the population lacks sufficient food. Agricultural exports used to provide revenues, which now vanished. Western sanctions exacerbated the financial and economic situation. Life expectancy dropped and the unemployment rate hit 95%. One-fourth of the population escaped via emigration. What went wrong? Firstly, the new black landowners lacked the know-how of running these enterprises and equipment. Second, they lacked access to capital, because the banks did not consider the land as theirs, which prevented the farmers from using the land as collateral. The third problem was the already mentioned corruption. By grabbing all the land held by the whites, 4.8% of the land went to well–connected businesspeople, 3.7% to military and security service personnel and 5% to other well-connected officials of ZANU-PF (probably an underestimate).

With the economy collapsing, Zimbabwe continued to have to pay veterans pensions if it did not want to risk an uprising, so the central bank resorted to money-printing to pay the government's bills, which resulted in hyperinflation. Soon, people had to push wheelbarrows of cash to acquire basic necessities like bread. Investments diminished to negligible amounts and household savings were essentially eliminated. In 2009, the government, now in a power-sharing agreement with opposition leader Tsvangirai, finally abandoned its currency and took on the US dollar as official currency. There was, ultimately, some economic recovery, because China became a major buyer of Zimbabwe's goods. Zimbabwe also had their international credit lines opened when they signed away mineral rights to foreign corporations (platinum, coal, iron ore, gold, diamonds).

The temporary economic stabilization via dollarization came to an end as the 2013 elections returned the ZANU-PF with a landslide victory (with vote rigging as part of the opposition's accusation). Mugabe promptly increased the size of his civil service and pushed for the further indigenization of the economy, by requiring non-black owned enterprises to be handed over to blacks. In 2016, resource constraints resulted in the laying off of 25,000 civil servants, and pleas to international donors like the IMF and the World Bank to re-open their credit lines. Besides bad political institutions, droughts as a result of climate change have become more severe, thus putting even more stress on a weakened agricultural system. Health indicators like life expectancy, cholera cases and HIV show signs of deterioration and the mass unemployment problem has not really been resolved.

In conclusion, Robert Mugabe's economic policy, which is built on racial resentment, corruption and incompetence, proved to be so catastrophic that his rule was no longer tolerable, even for the ruling class itself. There was no mass uprising to remove Mugabe, with the proximate cause being the ouster of his vice president Emmerson Mnangagwa, but it is really quite astounding how he could remain in power for so long.

Regressive New Administration in Vienna
Posted on <u>December 25, 2017</u>

With the onset of the new administration in Austria, it is worthwhile to examine parts of their government agenda, some of which makes sense. The administration shows commitment to shift to alternative energy and away from fossil fuels. They want to increase the speed of approving infrastructure programs, and want to strengthen the dual-track vocational/ educational program (DerStandard 2017). All of these things do make sense.

But the problem is that the new government is a notable shift to the right (Schulmeister 2017). They have appealed to the voting masses by promising to be harsh on refugees, even as the number of refugees has substantially declined with the migrant deal with Turkey, which involved a bribe to Turkey so they don't release any more Middle East refugees. Their major promise has been to slash the refugee payments in half, which would lower their standard of living if it does not get compensated by higher in-kind services. The logic is that the refugees shall have no better benefits than domestic nationals, which is a rather disingenuous claim, because in total nationals will always be entitled to greater benefits than foreign nationals, even if they are refugees. In addition, any refugee costs are necessary at the beginning because it takes time for the refugees to pick up the language, and the skills of refugees to become certified by local authorities such that they can find their way smoothly into the labor market. To exclude the refugees from essential benefits will complicate their integration, and could push them into criminality.

But even worse, the conservative-nationalist government is throwing sand in the eyes of the voters by pushing for a series of regressive measures, which include

1. A reduction of the corporation tax, which will lighten the tax burden on higher earners, i.e. people, who control vast fortunes in enterprises.

2. The hotel and tourism industry will get a tax break

3. The expansion of the child care tax credit is only applicable for people, who pay income taxes, which is not applicable to the lowest earners (less than 11,000 euros a year).

4. The new administration will re-introduce tuition fees of 500 euros a semester that were abolished under the SPO

administration in 2008 and would only have to be paid by students, who took more than an extra year to complete their studies (e.g. if bachelor studies take 3 years, the first 4 years are free, but the fifth year and above costs 363 euros a semester). This could discourage some people from working class families to study, or force them to take part-time jobs, which they are obliged to in the current system to afford living expenses, but it will just become harder.

5. Permission of a 12-hour work day at the plant level. Previously, employers could impose a 12-hour work day only with the approval of the trade union, which would then come with overtime pay, but if discretion is given to the employers at the plant level to impose a 12-hour work day those overtime regulations will fall by the wayside, making the workers worse off. At a time when automation and digitalization threaten jobs, it is questionable why working time shall be expanded at all. The administration claims that the 12-hour rule will only come with the consent of employees, but in a slack labor market it is not clear whether it will be all that voluntary and even if it were, it won't be good for worker health.

6. A current law prohibiting the arbitrary rise in rents in inner cities will be repealed. Landlords should also be able to raise their rents if they can prove an upgrading of the property, which could create an upward market pressure for rents and make cities like Vienna as expensive to live in as many other western European cities. It should be remarked that the OVP (conservatives) is serving their landlord clientele with these legislative changes.

7. The long-term unemployment benefit ("Notstand", best translated as emergency welfare), which can currently be drawn indefinitely after the expiry of the regular unemployment benefit (after a year), taking up 92% of the value of the unemployment benefit, will be abolished. It will be replaced by the minimum security welfare ("Mindestsicherung"), which is subject to strict asset tests. Henceforth, benefit claimants have to meet an asset test of 4,300 euros that they cannot exceed to qualify. The size of the benefit is also no longer tied to

the past unemployment benefit, but to the length of time paying into the system, which might benefit older workers with longer work histories more than younger workers. The Austrian government is taking the German Hartz reforms of the early 2000s as role model, which converted long-term unemployed people into low-income workers.

8. The previous government's policy to create 20,000 jobs for workers 50+, who tend to fall into the category of long-term unemployed is scrapped. Employers no longer find these older workers valuable given their high wage costs. The scrapping of these public jobs for older workers is doubly cruel when combined with the scrapping of the unemployment benefit.

9. The maximum commute time for workers will be increased to 2.5 hours a day and the requirement to claim jobs in one's area of training will be scrapped.

10. The number of occupations that companies can draw workers from non-EU countries will increase from 11 to 63, which will further increase labor competition in the domestic labor market. (No such laws apply to EU countries for whom there is freedom of movement.)

11. The social security contributions are going to be reduced. The question is what will happen to social spending when this occurs. There are already indications that the welfare state will be more restricted at a time when there are many more precarious employees.

There is no doubt that the voters have involuntary voted for a more neoliberal administration.

Hikikomori: Isolated By Choice or Force?
Posted on December 30, 2017

One interesting social phenomenon in Japan involve so-called hikikomori, which is best translated as acute social withdrawal, loners, hermits. These are young people from their teens into their 40s, mostly male, who don't leave their bedroom, usually in their parents' house. There are estimates of a million people in this condition. What are they doing in the comfort of their bedroom? They may be playing video games, watching TV, listening to music, reading their favorite comics or simply staring at the ceiling most of the day. For some introverted people in the West this might be a desirable way of living, but for me this would be like a boring hell over time. The ideal lifestyle is a mixture of solitude and reflection mixed with intermittent periods of social interaction. Schopenhauer had argued that the intelligent person is happy to live alone, but Aristotle was also right in pointing out that we are political and therefore social animals.

More importantly, we have to ask ourselves how it is that young Japanese men remove themselves so far from society in a way that does not happen in other similarly high industrialized countries in the West. These are the factors favoring hikikomori (acute social withdrawal, loners, hermits):

Middle class affluence and strong family values
It could be that living in a rich society among middle class people it is possible to keep children into adulthood. Not all middle class societies parents want to keep their children for such an extended period of time, but among Latino and eastern European culture I can tell anecdotally that it would be inconceivable for these middle class people to charge their children to live with them if they can afford to keep them on for longer. But staying with parents into adulthood (a phenomenon that is spreading all over the west) does not necessarily mean that one turns into a hikikomori. If I decided to stay with my parents into adulthood (not a desirable prospect), I would certainly want to spend as much time as I can outside the house.

Parental overprotectiveness
One of the reasons that Japanese children can cut themselves off from society is because their overprotective parents would not dare to interfere with the "home life" of their children. Parents certainly

do notice that the children refuse to get out of their room, but the hesitancy of parents to drag out their children makes this phenomenon possible to begin with. One might counter that children will be resistant, but it is the confrontation that would have an impact on their behavior. But this factor merely explains how children can be stuck in their rooms, and not why they decide to stay in their rooms in the first place.

Deteriorating job opportunities for the youth and negative impacts on the marriage market

There is an important economic trajectory that is ongoing in the most developed capitalist countries: there no longer is rapid economic growth, which could provide the cushy, stable middle-class jobs for males. Automation and offshoring are further factors disadvantaging middle class employment in rich countries. In addition, another negative drag on the economy is the fact that the population is shrinking as women are not having enough children and the Japanese government is unwilling to sacrifice the ethnic homogeneity of the Japanese people. The lack of employment security has a negative consequence in the marriage and dating market for men all over the developed world, but has an even greater negative impact in Confucian societies like in Japan, where the inability of the male breadwinner to get stable employment discredits them in the eyes of women to provide for family life.

The lack of a female partner provides an incentive to stay in the parents' house, while active family formation tends to result in new household formation. The lack of marriageable men, in turn, forces women to also seek for employment and greater economic independence could also reduce the pressure to get married and wait longer. (It is by no means argued that women are having a better time in the job market than men given the gender pay gap and employment discrimination against women.)

Competitive school system

Increased competitiveness in the job market with the decline of stable, middle class jobs also affects the competitive school system. In a Confucian society, parents and the society highly value their children to be as educated as is possible. As such the pressure on each child is enormous to perform well academically. Even as some education ministry officials are recognizing the importance of rest and reduce weekend schooling, parents compensate by sending their children to attend cram schools over the weekend and evenings every day. There is a lot to be criticized about an education system that overvalues rote memorization over individual creativity, but one could imagine how much worse it becomes when the number and proportion of good jobs are decreasing.

People's internal push to get another credential increases, and as more people are getting a degree it becomes less valuable, a classic case of credential inflation (Collins 1979). But as educational expectations increase, so does the frustration of children, who cannot perform up to those high standards set by their parents. To escape the education pressure, children opt to stay at home. Given that they lack the credential to get taken at a regular job, they are forced to either work low-skilled jobs or for the more fortunate children of middle class families become devoted hikikomori.

Collectivist Culture

In a collectivist culture it is very important to fit in with the dominant cultural values of the society, including high educational performance and attaining a decent middle class job, and in the absence of such face rumor, ostracism and bullying. The extreme sense of collectivism is also remarked by Japanese-Americans or Japanese-Brazilians, who don't really feel at home when setting foot on their ancestral homeland, because they don't speak Japanese so well or don't understand all the cultural mores, which makes them different in the eyes of the indigenous Japanese (Lie 2004). The high cost of collectivism is the lack of individuality, and the inevitable non-conformism leaves no other social space other than the bedroom in the parental house. In a largely individualist society within urban contexts, other people don't really care about your individual life choices, which offers freedom to pursue one's life choices without social exclusion, which Simmel (1903) had remarked as one of the positive elements of city life in the west.

What to Do?

Given that it is undesirable to have so many lives wasted the challenge will be to get these men out of their bedrooms. It will be an acute problem for people who have stayed at home for decades and then their parents die, in which case they will inherit the house and savings, but what happens when the savings are used up? The irony is that once the hermits become too comfortable in their nest they will have lost much of their socializing skills, and are not very receptive to outsiders coming in to tell them to get out. What almost certainly has to happen is that people have to have economic perspectives, which would allow them to participate in society. When robots take over the jobs, which is most acutely the case in Japan, it might not be feasible to think of employment opportunities, but volunteer activities funded by a universal basic income are certainly feasible. There are also psychologists, some of which were former hikikomori, who are trying to convince other hikikomori to leave their caves.

To some extent, if late-capitalism enforces such a fate of social exclusion and atomization to such a portion of society, this might bode well for our capitalist rulers, who have nothing to fear from this discarded surplus population that has no centralized organization to vent frustration against a system that so thoroughly mistreats them.

Elton John: A Music Career with High Emotional Energy
Posted on January 16, 2018

Elton John has long been part of my music repertoire, and up until a few weeks ago I knew that he was no one-hit wonder, and had written a lot of very interesting songs that were nice to hear. Then I began to play the Youtube playlists of Elton John, which- for people who don't know- is an endless playlist with a series of songs by that musician mixed with similar musicians (like Phil Collins, Cyndi Lauper, Sting and so forth). Through that tool I discovered and rediscovered many songs composed by Elton John, and so I began to put together my own Youtube playlists aggregating all my favorite singers, and with Elton John, I am currently at 43 songs, more than for any other interpreter.[24] How can I be so electrified and fascinated by the songs of this one British musician? So I thought it was time to dig into some video interviews with Elton John and explore some biographical data.

My knowledge of music is so rudimentary that I cannot describe in words feelings about his music. It either makes you feel good or not and you don't really know why. Not even John can describe his music writing process, as it is intuitive rather than logical-rational. Music is one of those things where the human language cannot really penetrate though it is real and can be perceived, which may be described as a cognitive limitation. Ludwig Wittgenstein (1961) claimed "the limits of my language mean the limits of my world". Fortunately, I can make some sociological statements about Elton John's success, using the framework of the sociology of emotions. In short, John gets energized in the act of writing a song, and this internal energy gets reinforced via his live concert performances in front of large audiences, who sing along with him, and inspire him in his work.

Sociology of Emotions
Let us first recall the key tenets in the sociology of emotions as laid out in Collins (2004): people are in social interactions and transfer emotional energy to each other based on the characteristics of the social situation and the given social and cultural capital of each

---

[24] Playlist available here
https://www.youtube.com/playlist?list=PLQkt-6c5Frv_8m1vgAUI86B7xHHs1C65h

individual. Picture yourself going to a party, and meet this really important big shot that everyone should pay deference to, and it turns out that he is a smooth talker, but doesn't have much brains, but you do, so you feel dejected and want to escape the conversation. You meet the next person, initially very shy and withdrawn in body language, but you both discover that you like oldtimer cars and discuss that topic animatedly for the next two hours, which you perceive as if mere minutes went by. Sympathy for the other person is strengthened via rhythmic entrainment, which is the copying of body rhythms, tone of language and body language to create positive interactional energy. These are micro-situations, where only individuals meet each other, but in large groups so-called interaction ritual chains become possible. Picture a church congregation that is looking forward to the Sunday preachings, because the pastor is so charismatic and leave the congregants with a sense of inspiration that can reverberate outside the context, because some of the congregants share the vibe of that pastor outside the church walls, and that may attract more people to attend that church. *Emotions are getting transmitted via social interaction.* This is the key thesis that should be kept at the back of our minds.

A Biographical Sketch

Reginald Kenneth Dwight was born in north-west London in 1947 into a largely lower middle class household. He was mostly raised by his maternal grandparents in council housing, which is the British version of public housing. His father, a Royal Air Force lieutenant, was not emotionally close to John, and wanted him to pursue a conventional career as a banker. The father was often away, and when his parents were together they often quarreled with each other, thus creating John's desire for his parents to get divorced (Interview, 1994).[25] The conventional thinking of his father coupled with the emotional distance with John (John did not even bother to show up at his father's funeral) created in him the desire not only to become a musician but to wear fancy clothes during his many stage performances, to be considered shrill and unconventional.

Being musically inclined, his family bought a lot of records of contemporary music, which gave him a taste for music. Being very talented on the piano, he was discovered in school and at age 11 received a scholarship at the Royal Academy for Music in London,

---

[25]https://www.youtube.com/watch?v=qiTzpPpGTEU

where he spent about 5 years. While at the Royal Academy, he enjoyed playing classical music, but was not a very diligent student, and often rode around the subway rather than practice or attend class. His rare musical talent, however, allowed him to pass classes, as he could play compositions after hearing them once. John's domestic situation improved when the father divorced his mother, and she then got married to the painter Fred Farebrother, a caring and supportive stepfather. John wrote his early songs in Farebrother's house before he moved out.

His early musical forays began when he became a weekend pianist at a pub. He formed a band with his friends called Bluesology, and while writing songs also went on tours with them. He divided his time between running errands for a music publishing company, performing solo at a hotel bar and working with his band. John was so serious with his music that by age 17 he had dropped out of school. In 1967, John and Bernie Taupin answered the same ad for a British magazine, seeking for song composers. John admitted to Ray Williams, record company manager, that he was a good melody composer but a bad lyricist and needed help from a lyricist. Williams gave him an envelope from another person that had been rejected, Bernie Taupin. John left and took a look at Taupin's lyrics and was enamored by it and immediately contacted Taupin (Interview, 2017). [26]

Taupin and John became close collaborators, as Taupin wrote all the lyrics in an hour and send them to John, who would read the lyrics and produce the melody in another half hour. Some lyrics do not inspire John, and he throws it out, finding it not worthwhile to waste his time pondering over uninspiring text. While reading the lyrics, John would have an immediate feel for the mood, the speed and the tone of the song (Interview, 1999),[27] which distinguishes musical geniuses from the average musician. Around that time Dwight also changed his name to Elton John in homage to two members of Bluesology, saxophonist Elton Dean and vocalist Lohn John Baldry. John and Taupin became staff songwriters for Dick James' DJM Records in 1968, setting off the pattern of collaboration. Taupin writes the lyrics, and John comes up with the melody. As staff writers they primarily wrote songs for other people, but also increasingly produced their own songs. By 1970, they had put out their first album titled "Elton John", and the second song in the

---

[26] https://www.youtube.com/watch?v=VHjxxMJLaQ4
[27] https://www.youtube.com/watch?v=QzFSZmn9v-k

album "Your Song" became the first hit single, landing number 7 in the UK charts and 8 in the US charts. However, John had almost been a failure in the UK, and it was only when his record company contacted an American record producer, Russ Regan, who really liked the song that he got his breakthrough (BBC documentary, 2010).[28]

Predicting Success

The rest, as the proverb says, is history (which can be read in Wikipedia, "Elton John"), because the first successful hit generates revenue to allow John to concentrate more on his own work composing new songs, and name recognition would grant him invitations for music concerts at popular venues, which increases his listenership further, thus generating even more revenues and social attention. The Matthew effect is clearly at work here, as initial success is converted into more success (Merton 1968). But it is not enough to have initial advantage, as that initial advantage is also tied to personal talent and knowing the right people at the right time (such as knowing the lyricist Taupin, or knowing Russ Regan, the American record producer; or being in close proximity to other great artists forming a huge network and generating more creativity, as had been the case with philosophers: Collins [1998]). John had all of these factors speaking for him.

So how come John could nourish his ability to write one great song after another? Here economic explanations are insufficient. We can't just say that John was driven by the money, and in his labor-leisure tradeoff he placed a low value of utility on leisure, and thus favored the labor income by writing great hits and performing at live concerts. The problem with this explanation is that the homo economicus is showing up nowhere in the interviews that I have watched of John. Money cannot be the key driver for John's internal drive to success, though he has enjoyed a great material life, owning multiple large residences and nice cars that he mostly resold because he wasn't using them.

Fame, which is a form of social recognition, is already closer to the truth, but fame for its own sake was not what John had emphasized in the TV interviews. Rather there were three crucial factors that he emphasized in his conversations with journalists: (1) the need to be loved/ recognized for which fame was one tool to get

---

[28] https://www.youtube.com/watch?v=oNZHA5eMEw8

there; (2) the love and skill of writing music and performing; and (3) the emotional energy generated from audience feedback. In short, the productive use of emotions works out very well for John, thus allowing him to coast from one great hit to another, and endure even during career stretches of less success.

Love and Fame

John's need for fame and recognition really came from his need to be loved. In his interview with Barbara Walters, he described the trauma of seeing his parents get divorced. He explained how he got tremors when his father came home, as he had a tense relationship with him. "The only thing I would get excited about was playing the piano and singing. I would go out. It would be easy for me to get recognition from 20,000 people, and I loved it. Then I would come home and it was me [alone] again. And that wasn't enough." (Interview, 1994)[29] Continuing the line of tense household relations and the importance of music, he states in another interview "I used to find solace in music. When my parents used to argue, I would go to my room and listen to radio Luxembourg." (Interview, 2010)[30]

It is not clear whether all successful people must have gone through a traumatic childhood, but in John's case he converted his childhood trauma into productivity in the world of music. How could he know that he was being loved? Only via the constant infusion of emotional energy from the audience, and it became a potent drug. To be clear, there was a very negative phase in John's life that a career civil servant with a predictable schedule would unlikely face. In the 1980s, John was suffering from alcohol and drug addiction, and only successfully battled it after an epiphany moment when he attended the ceremony of a gay young man, who had died from HIV/AIDS. John being a homosexual himself felt that he didn't do enough to combat HIV, so to do something productive he had to first get his act together by becoming sober again, which succeeded about 1990 (Interview, 2008).[31] Charlie Rose suggested in his John interview that John's obsessive-compulsive personality can only be accommodated via music, which keeps him alive, which John agreed with (Interview, 1999).[32]

---

[29] https://www.youtube.com/watch?v=qiTzpPpGTEU

[30] https://www.youtube.com/watch?v=oNZHA5eMEw8

[31] https://www.youtube.com/watch?v=2-irykwf_YA

[32] https://www.youtube.com/watch?v=QzFSZmn9v-k

Love for Writing Music

Accommodating this obsessive-compulsive personality via music is a good transition to John's love for writing music. There are many ways to get fame and attention, but for John, a very effective method for being successful has been to simply enjoy writing good music. In his interview with Stephen Colbert, John stated, "we love what we were doing and didn't stop for pause. We were having so much fun. When you have that adrenaline. When you have that impetus and you are successful- we were like kids in the candy store. I just loved what we were doing. That helps." (Interview, 2017) [33]

It is rare for a person to find a career that is completely fulfilling, and the profession of the artist, who also happens to be successful, belongs to that category. Once John was successful, he was able to devote himself completely to writing good music. Being so obsessed about the music also does not leave much time for reflection. As an artist, it is impossible to know whether that song that was just composed, will become a big hit, but one has to be relentless and not really care about temporary setbacks or disappointments. Truly successful people, like competitive swimmers, have to regard their success as mundane, focusing on their craft rather than other distractions like comparison with other successful people (Chambliss 1989). In a separate interview, John stressed the importance of coming up with new ideas and staying innovative. "I am always promoting new things. I am trying not to be an old fart." (Interview, 2017).[34]

John also does not get obsessed about a single song, which may excite him when it is written, but not really when he plays it for many times in front of live audiences, unless there is a lot of public enthusiasm that he can sense there. "When you first write that song and you have the birth of that song. That gives you chills. And then to be honest, when you are playing a song 1,000 times it's hard to get chills except on certain occasions...[having] the most incredible crowd [at a recent concert]. That gave me the chills. That was the event, more than the songs." (Interview, 1992)[35]

Emotional Energy from Live Performances

---

[33] https://www.youtube.com/watch?v=VHjxxMJLaQ4

[34] https://www.youtube.com/watch?v=9bIDdi1vv-g

[35] https://www.youtube.com/watch?v=rX6qiHjqzao&t=195s

That is an interesting transition to the last point. How can John know that he has been vindicated as an artist? It can't be merely the record sales that change the value in his bank account, but the positive reactions from a large audience during a live performance. In an Australian interview, John was asked whether he would tire out performing so many concerts. "It is exhausting, but it is not exhausting playing. It is exhausting traveling."

This suggests that playing music is part of his natural identity, and the positive audience feedback compensates for any physical exhaustion of the live performance. On the other hand, sitting at the back of the van or in an airplane traveling across different countries may not strain his voice, but the lack of audience interaction and the solitude of the travel does not lend much emotional energy. Therefore, live performances are not incidental to John's success, but an important part of it. "The career has lasted so long because I do play live... Some nights I play and it's horrendous. Some nights I play and it is miraculous. That's the drug that keeps you performing, because you never know what great performance will come out of nothing. And that's the reason you are doing it, and to get the feedback from the audience." (Interview, 2017)[36]

John understood the importance of live performances, claiming that it gives him the resolve and the skills to play, and stated in an interview, "Nothing is better for you than to go out and play live, even if it is to 20 people. Because it gives you resolve, it hardens you up. It makes you a better songwriter. It gives you the experience, the backbone." (Interview, 2010)[37] Live performances generate public approval, which in turn generates the emotional energy that he needs to continue churning out new hits.

Even though John had enjoyed the interaction with the audience, which transmitted positive energy to him, John is by no means an extroverted person, preferring to keep to himself and have his thoughts expressed in the music. It might be said that the most talented people tend to be introverts, as creativity of scientists is expressed in the lab or in front of a computer screen, or painters drawing up their still life need the alone-time with the fruits as objects. For John, his most important partner, the lyricist Bernie Taupin, was not even physically in the same room with John when writing the songs. Taupin sends the lyrics to John. John would sit in

---

[36] https://www.youtube.com/watch?v=9bIDdi1vv-g
[37] https://www.youtube.com/watch?v=oNZHA5eMEw8

his room alone in front of his piano, read the lyrics, brood over it and hit the piano keys with the lyric for inspiration before writing down the notes (John provides some description of how he got the melody for "Tiny Dancer" in a 1971 performance).[38]

Conclusion

To be sure, John's career was not as productive from 1975 onward compared to his early years of performance (between 1970 and 1975), but he was still able to keep the flow of good songs coming. Even the brilliant scientists have their greatest work published relatively early in their career. But the fact that John kept on producing good records makes him very different from one-hit wonders, whose flame perishes soon after their commercial success. A mixture of talent, knowing the right people at the right time, early success coupled with the need for recognition, the love and skill for music and the positive emotional energy generated from audience interactions produce the music success story of Elton John. Emotions within social contexts are, therefore, an important component for achievement at the top. The benefit to Elton John fans is a long and extended track record of songs that are enlivening our daily experience.

---

[38] https://www.youtube.com/watch?v=cbZmPdu8Vko

The Tragedy of Welfare Reform Austrian-Style
Posted on January 22, 2018

I had argued previously that whenever people are given the chance to punish the political establishment, usually by voting, it happens (Liu, "The Politics of Populism: Technology and Inequality", this volume). Regular political commentators had remarked that with both Brexit and Trump there was a certain pattern in western democracies, that was designed to upset the political calculations of the neoliberal establishment that is perfectly happy with the continuous economic insecurity and dislocation of the population despite continuous economic expansion and declining headline unemployment rates. But don't forget that averages are very different than the personal economic experiences of the bottom third of the income distribution. I won't cite again the many relevant statistics that point to a decline of working class wages or a rise in income and wealth inequality, which are all well-known trends that create the volatile political system.

But what is worse is that the so-called populists, as in Austria, who think that they have any genuine solutions for the economic anxiety of the masses, do not have any effective solutions whatsoever, but, in fact, want to make things even worse for the masses. Given my political bias, Facebook ensures that I get to read all of the posts by the Social Democratic Party in Austria (SPO), which keeps the stream of criticism against the conservative (OVP)-nationalist (FPO) coalition government going. But to get the full picture, I began liking many posts by the chancellor (Sebastian Kurz) and the vice chancellor (Heinz-Christian Strache), who both agree on securing the borders, reducing immigration, enforcing deportation and opposing the growth of refugees. The slight difference is not the content but the style of delivery: Kurz is more careful and bourgeois in his terminology, while Strache is more explicitly provocative. One of Strache's favorite topics, for instance, had been to demand the cancellation of Austrian-Turkish dual citizenships. Though to be fair, his provocation is nothing compared to the FPO interior minister (in charge of the police departments and internal security), Herbert Kickl, who thinks it is a good idea to "concentrate" refugees physically, a very peculiar language for a country that not too long ago had endorsed concentration camps for Jews and other political enemies.

While the nationalist topics have broad voter support (except for social democrats, greens and other more educated circles), social policy retrenchment has much less popular support as many Austrians have gotten used to the generous welfare system. The most radical reform will be the abolition of the *Notstand* (emergency standing, or the long-term unemployment benefit), which is drawn after the expiration of the regular unemployment benefit without time limitations or asset tests until a new job is found or until retirement. There are currently about 170,000 long-term unemployment recipients, who have to regularly look for jobs or risk having their benefit terminated, though only 2% of recipients lose their benefits because of non-compliance with the employment bureaucracy requirements.

Notstand is part of the unemployment benefit system and as such has a higher social standing and less stigmatization compared to *Mindestsicherung* (minimum security, or welfare), which has strict asset tests (no more than 4,300 euros) and is given to people, who have not worked enough to collect unemployment insurance (less than 2 years). Under the administration's plan, the expiration of the long-term unemployment benefit will force unemployed people to spend down all their assets before being entitled to welfare, which imposes the welfare bureaucracy permanently on those welfare recipients. This corresponds to the German Hartz IV system that has been implemented in 2003, and has created an abundant low-wage sector, labor precarization and greater stigmatization for these low-income people (because the insurance principle of unemployment benefits communicates deservingness of collecting benefits one has paid into, while the welfare system is explicitly about recipients "mooching on the backs of hardworking taxpayers").

The neoliberal argument used by the administration to justify the scrapping of the long-term unemployment benefit is that *the unemployed should not lose their incentives to look for work*, which is apparently the case in the current system. By bringing more people into paid work (about 380,000 unemployed in Austria in a labor force of 4.2 million), the calculation is that more taxes will be paid and less welfare will be consumed, which will relieve the national budget and will give the Austrian people more dignity. Yet this argument is flawed, because it relies on the assumption of full employment with an abundance of high-paying jobs, thus allowing the government to argue that the unemployed people are lazy moochers, who need sanctioning to accept these jobs. Yet, there are only about 60,000 open positions in the Austrian labor market, which suggests that even if all unemployed Austrians were accommodated with the given openings, ⅚ will still be out of work. Neoliberals and government supporters will object that the 60,000 openings show that the unemployed are either not interested, not skilled enough for these jobs, or older workers are too expensive to employ. But it does not solve the scale of the unemployment problem. First, the *Arbeiterkammer* (labor chamber) clarifies that only 2% of Notstand recipients have their benefits cancelled because of a refusal to accept a jobs. Second, qualification has long been an employer excuse to refuse training and hiring employees. Third, it is true that collective bargaining agreements ensure higher wages for older workers, but that is not applicable in all sectors. White-collar workers generally have rising age-earning profiles, while it is pretty flat for blue-collar workers, where greater unemployment problems exist.

The real issue for the long-term unemployment of older workers (above age 50) is simply that companies have no interest to hire older employees, and the implicit social contract since the era of company retrenchments in the 1980s is that the government would rescue these older workers with generous early retirement provisions. These have been retrenched since the mid-1990s, and the 2003 pension reform completely closed the early retirement pathway by 2010 and all cohorts born on and after 1955. Now life between 50 and 65 can be rather precarious for many unemployed, who under the current system are pushed from the unemployment to the long-term unemployment benefit. After closing the early retirement pathway, the new administration is now closing the long-term unemployment pathway too, thus creating more insecurity for older workers.

The outgoing social democratic administration was able to get the *Aktion 20,000+* passed, which was a public employment program for older unemployed people. The OVP, back then junior partner, now the leading governing party, ridiculed the measure as a temporary fix to unemployment, which was an expensive electoral gift, and scrapped the public works program. Timewise, the OVP is correct, because in case the SPO was pushed into opposition, the SPO would be able to politically blame the OVP for cancelling a rather popular program to create jobs for older workers. But in substance, the burden of blame is on the OVP, which takes away the newly created options for older workers, who are everything but lazy moochers.

Thus, the real unemployment problem, as in most capitalist countries, is not the motivation and work ethic of the long-term unemployed, but the regulating function of unemployment within capitalism. Marx had argued that the bigger the reserve army of the unemployed the capitalists can draw from the lower wages become, as desperate workers are in no bargaining position to press for higher wages. By flooding the labor market with unemployed people desperate for work, reservation wages are lowered (the minimum wage that will induce work from workers). While the administration ridicules the public employment program a waste of tax money and an expensive election gift, reducing the reserve army of the unemployed could create upward wage pressures, which the capitalists thought they had defeated with the end of Austro-Keynesianism (which is summarized simplistically by the Bruno Kreisky- chancellor in the 1970s and early 1980s- quote that a few billion shilling in debt is not as troublesome as hundreds of thousands of unemployed people).

Ending the public employment program is not the only policy that has pushed up labor supply. Austria's membership in the European Union means that low-wage Eastern European workers have unlimited access to the Austrian labor market, which has been phased in steps from 2004 to 2014. The current administration has also approved extending the types and number of jobs, where firms can attract workers from non-EU countries, to 63 (originally passed still under SPO administration), which is another increase in the labor supply that is favorable to employers. Labor migration is on net beneficial to any society, however, it will do nothing to relieve the problem facing the long-term unemployed and may create more resentment against foreigners. It is also peculiar that the nationalist FPO has accepted this policy change after having argued against EU and non-EU labor migration during their opposition time. The FPO can't escape the neoliberal logic, and they will be punished electorally next time.

A second neoliberal argument in favor of ending the long-term unemployment benefit is that *means-testing welfare ensures that tax money is not given to millionaires or heirs*, who have wealth but no income. But this is the weakest of all arguments. Even if all the rich people in Austria did their best to report no income, why would they ever want to bother dealing with the intrusive state bureaucracy doling out the Notstand? And even if all of them wanted to do so, there just are not enough rich people in the country to make a big dent in the social spending budget. This is a classic distraction, where neoliberals hide their true intentions (i.e. pro-rich policies) based on class confusion/ obfuscation. Policies that benefit the masses are rejected based on their alleged pro-rich bias, and policies that benefit the rich are embraced because they have a supposedly desirable pro-poor bias. For an example of the second example one may take the US inheritance tax debate. Opponents of what they call "death tax" claim that small business owners and middle class homeowners should not be asked to pay a tax upon their death. The semantics is very crucial here, because inheritance has a neutral connotation, while death has a universal connotation. Since all of us have to die at some point, do we now all have to pay the "death" tax? Politically uninformed people will likely think so and will, therefore, oppose the inheritance tax, even though most people (98%) pay absolutely no inheritance tax, because the threshold is really high (currently 5.5 million dollars for single and 11 million for couples).

I conclude that there is a long-term political campaign to blind the voters with refugee, immigration and cultural identity issues, but not address their underlying economic uncertainty. In a very developed country with an expansive social net, as it exists in Austria, there is a lot of room for things to continue to get worse without creating third world conditions (compare in the US south, where lack of proper sanitation and access to medical care has resulted in the resurgence of the hookworm disease). Nonetheless, the Germanization of the social safety net cannot be considered a desirable political outcome for the unemployed and underemployed Austrians. While in Finland and in Canada, there is an acknowledgment that it would make sense to experiment with a basic income to address growing insecurity from economic dislocation (globalization, automation, rationalization), the mainstream debate in the western world is still trapped in a semi-Keynesian, semi-neoliberal ideological framework, assuming each for very different reasons that maximizing employment participation is desirable (though the former is more humane in at least creating the aggregate demand to make it feasible, while the latter radically pushes down reservation wages to accomplish that outcome), rather than the enhanced freedom for individuals to shape their own life objectives with a basic income.

Social Progress in Gender Relations (and Class Retrogression)

Posted on January 24, 2018

As a male person, it is rather difficult to claim that social progress in gender relations has been achieved, which some people might object would be like white people arguing that racism has been solved and rich people saying that inequality is no longer a problem. The privileged oppressor cannot speak adequately as to whether the oppressed lives well. But I can hedge myself by phrasing gender relations as being *directionally* toward progress, and not that equality has been achieved. The gender pay gap still exists, whereby women are pushed into jobs that happen to lack economic and political power, though there are more women in high executive business and political positions. (As an ardent critic of neoliberalism, I would question, however, how much sense it makes to only shift the gender or racial balance in corporate boards, while the gap between the rich and poor, executives and rank-and-file workers is rising.)

But to some extent, gender progress has been achieved both in the sense of the socio-economic position of the woman, and with regard to the problem of highlighting and ultimately combating sexual harassment that has galvanized social media and discourse. There are two factors that are important in explaining this social change: capitalism and technology. This post will explore these two factors.

With regard to capitalism, we have to remind ourselves of an important element in the economic system: the endless need for changing methods of production to generate economic growth, which satisfies the capital accumulation requirement for the corporate actors in society. Even the common people are condemned to identify with the capital accumulation model, because we rely on jobs from the capitalist to pay our bills, and these capitalists only give us jobs if there is a sufficiently growing market fed by a growing population and/ or rising per capita consumption. This growth-oriented economic system sooner or later has to shift gender relations. Some feminists and Marxists might object by pointing to the perpetuation of female oppression by locking women into the passive housewife, nourishing the husband, who was the sole breadwinner for the family, while the woman would bear and nurture the future workers (children).

But that has only been true during a very limited time period, and mostly for families with the man in a bourgeois position who can afford a decent lifestyle to the family with one income. In the later phase, women are expected to join the workforce, and for the poorest families women had always worked. In advanced capitalist countries, where natural demographic growth has come to an end (partly as a result of greater female labor opportunities, which competes with child-bearing demands), capitalists become desperate to entangle more women into the workforce, who participate in lower rates in paid work than men. Women are pulled into the labor market, not so much out of their own volition, but because the husband's earnings are falling, as deindustrialization kills the nice male unskilled jobs.

Therefore, the second line of feminist critique is that women in the labor force are relegated to the lowest economic positions with the least pay. There is, indeed, an absurdity in the way how a society decides to reward workers in different occupations. It can hardly be argued that college professors (still very male) deliver a more important service to society than kindergarten instructors (mostly female), but the difference is merely that the former teach older individuals and the latter younger. One might counter that it takes multiple years of schooling and credentialing, i.e. going through a torturous PhD program (speaking with personal experience), in order to become a college professor, while a few pedagogy classes are sufficient to become a kindergarten instructor. But pedagogy is simply another specific skill that needs to be acquired, and given that people who can't relate to toddlers (myself included) will simply be unqualified for this socially vital position, it will be hard for those people to decide to look down on kindergarten instructors. Thus, demand and supply does not get us at gender pay inequality, but different political power.

It is true, however, that women are traditionally self-inhibiting in their ability to attain job skills, because their desire and social expectation to raise children makes them less attached to the labor market, thus also making employers skeptical of hiring women for highly complex positions requiring extensive training. Labor history has plenty of evidence for managers keeping women in low-skilled jobs, knowing that pregnancy can remove them from the labor force altogether. But even this pattern is changing. The initial motivation for women joining the workforce might be to supplement the family income, but as women gain confidence in their skills, they want to attain higher and higher positions. The fact that some very ambitious women do make it to the top, thus breaking the "glass ceiling", then provides a positive role model for other women to also work hard to succeed. They also might get the idea to push for more equal compensation with their male colleagues. In the absence of pro-natalist government policies (which themselves sometimes prove ineffective), the capitalist requirement for more women in the labor force to make up for the lack of children will merely increase.

And now onto sexual harassment, which is notably the most common when economic power is very unbalanced across gender. In other words, a powerful male boss and his female secretary. But here the capitalist logic works too: more women get promoted into more powerful positions, and the powerful women complain more about sexual harassment, thus pressuring the men to better behave themselves. People might counter there is nothing intrinsic to capitalist society, which improves women's status. I might as well sound like Milton Friedman, who argued the free market has to benefit black people, because it doesn't care whether products are created by blacks or whites (though employers, customers and workers do care, thus perpetuating discrimination as a social channel).

I certainly will not deny that the gender pay gap and sexual harassment can perpetuate itself for a very long time within capitalist society, but for my argument to work the relevant counterfactual is a self-sufficient agricultural society, where primogeniture has locked down any material inheritance to sons rather than daughters. Thus, to sum up, it might be the case that gender power differentials get magnified under capitalism (most capitalists are still men), but it simultaneously creates the mechanism by which later equalization can get realized, first by sucking more women into the labor force, and second by women discovering their skills to make their way to the top. I should qualify that there is no automatism, i.e. things can look very bad for women unless they organize and struggle, but the avenues are open to them in a way that would not be feasible if they remained homemakers.

For sexual harassment, there is another important tool that has increased the organizational power of women: technology and especially social media. The sexual harassment debate has taken on a different quality with the effective use of hashtags. The MeToo campaign has worked because influential women (think of Hollywood actresses with gazillions of Twitter followers) shared their sexual abuse stories, and then less important women also had lower barriers to share their harassment stories. Now having women in strategic positions of society (even if they are not half the profession) is crucial. Female journalists with the power of the pen and the public attention of readership and viewership began to influence public discourse with their own take on MeToo, and that gets replicated in business and politics. Cynics might claim that despite the greater public attention on sexual harassment at work and elsewhere there is insufficient action to address this issue, but public attention is often the first step, which in some cases could result in overshooting. Brigitte Bardot, Catherine Deneuve and some other prominent women are pointing to the feminist campaigners unrightful attacks against all men as opposed to the genuine sexual harassers in power.

While the public focus on gender inequality might make some feminist activists depressed about the prospects for gender equality, it cannot be denied that capitalism and social media have created the openings for gender progress. There is still a long way to go, but there is some improvement. On the racial front, we might be encountering terrible headwinds, as our bigoted administration is ramping up the deportation of mostly Latino undocumented immigrants (most recently many El Salvadoran refugees will no longer have their status renewed and thus become liable for deportation too). But even with all the deporations the Latino population is continuously increasing with many US-born children locked into the country with US citizenship. (Trump wants to remove birthright citizenship too, but that would create enormous resistance even within his own party.) White supremacy, long a rather suppressed force, has become a potent form of mobilization in this country, but minorities in important political positions make overt racist positions rather difficult. While Donald Trump made himself infamous again with the "shithole" country comment with regard to black migrants from Haiti, West Indies and Africa, the two black US senators, Kamala Harris and Corey Booker, hit right back, not at Trump directly, but at his Homeland Security secretary in a hearing. Granted, this might just be symbolism, but people should recall that there were practically no institutional channels for non-whites to protest bigotry not too long ago.

The only clear retrogression we observe is in terms of class, and here capitalism has no automatically redemptive feature, because the entire point of capital accumulation is to concentrate wealth into the hands of the few, while outsourcing of jobs, automation and technological progress continuously keep a check on the ambitions of the working class. While the capitalist ship is sinking as more and more people are pushed into insecure, contract, part-time work or into technological unemployment (e.g. cashiers displaced by cashierless Amazon supermarket; driverless cars etc.), it might be possible that some more ethnic minorities and women are accommodated on the sunny side of it (like Sheryl Sandberg [2013], who leans in), but it won't save us from the social catastrophe of a gradually expanding precariat.

Why Did South Sudan Split From Sudan?
Posted on February 12, 2018

It was a total puzzle to me why this large country called Sudan suddenly decided to split itself in 2011, thus ushering in a new country of South Sudan. Foreign investors were happy nonetheless as they rained into the country to grab the most desirable farm land for their own purposes. On the face of it the split between the two parts is based on different tribal affiliations, as the north was mostly Arab Muslim and the south was mostly sub-Saharan African with Christian and animist beliefs. The political mobilization based on tribal affiliations has long plagued Africa, and Sudan has been no exception to this worrisome trend, but there are other noteworthy creases in Sudan's history. In addition to tribal divisions based on ethnicity, race and religion, Sudan has also been plagued by a permanent economic crisis, an incompetent, corrupt political leadership and continuous civil war.

There has been an extended history of foreign domination in Sudan. Sudan is immediately to the south of Egypt, and has thus benefited from the Egyptian civilization. The Nubians were one of the original rulers in Sudan (3,000 BC) until the Assyrian army under Sennacherib defeated the Nubians in a military campaign around 700 BC. By the sixth century AD, there were three successor states to what was called the Meroitic Kingdom: Nobatia, Muqurra and Alawa. Christianity spread to that region and a little later Islam. Islam primarily spread via Arab merchants marrying into the local population. There was a material interest for the population to convert to Islam, as they did not have to pay taxes to the king. What is now called northern Sudan is still the result of a mixture of Nubian and Arab culture, while the south was made up of east African tribes and ethnicities.

In 1821, the Ottoman ruler of Egypt Muhammad Ali invaded and conquered northern Sudan, and promptly worked on improving the country's infrastructure. Over the course of the nineteenth century, the European colonial powers had increased their influence over the region, and in 1879 they initiated a coup against Ismail Pasha, the Ottoman Khedive of Egypt and Sudan. The desired successor Tewfik Pasha turned out to be a corrupt and bad ruler, which incited the Urabi Revolt. The British used the revolt as a pretext in 1882 to formally annex Egypt, while leaving Sudan under Pasha's rule. Sudan was badly managed, as taxes on farms became unbearably high, and

European initiatives against slave trade adversely affected the Sudanese economy. The Mahdists, a group of Sharia-law supporting forces led by Muhammad Ahmad ibn Abd Allah, became popular and successfully conquered Khartoum (capital) and Sudan. The Mahdists promptly planned conquests of neighboring states (Eritrea, Ethiopia, Egypt), but each time were repelled by the European forces. By the 1890s, the British have had enough and they defeated the Mahdists in a military conquest in 1898. The British were acting under the indirect pressure of the French and the Belgians, who were also interested in controlling the Nile, and so the British had to be quick to snap up Sudan as well.

But British colonization meant new challenges, because Egypt and the Ottoman Empire had insisted in a union between Egypt and Sudan, while the British wanted to prevent any strengthening of potential adversaries, so they were intent on keeping the two countries apart. The British also separated Sudan into a northern and a southern province, which was in effect from 1924 to 1956. The game changer was in 1952, when the Egyptian revolution restored independence from British rule. The Egyptian leaders Muhammad Naguib and Gamal Abdel Nasser abandoned sovereignty claims on Sudan, but nonetheless demanded the full independence of Sudan from British rule. The British continued to support Abd al-Rahman al-Mahdi, but his regime suffered from political mismanagement as well, which reduced support for the regime. In 1956, the British relented by allowing the Sudanese people to vote on an independence referendum.

The first prime minister of the newly independent Sudan was Ismail al-Azhari, but his regime was not stable and a new faction led by Abdallah Khalil took over forming a coalition between Umma and PDP (People's Democratic Party), the two political parties formed post-independence. Umma wanted more foreign aid and a strong presidential constitution, while the PDP objected to foreign aid as a form of undue foreign influence and did not want to empower the president. Factionalism, corruption and vote fraud dominate political life. A 1958 military coup led by Ibrahim Abbud and Ahmad Abd al Wahab ended democratic governance. The military regime was briefly boosted by scrapping the high cotton price policy, which made Sudanese cotton exports too expensive to be competitive, and ending Nile water disputes with Egypt. Nonetheless, the Abbud regime was not stable either as they neither implemented an economic development strategy nor were they able to prevent coup attempts against it. The fatal mistake of the Abbud regime was to suppress Christianity and its support of Arabizing the south of the country, which alienated the non-Arab south. Thus, the political conflict between the central government in Khartoum and the southern province became the defining feature of political tension that culminated in two lengthy civil wars and South Sudan's independence in 2011.

Popular discontent unloaded against Abbud, which was reinforced by civil servants, teachers and students were unhappy with Abbud's education and economic policies. Abbud resigned amid political pressure and appointed a non-political civil servant, Sirr Al-Khatim Al-Khalifa as prime minister in 1964. A scheduled 1965 election lacked overall political legitimacy as the PDP and SCP (communists), two major parties boycotted the vote because the southern security situation was so bad that ballots could not be held. The Umma and NUP under Muhammad Ahmad Mahjub took power, and quickly worked to pacify unrest in the south, yet that meant using the military to crush organized protest, which increased southern resentment against the Sudanese military. Mahjub was replaced by Sadiq al Mahdi, who was replaced by Mahjub again. The two men, both leading different factions of Umma, clashed with each other, as the country had two government for a brief time. The situation was resolved when a new parliamentary election removed Sadiq from his seat.

In 1969, there was a second military coup d'etat led by Col. Gaafar Nimeiry. Socialists were a substantial force within the military government. Conservative forces called 'Ansar' resisted the new military government, and their Imam al Hadi al Mahdi demanded a return to democratic government, which resulted in a battle between Ansar and the Sudanese military, which was won by the military. Nimeiry, the military leader, then turned against the Marxists and socialists by putting trade unions under national control and suppressing the communist party (SCP). Several Marxist factions within the military led by Major Hisham al Atta then tried to overthrow Nimeiry in 1971, but he was restored to power. Nimeiry was determined to end the southern insurgency led by the Southern Sudan Liberation Movement (SSLM) by granting more political autonomy to the south and by promoting its economic development. With the help of Ethiopia's Emperor Haile Selassie, the two sides reached an agreement called the Addis Ababa accords in 1972, which created a regional government in the three southern provinces of

Sudan and strengthened southern representation in the central government in Khartoum. To appease the Arab Muslims in the north, Nimeiry also reaffirmed Islam as having a special position and granted administrative decentralization in the northern provinces. Nonetheless, many Arab Sudanese were offended by the agreement with the south and leftist students also opposed the government. A coup attempt by the Muslim brotherhood/ Ansar in 1976 was thwarted by the military.

In 1978, Nimeiri tried a return to parliamentary rule, but the elected representatives in the assembly defected from party discipline and furthered their own financial interest over that of the country. Continued corruption undermined Nimeiri's legitimacy, who subsequently returned to a more dictatorial leadership style of imprisoning opponents and dissidents without trial. To counter the growing political power of the south, he redivided the south into the three old provinces and suspended their assembly in 1983. A little later, he imposed sharia law, which was resented by secular Muslims and non-Muslim southerners. By the end of 1983, the next civil war began. Nimeiri was ultimately toppled in 1985 as rising food, gasoline and transport costs brought people out on the streets. The coup was led by General Abdel Rahman Swar al-Dahab, who then promoted Sadiq al-Mahdi to become prime minister after elections.

Sadiq was a weak leader, who had already been deposed back in 1969. His Umma, DUP, NIF and 4 southern party coalition was internally divided, while corruption scandals bogged down any effective governing and worst of all did not resolve the civil war. The DUP was intent on signing a cease-fire agreement with the southern party (SPLM), which would also have ended sharia law and lifted the state of emergency, but NIF rejected the deal. DUP then pulled out of the coalition, which infuriated the military generals, who wanted to see terms to end the civil war. Under military pressure, Sadiq then invited DUP back into the government and vowed to implement the DUP-SPLM cease-fire agreement, but the government was too weak to implement the ceasefire. In 1989, Lieutenant General Umar Hassan Ahmad al Bashir then overthrew the Sadiq regime, though he was not a very peaceful ruler himself, as he pushed for the continuation of sharia law, which was not acceptable in southern Sudan that was barely Muslim. Bashir called out the Revolutionary Command Council for National Salvation to rule Sudan, which was dissolved in 1993 upon which Bashir became the president. Bashir has continuously ruled Sudan since his takeover, and has been indicted by the International Criminal Court for genocide, war crimes and crimes against humanity in Darfur. His presidential term runs until 2020. Bashir is no less corrupt than his predecessors, as he transferred 9 billion dollars from the public treasury into foreign bank accounts.

In addition to the civil war with the south, which had displaced over 4 million southerners, the western province of Darfur also became engulfed in a rebellion in 2003 led by the Sudan Liberation Movement (SLM) and the Justice and Equality Movement (JEM). SLM and JEM had accused the central government of economically neglecting the Darfur region. Arab militias (Janjaweed) supported by the central government committed atrocities and killings of many people, and the rebels also killed many people. Only in 2004 was there a ceasefire agreement, between the different parties, which was monitored by the African Union and the Ceasefire Commission. Rwanda and Nigeria dispatched troops to ensure the ceasefire. Sudanese militia attacked villages in eastern Chad, which induced Chad to fight a war with Sudan at the end of 2005, which was not ended until 2010. The Darfur conflict ended in 2010 as well, though there continue to be millions of displaced people in camps.

With the southern provinces the situation stabilized somewhat with the peace treaty of Nairobi in 2005, which would grant 6 years of autonomy to southern Sudan followed by an independence referendum. Income from the oil fields should be shared. Islamic law would continue in the north, while in the south it was decided by the local assembly. The January 2011 referendum in the south approved independence and on July 9, 2011, South Sudan became an independent country with Kiir Mayardit as first president. Bashir accepted the independence vote, but fighting broke out in Abyei, a territory along the border of both countries and claimed by both. Both sides then decided to demilitarize Abyei and deploy Ethiopian peacekeepers.

This account of Sudan's history shows that the South Sudanese independence likely made sense. Since independence in 1956, Sudan had been almost continuously in a civil war. The first ranged from 1955 to 1972, the second ranged from 1983 to 2005. The first civil war had killed 500,000 people, of which 4 out of 5 were civilians. The decade of peace in the 1970s, was not really peaceful, as there were continuous incursions from the north, which resulted in mutual hostilities. The resumption of open conflicts with the second civil war resulted in 1 to 2 million deaths, again mostly civilians whose economic lives became disrupted with the war, which resulted in starvation. The two sides were too different: the north was Muslim, Arabic and lighter skinned, while the south was sub-Saharan, east African, darker-skinned and English-speaking. The north monopolized political positions, and the exclusion of southern elites in the leading posts of the bureaucracy created sufficient alienation to mobilize the south for civil war and the quest for independence.

Another sticking point is the existence of oil reserves, which are mostly concentrated in the south (75%), yet the oil pipelines and refineries connecting to the Port Sudan along the Red Sea are in the north. Given the desert conditions in the north of Sudan, the central government had good reasons to retain authority in the south. With the southern independence, the north has focused on drilling more in the oil fields they still have and also exploring the Red Sea deposits. Post-independence both sides still rely on each other, because the south has the oil fields and the north has the refineries and the port. Sudan still has the upper-hand as final sellers, they determine the price. Although there is a certain quota that has to be shared with South Sudan, Khartoum can effectively screw the south by misreporting prices and skimming from the top. 90% of the foreign exchange is earned by the sale of oil (Summers 2011), which would be fine if there were existing political institutions to responsibly shepherd these abundant natural resources, like in Norway. In Sudan, a substantial share of the oil revenues is siphoned off by officials. South Sudanese president Salva Kiir admits in a letter to his officials, "An estimated $4-billion are unaccounted for or, simply put, stolen by current and former officials, as well as corrupt individuals with close ties to government officials." (York 2012) Foreign oil corporations, who provide the equipment and investment, are also the primary beneficiaries of the two countries' oil wealth. Most recently, China has become the largest importer of Sudanese and South Sudanese oil, indicating a shift in global political relations.

Cross-border clashes continued after South Sudanese independence. In March 2012, South Sudanese forces seized Heglig oil fields, which are claimed on both sides. A few weeks later, they withdrew as the Sudanese Army seized the oil fields. On the other hand, bilateral tensions have been restricted to border clashes, while for the multi-ethnic South Sudan it meant that there was no longer any Arab opponent to fight against. With the lack of a common enemy, internal tribal divisions in South Sudan broke out with a vengeance. Since 2013, the political power struggle between president Kiir and his former deputy Riek Machar engulfed the country in the South Sudanese Civil War. The UN put pressure on Kiir and Machar to end their conflict, and in 2016, Machar was invited back to the capital Juba to take up a post as vice president. The power-sharing agreement failed as violence broke out in Juba, and Machar was forced to flee the country. Out of a population of 12 million people, 3 million had become displaced and 300,000 have died with the number continuing to rise. Although Kiir and Machar have supporters from each tribe, Kiir is an ethnic Dinka (38%, largest ethnic group) and Machar is an ethnic Nuer (27%, second largest ethnic group), thus pro-Kiir government troops tend to target Nuer and the anti-government rebels tend to target the Dinkas.

The deeply entrenched tribal divisions along race, ethnicity and religion along with a permanent economic crisis, an incompetent and corrupt political leadership and near permanent civil war explains the break-up of Sudan and continued political instability. As with the problems of post-colonialism after independence across sub-Saharan Africa, creating a new country does not solve underlying political problems and the fighting will rage on.

What's the Problem with the Universal Basic Income?
Posted on <u>February 12, 2018</u>

Ian Goldin (2018) claims that even with accelerating technological change and the displacement of workers, we should not introduce a universal basic income (UBI), which he had called a "red herring". I counter, in brief, that *while his concerns about the UBI are valid, his reasoning is insufficient to reject UBI as a necessary social policy tool to mitigate the problems in the labor market and society* we all acknowledge. Let us examine his arguments.

UBI is financially irresponsible

Essentially, UBI is really expensive and would result in enormous tax increases. The proof is in the pudding, though. The more generous the UBI is the higher the taxes would have to go and the less sustainable the policy becomes. If our national GDP is 60,000 dollars per capita, I would doubt that the UBI per person can equal to 60,000 (we are assuming non-inflationary payment of the UBI), as there has never been an economy that exactly consumed what it produced. If we reserved a quarter of the national income about 15,000 dollars as a basic income payment that does not sound too bad, and will leave enough income for other purposes like investment. Naturally, the role of the state will have to increase, and to some extent we have gotten used to the state taking up nearly 40% of the national economy, in some European countries even more than half. Fair accounting of UBI would also have to mention other social programs that are folded into the UBI. In other words, these other social programs are either eliminated or reduced in size once the UBI exists to take care of people's needs.

I don't advocate for the most right-wing interpretation of the UBI, as is formulated by Charles Murray. 10,000 dollars for everyone annually, and then get rid of all other social spending. In that case, social spending by the government might be expected to stay the same or fall, and that would be a very regressive perspective, as declining social wages for poor people means that the 10,000 dollar UBI grant they get will quickly be spent before the year is over (e.g. expensive kindergarten for families with young children), and we have not done anything to reduce poverty or insecurity. A basic pension granted via social security may very well become displaced by the UBI, because UBI is an expansion of social security to all individuals rather than only old people. With Food Stamps, we might have to see whether it will lower the standard of living of current recipients if it gets cut. For health care, it obviously makes no sense to privatize it, when single-payer health care systems all over the developed world have done a great job in curing people's illness without bankrupting them (as in the US).

UBI will lead to higher inequality and poverty

The reasoning here is that the displacement of targeted economic transfers (unemployment insurance, disability and housing benefits etc.) with a UBI will disproportionately help the rich more than the poor. A billionaire does not get unemployment insurance, but he will surely get a UBI, which would be a waste of resources. But among social policy scholars, there has long been the paradox of redistribution in that earning-related social insurance tend to be more effective than poverty-targeting or flat-rate benefits (Korpi and Palme 1998). Thus, poverty-targeted programs that lack the broad middle class support do not necessarily help in redistributing income and reducing poverty either. Granted, UBI is a flat-rate benefit and might not dent inequality. Imagine an inflation-adjusted UBI paid out into eternity which does not change the amount of goods you can buy with it, but productivity continues to rise and the Zuckerbergs and Gates of the world continue to make their fortunes. For UBI to make sense, the state would also have to raise more taxes on capital, which also forms the basis for raising the UBI with the rate of productivity rather than just by inflation. If we don't want to sacrifice the U in UBI, yet hoping to dent inequality, the UBI will have to be supplemented by other government policies, and I reiterate my opposition to the Murray position that restricts all social policy to solely UBI.

UBI will undermine social cohesion

Work is identity-forming and creates social integration, while the subsidization of non-work via UBI will foster laziness, moral decay, the break-up of families, crime and drug addiction. He cites the US as an example where the contemporary inexistence of work among some social quarters has produced that outcome. But the US is a strange example to pick, because it does not have a UBI, and for his reasoning to be effective, Goldin has to pick an example where the UBI contributes to less work and to social disorder. Right now we only know that less work leads to social disorder, a point that is well-taken. In the absence of solid evidence to the contrary, we might argue that the UBI will encourage economic activity (or at least not reduce it). Perhaps not of a wage-labor kind, but there are two other economic activities that might increase: entrepreneurship and volunteer work.

Today, there are wannabe novelists toiling away as corporate accountants, because that is the best way to pay their bills. Naturally, if you have a Protestant inclination and argue that any work is better than no work, an accountant is a fine way of making a living, but for that wannabe novelist it is a huge opportunity cost. They are wasting their time crunching numbers in the office, when they could have spent that time typing their novel. Perhaps society would enjoy such a novel if only that person were paid a UBI, and can afford to point the middle finger to a boring, meaningless job. Entrepreneurial ventures, whether it is writing a book, selling and designing skirts or inventing a new twist to barbecue sauce, can become possible with UBI, which will actually enhance economic life. People can also afford to volunteer for after-school programs for kids or old people's homes, which incidentally reduces the social cost for caring for kids and old people, because volunteers are not necessarily paid a wage.

Unstructured lives may very well lead to social dislocation and disorder, but it is questionable why most people receiving the basic income would have to fall into this trap. Community centers and NGOs have to become more proactive in offering meaningful activities for an unemployed population, but let us not forget the basic premise of the UBI: the lack of good job opportunities because of technological displacement. It is given the lack of good employment options that the basic income is needed as social stabilizer.

UBI undermines incentives to participate

In other words, UBI creates dependence on the welfare state rather than independent living. But the reality under contemporary capitalism is that independent living is made impossible for people, who lack affluent parents or a huge stock or real estate portfolio. In that context, why is UBI defined as dependence on the welfare state rather than freedom from capitalist control? One may argue that the expansion of the social safety net with a UBI means an empowerment of the public bureaucracy, which is another monster of rationalized modern existence besides the big corporation. But UBI would work similarly to Social Security in that the benefit administration that is tasked with administering the payout of the

UBI is much smaller than the drug-testing welfare bureaucracy and other shenanigans invented by right-wing administrations. Therefore, we should not underestimate the importance of positive freedoms that can be afforded only by the attainment of material security, which is at most precarious for wage laborers under capitalism.

UBI postpones discussions on the future of jobs

Goldin thinks that discussions of the UBI distract from necessary changes to a bad labor market and the promotion of things like shorter work weeks, part-time work, reward for tele-working and the promotion of caring and creative industries. But if you believe in my foregoing discussion of people becoming liberated under UBI to pursue caring and creative work, then this argument collapses in itself. Besides if we think that the low quality jobs originate from worker inability to say no to bad employment relationships, then the introduction of a UBI would naturally force employers to offer better wages and working conditions to attract enough workers.

But let us assume the correctness of the premise of the argument, namely that UBI distracts from bad employment relationships and these relationships stay bad, because employers know they can pay their workers little and they will still survive because of the UBI. That would, indeed, be a less than desirable outcome, but the relevant comparison is not some ideal utopia but the present moment of bad employment relations without UBI, and I prefer a world with bad employment relations with a UBI to one without UBI.

I do understand the argument that UBI is a cop-out for the political impetus to improve work relations, which is part of the reason that trade unions tend to view UBI also quite skeptically, but here I want to question the moral premise of our social economy: is our desire to create ideal employment relationships or to live a good life? And if I say good life, I don't mean pure hedonism and the pursuit of frivolity, but the ancient Greek idea of minimizing work and pursuing leisure for the increase of knowledge, friendships, social relationships and the admittedly ill-defined 'virtue' (which I won't define here). I would prefer the latter.

I don't detest all notions of work. Let us reflect again what we mean by work, which I treat separately from a job. Work is the activity requiring physical, emotional and mental exertion to produce something of value to somebody, which may be hunting animals for food, growing crops for food or loading carts with merchandise in a retail store. This is tied to human activity from the beginning, which may co-exist with leisure and we shall pursue as long as humans exist. A job is a social formation, where one group of people works for somebody else for hire, and has existed for extended parts of human history, but radically took off not until the Industrial Revolution. The job is thus a particular historical formation that is built on domination and exploitation, because there are people who provide the work, and there are other people who benefit from the work thanks to their ownership claims over the means of production.

If the UBI has the capacity to kill the job- a prospect that Goldin and others seem to detest- then go ahead with the UBI. If UBI maintains bad jobs, we at least no longer struggle with existential problems and the unrestrained power of our bosses. Though I cannot confirm my suspicions, it is for that reason, perhaps, that anti-UBI ideologues are so fierce in their stance: don't mess with the social order of the status quo!

The Problem of Gun Control
Posted on February 18, 2018

It almost becomes a waste of time to have another dinner conversation around another school shooting carried out by a deranged person, who had access to guns. An examination of public polls shows that there is a solid majority of the population that favors stricter gun control.

The relevant question, thus, becomes why the US cannot copy countries like Australia or the UK that had mass shootings that became restricted by the passage of strict gun control laws. There might be some people, who argue that the government should not take the freedom from people to own property, including guns, but to not distinguish ordinary property from guns is highly questionable, because of the potential harm to other people guns produce. And the ability to kill other people is the greatest restriction in the freedom of other people. I would scarcely deny Robinson Crusoe gun ownership rights, but the moment he joins society, we do want to minimize homicide possibilities.

Some people might respond that cars kill many more people than guns, and my logic would require the prohibition of cars too. But here the comparison to utility matters. To the extent that we have built our cities and villages in ways that make us reliant on cars to get around (as opposed to have reliable public transit), the benefit of a car is still greater than the cost of potential car crash. The benefit of owning a gun is negligible, e.g. the *feeling* of safety (which is more than offset by the *experience* of unsafety when insane people get to run around with machine guns). The second factor is intentionality, as there is virtually no one that wants to kill himself or others in a car crash, but gun deaths are in most cases purposeful, which is more problematic.

Some people would suggest that the existence of the second amendment and the popular belief in becoming safer after owning guns makes effective gun control legislation very difficult. In addition, every school school shooting seems to strengthen the irrational belief that one's own security is increased by clutching tightly to a gun.

But these reasons are insufficient to explain the lack of movement on gun control. Gun control would include a stricter background check on the purchase of guns; the prohibition of selling automatic weapons; and a government policy to re-purchase any guns under private ownership. So why is it so hard to pass these restrictions? The power of the NRA, the National Rifle Association, makes any movement on gun policy self-defeating for politicians, who dump enormous sums of money in the electoral process to ensure that the politicians vote in the "right" way.

The absurdity of the liberal gun laws are not even challenged when one of the power holders, Rep. Steve Scalise, was shot during a baseball game. Former Congresswoman Gaby Giffords was also shot during an event. It can, thus, be said that no one is formally safe from crazy people using guns to kill other people.

The NRA naturally does not demand lighter sentences on mass murderers. In fact, they are in favor of strictly punishing gun abusers, but that can only be stated after the fact, i.e. after the mass murder happened. There are plenty of social problems in this country that create victims rather than focus on prevention. Our health care system, for instance, still makes the purchase of good health insurance difficult, and thus encourages people, who are not able or willing to make the financial trade-off to purchase insurance to wait until they become very sick before they go to the emergency room, where doctors might discover that the disease is so advanced that they can't really do anything for the patient anymore. A preventive health care system would guarantee health care to all people, such as via a single-payer system.

A major cause of sickness in turn is the unhealthy diet of most Americans, who have to consume excessive amounts of sugar, high fructose corn syrup and fat because they happen to be cheap and convenient to get. While in Europe and Asia, obesity is increasingly becoming a major health threat too, I do notice that there are cheap alternatives that do not nearly produce the same amount of plaque around the arteries and fat on the body as in the US. Europe has many bakery shops that sell cold sandwiches with plenty of salad. China has many restaurants that dish out the balanced meals of plenty of vegetables, some meat and rice or noodles. A preventive food system would offer cheap, healthy options and make unhealthy options expensive and harder to acquire.

Subsequently, a preventive approach to mass shootings would be to minimize popular access to guns. Some people might suggest that taking away guns from law-abiding citizens goes too far, while no one would oppose background checks on mentally troubled individuals. But there are two problems with this argument. First, I might be a sane person who becomes insane as a form of affect. Second, I might be a sane person, who illegally resells the gun to an insane person. The first case is not as rare as one might think. I cite the gun violence statistics here.

In 2013, there were 73,505 nonfatal firearm injuries (23.2 injuries per 100,000 U.S. citizens),[2][3] and 33,636 deaths due to "injury by firearms" (10.6 deaths per 100,000 U.S. citizens).[4]These deaths consisted of 11,208 homicides,[5] 21,175 suicides,[4] 505 deaths due to accidental or negligent discharge of a firearm, and 281 deaths due to firearms use with "undetermined intent".[4] Of the 2,596,993 total deaths in the US in 2013, 1.3% were related to firearms.

Source: Wikipedia ("Gun violence in the United States")

In the second case, it might be hard to measure because it is an illegal activity, but the possibility is just there compared to when most people cannot acquire guns. Critics will object that insane people can still acquire guns regardless. But the relevant comparison is not to a perfect society, but to a society that prohibits guns to the masses, and you will see that most countries with the stricter gun laws have fewer gun deaths, which suggests that in those cases insane people are less likely to have access to guns, and that itself is a justification for stricter gun laws.

What might change the dynamics on gun laws? It is hard to say, but without public mobilization it will be impossible. Mancur Olson (1971) had pointed out that the beneficiaries of a dysfunctional policy are small in number and are part of a concentrated organization, while the losers are many in number, the cost is widely dispersed and it is hard for the multitude to mobilize on any particular issue. Not all hope is lost, though, because there has been a limited gun control law in 1994, which was allowed to expire in 2004, but with changing circumstance it does become possible to rein in guns.

The Wind of Authoritarian Rule
Posted on March 4, 2018

While one may not be surprised that President Xi Jinping has now decided to scrap the two-term limit on his office, there is an element of discontent among the liberal portions of the Chinese society (among the Chinese overseas students, I have yet to hear an enthusiastic Xi supporter). The lack of surprise lies in the fact that the 19th Party Congress last November had not resulted in the anointing of a potential successor to Xi Jinping. While superficial observers of China may be shocked by the abolition of the term limit for the presidency, keen observers know that there is not much historical precedent for term limits. In the nearly 70 years of Chinese Communist Party rule, only the past three leaders over the last 25 years had an orderly transition.

If you want to be really strict and exclude Jiang Zemin (de facto ruler from 1989 to 2002, while his presidency was limited to after 1993), then we are only talking about the last two leaders over the last 15 years. Jiang had been the hand-picked successor of Deng Xiaoping, the undisputed Chinese leader since 1978, following on the heels of the infamous Mao Zedong, who ruled for his entire life, and his own weak hand-picked successor Hua Guofeng. Deng had the hope that by instituting collective leadership (i.e. multiple leaders within the Politburo rather than have one strongman) and term-limits on the leading positions the excesses of Maoist rule could be prevented. Jiang, thus, became the first leader to peacefully pass the power to Hu Jintao, who in turn accepted his 10 year term and handed power to Xi Jinping. Among all the leaders in Chinese history only Hu can be said to have fully complied with the term limit and fulfill the aspirations of a collective leadership.

Political scientists claim that the pursuit of a particular policy would result in path dependence, i.e. increasing returns to scale for the present system, and high costs of switching to an alternative system (e.g. electoral backlash). In the Chinese case of presidential term limits, this principle is difficult to apply, because firstly China still has an authoritarian government, i.e. does not rely on popular, democratic elections to change the rules of the game. If the party wants a change in the statute, then it will happen. Thus, the key challenge becomes how to wrest control over the party. Second, to have only two neat leadership transitions is not enough time for institutionalizing the term limit.

With the advent of a strong leader like Xi Jinping the term limit has been formally removed, and there are no visible forces within the Communist Party to challenge Xi's leadership. The last formal challenge came with the fairly charismatic Bo Xilai, the former party chief in Chongqing, who had been removed from office in 2012 because of corruption charges and accusations against his wife of killing a foreign businessman. Xi followed up with a brutal crackdown on corruption, which no longer only targeted the lowest officials, but also high generals and party officials. Xi argued that in order to retain popular legitimacy the state-capitalistic corruption and self-dealing had to be contained, and the people supported him. But the side effect is that anyone, who could potentially oppose and challenge Xi, would also be pushed to the wayside.

Popular support for Xi

What forces allow Xi Jinping to cement his power for life? Evidently, removing his political opponents with the anti-corruption crackdown have helped his cause, but as with Mencius, the Chinese political philosopher, who stated that the ruler can legitimately rule only if he has the support of the masses, Xi can only hope to retain power if people are unlikely to want him to step down. Can we infer people's support for Xi? Social researchers, evidently, have trouble to study public opinion in authoritarian countries (already hard enough in democratic societies), because social desirability bias (or the inclination to not be punished by the state) will make respondents lie to pollsters collecting data on people's views on the political climate. (A highly educated Chinese person admitted to me that it is not particularly safe to comment on Chinese politics via Wechat, their version of social media, which is algorithmically tracked by authorities.)

But can we infer people's support for the current leadership? The TV interviews tend to exhibit broad Chinese support for Xi, because he is fighting corruption, improving the economic fortunes for the masses and returning China as the proud, outward-looking dragon on the international arena, which it deserves to be. Surely, people might be discontent about land grabs or environmental pollution, but the positives that the Xi administration has delivered outweigh any weaknesses. And it surely can't be so bad that he will now get to rule for life. Isn't that what Chinese people are used to with the dynasties lasting 250 to 300 years, handing power from father to son until conditions led to their toppling by a different set of rulers?

While for the common working class, which has escaped the worst poverty during the Mao era, economic improvement is the single most important factor for contentment with the present political system, the emerging middle class is more heterogeneous, as they might travel abroad, and become exposed to the "subversive" western influence of democracy, rule of law and strong civil society. We will turn to this point next.

Weakly developed civil society

A foreign journalist, who covered China during most of Hu's rule in the 2000s, reported on the relative freedom that she had experienced in Chinese academia, journalism and civil society. The rather liberal and open framework for Chinese circumstances (there still were no free elections, free media or freedom of speech) came to an abrupt halt with Xi's ascendancy to power. Civil society organizations- focused on labor, environment and social welfare that were hoping to expand- now faced much harsher conditions. They have to register with various government branches, which in turn were staffed by officials, who received directives to crack down on too much independent civil society activity. Government funding became focused on specific organizations that were most closely allied with the government, and some organizations refused funding from foreign organizations for fear of state reprisal.

The 2014 Umbrella Movement in Hong Kong resulted in a government backlash against civil society organizations. The Umbrella Movement was a culmination of popular and student-led discontent against the increasing power of Beijing, which interfered in Hong Kong's domestic affairs despite the 1985 agreement to retain Hong Kong autonomy until 2047. After a few months, Hong Kong authorities began to crack down on the movement and put their leaders on trial. Hong Kong elections resulted in three movement members being elected, but the executives refused to swear them in for not conforming to some protocol. (The Hong Kong parliament is a sham anyway, as most members are either appointed by Beijing or by organized big business interests in Hong Kong.)

There was some spillover of protest action to the mainland, especially in adjacent Guangzhou. But more so than any practical action on the ground, the Xi administration became alarmed that there could be organized protest culminating in a challenge to the CCP power monopoly, which had to be prevented by all means. The first step was to replace the provincial leader in Guangdong to ensure that a party hardliner would hold the position. Then rules were tightened on many NGOs, some were closed down and/ or defunded, leaders were put on trial and jailed. As independent NGOs move to the defensive, some of them adjust by increasing cooperation with government officials and changing their advocacy to less politically controversial topics, but also sacrificing some of their original objectives.

The poor fate of the Chinese NGOs produces the question whether a liberal middle class is in a position to challenge the political leadership. There is no immediate indication for it, and as long as less politically active classes (e.g. workers, farmers, bureaucrats) are mostly dispersed and quiet, the liberal middle class is not in a position to challenge the party, thus ensuring further power consolidation for Xi. But there is another reason why liberal mobilization against Xi will be difficult.

Increasing surveillance power of the Chinese state
With the increasing uncertainty over economic growth and rising economic inequality, potential domestic discontent is on the rise. This is so much so that the Chinese government has refused to publish mass public incidents (usually protests or strikes) since 2010, fearing that the statistic could give more momentum to the regime critics. Fortunately for the regime, improvements in computer technology and the emerging field of artificial intelligence are giving the Chinese government the opportunity to surveil the population ever better.

Social movements have taken advantage of social media in order to mobilize large crowds for protest action or even just to raise awareness of political issues. While social media cannot be considered the root cause for the Arab Spring, it has catalyzed more activism than would be possible otherwise. Knowledge of foreign discontent could also provide the impetus for the Chinese middle class to mobilize discontent against the authoritarian state, or at least against undesirable trends like environmental pollution, worker exploitation or land grabs.

The reaction of the Chinese state was to delete activist posts, hire a 50 cent army to make distracting posts to inundate people's social media walls with non-political messages, and in the most recent development indict and jail some bloggers and activists. The regime also holds a tight leash on information, ensuring that Chinese people cannot access western media sources that have often reported quite critically on the regime. The only way to circumvent the Great Firewall has been to acquire a foreign VPN (virtual private network). Generally, the government had been quite reluctant to abolish VPNs as foreign businesses insisted that it would be necessary to access an unfiltered internet. But just in the last year, the government decided to also crack down on VPNs, putting many of them out of business and banning them. While I had been in China, the VPN service was mostly reliable, but not all the time, which suggests that the Chinese state is finding ways to control people's access to information.

As algorithmic tracking capabilities continue to increase, the state will be better capable of cracking down on what they regard as social misfits, i.e. people who can mobilize discontent against the state actors. State surveillance would not be possible if it were not for the cooperation of the major private communications firms such as Alibaba and Tencent. State officials generally approve of concentrated economic power in the private sector, but only if the party can continue to appoint high officials in those firms. Furthermore, these firms have to cooperate closely with the state and disclose all information of individual users to the state. This allows the state to imprison people, who write negative things about the regime. This strategy of state-corporate cooperation has been pursued even in western developed countries, though not as systematic as in China.

The surveillance power of the Chinese state also increases to the extent that the Chinese people become more and more dependent on their smartphones for all of their personal and commercial needs. Wechat is a single service that combines the payment of bills, communication with friends and family, online gaming, work payroll, newsfeed, booking doctor appointments, paying electricity fees, booking transportation and a so-called heat map. The heat map shows users about the number of people in a certain location, which also allows the government to monitor mass assemblies, which are generally prohibited.

While high technology use allows the Chinese to leapfrog into higher stages of economic development compared to western countries, who still use older methods of electronic payment, it also permits the state to more completely monitor the population to an extent that was not possible in the past. Even during the height of the Cultural Revolution of the 1960s, Mao Zedong had to rely on the social willingness of his Red Guard to out and prosecute the "capitalist reactionary traitors" (i.e. enemies of the regime). Now, every move that is somehow electronically recorded can make individuals liable for prosecution.

Does every somewhat liberal person in China now fear immediate prosecution by the state? Not necessarily. If the Chinese state wanted to prosecute everyone for the smallest infraction, jail cells would have to be filled many times over and the entire society might collapse. We still have to keep in mind that despite the harsh human rights regime, there are fewer Chinese in jail than in the US with only a quarter of the Chinese population. What is more pernicious than the prospect of landing in jail for criticizing the regime is the fear or expectation of landing in jail, which then re-structures people's behavior to avoid making political statements in public or even in private messages, which are surely monitored. Another pernicious element is the extent of algorithmic power, because there are not enough state bureaucrats to monitor all people's behavior, but if algorithms can automatically evaluate people's messages and flag them for the police, then it will be hard for regime critics to remain under the radar.

For social scientists it is practically impossible to measure people's extent of self-censorship. Perhaps you need to track people that were outspoken on social media and then they turn silent, but there could be any number of reasons when that happens, e.g. death or switching accounts. But self-censorship imperceptibly happens as people consciously state they cannot talk about political issues online, which had happened to me several times. I also recognize that the extensive political statements that fill my Facebook wall don't tend to be replicated on the Wechat wall, which is mostly perfunctory political commentary and mostly non-political talk. Some Chinese friends tell me that they are socialized to not discuss politics, and that sentiment exists in some circles in my own family as well. Naturally, depoliticization of the public is a godsend for the government, which does not want to see the status quo overturned. The turn toward authoritarianism is, however, not merely restricted to China.

International examples of populist authoritarianism on the rise

In a globalized world economy with improved transportation and communication technology it is really difficult to conceive of different geographic spheres that lack interconnection. It might have been the case that the Mesopotamian, Indus Valley and Chinese civilization had each developed distinctly, but today any kind of development is embedded in a global economy and subsequently a global culture. As such, the political observer notes a rise of populist authoritarianism that transcends the borders of the nation state.

Within democratic societies, populist authoritarians generally use similar strategies of getting their way. Firstly, they wage a political campaign based on hatred toward outsiders, whether they be globalists, liberal elitists, foreign trade, ethnic minorities, homosexuals or immigrants. Interestingly, these authoritarians can get away without a positive ideology, suggesting that it can't be worse for the masses if they are in power. If they do offer a positive vision it tends to be nebulous and zero-sum. "We will take from the immigrants and give it to you."

Second, they aim to win the elections, which tends to be quite successful, as the popular masses are upset about a political establishment that promotes neoliberalism, i.e. more inequality, lower wages, more precarity at work, weaker social policy and more gifts for the rich. Third, once they win the elections, they gang up against democratic institutions that could criticize their policies, usually the media, parliament and the court system. Once those control institutions become compliant with the ruling government, the turn toward authoritarianism has become successful, even if it isn't so obvious that the common people will benefit from it.

Some Germans have surely benefited from Nazi full employment policies, but firstly labor unions were prohibited under the Nazi regime, which was reflected in stagnant wages even during full employment; second all excess economic surplus was invested in the armament industry, which yields less economic benefit than other civilian economic sectors; and third, the German people were dragged into a world war, which ultimately resulted in their defeat and the death of over 50 million people.

The only reassuring trend is that we don't have a populist authoritarian as strong or as megalomaniac as Adolf Hitler. What we will likely see in the immediate future is a continuous chipping away of freedoms and democratic institutions, as we see in Hungary, Poland, Russia, Turkey and even the United States (where president Trump had praised Xi for becoming president for life). Even in my native Austria, a supposedly stable democracy, the right-wing populist vice chancellor HC Strache has made "satirical" posts attacking the public media and journalists (ORF) as liars. His government also wants to end mandatory user fees for public media and replace it with direct treasury funding, which is a prelude to make its reporting more compliant to the government.

As more evidence of authoritarian control emerges, pro-capitalist free traders might be inclined to double down on their neoliberal version of globalization, though they are clearly on the political defensive. Disembedded liberalism, which only prioritizes corporate access to markets while ignoring citizens' demand for economic security, has provided the necessary fuel for populist authoritarians to gain political power.

Marx has been right in critiquing bourgeois democracy in that one cannot speak simultaneously of freedom and rights for the individual and combine that with the private appropriation of the means of production. Political democracy (one man, one vote) stands in contradiction to economic authoritarianism (wealth only accrues to capitalists, not workers and citizens), which defines contemporary capitalism, whether it be of the more democratic (western) or authoritarian (eastern) variety. As the social contradictions (extreme inequality) increase, I predict a stronger pull toward authoritarianism. In other words, rather than China adopting democratic institutions, the west will increasingly adopt authoritarian institutions. The technological surveillance tools are certainly available for that to happen.

Meta-stability of authoritarian regimes

Even as neoliberalism is in shambles, the question remains whether the Chinese leadership can retain political stability. Observers, who believe in static conditions, might be inclined to argue that Xi Jinping's power grab implies the strengthening of the political status quo. But I should remind people that history is actually quite dynamic. Over the short-term the end of the term limit means that Xi will be able to rule for the rest of his life, and we are back to a quasi-monarchical system (though without family inheritance as in the North Korean regime). But over the long term, there are dynamic social forces that could predict instability for the regime. While democratic regimes tend to adjust to the wind of popular pressure, this is much harder in an authoritarian regime, where there are no elections to capture and channel popular sentiment.

To adjust for this weakness, the Chinese government allows restricted channels for the airing of public discontent, usually in the form of petitions or a customer service department, where citizens can call in and make complaints. What is notable is that customer service representatives are instructed to not hang up on the callers and perform emotional labor to calm down the caller. The Chinese might not be so concerned about functioning democratic institutions as much as having responsive institutions in general. With the right balance of carrots and sticks, the government hopes to steer the public in ways that will maintain the political hegemony of the Communist Party and whoever is in charge at the helm of it.

But there are limits to this kind of political stability under authoritarianism. A completely stable political regime has to apply almost no coercion on the populace and receive high levels of popular approval. A meta-stable political regime has to increase surveillance and punishment to keep the public under a tight leash. In this way, the regime can maintain some political stability until the entire structure blows up and disintegrates, as had happened during the Arab Spring in many north African states. Once the military sides with the public masses on the street, the regime can no longer hold. What will provide the spark for such a social explosion? This is as hard to predict as the next economic crisis. We can talk about underlying fundamentals (e.g. economic inequality, riots, protests, house prices etc.) that favor disintegration, but we cannot predict a certain timeline. Until that happens, hail to our overlord rulers!

From Wage Labor to a Gift Economy: Contradiction of Capital Accumulation

Posted on March 21, 2018

While reading *Profit and Gift in the Digital Economy* by Dave Elder-Vass (2016), I was reminded of a contradictory development within modern capitalist economies. We are shifting from an economy based on wage labor, which simultaneously fueled production and consumption, which has been keeping the capital accumulation regime going, to an economy based on unilateral gifts given by individuals to powerful monopoly corporations, who have to pay us virtually nothing in return, thus feeding a cycle of growing income inequality, reactionary populism and frustration with the status quo among what Donald Trump described as the "forgotten men and women". Declining purchasing power among consumers in developed countries subsequently pushes down rates of economic growth, which will produce not only a crisis of legitimacy but also a crisis of accumulation. To understand this contradiction we have to remind ourselves of the major trends happening in the economy.

The digital revolution implies greater dependence on major monopoly capitalist firms like Amazon, Apple, Google, Facebook and Microsoft. They get to consume a greater share of our attention, and can control the channels of a giant networked customer base (as opposed to e.g. Halal food carts), thus earning more profits than any other firm can. Amazon is a giant bazar displacing the big retail competitors. Apple/ Microsoft are giant suppliers of computers, smartphones and what forms the hardware of consuming many online services. Google is a giant library, which contains all of the world's knowledge with steadily improving algorithms. Google also runs Youtube, which is a way to access our media entertainment. Facebook is a giant social network that we use to keep in touch with people and share silly thoughts and experiences with others in the network.

In addition to the monopoly power of these internet giants increasing, the invention of self-driving cars, self checkout kiosks, free media streaming (as opposed to buying CDs, DVDs etc.), automated warehouses, software in the service sector and robots in factories implies a mass displacement of mostly routine jobs, which are not growing since the last great recession of 2008. Considering the fact that the labor force is continuously growing, the absence of routine jobs means that there will be more frustrated unemployed and underemployed workers, who will vote for the next Donald Trump that hails from some corner in the country. Capitalism is built on labor-saving technology, which pushes out the frontier of production, while eliminating old jobs with the potential promise of creating jobs elsewhere in the chain.

Managerial and professional positions may be on the rise, and if we follow the "bullshit job" argument by David Graeber (2013), they can technically be endlessly extended. What he is referring to is the growth of unproductive service jobs that don't exist to feed, clothe and shelter us, but to entrap us in extended periods of busyness, e.g. advertising, contract lawyers, financial services, education and health care administration, human resources or public relations. While some may object that these are all necessary aspects to a modern economy, one should be reminded that many health care jobs don't contribute to the health and welfare of the citizenry. The lack of an efficient single-payer health care system bloats up profits and administrative expenses in the US.

But while we may be inclined to criticize these jobs, our laborist political economy ("work or starve") convinces us that given the strong force of automation coming down our way, we should defend these jobs as long as possible, no matter how useless they are. As long as we can convince some powerful employer to buy our labor services, we should shut up and be grateful that we can get the means to fill up the gas tanks and keep the lights on at home, even if we perceive our job as socially meaningless. That is how absurd our economic system has become.

The devalorization of labor (either in the form of displacement of expensive, organized labor or in the maintenance of deskilled, low-cost workers with little or no rights) is also connected to an increasing donations/ gifts. Amazon Mechanical Turk, Uber, Google, Facebook, Youtube and Wikipedia are useful representations of this gift economy. But what do I mean by gifts? One may argue that gifts are given in exchange for another favor from that person in the future. Think of lobbyists bribing politicians to make them pass a law friendly to the lobbyists' industry. But gifts may also be given without any expectation of return. Think of giving the street beggar some small change. For most of us engaging in the internet economy, donating our time for free, we never expect any monetary returns, even as the platforms we are on and their investors make money like there is no tomorrow. Let's take a look at what I will call the "unilateral gift economy".

In Amazon Mechanical Turk, one can fill out surveys or complete any tasks that can be done online, which are demanded by requesters. Pay is often very low, in part because there are so many MTurkers (supply) relative to requests (demand). A recent paper by Dube et al. (2018) found that there is substantial monopsony power by MTurk requesters. A monopsony is a market condition where there is only one buyer (i.e. Amazon). Monopsony power is reflected in the inelastic labor supply, which means that regardless of what the price is, the number of MTurkers does not change. In a very elastic labor supply situation small price changes result in substantial shifts in the labor supply. There are simply too many MTurkers, who are desperate for any job that they accept any compensation even if very low.

Now you might object that MTurk sounds like just another job, because responding to a request means work and that becomes compensated even if that is not enough to live on. In a technical economic sense those critics are right. But from a critical perspective, isn't it also true that once one becomes so absorbed in doing MTurk jobs with so little compensation that MTurkers might use reasons other than making money and paying bills to continue doing it? Subjectivity is very important here. Scholz (2016) reported surveys/ interviews of MTurkers, who participated on the platform because filling out surveys would "benefit science". These are MTurkers, who used a higher non-economic rationale to justify why they continue to do a lousily-paid job.

Uber is another example of a job, whereby the sheer scale of the number of drivers in the industry pushes down the total compensation in the industry (Schor and Attwood-Charles 2017). Subsequently, many Uber drivers that I had encountered were not using earning money as a primary reason to drive, but their ability to communicate with customers, being out of the house, having something to do. As such, drivers are pre-emptively undervaluing their labor, and consent to the unilateral transfer of gifts to the powerful company. It turns out that Uber has also developed algorithms to encourage their drivers to drive more hours to hit certain earning targets, which becomes the gamification of work. Perceive what you are doing as entertainment or fun competition and not work, which eases the unilateral gift transfer to Uber.

Google seems to deliver users the best of all worlds: access to the world's combined knowledge for free. Even just 30 years ago, knowledge was concentrated in a few minds and a few education institutions. Encyclopedia Britannica and Brockhaus were encyclopedias that were compiled by some very educated people, who then have their works read by an audience of other educated people. But Wikipedia and Google open up knowledge to anyone with an internet connection. Now, we can critique that only educated people will look for interesting information, while others will search for computer games and online porn. But that is beside the point. The key point is that the free receipt of information is not so free.

The famous saying is that if the product does not cost anything you become the product. That is the world of Google, Facebook and Youtube. The economic success of Google despite the free offering of their product is the targeted advertising that is made possible by tracing any online web searches to your individual account. My entire web search history is tied to Google Chrome and I am always logged in with my email account. That is very convenient, because all of my web searches and bookmarks can be pulled up anytime and anywhere that I am logged in. If I have recently searched for neckties, then lo and behold I will see many commercials of neckties on the sidebar. As a result, advertisers who are greedy for user data to target their products to potential customers know that they have to advertise via Google and may even pay a premium to do so. Thus, Google takes a huge chunk of the globally available online ad revenues.

Elder-Vass (2014: 189) claims that Google is embedded in both the capitalist and the gift economy, which does make sense. Targeted ads make Google capitalist, while the free user service and the need to please users with fancy, convenient features make it part of the gift economy. But this demarcation does not allow us to weigh which economic aspect dominates. To the extent that users are providing free data to Google, which profits indirectly from users, the users are uncompensated workers, thus providing a giant gift to Google.

A similar principle exists for Facebook, which is perhaps even more pernicious than Google in aggregating information on individual users. While Google has to infer my tastes and preferences indirectly via my search preferences, any Facebook comment, like/ hate/ love/ disgust etc., sharing of link and inputting of personal data into the profile produces a very explicit and direct expression of my tastes and preferences. Thus, Facebook is as good if not better poised than Google to profit from individual user data.

In the case of Youtube, our video preferences get saved to an individual account, which is often tied to the Google account, and as such it ensures that we constantly watch things on Youtube. In that sense, it is similar to Facebook, Twitter or Gmail in that it can permanently occupy our attention space, which confronts us with more commercials, which showers Youtube with even more profits. While writing this post, I listen to my favorite pop song playlist, getting advertisements in regular intervals (perhaps every 2-3 videos). Video content creators might be put in a position to earn a share of the advertising royalties in pay-per-view agreements. But video creators have to individually negotiate that with Youtube if they want to get any royalties. In the absence of such agreements, Youtube collects all the revenues. It can, therefore, not be surprising that many hobby video creators (e.g. people doing Jackass-style stunts, share their family cooking recipes, or just tell stories) just treat their activity as an entertaining hobby that will enliven the life of their viewers (i.e. a gift) rather than a way to earn royalties.

Music producers, in a classic "if you can't fight them, join them" manner, had first tried to sue Youtube for copyright infringement for posting music videos, but then realized that it was too stressful/ uneconomic to force removal every time someone uploaded a bootlegged copy of a song. Youtube could not be held to account for such copyright infringement so long as it removed unlawful use of copyrighted songs when told to remove them. The music producers (there are only very few, and the official music videos on Youtube are sponsored in VEVO) partnered with Youtube and are back to making money, though the total revenues in the music industry have declined, making artists more dependent on live performances to make a living.

Among all of the major examples of the online gift economy (with capitalist underpinnings), only Wikipedia is unambiguously not for profit. It is not listed in the stock market, and is operated by the non-profit Wikimedia Foundation. When going to the Wikipedia page (which had been very useful to me in many of my investigative blogs), you will find the regular pleas for donations from users. There are no ads, and thus no other way to generate revenues to keep the staff which maintains and hosts the site. But it is precisely because of the pure gift economy ethos that all the Wikipedia contributors (which is, again, anyone with internet/ computer access) will ask for nothing more than the feeling of benefiting the community with knowledge in their respective areas of expertise as opposed to any material compensation, as was the case with contributors to other professionally curated encyclopedias. One donates his/ her time and knowledge to contribute to publicly available knowledge, and this is a pure gift economy.

So what are the implications of these three large forces? These forces include (1) the intensification of monopoly capitalism with the giant internet providers; (2) the decline of routine and productive jobs; and (3) the rise of a unilateral gift economy to the benefit of these monopoly companies.

Concerns about surveillance are certainly becoming louder. In China, the social credit system bars people with unpaid financial debts to purchase flight or train tickets (TodayOnline 2018). Facebook is drawing intense public scrutiny for allowing Cambridge Analytica to draw on Facebook profile data for political influencing in the 2016 presidential elections (Tam and DelReal 2018). When the trolls take over or the state with its own controlling needs, then civil society is besieged because it is unlikely that such a large, complex social network can be democratically held accountable. The few thousand employees in Silicon Valley, who create the products that we all need, hold tremendous amounts of power over the rest of us, who cannot afford to quit Gmail or Facebook for fear of becoming a social isolate. Citizens groups might want to pressure lawmakers and the internet giants themselves to subscribe to a code of conduct that will avoid excesses in surveillance and opinion manipulation, but I doubt how effective that can be.

With respect to the economic forces at play here, we are reminded of the contradiction of capitalism. The growth of monopoly internet firms reflects not the initial failure of capitalism but its success, because it is the objective of firms to control the entire market. Rockefeller had attempted this by consolidating the oil and railroad industry, and in today's economy it means the control over the digital information channels, but also the centralized controls over the productive portions of our economy (extraction, manufacturing and agriculture). The fact that Silicon Valley firms are swimming in cash should be a source of happiness if that wealth can feasibly trickle down to the rest of us. But the decline of productive/ routine jobs and the rise of the gift economy (i.e. our contributions of time and data to internet companies) imply that there is no such trickle down to be expected.

On the contrary, the existence of a homelessness crisis in cities like San Francisco and Los Angeles indicates a microcosm of a failing social economy. As the tech giants continue to attract more investor capital and grow their user networks, they attract a few thousand engineers form the elite universities, who use their high salaries to buy the scarce attractive residencies in the Bay Area, thus driving up home and rental values for everyone living there, even poor people with minimum wage jobs that have lived in the Bay Area for their entire life. No wonder there is a homelessness crisis. The internet monopoly firms' drive to accumulate capital is an utter success, but this will be the utter failure as the lack of broad purchasing power in the economy will diminish any future sources of growth, which can by itself negatively affect investor animal spirits and push down ad revenues for these internet giants. Add to that demographic aging and decline, and I can hardly see how the economic growth mantra shall continue indefinitely.

From the perspective of social theory, the unilateral gift economy is even worse than Marxist labor exploitation, because labor is at least compensated for part of their labor, but now we are being paid nothing for any information that we hand to the internet giants.

What is to be done? We certainly know that the endless accumulation of academic credentials or a massive jobs program are no longer sensible tools to ensure broad-based economic benefits. The removal of mass routine production jobs is probably for good. Even as we still have unmet needs in public infrastructure (roads and rail lines have been left to decay), these are temporary priming the pump mechanisms that won't generate sustainable full employment.

I would also argue that we should stop second-guessing about finding new mass employment industries, because the goal in life is not to have a job for its own sake. Reasonable policies would be to increase paid vacation benefits and shorten weekly work hours so that we can distribute work that is not automated to a broader set in the population. This step might have to to be financed from profits, though- as Kalecki (1943) noted- a full employment equilibrium might produce higher profits as both production and consumption increases. If the market does not generate full employment (as it never does), then the state might have to step in by creating public employment financed by the giant revenues from the internet firms. Because how likely is it that Facebook will hire millions of social media app developers, which it could easily afford at the moment?

In the absence of the full employment option, there are still two other alternatives: Jaron Lanier (2014) is a supporter of so-called micro-payments, which means that we are no longer treated as Facebook's and Google's consumers, who are passively benefiting from their service, but we are treated as workers, deserving of financial compensation for inputting our data. To the extent, that we are wasting more and more hours of the day with those internet companies, the survival of the masses might be made possible via these micro-payments. The difficulty lies in the indeterminancy of "fair" compensation levels. Should you just be paid a flat-rate for owning an account (which almost works like a basic income), or should you be paid for the number of likes/ views you get on your post? What happens to very poor people lacking stable internet access, or people who are not voyeuristic enough to display all their life stories on social media or use other non-internet sources for gathering information? Therefore, I think that micro-payments are an interesting idea, but hard to define in practice.

So far we are still assuming that we can rely on a market mechanism to ensure the fair distribution of economic resources. But I find that perspective deeply troubling, because in a market the best networked people will earn the most income compared to those with fewer networks, thus continuously reproducing socially undesirable concentrations of wealth. Mark Zuckerberg, CEO of Facebook, knows that he is not going to create millions of Facebook jobs to cushion the social dislocation of low-wage jobs or lack of jobs, so he supported the universal basic income (UBI), which is in part financed by a wealth tax that would burden people like himself and other similarly situated people. Zuckerberg frames this position as allowing people to experiment with entrepreneurship the same way he has (Gillespie 2017).

It is probably true that there are a lot of people working boring jobs to keep their pensions and health care, while they really want to become independent entrepreneurs like Zuckerberg. But there are also people, who want to take it easy, spend more time with the family and work a job without the threat of being fired becoming an existential threat. But that is not inconsistent with the principle of a UBI. Only when a basic income is conditional, as with the conditional cash transfers in developing countries requiring parents to send their children to be vaccinated and to school, can we mandate desirable behavioral traits on benefit recipients. But conditional cash transfers, even if well intentioned, are still constraining the behavior of individuals.

UBI will decouple economic survival from work and wage labor and has the positive side effect that we don't have to intervene in the labor market to ensure more job opportunities. We also don't have to get bogged down by complicated evaluations of how many likes or how many web searches we do to get "fair" compensation. The only question that arises is whether s UBI can weaken the pillars of capitalism, which is based on the exploitation of wage labor. But to some extent, if the only economic benefit that individuals can generate is like Wikipedia, where we gift our knowledge to the broader world community, and not producing food or cars, then it should be possible to subsidize this gifting, which is not based on economic greed but the love of sharing information with others. Payment for service as opposed to payment for time can negatively influence professional autonomy (Crouch 2015). Take, for instance, the doctor, who gets more money for prescribing more medical tests to patients even if they are not medically necessary as opposed to a doctor, who gets paid a fixed salary, and autonomously decides to prescribe tests in accordance to what he/she thinks is necessary for the patient's health.

This would suggest that it is okay for Facebook, Google, Wikipedia and co. not to sponsor our free work for them as long as those wealthy and powerful entities pay their taxes to fund a universal basic income. The question is merely whether the state actors can be convinced to embrace that solution.

Low Productivity Service Jobs in an Automated Economy
Posted on <u>April 1, 2018</u>

In a raging debate on whether machines and robots will wipe out all jobs, the judge is still out. The economic forecasters strongly believe in the possibility of displacing anywhere between 10 to about 50% of all jobs given the advancements of robotics and artificial intelligence. Other scholars argue that rising productivity pushes down costs, which raises consumer savings, which then become redeployed in other economic areas, which creates new jobs, especially in the service sector.

A decline in the overall unemployment rate and a modest decline in the number of long-term unemployed that have been excluded during the era of "jobless recovery" might suggest that the capitalist economy has not exhausted all means of generating new jobs for people. This positive labor market trend may be limited by the fact that we are simply waiting for another major economic bubble to burst, perhaps this time in China. But even if we assume that the optimists are correct and we have found a sustainable job recovery, the headwinds lie in the quality of new jobs that are created.

The expansion of a digital labor market interestingly takes the form of low-wage work, like Uber, Lyft, Mechanical Turk or Task Rabbit. Online mediated services undermine the potential for social solidarity, because they lack the face-to-face interaction which is required to create sympathy and a worker organization. As such, any firm rents that these internet platforms generate will unlikely be shared with the workers.

The vast bulk of jobs that exist even in the non-digital economy, like being a substitute teacher in high school, care worker in a veteran's hospital or a food service worker in a big company, are also rather poorly paid and unionization has been difficult. Progressive political forces have pushed for a higher minimum wage to ensure a socially acceptable standard of living for these low-paid workers. It certainly makes no sense for a single mother to receive 7.25 dollars an hour, when despite her full-time work half the income already goes to childcare, let alone paying for rent and food. The dismantling of basic welfare programs (like AFDC, Aid for Families with Dependent Children) has removed any last economic cushion for the lower class confronting a very bad labor market.

The capitalists' response to a higher minimum wage is that payment of wages above total worker productivity would result in a cutback in hiring. Naturally we have to ask ourselves how much of the low-payment of wages is linked to worker productivity and how much to the monopsony power of the company. (A monopsony is where the buyer of labor services has a lot of power, because that employer is an employer of last resort, and there are not many other jobs available.) In the case of Walmart, the giant bonuses for managers and the Walton owners suggests that many workers can gain additional thousands of dollars a year without turning up a loss for the company (profits might even increase with reduced turnover and training costs, as well as a spillover effect of larger wages in similar retail companies raising aggregate demand in the economy).

But let us assume that the capitalist is right and that any higher payment of wages for workers in the service sector would induce Baumol's (2013) cost disease, i.e. higher wages have to be compensated by higher product prices. Professors in universities are a classic example: the highly recognized professional status has allowed professors to command increased incomes, which has to be passed down to students facing increased tuition (which increases even more with cuts in state subsidies for public colleges). But what might work for the professor might not work so well for the food-service worker, where automation potential exists, or it might not work for strange service sector jobs like dog walkers, whose high prices lead to substitution with one's own labor (people walk their own dog instead of hiring someone else).

The key problem in the Baumol cost "disease" (a notably pejorative label) is that workers in those occupations with rising wages experience no increase in labor productivity. Auto workers don't suffer from such cost disease, because the continuous innovation in production methods, especially the use of industrial robots, results in rising productivity, which would justify rising wages. (Given the lack of political power of the auto unions, who have been battered by outsourcing and automation, productivity rises are often not even matched by rising wages, but instead rising profits for shareholders and executives.)

But it seems to be that rising productivity is not desirable for two different reasons: service decline and technological displacement. In the first case, think of Massive Open Online Courses that can displace brick-and-mortar education. In the latter case, most teachers might have 30 students in a classroom and they won't be teaching more than 2-3 courses a semester. And that ratio has never really changed over time. But the online education revolution has promised to give more and more people an education where one teacher can teach tens of thousands of students.

But the initial enthusiasm for MOOCs has by now abated. It might come back later, but the issue seems to be that universities are still controlling the conferral of degrees, which is restricted to the brick-and-mortar experience. Another factor is that a functioning educational experience cannot do away with the personal encounters with teachers. As someone, who has spent his entire life inside the walls of the education system, I can confirm that the entire value-added of my educational experience comes from my direct interaction with teachers and professors, some of which became my mentors. I have once enrolled in a MOOC, watched a few videos, but did nothing else, and there is no penalty to it. Productivity rises in education, thus, make no sense, and might even diminish the quality of education.

On the other hand, the food service sector, custodians, cashiers or the border control officials at airports or any other perfunctory service job, where the things that customers want to have done for them require no specialized attention, but where robots and artificial intelligence have not gotten around to do them yet, productivity rises could make sense. In some cases, the low wages accompanying those sectors might discourage the increased diffusion of robot innovation. There might come a time of technological breakthrough, which will reduce the cost of robots, upon which the technological displacement of those service workers becomes feasible.

But a rising minimum wage in the low-productivity service sector could accelerate the employer demand for service automation. At this point, very few people would suggest that perfunctory service jobs cannot be automated. Some right-wingers might use this situation as evidence for not wanting to raise the minimum wage, but naturally the premise of their argument is quite absurd: heads, you work a miserable, low wage job. Tails, you have no job. The cruelty of this economic logic creates the kinds of economic dislocation that creates political monsters like Donald Trump, Brexit, nationalism, racism and xenophobia.

In some sense, we should celebrate the fact that agricultural and manufacturing work have become more and more productive, which means that we can have material goods and food without having to work that much. As such, we can only slot most people into low-productivity service jobs, which don't have much wiggle room for higher wages. In the meantime, the high cost of living still requires us to earn sufficiently high wages to afford the services that we need (services are especially expensive in health care and education, where the Baumol cost disease is the most acute). Given that we have a laborist political economy, which forces people to make a living from wage work, we are trapped in a contradiction of rising productivity across most industries and too many low wage jobs for most people in the service sector. And the solution of rising productivity for service workers creates a new unemployment problem.

Defenders of the status quo will counter that the solution has to be to slot more people into higher-skilled jobs. After all, the economic evidence shows skill-biased technological change, which means that high skilled workers, whose work is not (yet) automated, continue to command higher returns to their skills (Bekman et al. 1998). I am certainly not opposed to a mass education and training program, but it is simply wishful thinking to suggest that training and education will solve our fundamental problem of economic inequality. The entire point of advanced technology is that we don't need more than 10-15% of the workforce that does a highly-skilled occupation.

Shortening the work week would certainly make sense to distribute these high-productivity jobs across a larger amount of people, and that might defuse some of the economic anxieties. If that solution is not so feasible (as it does not do anything for people, who are still trapped in low-productivity service occupations), then a massive expansion of social services, which lowers the general cost of living, or a universal basic income are ways out of the problem. If we had free health care and free higher education and really cheap housing, then it doesn't matter if you only make 7 bucks an hour, because the important stuff you get for free. Critics of the enlarged welfare state will counter that we have to collectively pay for these services with higher taxes, but in a functioning progressive tax system the burden of the spending would be shifted from workers to capitalists, who really can't complain about the neat profits they have made with increased automation and outsourcing to cheaper labor countries.

The expansion of social welfare, including a universal basic income, implies that we would maintain poorly paid employment, but if we wanted to make sure that all people shall somehow benefit from a high productivity economy with low employment in highly productive sectors and high employment in less productive sectors, then I see few alternatives available to us.

Hungarian Elections and Viktor Orban
Posted on April 8, 2018

This Sunday Hungarians were asked to vote in the parliamentary elections, which the national-conservative Fidesz party won with a larger majority, thus retaining their two-thirds constitutional majority. The ruling prime minister, Viktor Orban, had done so much to consolidate his power and shut out and weaken the power of unfavorable institutions or fill them with his associates. The seeming invincibility of Fidesz has resulted in a strange electoral coalition among all the opposition parties (Jobbik, the socialists or MSZP and Green LMP) in the mayoral election of the southern town of Hodmezovasarhely, which led to the victory of Peter Marik-Zay, who led the grass-roots Country for All movement (Witte 2018). Such electoral coalition is unlikely to be repeated at the national level, where Orban's Fidesz had controlled the levers of government since 2010.

What explains Orban's political power? The first reason, as indicated above, is the fracturing of the political opposition. There are two smaller parties (the Greens and the Christian KDNP, the latter of which sits as junior partner in the coalition), and two larger opposition parties, including the socialist MSZP and the right-wing, anti-immigrant Jobbik. It is rather unlikely for the MSZP and Jobbik to enter a broad electoral coalition given their philosophical disagreements. The second reason is that the credible alternative to Fidesz, the MSZP had itself been discredited by corruption and bad economic management during the 2008 economic crisis, which happened during its rule from 2002 to 2010. Jobbik, which contested its first election in 2006, may be considered a credible right-wing challenger, running on a platform of ethnic nationalism, and gaining 20% of the vote in 2014. But even here, Orban outgunned the anti-immigrant platform of Jobbik by harping on law and order, such that Jobbik has to shift to left-wing economic policies to get popular attention.

The third reason is the somewhat successful economic record of the Fidesz-led administration, which feeds its job growth primarily from subsidies in the EU budget for economically weak regions in the EU (from which poorer countries like Hungary benefit disproportionately). This is all the more ironic given that his declared enemies are an all-powerful Brussels and the liberal cabal financed by George Soros, a Hungarian-American investor and philanthropist. That is perhaps the fourth reason for Orban's political power: he permanently agitates against some external enemies, whether it is the liberal establishment elite, the European bureaucrats or the refugees that "invaded" Hungary via the Balkan route in 2015 and 2016. Among a frightened and angry electorate that feels left behind by economic globalization and the rapid pace of change in a neo-capitalist society, which was communist for two generations, this agitation seems to work quite well. The fifth reason is that Orban's pan-Hungarianism, which resulted in the handing out of hundreds of thousands of Hungarian citizenships to ethnic Hungarians in neighboring countries boosted the electoral fortunes of Fidesz, which receives almost all the overseas votes (95%).

I want to explore a sixth reason, which is related to the charisma and dogged determination for power of Viktor Orban. He has been the face of Fidesz since it fought its first election in the post-communist era in 1990. It was not clear initially that Orban would become a power-hungry politician. During his university days he wanted to be an academic intellectual. He was born into a rural lower middle class family in 1963 and was interested in communism, but his military service had disillusioned him from communism. In 1988, at the age of 24 he became one of the founding members of Fidesz, the Alliance of Young Democrats, which initially only admitted people below the age of 35. The vision was clear: usher in liberal democracy into the decaying communist structures.

There were two factors that favored the end of Hungarian communism: first, Mikhail Gorbachev's takeover of power in the Soviet Union in 1985 displaced the old generation that had grown up under the yoke of Stalin and initiated liberal reforms in the economy and the polity, which was a signal to the other Warsaw Pact countries that the Soviet Union, which still had hundreds of thousands of military troops stationed in Eastern Europe, would not use violence to suppress communist regime critics. That was a huge blow to all communist leaders from Honecker in Germany to Ceausescu in Romania. Orban himself became emboldened enough during a speech in the reburial of Imre Nagy on June 16, 1989, the tragic Hungarian leader, who was felled in 1956 by invading Soviet tanks which crushed the Hungarian uprising, to demand free elections and the removal of Soviet troops from Hungary. That speech brought Orban much fame in the country and perhaps made him the undisputed leader of Fidesz. In fact, Orban has been the only

Hungarian party leader, who has consistently fought every single election since 1990.

The second reason was that Hungary became known for its goulash-communism approach, especially during the long rule of Janos Kadar, who was supposed to be a Soviet henchman after crushing the Hungarian uprising. The essence of goulash communism is to retain broad state ownership over the economy, but relax some central controls by allowing individuals to trade in the market, which resulted in a somewhat consumer-oriented marketplace. In the political sphere this meant that there was some freedom of speech (as long as critique was not directly addressed at the ruling government) and even freedom of travel. As such, it was not too far fetched for Hungary to transition into a capitalist democracy once Soviet control relaxed.

In the fall of 1989, Orban had accepted a Soros-funded scholarship to study politics in Pembroke College, Oxford. It is all the more ironic that Orban would turn so drastically against his funder in order to score political points. But only four months into the course (which really means after 8 weeks of courses, or one trimester- Michaelmas), Orban disrupted his studies to contest as leader of Fidesz in the first parliamentary elections scheduled in 1990. With only 9%, Fidesz only became the fifth-largest party, and Orban became opposition leader. In the following elections in 1994, Fidesz only received 7% of the vote. Orban realized that he had to change his strategy.

Instead of promoting liberal democracy (which had de-facto been achieved with the introduction of elections), Orban shifted to a more right-wing nationalist platform, which fellow party leaders Peter Molnar, Gabor Fodor and Zsuzsanna Szelenyi disagreed with. These more liberal leaders then left the party, leaving the party to Orban. Was Orban a plain racist, who was using his early support for liberalism as an excuse to become elected to power and then promote an anti-immigrant, anti-foreign agenda? I have not found any evidence in favor of this reasoning, but we can state that the rightward shift of Fidesz came from Orban's belief that political power can only be attained when voters can agitate against an external enemy. Carl Schmitt would have been proud of Orban.

The following exchange that is quoted in BBC (2018) is quite instructive

"We were sitting in the Angelika cafe, across the Danube from parliament," economist *Peter Rona remembers. Orban was*

describing how he wanted to turn Fidesz into a modern conservative party, but Rona warned of the danger of abandoning the "modern" at the first sign of electoral trouble.

"'I will not fall into that trap, but if necessary, so be it,' replied Orban, to my surprise. What mattered to him was to win power, and keep it, at any cost."

Orban's electoral strategy to channel the mass resentment against foreign investors, who were not interested in the unproductive socialist-era factories, resulting in a rise in unemployment, and gained sufficient electoral support in the 1998 elections to win power despite fewer electoral votes (because of winning more constituencies, especially the rural ones). Upon election, Orban pushed for lower taxes and lower social insurance contributions. He abolished university tuition fees and reintroduced universal maternity benefits. However, the Fidesz government also continued budget consolidation from the previous administration and did not reverse the privatization begun under the previous administration, which is in line with the liberal economic policy preferred by the EU (which Hungary was about to join) and the IMF.

Orban promptly lost the next elections in 2002 and was pushed into opposition (Fidesz got the most seats, but the socialists formed a coalition with the Free Democrats). This had enraged Orban so much that he vowed not only to return to power later on but also to change the institutions to make it difficult for the other opposition parties to defeat him again. So much for his avid demand for democracy from his student days in the 1980s! Orban doubled down on the national identity agenda, hired a communications guru to talk like the common man and received generous funding from his former schoolfriend Lajos Simicska to finance the next elections (Simicska's companies were then handsomely rewarded with generous government contracts once Fidesz returned to power). Fidesz was defeated again in 2006. The next opportunity for power came with the 2010 elections after the poor handling of the financial crisis in 2008 of the socialist government (unemployment increased, while corruption charges against high administration officials blew up).

Once back in power, Orban went to the EU and demanded more time to tackle the budget deficit, but was rejected by Brussels, which fueled his rage against the EU. To plug the budget hole, Orban increased taxes on foreign companies, a bank transaction tax and mobile phone charges. He also forced a conversion of private pensions into public pensions, which immediately made funds available for the administration. A 5.5% of GDP budget deficit in 2011 was lowered to 1.6% in 2015. His economic agenda was to reduce unemployment with the help of public works schemes financed by the EU. The emigration of unemployed workers also helped reduce tensions in the domestic labor market, though it created a brain drain of higher skilled talent. Employment was further boosted by slashing welfare for the long-term unemployed, though family benefits continued to increase in the hope of countering the low birth rate (which increased from 1.34 to 1.44 from 2010 to 2015). The government implemented a flat tax and a very high VAT, following in line with liberal policy prescriptions. What endeared voters to Fidesz was that the majority of the tax increases (with the exception of VAT, which is a consumption tax) were focused on foreign banks and commercial chain stores rather than the general population (Kowalczyk 2017).

To realize his power consolidation, Orban instituted a new constitution, which stressed nation state and family. The Constitutional court was weakened, the TV and radio news media were put under direct state control, and ethnic Hungarians in neighboring countries were given citizenship. Orban also purged opponents and critics in the civil service, state companies, schools and hospitals. NGOs were put under tight supervision, and the Soros-funded flagship university Central European University is threatened with outright expulsion, which motivates the university officials to open up a branch in Vienna. Finally, electoral reform reduced the parliamentary seats from 386 to 199 and abolished second-round runoff elections, which has so far favored Fidesz.

In a mature and consolidated democracy one would think that rabid nationalism won't work, but even this cozy assumption has been shattered by Brexit and the Trump elections. Western capitalist countries seem to have a problem to deliver a basic standard of living for the masses. In the Hungarian case, it might be true that greater western corporate investments have created growth and needed jobs (especially from Austrian and German firms), but a more market-driven labor market also means more uncertainty relative to the experience of communism. To some extent, Hungarian nationalism provided the same mantle of rhetorical protection to the population that state socialism used to provide, even as the nationalist mantle claims to fundamentally oppose state socialism. But this similarity is not so surprising insofar as both ideologies deny the premise of liberalism and the primacy of individual rights.

Orban's electoral strategy worked and his coalition government retained a two-thirds majority in the 2014 elections. The opposition worked together to field single candidates against Fidesz as opposed to split the opposition vote, which benefits Fidesz. Even though there was an electoral coalition between the socialists, the Together Party, the Democratic Coalition, the Dialogue for Hungary and the Liberal Party, it wasn't enough to break the electoral control of Fidesz. The center-left bloc also did not include a coalition with the right-wing Jobbik, which had received 23 seats on its own right (primarily via the proportional party list rather than first-past-the-post constituency).

The next test to the Hungarian government was the influx of refugees over the course of 2015, which escalated in the fall of that year. Orban announced in June 2015 that it would construct a border fence with Serbia, where most of the Iraqi and Syrian refugees on the West Balkan route were trying to head toward western Europe (i.e. Austria, Germany and Sweden). The EU had criticized that step, but Hungary claimed that Serbia was not part of the EU and also not part of Schengen. The flow had intensified going into the fall, reaching 30,000 a week in September (compared to 2-3,000 in May), and refugees were forcibly trying to cross the border, which induced Hungarian police to use teargas and batons to halt the flows. In October, Orban announced the closure of the border with Croatia, an EU member, but not part of Schengen.

But it just wasn't physically possible to halt the strong flows, which resulted in people flooding the train stations in Budapest. Hoping to remove these refugees, the government encouraged the refugees to move onto Austria. Fortunately for Orban, the widely publicized photos of an infant death in Syria and the suffocation of dozens of refugees on the back of an unventilated truck in Austria had convinced both the Austrian and the German chancellor to temporarily open up the borders and admit a large number of refugees.

In December 2015, Hungary challenged EU plans to distribute the asylum seekers across Europe, which would have provided relief to the main refugee-takers in the EU. In March 2016, the government declared a state of emergency, which has been extended to today. 60 refugees per day were permitted in 2016. In February 2018, the government announced to only take in 2 refugees per day, while deporting most of the rest of the refugees. In the meantime, the border fence kept on being reinforced with barbed wire, heat sensors, video cameras and armed police patrol (Nelson 2018). There are many refugees who are trapped in the Serbian-Hungarian border, receiving poor supplies of food in camps without much protection from the winds during the winter season.

From an electoral standpoint, will Hungarians punish their ruling government for the handling of the refugee crisis? This is the first election since the refugee crisis, and the polls have not suggested any dips for Fidesz, which means that the tough anti-refugee position paid off for Orban. In contrast, Austrian chancellor Faymann's party lost the first round of the presidential elections, which had increased the pressure against him to resign, which he promptly did in May 2016. Chancellor Merkel's CDU and the SPD coalition partner in Germany dramatically lost voter support in the fall 2017 elections, which explains in part why it took so long for them to form another new government. The right-wing parties (FPO and AfD) gained a lot of electoral support, though in Austria, the FPO was surpassed by the conservative OVP, which ran an anti-refugee, anti-immigrant campaign, thus resulting in an "Orbanization" of the political process in Austria.

The 2018 electoral campaign in Hungary continues on the anti-refugee sentiment, which is driven by both Fidesz and Jobbik, but given that those themes don't differ, I doubt that Jobbik can substantially gain in the vote share. Jobbik is somewhat more progressive in social policy, demanding much higher minimum wages, full pensions after 40 years of work for everyone (only for women in the Fidesz program), and the modernization of the education and health systems. Fidesz pushes for higher pensions, family tax allowances and a modern village program to boost the rural vote.

The socialist party does not mention the refugees at all and focuses on bread and butter issues, i.e. higher wages, tax credits for low-income households, inflation indexation for pensions, higher family allowance and gas/ electricity subsidies for poor households. If refugees are a main driver for electoral shifts, we can't find that they would work to the detriment for Orban. The major weakness in the Orban strategy, which the opposition is hammering him on, is political corruption, which results in the loss of national funds to Orban's political cronies. But such corruption is not out of line with other eastern European countries or his socialist predecessors.

It may be stated that the electoral success for Orban lies in his ability to manipulate the electorate with a strong anti-immigrant and national identity platform, which is additionally bolstered by his hardline stance during the refugee wave, his persistent verbal attacks against the liberal elites abroad (especially the EU, that finance most of the country's infrastructure projects, and George Soros, who had financed his Oxford studies), economic policies that favor families and the lower middle class, especially in rural areas, the weakness/internal division of the political opposition, and making the democratic control institutions (primarily the media and the supreme court) compliant to the government.

For the immediate future we cannot realistically expect a democratic awakening for Hungary nor for any other Eastern European country, which had suffered from various national trauma (from Austria, Germany or the Soviet Union), and recently escaped the comforts of state socialism to be plunged into what Francis Fukuyama (1989) alleged to be the end of history, i.e. the triumph of liberal democracy (or neoliberal capitalism for people on the political left). Nationalism is cleverly combined with selective liberalization and a family-oriented welfare state, while the socialist opposition is discredited in part by the state socialist past and the lack of credibility for implementing neoliberal reforms of privatization and deregulation.

But how sustainable is Orban's strategy? There is a certain economic contradiction in the Fidesz project, which is chiefly related to demographics. Over the short-term, Hungary and other post-socialist states have benefited from western corporate investments into a cheap but (thanks to state socialism) highly educated population/ labor force, but any long-term economic gains are dependent on a population growth strategy, which is not compatible with the anti-immigrant policies of the government. The pro-natalist policies have slightly increased the birth rate but insufficient to halt population decline. In addition, as long as there is a wage and living standard gap between the rich west and the poor east, eastern Europe will continue to lose workers, which in some cases is permanent. To the extent that it is the young and educated people, who prefer to work in Germany than in their native Hungary, population decline is compounded by labor force decline. The implication is that once the easy avenues for growth disappear, then population decline will be felt in the form of economic decline, in which case the argument for limiting foreign migration become even more acute, though there won't be many scapegoats left to blame.

For arrogant western liberal elites lecturing down on the democratic deficiencies of Hungary and their political cousins in Poland (which are undoubtedly concerning and ought to be criticized), they should be reminded not only of the specific historical context of eastern European, but also the electoral upheaval in their own country, which delegitimate democratic political and social institutions. Donald Trump wants a giant military parade. Donald Trump wants to build a giant border wall to keep out immigrants (even as their numbers are pretty stagnant and in some cases declining). Donald Trump congratulates Vladimir Putin on his re-election (without any credible alternative candidate) and Xi Jinping on ending his term limit in power, and maybe the US should do something like that too.

Thus, Orban and other more authoritarian leaders, who prefer not to surrender their power are vindicated in their strategy, as the liberal political order continues to crumble. Though to be clear, I still find it unlikely that Orban will push for a complete abolition of democracy, so long as curtailments of democratic institutions to retain his power monopoly are sufficient and as long as the EU continues to act as external constraint. Though the paradox in the latter is that the harsher the EU cracks down on the Hungarian government, the more the EU will be delegitimated in the eyes of the electorate that feel closer to Budapest than to Brussels.

In other words, Hungary and the "Orbanization" of politics in the absence of progressive alternatives is the new normal.

The Charismatic Musician: Nile Rodgers
Posted on April 29, 2018

I had previously pointed out that Elton John, whose career spanned several decades was a talented musician, who had derived much of his emotional energy from live performances (Liu, "Elton John: A Music Career with High Emotional Energy", this volume). For social theorists, the greatest satisfaction comes from a theoretical prediction that is more generalizable, and I have made it easy for myself by picking another interesting and fascinating musician and producer: Nile Rodgers (2011). There are some commonalities and some differences in each of their characteristics, but they are not so different overall.

John is white British, while Rodgers is black American. John plays the piano and integrates it into pop music, while Rodgers plays the guitar (his Fender '59) and is associated with funk, disco and the early version of Hip Hop. John composed the music (with the help of his friend Bernard Taupin) and became a solo artist, which Rodgers also did with the help of his friend and bassist Bernard Edwards. But Rodgers musician career in the funk band Chic was disrupted by the Disco Sucks movement in 1979, which he described in his autobiography as an uprising of white male rock fans against disco music, which was attached to racial minorities, women and gays. Rodgers continued writing and producing music, first for black artists (like Sister Sledge and Diana Ross), followed by mainly white artists (David Bowie, Duran Duran and Madonna being the most prominent ones).

John and Rodgers also shared their proclivity for drugs and alcohol, which had nearly destroyed their lives. Once they reached their mid-40s, their bodies could no longer handle that lifestyle and they checked into rehab, and as such got another lease on life. Most importantly, John and Rodgers had shared an obsession with their musical work. John would spend a balanced time recording songs in the studio and doing live performances in concerts, which he thought had also saved his life, because otherwise he would have spent even more time getting wasted. Rodgers did very few live performances, and focused most of his energy in the recording studio putting together the music and working with other artists.

To become an expert, one would have to spend a lot of time doing the same things and gradually become very good at what one is doing. Rodgers and his colleague Edwards had come up with the idea that the music they were writing contained some deep hidden meaning, which is the amalgamation of their musical influences and thinking about producing new music with it. But they never really specified what they meant by this deep hidden meaning. To some extent, it becomes difficult to verbalize the creative process, which from the consumer end can only be judged by the product.

Funk and disco music brought many people regardless of their skin color onto the dance floor. What is the secret sauce? Firstly, it is the combination of the guitar and the bass, which were complementing each other very well, which is also related to the fact that Rodgers and Edwards very terrific musicians. Second, the guitar has a constant strumming pattern, focusing the pick on three strings and frequent scratches, which means to lift the finger slightly from the strings, but still touching them. The mix of normal strumming with scratches, and the constant repetition of the 4 chord structure produced the very attractive tune that would take people out onto the dance floor. Third, while there were lyrics and singers, those would be secondary to the combination of guitar, bass and drums (with the occasional electric piano or violin tossed in between).

Even in the music writing process, Rodgers usually single-handedly writes the songs with some input by Edwards to make it even more appealing while Sister Sledge and the Chic singers were just handed the final product to perform. With many of the other musicians Rodgers had worked with, there was more interchange and input of the musicians, because the general song idea would come from the artist, but it was still Rodgers who would take the clay and form it into shape.

The creative process with David Bowie is a case in point. Bowie took out his guitar and played a country-music style riff, which he wanted to call "Let's Dance". Rodgers freaked out and said this can't possibly be played. He asked Bowie to play the riff again, so that Rodgers could write it down and reflect on it. Rodgers then went to his room, picked up the guitar, looked at the chords that Bowie played him, and began experimenting. When he liked what he composed, he played it to Bowie, who was immediately impressed (which shows the great musical quality of Bowie, who could tell the difference between what music could work and what would not). They immediately hired a band and recorded the song and the album on the spot, and the end result is "Let's Dance".

Madonna had also made a deep impression on Rodgers. When they first met in the studio they sat in the room and listened to

Madonna's previous records. Rodgers reflected on the harmony of the instruments and the style of Madonna's voice, but when they were finished listening, Madonna looked very seriously at Rodgers and said, "If you don't love all my music, then we can't work together." That came as a great shock to Rodgers as each side had just agreed to sign a record deal (which provided very hefty royalties to Rodgers once the album became a hit record). Rodgers said, "I don't love all of your music, but once we are finished recording I will love all of them." That was apparently enough to reassure Madonna. Madonna was a very decisive musician, often making verbal abuses to Rodgers' recording team when things were not done her way. One important disagreement was with respect to the selection of the lead single, which would become the name of the album. Rodgers thought "Material Girl" should be the lead single, while Madonna insisted on "Like a Virgin". Both songs became great hits, but because it was Madonna's album her view prevailed.

But musicians rarely made a mistake when they had decided to collaborate with Rodgers. Rodgers had a great sense of what music would catch fire and which didn't, and that is what defines a great musician. Most musicians in their old age begin to take it easy. They might still be performing to get a thrill, but it would be the old songs that become heated up, just like Billy Joel, who stopped composing new things in the early 1990s. But for the workaholic Nile Rodgers that was inconceivable. In 2013, his hit single "Get Lucky" that came out of collaboration with Daft Punk and Pharrell Williams brought him back to prominence. Daft Punk, the two French musicians in robot outfit, had approached Rodgers, and they were eager to collaborate with Rodgers, thus bringing the funk back alive (it was never really dead, maybe dormant over some stretches of time). "How did you make the Chic record?", Daft Punk had asked Rodgers. Rodgers took the basic riff for Get Lucky and created two guitar riffs recorded separately, but played alongside each other, thus producing the distinctive four-chord structure in Get Lucky (for which I recommend listening to the long version on the album, not the radio version). What I find remarkable about "Get Lucky" is that the lyrics is awful (sorry Pharrell), but it is the instrumental which makes it so worthwhile listening to. There, indeed, is a deep hidden meaning.

The decisiveness and quickness with which Rodgers had justified his choice of chords and structures to the song ("Good Times" by Chic was composed the night before it was recorded) he had explained with respect to the competitive music business, where you have to get things right immediately, because there wasn't the advanced technology that allows for the easy recording and manipulation of the music. But this quickness may also just be a reflection of the musical genius of Rodgers. Even Elton John did not take much time to compose his songs. He would get the lyrics faxed over by Taupin, and he would sit on the piano just hitting the keys, and either figuring the song out in 15 minutes or throw away the lyric.

Rodgers was once asked in an interview about how he thought about talent and genius, and he used the Albert Einstein metaphor, who created the relativity theory in his mid-20s, and then spent the rest of his life defending it. There is not much space for creativity and it has to be fully exploited. Rodgers is now well into his 60s, but he can talk about his formative time at Chic in the late-1970s as if it just happened yesterday.

Thus, to be defined as a musical genius- the charismatic musician- it is not enough to be a good and passionate instrumentalist (though, no doubt a prerequisite), but one has to have a quick, discriminatory taste and judgment, and also be connected to the right networks at the right time. For posterity, the benefit comes in the form of addicting music.[39]

---

[39] My personal Rodgers playlist is here:
https://www.youtube.com/playlist?list=PLQkt-6c5Frv-du_DZ0AxTDuc2SS4cQxDI

The Gates-Buffett-Bezos-Zuckerberg Bullshit Job Creation Act

Posted on May 9, 2018

I had this rather strange dream that I had been summoned to meet the country's richest people (Gates, Buffett, Bezos, Zuckerberg) and put in charge of a giant fund endowed by them to create a giant basic income program funded from the successive sale of half of the stocks held by these individuals (which generates close to $200 billion, which still leaves them with nearly the same amount in net worth). But because they also believed that people had to be made useful they made the receipt of this basic income dependent on people doing "something useful". They would leave the details of the program to me.

I was sweating as I approached the boardroom, where I was supposed to give a powerpoint and distribute an accompanying document, which outlines my plans for the many low-wage workers and unemployed individuals, whose basic economic needs could now be fulfilled with the basic income. To gain more legitimacy, the inactive Congress, which, thus far, can agree on fully funding a military budget to fight foreign wars and give tax breaks to the rich, but not on benefiting the working class with better social policy, had also sent a small delegation (including Senator Bernie Sanders) to attend the meeting. Politicians were hoping to use the oligarch money to codify this donation as law, and perhaps even expand the program at a federal level. At least that is what Sanders hoped to do, co-sponsoring this legislation in the senate.

I was even asked to propose what to call the law. I was baffled for a while but then replied confidently, "The Gates-Buffett-Bezos-Zuckerberg Bullshit Job Creation Act". I could see the laughter in each of the oligarch's faces. Zuckerberg had objected that he wanted to be somewhat more low-key, but I had insisted on that name, because it should be clear where that money had come from. There is a little bit of self-deception here, because any person can only get rich by taking advantage of many customers and workers, so I was aware that the money of the oligarchs is returning the money they had taken from society, but I was willing to stroke their egos for the good cause.

Gates was more troubled by the latter half of the name. I then briefly summarized the research of the anthropologist David Graeber (2018), who had remarked that the vast majority of jobs that are created in the contemporary service economy are regarded as utterly useless to the workers and the society. These may be telemarketers, PR lobbyists, corporate lawyers or financial accountants. Take any service and then find things to do for people rather than how to help the society (like collecting garbage, curing patients or teaching students). I understood that Gates was funding projects worldwide, where he thought that by curing basic diseases via better sanitation and access to medicine in poor countries that the people will help others after having themselves be helped. It was hard to drill into his head that the vast majority of jobs are utterly useless to society, but that conservative political norms would prohibit us to call out the bullshit jobs for what they are.

While by using the names of the oligarchs I was lying and flattering their conscience, I decided to be brutally honest about the intention of what my proposal was going to do. My first preference was to get a universal basic income grant, which would place absolutely no restrictions on what people could and could not do with the money. But the oligarch requirement was for the people to do something "useful". The funders were also not interested in giving every person in the country the basic income, but selected their targets to be the bottom fifth of the income distribution. I suppose they were hoping that the politicians would jump at it and have the state fund a basic income for the rest of the population. Only Sen. Sanders gave me an approving nod, when revealing my intentions.

So what kind of bullshit jobs did I plan for the masses? Everyone would be given a basic income grant, but they have to show up once a month in a local gathering, which may happen in a church, school or any other institution and report what they have done this past month. Some people may do a formal powerpoint, others just talk about it, but it has to be a coherent oral presentation of at least 10 minutes. There is no restriction on what one can report on. You can compose rap songs and impress the 20 people in the gathering with your rap skills. You can cut your own and your neighbor's grass and show images of having done so. You can go kite-fishing and try to teach others the technique of how to do it. You can go on a Harley Davidson biking trip with your buddies and show videos and photos of your exploits. You can go bird watching in the forest and explain the different features of birds. You can volunteer in an after-school program teaching kids how to read. You can write a crime fiction, and read the most salient passages to the group. You can go the

Muslim hajj in Mecca or walk Santiago de Compostela in Spain as Catholic, and share your religious experience.

To make sure you don't get bored, the computer assigns you to a new group of 15-20 people all over the country. For people with severe disabilities, there is the option to restrict meetings to within one's living area, but for the rest of the basic income recipients they will be required to travel, and when their location for the next meeting is disclosed, they also receive a plane/ rail/ bus ticket funded by the oligarchs to reach that location, including two nights of accommodation in a budget hotel. When the presentations are finished, there would be a funded restaurant meal for all participants before taking off later that afternoon or the next day.

Some people might counter that there really is no bullshit job that people are subjected to. After all, if I only have to share what I am passionate doing to strangers, then this cannot be considered bullshit work, right? Yes, but the fact that you are required to report back to them or otherwise risk losing your benefit makes it a bullshit job. A more ideal version of the basic income would be to do whatever you want to without having to be accountable to others.

But that design could still satisfy the funders, who want their beneficiaries to still do something useful. I did not want people to go through unnecessary busywork like emptying trash cans on the ground and then picking it up again. I did not want to hire an army of security guards, who would stand around building entrances looking at each other. I did not want to put people into administrative offices, so they can be glued to a desk, shuffle papers pretending to be busy, and obsessively check out their emails and Facebook. Even the useful work which lacks enough people doing things like advocating for homeless persons or alcohol addicts, I would have trouble forcing people to do it. If they decided to do it on their own account, because they now get the basic income grant, all the better.

So I think I have a proposal that satisfies the big funders while giving people still enough freedom to do what they want. The funders asked me to leave the room, and I waited half an hour in the hallway. When I was called back in, Bezos said, "You're fired." It came a bit as a shock, and my mind was looking for potential responses, but all I could think of were lawyers coming up with counter-arguments. The Socratic method. Where is the Socratic method? But the big smile on his face made me feel at ease. Buffett replied, "Relax, Jeff is just pulling your leg. You're hired." I was pulled a Donald-Trump.

In the background of this big room, there was a big flatscreen TV with CNN running. The camera honed in on President Trump during a press announcement, "Nobody takes more care of the little people than me. I take care of the little people. Believe me. No one can do that better than- And I am telling you, we are going to do this huge program, fully funded. We have this program fully funded. Trust me. No one has done before what I am about to do now. People are like 'Donald Trump can't do this thing. He is not going to be able to do this thing.' But they are wrong. They will say wrong things. The mainstream media will tell lies and go on a witch hunt against me. They are doing a witch hunt. They say it's Russia, Vladimir Putin. I got along really well with Putin. We negotiate, and I get along very well with Putin. So are you ready for it? Are you ready? I, Donald J. Trump, am going to announce the creation of a universal basic income. We want to do the universal basic income [when reading these three words, one can see this is the only time Trump is on script and he says it slower than the rest of his speech]. You know what the best thing about it is? The best thing? I came up with it. You know, I should be getting the Nobel Prize for it. The Nobel Prize."

We all had a great laugh.

Warpath in Iran vs. Peace in Korea?
Posted on May 13, 2018

In a rather confusing turn of events, we might see a resolution to the Korea conflict, but might be drifting into war over Iran. There are very different strategic considerations which would favor each political outcome, but there is sufficient evidence to suggest that the arbitrary behavior of US president Trump plays a substantial role in this uncertainty in international relations. Pre-existing political fault lines in addition to short-term political calculations of Trump will shape how the contemporary political challenges are dealt with, and it will really be anybody's guess how it will turn out.

Up until last year, we had been contemplating the escalation toward a world war based on the heated verbal exchange between North Korean leader Kim Jong-un and Donald Trump (Liu, "North Korean Woes and the US", this volume). Kim was threatening to attack a US island, while Trump had responded with off-the-cuff remarks to inflict 'fire and fury' on the North Koreans (which was not incidentally the chosen title for the Michael Wolff expose book of the Trump administration), then doubled down in the UN speech by promising to inflict the "total destruction" of North Korea if "rocket man" didn't know how to behave himself, i.e. continue to do ballistic missile and nuclear tests.

But in a surprising turn of events, Kim decided to de-escalate. Now that he had acquired nuclear capacity, he thought he would have an effective bargaining chip to get South Korea and the Americans to hand them more economic concessions. Another argument is that the mountain where the atomic tests have taken place has collapsed, thus making it technically difficult to continue the tests (McCurry 2018). Kim promptly cancelled all future nuclear tests and scheduled a meeting with the South Korean president Moon Jae-in on the Demilitarized Zone (indicating the continuing war status between both Koreas). Moon is eager for hammering out a peace agreement, very much unlike his predecessors. It was the first meeting of each country's leader since 2007, when there were futile talks to get the North Koreans away from nuclear weapons. Perhaps this time it will be an earnest attempt toward reconciliation, though we should not forget that it cannot be in Kim's interest to surrender toward reunification.

Any attempt toward reunification would be led by South Korea, which not only has the larger relative population, but also the economic wealth to support a deeply impoverished population in the north. It would be similar to German reunification, though the burden on the south will be larger, as the west to east population ratio in Germany was 3-1 while in the south-north in Korea is only 2-1. In the first stage of reunification, West Germany sent its civil servants to occupy the bureaucratic positions held by East Germans. They then created a "Treuhandfond", which took over the unproductive East German industries and sold them off, which resulted in massive job cuts, which was quite a bad welcome of East Germans to capitalism.

To cushion the difficult economic adjustment, the federal government also imposed a solidarity tax on West German taxpayers, which has generated 343 billion euros in subsidies to East Germany, a large portion of which is concentrated on paying welfare, maintaining city services, strengthening universities and building infrastructure. West German taxpayers are hoping to get rid of the solidarity tax nearly 30 years since inception, yet East German economy per capita is only 72% of West German levels, so it is hard to argue for less support to the East (though the critic of the West is that a declining fraction of the solidarity tax is flowing to benefit the East, and more goes toward other projects and budget consolidation, Chase 2017).

The Koreas are still quite far off from contemplating reunification, but it won't come cheaply. And if Kim is unwilling to hand over power, it will take some time before reunification is possible. It could just be that the Kim regime is temporarily bluffing to buy themselves some more time until they have developed a new nuclear testing site. But Donald Trump sells himself as the savior by agreeing to meet with Kim in Singapore in June. Secretary of State Mike Pompeo has already traveled to Pyongyang for a personal encounter with Kim to prepare the ground for meeting between the two leaders. The goal is to denuclearize the Korean peninsula and declare an end to the Korean War, which is still happening on the books (and sometimes Korean soldiers along the DMZ get killed because of altercations).

For China, a denuclearized Korean peninsula may be hailed as a good outcome, which could contribute to more stability in their backyard. On the other hand, the prospect of good North Korea-US relations and potential reunification could push US troops up to the Yalu river along the border of China. Russia has had to make that experience after all the former Warsaw Pact countries have joined

NATO (exceptions are Belarus and Ukraine, though the latter now has a pro-western government with active NATO collaboration). China will, therefore, hope to continue having a place in the bargaining table.

If the picture in Korea is slightly optimistic, then why is it deteriorating in Iran? The 2015 Iran nuclear deal (Joint Comprehensive Plan of Action), which was negotiated by Iran along with the US, UK, France, Germany, Russia, China and the EU, had required Iran to give up its nuclear program, enrich very limited amounts of uranium (primarily for industrial purposes) and allow full monitoring by foreign agencies. In exchange, the economic sanctions on Iran would be lifted. From the US perspective, the deal was negotiated by President Barack Obama and his secretary of state John Kerry. In the campaign trail, most Republican presidential candidates, including Trump had vowed to overturn the Iran nuclear deal, because they thought that the restrictions on uranium enrichment were not strict enough. They had bemoaned the time limit on the provisions (gas centrifuges are restricted for 13 years). But clearly this was an excuse. The Iran nuclear deal had just been cancelled by the US. Why is Trump so hawkish on Iran?

First, he had fired Stephen Bannon as personal adviser and appointed John Bolton as national security adviser, which gives an indication of wanting to be more confrontational. Bannon represented the white nationalist wing, which campaigned for domestic nation-building and shunning foreign political interventions. These vague promises generated the enormous primary and general election support for Trump, which put him into the White House. Bolton, on the other hand, has been calling for war against Iraq and later against Iran. He openly touts regime change in the Middle East. Any sane leader would keep him as far away from any position of power as possible, but George W. Bush and now Donald Trump have put him in charge. Second, the budget request, which increased the public budget deficit to over $1 trillion, included enormous funding increases for the military. Why would you invest in the military if not for war?

A third important factor is related to geo-political considerations of Israel and Saudi Arabia. Both countries hate the Iranian regime, and think that their outsize political influence, military/ logistical/ financial support in Lebanon, Syria, Bahrain, Yemen and Iraq have undermined the interests of Israel and Saudi Arabia. Israeli prime minister Benjamin Netanyahu has openly torpedoed the Iran nuclear deal, seeing it as unwarranted support for an enemy regime. The US has traditionally sided with Israel and Saudi Arabia, which was no different from the Obama administration, though Obama was often willing to ignore the hawkish positions of their allies in the region.

Fourth, Iran had converted their oil transactions from the US dollar to the euro (Jalili 2018), which could undermine the reserve currency power of the US dollar. When Saddam Hussein quit the US dollar in favor of the euro in 2000, he was invaded by the US only three years later upon which oil trade became reported in dollar again (Liu 2014a). To some extent, the US had to blame itself for this step, because continued US sanctions, which the EU had long ago lifted created more currency uncertainty between the Iranian rial and the dollar, so it was more predictable for the Iranians to switch their trade accounts to the euro.

But what are the prospects for war? It appears to be much slimmer than in the case of Iraq. First, Iraq was a weaker military power than Iran. Iraq only had 25 million people when it was invaded, while Iran stands at 80 million. Second, during the Iraq invasion the Bush administration could still cobble a multinational coalition of troops from 46 countries, including big countries like UK, Japan, Spain and Italy.

But who will support a war with Iran now? When Trump won the elections, German chancellor Angela Merkel promptly gave a speech to assert that the EU had to rely more on its own and less on the US. Trump's disparaging comments on NATO were driving her statement. French President Emmanuel Macron would favor continued rapprochement with Iran, partly because of the Iranian shift to euro trading. The Iraq War had not been in the interest of the EU, but now it will be even less so. China and Russia have already indicated their continued support for the Iran agreement.

The key link will be the EU. EU foreign commissioner Federica Mogherini issued a statement supporting the continuation of the Iran nuclear deal. Foreign minister of Iran, Javad Zarif, had been dispatched to Europe to confirm the continuation of the nuclear deal. Some critics suggest that the deal can't be kept alive without the support of the US, but the Paris climate accord also continues without the US. The crucial player is the EU, which by refusing to surrender on the terms of the agreement can neutralize US actions. Trump might be expecting that the Iranian regime will break the agreement and enrich uranium, which would give Trump the justification to start an Iran War. The irony can't be lost on observers. Step one: give up the agreement. Step two: motivate Iran to enrich uranium. Step three: declare war on Iran. Pour out the gas canister, light the fire and burn down the building, while blaming it all on the other party. This is how deranged the US political leader is.

What will be the ripple effect of the US pulling out of the Iran deal on North Korea? What signals are sent to Kim Jong-un? Trump thinks that the crackdown on Iran will remind Kim to be compliant with Trump's request for denuclearization, but if anything the opposite incentive is created. By abrogating on an international agreement, there will also be no reassurance for Kim that his compliance with US demands will not result in a US abrogation. This might kill any multilateral agreements to solve the Korea crisis.

One can only hope that the international problems in Iran and North Korea can be contained to manageable levels, though this sounds only feasible when all parties take on a more rational frame. It is startling that one wishes back Henry Kissinger (despite the many deaths he was, in part, responsible for causing all over the world) in an era of Donald Trump.

Israel and Palestine: A Seemingly Never-Ending Conflict
Posted on May 17, 2018

When Donald Trump had decided to move the US embassy from Tel Aviv to Jerusalem it happened to the dismay of many Palestinians, who had been protesting extensively against Israeli authorities controlling them in a chokehold, which is most severely the case in Gaza. Gaza is a densely populated strip of land, which is suffering from severe economic isolation coming from the heavy Israeli sanctions, control of borders, airspace, sea access and finances. Israel had justified this stance because of the fact that the Hamas, which has effectively controlled Gaza since 2006, had sent rocket fire and suicide missions targeted at Israel and not recognizing the state of Israel. But the strength of force is often quite one-sided, because the overarching power in the form of an occupying army and economic controls are exclusive to Israel.

Border protests in Gaza have begun in March 30 of this year and demanded that Palestinian refugees and their descendants be given the right to return to Israel and now to oppose the movement of the US embassy to Jerusalem. The outcome of the border protest thus far is that 111 Palestinian protesters (mostly children) had been killed and 12,000 had been injured. In comparison, 1 Israeli soldier had been wounded and none killed.

There is a bad catch-22 in Gaza, because as long as Hamas does not recognize the state of Israel and angry Palestinians are protesting against their blockade, Prime Minister Netanyahu has the excuse to crackdown militarily. But quieting down is also not a viable option given the continued chokehold of the Israeli authorities. For Hamas, the end game is to return to pre-1967 borders, which was the year when Israel had taken the West Bank and Gaza, which are territories that it effectively controls (despite the Israeli withdrawal from Gaza in 2005). This is not so realistic given that there are so many Jewish settlements interspersed in the West Bank. The end game for Netanyahu's Israel is to build more settlements in the West Bank and suppress any discontent in Gaza with military presence if necessary.

This attitude is merely a recipe for a further never-ending conflict, which reaches back as early as the late-19th century, when the number of Jewish settlers (mostly from Europe being shaped by Zionism) increased, thus competing for spaces with the Arab population. The conflict intensified with the declaration of the state of Israel (following on the heels of the Holocaust), the conquest of territories beyond what the UN mandate had provided, the 1967 conquest of Gaza, West Bank, Sinai and Golan Heights, and various Intifada (Palestinian protest, resistance) since the 1980s.

With regard to the resolution to the conflict, the bygone era where peace was possible seem far away. Gone are the 1990s, when Yitzhak Rabin (Israeli prime minister) and Yassir Arafat (Palestinian Liberation Organization chief) sat down to sign the Oslo Accords, which allowed for the creation of a Palestinian political authority which was recognized by Israel. Gone are the early-2000s, when there was some chance to negotiate a two-state solution during the Camp David Summit. Now there are no pretenses of compromise, as Hamas refuses to recognize Israel, and right-wing Netanyahu's hold on power over the past decade has made any overtures to compromise impossible. The Trump presidency has added more fuel to the fire, as he gave the American right-wing evangelical voters and rich Jewish donors to his campaign (especially Sheldon Adelson) what they wanted: the cancellation of the Iran nuclear deal, which they hope could weaken Iran's increased regional influence (like in Yemen, Iraq, Syria or Lebanon); and now the movement of the US embassy to Jerusalem, which sends the message to the Palestinians that what the international community regards as a politically divided city really belongs to Israel.

The lack of an even-handed approach by the US (which was never even-handed given the huge military aid to Israel and the refusal of UN security council sanctions against Israeli transgressions such as on the settlements) will result in more conflict, as the weaker side (Palestinians) receive no fair stake in the table. Lacking a stake, they feel they have nothing to lose by protesting, fighting Israeli security authorities, carrying out suicide attacks and throwing Molotov cocktails. The deteriorating economic situation, following the original Israeli withdrawal of 2005, the election victory of Hamas in 2006 and the Israeli blockade and sanctions, had created a veritable humanitarian crisis. The only thing that props up the Gaza economy is foreign aid, chiefly from US, EU and the Arab League.

Outside observers might argue in Samuel Huntington fashion that the driver of conflict is religious and cultural. Jews and Muslims can't get along with each other based on different interpretations of sacredness. But this is a rather strange explanation as the Northern Irish who were divided by sectarian lines (Protestant-Unionist vs Catholic-Republican) reconciled with the Good Friday Agreement and no one would nowadays claim that these religious divisions are salient.

While it is true that the Jew and Muslim divide was the beginning of the conflict and became the socially reinforced mental divisions in daily interaction, the real trouble comes from the question of who wields political power. In a peaceful state, the multitude of factions, tribes and interests rotate in power, emphasize national unity when holding political power and respect the rights of the political minority. In a civil-war state, the political leaders of one group mark themselves off from another group, and then argue that the other group has no right to exist, or at least not in this given territory. Another problem is the endless cycle of retaliation, as the death of one of my relatives needs to be avenged by the death of your relative. The cycle of hatred and violence can only be broken if powerful external actors broker a peace, and when the internal actors, i.e. their political leaders, believe that it is possible to negotiate peace and a lasting two-state solution. But with an erratic Trump foreign policy such a rational foreign policy appears to be unfeasible.

Goolsbee is Wrong on UBI
Posted on <u>May 28, 2018</u>

In the debate surrounding whether or not we should have a universal basic income it is at least heartening that even critics take that proposal seriously. One may think of Mahatma Gandhi's statement that "first [your enemies] will ignore you, then they laugh at you, then they fight you, then you win". We are somewhere between stage two and three.

The economist (and former White House economic adviser under Obama) Austan Goolsbee (2018) adds his voice to the UBI debate. He has proffered three counter-arguments to UBI:

First, if you accept the economists' basic labor supply model (that people value leisure and so generally need to be paid to work) then there are likely to be some sizable number of people who are working only because they absolutely have to.

In other words, we pay a UBI and universal laziness will break out. There are really two counter-arguments, which each cut in a different direction. The first is to directly question the economist assumption, which is that a UBI will make people more entrepreneurial and look for better employment opportunities while refusing the horrendous and most exploitative employers, who either have to improve working conditions or hike wages or do both to keep their workers. On the face of it, the selfishness assumption of economists is that people will retreat en masse into the private sphere and watch Netflix all day long. There might be a few people who do that, but for the vast majority of people, who are trying to find some meaning in their life, it does not seem like a plausible outcome. In fact, given that health and retirement benefits are tied to the job, potentially entrepreneurial people are prevented from taking the leap under the current regime.

The second counter-argument is related with the premise of the UBI. If we already assume that work is replaced by artificial intelligence, then to go out and demand the same high rates of employment participation with a 40 hour workweek is entirely outdated. In a time of economic abundance, it might even make sense for people to drop out of the paid labor force and do something more meaningful with their lives than to be controlled by a nasty employer. Read poetry, write a novel, read books, compose music, take up athletics, grow a garden, care for aging parents, go mountain hiking, do whatever. David Graeber also points out that a sizeable fraction (35-40%) of the workforce believe that their jobs have no useful purpose, and merely serve to keep us busy bees controlled by an employer. We can dispute how high that figure really is, but to the extent that they exist, we do want to get rid of these jobs, which a sufficiently generous UBI could accomplish.

In a telling piece of evidence Graeber (2018: 157) cites President Obama, who justified his choice not to push for single-payer health care, which could cut out administrative waste:

Everybody who supports single-payer health care says, 'Look at all this money we would be saving from insurance and paperwork.' That represents one million, two million, three million jobs [filled by] people who are working at Blue Cross Blue Shield or Kaiser or other places. What are we doing with them? Where are we employing them?

What the president is saying is that it is better to keep us as wage slaves than to maximize efficiency in the system and compensate the losers with a UBI so they can do things that are enjoyable to them. If we accept the Graeber hypothesis about bullshit jobs, then I don't find it problematic at all to have a receding labor supply after introducing a UBI.

To be fair to Goolsbee, it is not him, who moralizes on the declining labor participation of low-skilled workers, but the general public, which he is simply channelling in his essay. But again, why is it so problematic that people are pushed out of undesirable work? If they are so essential, yet not automatable, then wages would have to increase or if the community does not want to pay more for essential services, the state will have to tax the profitable industries to subsidize essential and low-skilled work.

Second, for a given amount of money to be used on redistribution, a UBI likely shifts money away from the very poor. To oversimplify, if you have $50B to alleviate poverty, the targeting approach followed in most countries today might use the $50B to help the poorest/sickest 25m people and give them the equivalent of $25,000 of benefits each. With a broad-based UBI, the same $50B would be spread out. It might involve, say, 100m people getting $5000 each.

The point that the poor will be hit hardest by a UBI really depends on what the size of the program is going to be and whether other social services are reduced. Social Security, for instance, could be folded into a UBI, which means that any SS payouts we currently have flow into a UBI without an increase in cost for that segment of the population (mostly seniors and disabled). For general poverty reduction efforts, the US really has a paltry welfare state. The mix of Food Stamps, Medicaid and in rare cases TANF (only for mothers with young children and only with a five-year lifetime limit) is nowhere near enough to care for the poor. It is thus, disingenuous to dock a UBI budget on current levels of social welfare spending, which has to substantially increase, perhaps to 20% of the GDP to be universal and alleviating poverty for the neediest. But the difficult politics of the UBI suggests that it is not clear whether UBI will turn out to be so generous.

Converting to a UBI and abolishing the in-kind safety net will lead to a situation where some people will blow their UBI money in unsympathetic ways—gambling, drugs, junk food, Ponzi schemes, whatever

Goolsbee's moral imagination, while a popular trope, assumes the worst form of behavior among the poor. It is this moral imagination of the depravity of the poor, which created an in-kind transfer benefit system, which I don't deny should exist. Single-payer health care has to be implemented on top of UBI, and they should not be seen as unachievable tradeoffs. But that is where another problematic assumption in Goolsbee's argument crops up, which is- as with point 2- that there is a limited amount of resources to care for the poor, which is just not true given that his entire essay is framed around the rise of artificial intelligence, i.e. the creation of economic abundance for humanity.

It is as if there is a cognitive dissonance, whereby economic developments are assumed to be very advanced while as soon as he talks about social policy, he again assumes a backward economy of the nineteenth century, where the idle poor have to be put into workhouses (while the idle rich landlords or -the modern equivalent- heirs, stock market investors, hedge fund managers and real estate tycoons can enjoy their fortunes which they always had). Goolsbee is not the only economist, going down that path, but without taking the AI economy to its fullest conclusion, the prejudice against the UBI as a policy solution will persist.

Troubled Land Reforms in South Africa
Posted on June 4, 2018

When in February Cyril Ramaphosa replaced Jacob Zuma as president of South Africa, he said that land reform became a major priority. The ANC (African National Congress) government had campaigned on land reform when the apartheid regime, which separated blacks and whites and discriminated the former group, was abolished in 1994. Back then whites made up 9% of the population and owned 85% of the land, while today they are only 8% of the population but still own 73% of all the land. There has been some expansion of black-owned land as in KwaZulu-Natal and Limpopo (Crowley 2018), but the sad reality is that nearly half of all black South Africans are living below the poverty line of 992 rand (75 dollars) a month, about 20% of colored people (i.e. mixed race), and negligible proportions of Asians and whites (Chutel 2017).

The slow pace of land reform comes from the government policy of "willing buyer- willing seller". The government was unwilling to force white landowners to surrender their land. But the slow pace of reform and the electoral pressure for the ANC to accelerate the pace of land reform resulted in calls for land expropriation as early as 2006. These calls for land expropriation were not formally taken up until December 2017, when an ANC conference stated that they wanted to amend the constitution to allow for land expropriation without compensation. This move has a precedent in Zimbabwe in the early-2000s, which had deleterious effects on the economy, as the land was primarily reallocated to the cronies of the government, who used it for their personal patronage, i.e. leasing it out to other people without caring whether these farmers were competent in running the farms. The attendant economic decline (reinforced by giddy foreign investors, who don't like expropriation of private property) convinced the Mugabe regime to put on the printing press to pay its bills, which resulted in hyperinflation and the abandonment of the Zimbabwe currency in favor of the US dollar.

Even in South Africa itself, land reallocation that has taken place the past 25 years have not borne much fruit. 5% of white-owned land had been transferred to blacks (Lahiff 2008). The government invested 60 billion rand in land reform projects, which had resulted in a 79% decline of crop production and job loss of 84-94% (Wikipedia, "Land Reform in South Africa"). Without sufficient equipment, financing and know-how, land reallocation to blacks is not going to result in economic stabilization. Ramaphosa and his government have promised that they are not going to repeat the mistakes of Zimbabwe, but how can they be so sure about it?

The white farmers are naturally outraged about the proposal for land expropriation, though they are politically sidelined. Within the South African parliament only the Democratic Alliance (DA), the main opposition, is a vocal opponent of land expropriation, and two of the past three leaders of the DA have been whites. The DA emerged out of the white liberal, anti-apartheid political opposition against the ruling National Party, which held onto power until the end of apartheid. The DA has therefore been considered a white party, though for obvious reasons (whites are only about 8% of the population) they deny this claim. With Msumi Maimane, the DA received its first black leader in 2015.

The presence of another political party shook up the political process. The Economic Freedom Fighters (EFF) was founded in 2013 by a faction of the ruling ANC, which championed far-left black nationalist causes and felt that the ANC was too accommodating to the interest of the wealth-owning whites. In their first parliamentary elections, they promptly took 25 out of 400 seats, which made them the third-largest party. To effectively prevent a loss of votes in the next elections, the ANC has begun to copy the rhetoric of the EFF and accepted their demand for land expropriation. This political dynamic is very troubling for whites, who might still hold most of the economic property, but no longer wield a dominant influence in the political process.

The struggle over land reform allows for a brief examination of South Africa's troubled racial history, which has been even more oppressive than in the US, which will also make it clear how land expropriation has arrived on the national agenda.

2.5 million years ago, the territory of what is now known as South Africa contained the Australopithecines, a forbear of the homo sapiens. Modern humans moved to South Africa in the Middle Stone Age about 125,000 years ago. The first human indigenous culture were the so-called Khoisan people, which now form a racial minority, and are called "colored" in the census classification system. Khoisan is a combination of San and Khoikhoi, two separate but related tribes. The San were hunter-gatherers while the Khoikhoi were pastoral herders. The Bantus, who originate in western Africa and are darker-skinned than the Khoisan, went on migration waves all over sub-Saharan Africa from 1000 BC onward, and have reached

South Africa by about 300 AD. Being more organized and militarily dominant, the Bantus drove away the Khoisan people, who were forced to move to more arid areas.

But the real trouble only came with European colonial expansion. The Portuguese used their shops to explore the coastlines in southern Africa in 1488. They were trying to discover a better trade route to the Far East, which would otherwise have to go through the Middle East. They set up the Cape of Good Hope at the South African coast, which became an important haven for trade with the Far East. But the Portuguese did not arrive in large numbers. This changed with Dutch colonization, which began as early as 1652. The Dutch West India company set up permanently in the Cape, also taking advantage of trade routes to the Far East. Upon encountering the Dutch, two things happened to the Khoisan people. Firstly, they were decimated by smallpox, an old European disease against which the Khoisan people had no resistance or medicine. Second, as the Dutch became greedy for more and more land. They fought three wars with the Khoisan to steal their goods and land and drive them out.

As the colony lacked agriculture, the Dutch brought over farmers from the homeland. As their numbers grew, they expanded northward to occupy land, which was previously held by black people. In order to work the land, the Dutch also brought over slaves from India, Indonesia, East Africa, Mauritius and Madagascar. (The British later brought even more Indians to South Africa.) The Dutch were later also joined by Germans and French Huguenots. The racial mixing that happened among all these groups created the racial category of 'colored' people that were ranked lower than whites but higher than blacks under apartheid.

When the French invaded the Netherlands in 1795 and the newly founded Batavian Republic (in the Cape) became loyal to the French, the enraged British demanded a Batavian surrender to the British. When France lost the Napoleonic wars in 1805, the British inherited the Cape. The British had little interest in the interior of South Africa and held onto the Cape as a strategic site for trade with India, the crown colony of the British empire. When Britain enforced an English language policy in 1815, when they formally bought the Cape from the Netherlands, the Dutch settlers felt sidelined and oppressed, and so they trekked to the north competing with blacks for land first in a trickle from 1805 onward and then in a huge stream from the 1830s onward. The Dutch were also upset that the

British banned the slave trade on which the Dutch settlers relied on. The Dutch founded three independent states that lived for a while (Republic of Transvaal/ South African Republic, Orange Free State and Natalia) before being crushed and incorporated by the British toward the turn to the twentieth century.

One ethnic group of the Bantu, the Zulu, were able to establish an empire with a centralized military that broke from clan traditions (which is a precondition to centralization). Their leader Shaka kaSenzangakhona had seized power in 1818, and went on an expansion drive of conquest, killing and pillaging in the surrounding regions. Shaka was killed by a dynastic intrigue in 1828, and his successor Dingaan was less militaristic. The Dutch and later the British ultimately put an end to Zulu expansion. When the Zulus attacked Dutch cattle and killed a group of Dutch settlers, the Dutch retaliated by killing 3,000 Zulu warriors in 1838. More importantly, the 1879 Anglo-Zulu war eliminated the Zulu empire as an independent political unit, though the Zulu had won the Battle of Isandlwana. But the British were clever enough to re-fashion their attacks with the help of Zulu collaborators who were opposed to centralized Zulu rule.

To some extent, conflict was fueled by the European desire for expansion and was undergirded by their fixed notions of private property, which had no precedent in traditional African societies. When the Europeans seized the land from blacks, they encountered resistance from them, which induced a series of frontier wars, also known as Xhosa Wars, which were won by the Europeans. The Basotho people, for instance, fought against the Orange Free State for territory, whereby both sides practiced destructive scorched-earth tactics with the Dutch being far superior in their military technology and agricultural productivity, which brought the Basotho to the brink of starvation. They signed a peace treaty in 1858 and again in 1866 (with some hostilities in between). Ultimately, Basotho was incorporated into the British empire and gained independence as Lesotho in 1966.

The Dutch were equally ruthless in their war with the Ndebele. After having killed 28 Boers (Dutch) accused for cattle rustling (stealing), the Ndebele retreated into the mountain caves. The Boers followed the Ndebele and laid siege on the caves, which resulted in the death of 1,000 to 3,000 Ndebele. By the time the remaining Ndebele surrendered, they were captured and enslaved by the Boers. The Bapedi were another black ethnicity under siege by first the

Dutch and then the British from 1876 to 1879. Cut off from supplies, the Bapedi were forced to surrender.

The British Cape Colony became an autonomously run part of the British Empire. They had their own parliament and non-racial laws, which was unusual for that time period. The discovery of diamonds (1866) and gold (1886) in the Transvaal and Kimberley, Dutch and black-held territories, and the ambitious Cecil Rhodes becoming Prime Minister of Cape Colony (1890-96), changed the quiet equilibrium. Rhodes got rid of the multi-racial franchise and sent British troops to conquer the Dutch-held territories, resulting in the two Anglo-Boer wars. The first war (1880-81) was won by the Boers, which forced the British to recognize the South African Republic and the Orange Free State, but the second war (1899-1902) was won by the British, which resulted in the dissolution of the Boer states and the British takeover of the Boer colonies. What was even worse for blacks was that they were conscripted and coerced to fight and die on behalf of either the British or the Dutch.

It was first the European greed for land followed by the greed for diamonds and gold, which had created severe military conflicts and the displacement of blacks. The gold discovery had attracted British, German and Austrian industrialists, which also included many Jews. The industrialists attempted to recruit black laborers, who refused to work in those dangerous and onerous conditions. They then turned to Chinese laborers, attracting 53,000 Chinese indentured servants who were willing to work in the mines for lower wages than was offered to Africans.

The Chinese were an ambiguous category, sometimes regarded as colored sometimes as Asian (which is reserved for Indians and South Asians), but were clearly discriminated under apartheid as they were non-white. The arrival of Taiwanese immigrants, especially businesspeople, in the 1980s created the weird situation that that the Taiwanese were considered honorary whites, while the Chinese were regarded as colored people. The end of apartheid restored civil rights to the Chinese, which coincided with the massive increase in immigration from mainland China, which swelled the Chinese population to over 400,000.

With the British victory in the Anglo-Boer war, the British set out to unify the country as South Africa in 1909, and in 1913 passed the Natives Land Act, which allocated a paltry 8% of the land to blacks, and 90% to whites, who were 20% of the population. This law was the basis for later laws on apartheid. British and Dutch tensions did not disappear, as South Africa developed two political parties, the pro-British South African Party and the pro-Dutch National Party. Dispossessed Boers attempted an uprising against the British in 1914, which the British successfully crushed. In the two world wars that were initiated by Europeans (chiefly the Germans), South Africans of all races were again called upon to serve in these wars, which had also resulted in the death of many blacks.

While South Africa as a nation solidly fought on the side of the British, i.e. the Allies, the Nazi Germans were able to infiltrate and nurture a pro-German Afrikaner-nationalist (i.e. Boer) movement, which were the Ossewa Brandwag (OB), which was later absorbed into the National Party that instituted and ruled over apartheid South Africa. The Afrikaner Weerstandsbeweging (AWB) was another white supremacist group emerging in the 1970s, which was inspired by OB and the Nazis.

The National Party, which was briefly in government from 1924 to 1938, and then without interruption from 1948 to 1994, formally instituted apartheid in 1948. But it was not a new system, but rather an extension of discriminatory policies implemented by the Boers and the British since the 1850s. The 1970 Homeland Citizens Act established homeland reserves, or Bantustans, which concentrated the black population while driving them out of cities, which whites monopolized for themselves. The forced segregation and inferior economic status of blacks not surprisingly created discontent, which culminated in the 1976 uprising, which resulted in a harsh military crackdown and a strengthening of white police and military at all levels of South African government. A large chunk of the South African government budget was devoted to military and security spending.

The UN had not approved of apartheid, and passed a 1966 resolution which held apartheid as a "crime against humanity". A 1973 apartheid convention was passed with 91 votes for and four against (Portugal, South Africa, UK and US), which resulted in a suspension of South Africa's UN membership. A 1977 Security Council resolution barred arms export to South Africa. The tacit support of the US, which thought that South Africa was a bulwark against communism, and the military support from Israeli arms manufacturers were crucial in maintaining apartheid. The US supported the South African regime for attempting to prevent communism in neighboring countries like Angola and Mozambique. Cuba had militarily supported the Angolan communists, while South

Africa supported the Angolan nationalists. The Angolan Civil War had resulted in the deaths of between 550,000 and 1.25 million people.

Apartheid was not simply about segregation, but also racial tensions and hostilities. Extra-judicial killings in the 1980s that were sponsored by the state led to hundreds of killings. The Truth and Reconciliation Commission, which was tasked to review the number of deaths during the apartheid period, found that 4,500 deaths were caused by the Inkatha Freedom Party (IFP, a Zulu nationalist group led by Mangosuthu Buthelezi), 2,700 by the (white) South African police and 1,300 by the ANC.

The ANC was the main political movement that opposed apartheid, though there were other organizations like the Pan-African Congress (which was explicitly anti-white) and the United Democratic Front (which used rent boycotts, student protest and labor strikes to fight apartheid). The key strategy against apartheid (at least initially) was passive resistance, which was influenced by Mahatma Gandhi and his Indian struggle for independence. The South African government reacted with harsh crackdowns and by the 1960s, the ANC and PAC were pushed into the underground.

External changes in the form of the end of the Cold War, ultimately, led to the downfall of the apartheid regime. The collapse of the Soviet Union meant that the ANC would no longer get weapons and funding, and the US no longer saw an incentive to support the apartheid regime. Domestic political opposition in the US similarly made it difficult for the US administration to continue supporting the apartheid regime. President Frederik de Klerk and ANC leader Nelson Mandela negotiated the end of apartheid laws in June 1991, and an election for 1994, which restored the franchise to black South Africans. The ANC and the IFP were also permitted to participate in the election, such that ANC (in a common ballot with the labor confederation COSATU and the South African Communist Party) promptly received 63% of the vote, while the ruling National Party (NP) dropped to only 20%.

Under a common agreement, Nelson Mandela was tasked to form a national unity government, which included the National Party and the Inkatha Freedom Party. Mandela gave the two deputy president positions to Thabo Mbeki (ANC), who succeeded Mandela, and F.W. de Klerk from the National Party. De Klerk ultimately withdrew from the government in 1996 after being disappointed that constitutional changes did not guarantee National Party rule until

2004. Interestingly, Mandela also reappointed Derek Keys as finance minister and Chris Stals as central bank governor, who had previously served under de Klerk's rule. It was clear to political observers that Mandela cared mostly about continuity in economic policy to maintain the economic status of South Africa, and that meant not to antagonize whites with land expropriation.

When the ANC was still in opposition it had demanded land expropriation, which was an electoral strategy to get the black electorate to support the ANC. Once in government one might argue that Mandela was tied by the coalition agreement with the NP, which would have blocked any radical moves toward land expropriation. But even more importantly, Mandela's temperament was moderate, calling for racial "reconciliation", i.e. no extreme moves to antagonize wealthy whites. Out of the more than 5 million whites in South Africa, 800,000 skilled whites permanently left South Africa, mostly migrating to other English-speaking countries (AUS, NZ, UK, US, Canada), citing concerns of personal safety after the end of white rule. Their emigration came to the chagrin of Mandela, as he feared that South Africa will be left with only impoverished blacks.

Dire fiscal and economic circumstances in the post-apartheid era also constrained political action. The South African government had a foreign debt of 86 billion rand (or 14 billion dollars) when the apartheid regime ended, which tied up 20% of the national budget for debt repayment. AIDS turned out to be another financial burden, as the spread of AIDS resulted in over 5 million people being infected by the disease, and the national health services being unable to cope with burgeoning health care needs. In 2014, 47% of South Africans (mostly black) were still living in poverty, which provides fertile ground for opposition to the ANC government that failed to deliver on economic development.

The ANC dashed any hopes for a socialist transformation (nationalization of industries, higher taxes on wealth, land expropriation) once elected to power, and stuck to broadly neoliberal policies, which meant the hope to attract foreign capital and secure the private property of investors, who themselves see little incentive to fund mass job creation. South Africa's primary export items are gold, platinum, coal and iron ore, which are hardly commodities that could transform the country to a high-income economy. It is also questionable whether foreign investors can be attracted with the poor availability of basic infrastructure like reliable electricity. South African economic growth was boosted during the initial post-apartheid years, but declined substantially since the 2008 economic crash, reaching 0.3% in 2016.

The lack of economic development naturally breeds distributional struggles, which are aggravated by the influx of refugees from the rest of Africa, ranging from countries like Zimbabwe, Burundi, Congo, Rwanda, Eritrea, Ethiopia and Somalia. Native people's perception of competition for jobs, business opportunities, public services and housing result in xenophobic attacks against refugees and migrants.

Popular legitimacy for the government is also impaired by perceptions of corruption, which ensnared Ramaphosa's predecessor Jacob Zuma. Zuma gave government contracts to the Gupta family, a South African family of Indian descent, running a business empire for computer equipment, media and mining. Zuma also appointed people to the government cabinet that were suggested by the Gupta family. The Gupta family in turn funded the election of Zuma, gave him other gifts and appointed family members of Zuma into highly paid positions in the company. Trade union leader Zwelinizima Vavi had called Gupta the "shadow government" of South Africa. Zuma's corruption was one of the reasons that the ANC no longer supported Zuma, so he was replaced by Ramaphosa.

Thus, we arrive in today's difficult political dilemma, where the perception of a lack of economic progress is combined with a lack of political trust in the ANC, which has held power for the past 24 years. As they sense political support among blacks slipping away, who are hungry for progress and redistribution, and the opposition EFF expose the ANC for being too accommodationist to whites, the ANC will seek to copy the strategy of the EFF to prevent electoral leakage to the EFF. In my native Austria, the conservative party gained 7 percentage points and won the elections on the basis of copying the rhetoric of the right wing FPO, focusing on excluding refugees and unwanted migrants from the polity. This strategy worked astoundingly well in the context of the refugee wave that came to Europe.

It may not not sound fair for white South Africans to lose their land simply because their forebears had driven out blacks from their ancestral homeland and solidified this injustice with formal apartheid laws. But in a largely rural population, the attainment of land is often a precondition for better economic livelihood. The poverty of blacks that are concentrated in shantytowns cannot be overcome unless they are given a stake in society, either via good jobs or access to fertile land. On the other hand, access to fertile land should not result in less production, which could happen if blacks do not receive enough funding, equipment or training to upkeep modern agricultural practices. As an outsider, there is no easy solution for it, because whites are unwilling to turn over the keys to their farm and then provide blacks with the support to run the farm, which whites think belongs to them.

Japan is cited as being a successful case for past land reform. The post-war American occupation of Japan had allowed authorities to hurt the interest of powerful landlords, who used to lease out land to farm laborers and small farmers and collect huge rents. The government forced the landlords to sell their land to the government, which in turn sold it to the farm laborers, who could benefit from ownership over land without the payment of rents to landlords. Japan had been successful in radical land redistribution. Obviously, the ANC is not an external party like the US, but it would have to be the responsible entity to force the sale of white-owned land, but crucially do it with (fixed) compensation. The harder part will be how to get the new black landowners to produce at high levels of output. This would convince me that any land reform has to take place gradually, which will piss off all sides (whites for being gradually squeezed out and blacks for feeling that it moves too slowly).

A forceful acquisition of white-owned land could also result in a further emigration of the remaining white population in South Africa. Mandela was right to be concerned about the outflow of talent, which South Africa-still one of the wealthier economies of sub-Saharan Africa- can ill-afford. Whether Mandela's moderate legacy can be preserved is largely questionable as he is dead, and the country will have to figure out what it wants to do in the years ahead. In the absence of employment generation or the establishment of industry, it is questionable whether existing social tensions and inequality along racial and class lines can be overcome.

Book Review: David Graeber, "Bullshit Jobs" (New York, Simon and Schuster, 2018)

Posted on June 12, 2018

Five years after Graeber submitted his provocative essay "On the Phenomenon of Bullshit Jobs" he had now written up a 300 page book describing a phenomenon in contemporary capitalism, which requires further elucidation. Graeber's simple argument is that the advancement of technology may have led to the displacement of production jobs (primarily in agriculture and manufacturing), but the number of total jobs keeps on increasing, because of the proliferation of bullshit jobs, which includes a lot of middle management, bankers, HR consultants, corporate lawyers, communications coordinators, PR managers, consultants. For Graeber, there are two definitions of a bullshit job: "if the position were eliminated, it would make no discernible difference in the world" (p.2), and a position where "the person doing that job considers [it] to be pointless, unnecessary, or even pernicious" (p.5).

For critics of Graeber, the two-pronged definition provides a fertile ground for critique. My job could make no discernible difference to the world, but I could think that it is useful. I met a private equity investor recently who thinks that her mergers and acquisition and leveraged buyout strategy create a win-win situation for all parties, even though workers are getting laid off once private equity enters the scene. To be fair to Graeber, his definition of bullshit jobs is quite strictly subjective, i.e. if a person thinks his own job is pointless, unnecessary or pernicious, then it is a bullshit job. The only way how you can attack that definition is by questioning how many people would think that, how many people do something valuable but think it is useless, or vice versa how many people do something useless but think it to be useful. Graeber cites two studies, a British survey where 37% of workers argued their job was bullshit and a Dutch survey where 40% of workers thought the same, but are these studies representative and meaningful?

As a social scientist and empiricist, we have an inclination to create objective measures to assign a bullshit score to occupations, though I doubt that any institute would want to fund such an empirical investigation, so we have to rely on the subjective evaluation of individual workers. The proof for bullshit jobs is in the pudding. If all the bullshit workers were going on strike, the system would not break down and life would continue as before. That automatically precludes doctors, teachers, police officers, firefighters, train operators etc. as bullshit job. The limitation in the social sciences is that we cannot organize such a grand experiment to test the bullshit job hypothesis, so we have to rely on the cultural stories that Graeber and other thinkers provide.

Bad jobs vs. bullshit jobs

One of the basic problems we might have with bullshit jobs is when people hear the word "bullshit" job, they mistake it for bad jobs, which happened to me twice, when I explained that concept to other people. A bad job is valuable work that is poorly paid and involves employer abuse and poor treatment. Think of home health aides or food service workers. A bullshit job is pointless, but may involve very high pay. Graeber, thus, points out an important problem in the labor market, which is that the pointless jobs can be paid well, while the valuable jobs are paid almost nothing.

In the framework of the mainstream economists, we are not entirely surprised about why that is the case. If you enjoy what you are doing, presumably because you think that your work is very valuable to the community, then you have a strong altruism preference, which works as a tradeoff with income. Because many people like altruistic work, the labor supply for these jobs is high, and equilibrium wages can be very low. On the other hand, if you do jobs that are troublesome and useless, then very few people want to do it, so the wages you command will be higher. In sociology, we think that power plays an important role in compensation too, because women are relegated to unpaid housework, while men can dominate the exchange-oriented occupations, which command high incomes. Thus capitalistic exchange reproduces gender inequality.

To some extent there is a conflict with mainstream economic theory. This account does not jive well with the marginal productivity thesis, according to which every person is essentially paid however much they produce for the economy. But let us recall the original premise of Graeber's argument, which is that the real production jobs are automated. There are some well-paid and productive jobs, for instance in the research wing of a technology company, developing the new technology, but their compensation is a fraction of what the company owners get. But if the production jobs are automated, then the bulk of the job creation would have to fall into service and professional work, i.e. the proliferation of middle management, which for firm accounting purposes is an addition to cost, not the generation of new revenue. Thus, the marginal productivity thesis is clearly not the basis upon which the payment of individuals is determined. For sociologists, this is not news, because we have long argued that tradition, network access and political power are other factors that influence compensation.

For Graeber, the generation of bullshit jobs is precisely about the degradation of corporate capitalism into corporate feudalism, where the drive toward greater efficiency is surpassed by the drive to pad the prestige and power of the feudal lords (or senior managers and administrators in contemporary parlance). The more inefficient corporate bureaucracies are, the more prestige is concentrated within each department and among each senior manager, and that itself becomes the end goal. The argument reminds us of Schumpeter (1942), who argued that capitalism could ultimately decline as entrepreneurs get displaced by corporate bureaucrats, though I would object that corporate capitalism still relies on the capture of new markets and the generation of new surplus value, but that is what technology in the production sector is good for.

Five types of bullshit jobs

If at the surface of it, Graeber has convinced his readers that a huge bulk of the jobs in our economy are bullshit, then the next question is what the range of bullshit jobs are. There are five types of bullshit jobs for Graeber. Flunkies are jobs that make someone else feel important (doormen, receptionist); goons exist only because other organizations have them too (e.g. lobbyists, PR managers, telemarketers, corporate lawyers); duct tapers fix up problems that exist because organizations don't want to create a permanent fix (e.g. software engineers creating free software with glitches, which corporations use and then have to hire these engineers to fix the glitches); box tickers certify that organizations are doing something, which they are not really doing (e.g. leisure coordinators, who send surveys to care home residents, knowing that these survey ideas will not become implemented); and taskmasters assign bullshit activities for other people or are unnecessary superiors (i.e. underlings can do the job without supervision; examples are higher ed administrators, sending performance surveys to measure "academic impact").

Why do these bullshit jobs proliferate?

It's about social control, at least for Graeber. Those at the top of the corporate pyramid control the flows of resources, and these flows do not have to be used for the maximization of more economic output, but bureaucratic busywork. As the number of people working below the top management increase, the reputation and prestige of top management increases relative to other departments and competitor firms. Graeber's political account of the proliferation of corporate bullshit jobs blocks other accounts that are centered on economic efficiency. A job can only exist if it produces a profit for the employer. Period. But the creation of profit is a property of the entire corporate organization, which can be read in the quarterly investor reports, not of particular individuals. Therefore, it could very much be that a giant pharmaceutical company has a small staff of people that produce the actual output, i.e. the pharmaceutical product, a larger size of the staff that support the activity of this smaller staff, which are essential, like some managerial staff, janitors or food service workers. The rest of the organization, which involves middle management for Graeber, is completely unnecessary and exist as cost, even though their high compensation suggests that they are the most productive workers.

What are the implications of proliferating bullshit jobs?
Some optimists might claim that it is okay that bullshit jobs exist. Because people need something to do. But here the question is how that work is organized. If most of the jobs require us to be subordinate to the whims of an employer, then reproducing bullshit jobs has very worrisome implications, because it means that most of us are not allowed to figure out what we are really interested in or are good at, even though technological progress would permit us to do so.

The National Bureau of Economic Research papers are increasingly filled with papers that predict the rise of robots and artificial intelligence having huge effects on labor markets. The pessimists think that many jobs will disappear and people will struggle to find new work. Optimists argue that we have to run faster and train for new skills and jobs. But if Graeber is right both sides of the spectrum have it wrong, because robots can only take over the production jobs, while bullshit jobs for humans can increase indefinitely. We are thus trapped as slaves to the system, and we can no longer find meaning in it, because production workers at least thought they were feeding, clothing, or sheltering people. There are no technical limits to how many bullshit jobs exist, only political limits, i.e. how socially acceptable is it to have a giant workforce of paper-pushers, ditch-diggers and box-checkers? There might come a time, when we have programmed the robots to do the bullshit jobs as well, but that is thinking one step too far ahead.

Solutions to bullshit jobs

For Graeber, the solution is to introduce a universal basic income, which if it is high enough to survive will shrink the supply of bullshit jobs. There might still be some people, who will continue working these bullshit jobs because of the prestige or high income, but it will be much fewer people. Those, who do should not be prevented from working bullshit jobs, but those, who do not want to work these jobs, should not feel that this is all they can do to pay the bills. Graeber is not a big fan of other solutions like a job guarantee (full employment) or short work schemes. In each case, Graeber, the anarchist, believes that there is a giant new bureaucracy that is required to steer people to work or to set limits to how much needs to be worked. In a full employment scheme, the generation of bullshit jobs (especially taskmasters) might become encoded in what the scheme entails. Central European countries that invest a lot of funds into labor market activation experience this growth to bullshit, because the unemployed are required to go training courses and get a stamp by an employer certifying they have applied for a job, and there are government bureaucrats, who have to oversee these unemployed people to make sure they are still hunting for work.

Short-work might be a successful labor market strategy, though Graeber thinks it won't destroy enough bullshit jobs. Capitalists can be driven to cut work hours only if they can cut the pay of their employees as well, and that tends to be difficult because wages are downwardly sticky. In a more coordinated market economy it might be possible to rearrange work hours, but even Germany has only done that during the recession. I myself have become increasingly skeptical of finding labor market-centric solutions to employment problems. In a very dystopian development we can have the proliferation of bullshit jobs along with the proliferation of unemployment and underemployment, which the declining labor participation rate of prime-age (25-54) males in the US shows, and that is because we need fewer and fewer production workers, and there might be limitations to how many bullshit jobs are created. It is in this context of the rise of bad jobs that most young people become grateful to work any kind of job, even if it is substantially meaningless.

I don't argue that labor market-centric solutions are impossible to attain, but it requires a lot of creativity and you have to get the capitalists to agree to it in a private ownership-based economy. In that context, I don't find it likely that the proliferating logic of bullshit jobs can be challenged sufficiently. I agree with Graeber that the universal basic income would provide a solution that could realize the condition of freedom, which is currently a luxury of people with accumulated, independent fortunes.

The Return to Incivility
Posted on June 14, 2018

Nga Than (2018), good friend of mine and Vietnamese researcher based in Germany, recounts her experience with two racist German teenagers, who said to her that foreigners have to leave Germany:

This incidence was different. It challenged my physical appearance, and it left a permanent psychological disturbance. It took place in the neighborhood of Friedrichshain in East Berlin, where the majority voted for the Green Party, or the Linke in the last state election. I didn't expect such a characteristically AfD behavior on the streets of the district. In the period of two years I had lived in Germany before, I never encountered such an incidence. Yet now as a tourist, the expression was directed to me, and it disturbed me tremendously. How daily civility has changed in this city!

It becomes worthwhile to think about where the rich societies of the world are going. In a timespan of a few years it is possible to normalize a discourse of detesting foreigners and blaming them for all the ills that exist in domestic society. One might argue that this has long been in the making. A lily-white German society had been transformed over half a century to a much more diverse and multicultural society, inviting many people of Middle Eastern and now also African and Asian origin to immigrate.

The official discourse had been rather welcoming of immigrants, imparting the cosmopolitan and technocratic consensus that an increase in the migrant population is structurally necessary to provide for the economic growth that maintains the pensions and the social welfare system.

But here the technocratic discourse will ultimately fall on deaf ears, because the native, domestic population consists of the many losers of globalization, automation and rationalization. The capitalist system creates so much economic dislocation and uncertainty that most workers can no longer be sure that they can live a similarly privileged life as their parents (many don't). People in developing countries might criticize the rich developed country people of complaining about first-world problems. Even to have employment instability, precarious work arrangements or rising rents might be a nicer problem to have than drought, famine and civil war. But relative deprivation, which is a driver of human behavior, is about the comparison with people, who are physically close to you. A lower middle class person in Dortmund thinks about the run-down neighborhoods in Dortmund, and not in Bombay. The neoliberal technocrats have failed the working people, who use their frustration to vote against the establishment: Brexit, Trump, Five Star Movement.

Relative deprivation and economic frustration merely provide the fertile ground for the political opposition toward immigration, but it would not explain that this anger and this collapse in public civility would happen right at this moment. Randall Collins (2009) had analyzed how physical violence gets carried out, and he argues that it is a difficult thing to accomplish and happens mostly when there is overarching emotional dominance among the perpetrators. Think of multiple rapists going at one defenseless female. Think of a dozen police officers beating a black guy lying on the ground. Once the violence happens the rhythmic entrainment between the perpetrator and victim, i.e. the emotional dominance and position of overwhelming strength of the former and the whimpering, surrendering pose of the latter, encourage the perpetrator to inflict even more and worse violence.

Is that analysis of the steps of violence useful to explain the growing incivility against foreigners? It is relevant to some extent. As I said, underlying tensions and resentment against foreigners has long existed in western society. Neoliberalism and the growth of foreigners take away the economic security of the domestic population, but the masses are not lashing out. The lashing out comes with permanent political agitation coming from a charismatic leader, who urges on his people that it is okay to hate the foreigners and to reclaim the country for your own people. The rhythmic entrainment, the use of body language for the escalation of a situation (which can be good or bad, e.g. sex or violence), happens on the campaign rallies of Marine LePen, AfD, Brexit, The Northern League, FPO and Trump. Finally, someone speaks to their heart. Yes, these false preachers might have no real solutions, but they feel my problem. The technocratic establishment does not.

The very well-attended Trump rallies provided the fertile ground and legitimation for denouncing Mexicans as rapists and even to inflict physical violence on mostly non-white anti-Trump protesters. Trump encourages his minions, "Get him out of here," referring to a protester in his rally. During one rally he encouraged his fans to take off a protester's winter coat and send him out into the freezing cold.

It is as if the protester was not a human being deserving of equal treatment and respect. What about after the elections? Post-Trump immigration officers feel vindicated to deny certain people entry into the country. Since his takeover, the refugee inflow has declined to a tiny trickle because of understaffing and increasing the already onerous vetting requirements. On an interpersonal level, viral Facebook videos show how white racists want all people to speak English in public or "go home".

In Germany, the refugee crisis provided the fertile ground for the AfD, which began as a party of intellectuals, who worried about the benefits of the euro membership, and then devolved into a nationalist, anti-immigrant party, emphasizing Das Volk, the people. That's how you become a big party. This Nazi discourse had long been suppressed, because of the German historical guilt, but economic dislocation and distance to the Nazi era means that the young Germans can now again be socialized in volkisch, nativist and xenophobic discourse. Once new behaviors become the norm, the escalation toward open violence against foreigners is only a matter of time.

The era of globalization and immediate interconnectedness also means that the nationalists, who provide the perception of security to the masses, celebrate each other's political victories and spur each other on. If it's okay to hate immigrants in the US, why is it not okay in Austria, Sweden or Greece? When Trump demands Putin to return to the G8 or praises Kim Jong-un as a great leader, the punditry and mainstream establishment claims to be shocked. How can the leader of the free world praise dictators? Perhaps because Trump does not care too much about democratic norms either. And why should he? The neoliberal establishment has done its best to make democratic elections virtually meaningless. Bill Clinton said in the 1990s that the Democrats would win elections based on neoliberal strategies that made the Republicans successful in the 1980s. Tony Blair's New Labour had something similar in Britain. Thus, the big parties converge on a political consensus that there are no alternatives to neoliberal globalization and endless immigration. In the absence of Bernie Sanders on the ballot, people prefer a self-obsessed billionaire, who threatens to overturn the liberal order, over the establishment candidate. For people like the Hungarian premier, Viktor Orban, this globalist agenda is driven by George Soros, a rich philanthropist.

As nationalists in one country succeed, their claim to power becomes fair game in the other countries until there no longer is any liberal bastion. The legitimation of a raw public discourse makes immigrants and foreigners an unwelcome piece of meat that need to be extinguished from the territory regardless of how many years or generations they had spent there or how much taxes they contributed to the welfare state. The outrage and fight against xenophobia can only be successful when the civil society is strong. And it is still strong, providing the bulwark against an even more uncivil turn over the short run. But the cracks in civil society are appearing and becoming greater every day. It is not inconceivable to experience a return to a fascist regime, where the strong ruler promises security to the masses in exchange for the surrender of individual liberty.

The liberal order is dying, yet the complicated thing is that some aspects of it are worth preserving (dignity to the individual, universal human rights, freedom of speech), while some things are not (like a capitalist system focused on accumulation for the global 1%, and misery and insecurity for the rest of us). Trump is throwing more fuel to the fire by picking trade wars with the countries of the western alliance. The rise of Hitler in the 1930s was not unrelated to America's Smoot-Hawley tariffs, which halted global trade integration and created autarkic fascist regimes bent on global military conquest.

What about the other countries? Theresa May still thinks Britain is stronger outside of the EU. Macron wants to double down on liberalizing the French labor market, but with Marine LePen ready to take over as most workers are bound to be disappointed. Merkel is limping on, but the two major governing parties are unpopular as ever with the AfD gaining ground in opposition. The Five Star Movement wants to challenge the existence of the euro and the Northern League wants to deport all refugees in Italy. We rarely get to choose how history is made, even though we are the only actors. In that statement, Marx is vindicated. We are not awaiting a liberal utopia but a tribalist nightmare.

Logic of Automation, Part 2 (and Constraints to Capitalism)
Posted on <u>June 21, 2018</u>

I had previously described a complex model in the logic of automation (Liu, "The Logic of Automation", this volume), which involved consumer finance, which is an important channel for understanding the potential fallout of the automation of jobs. I exclude this option in the more simpler version of the automation model, which is depicted below.

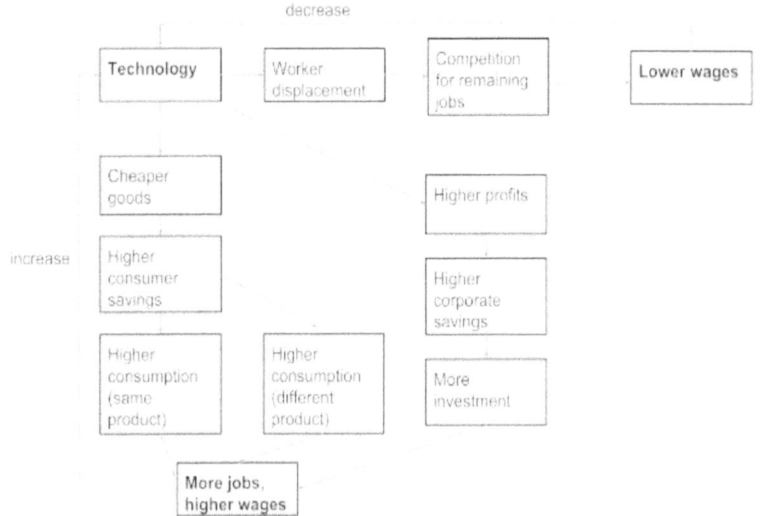

If workers are getting displaced by technology, as is the case in most production sectors, these workers are then pushed into non-production sectors that are labor-intensive and don't require much technology (as is the case with caring occupations in health care and education). The competition for remaining jobs increases and allows employers to pay very low wages. Perhaps political pressure will result in a rise in the minimum wage, though this can come at the risk of less employment, because employers with low profit margins would have to bear the burden of higher labor wages, while the highly productive monopoly sectors get away with high profits. Lower wages ultimately limit the extension of more automation, because it competes with high technology costs. Only when Rifkin's vision of a zero marginal cost society is realized will technological cost be so low that workers have to sell their work below subsistence level if there is no further political intervention to distribute the gains of technology.

What could prevent the realization of a dystopian vision of technology? It would be Say's Law according to which supply creates its own demand. Any increase in profits and savings arising from technological expansion is translated to higher consumer/ corporate savings, which will spur more investment and more consumption (either of the same or, after saturation occurs, in a different product). In that case, demand for labor increases, which will push up wages, which will increase the pressure for more automation.

Even if we assume that the capitalist game can continue indefinitely, it still entraps most of us as hamsters in the wheel. In the case, where the displacement-competition vision gets realized, workers are structurally too weak to advance their interests, and capitalists who make enough profits with cheap workers might slow down automation, which keeps us in a low-wage trap. Though to be fair, wherever capitalism has existed the long-term trajectory is an upward push in wages and a pushing along the innovation frontier. But even if we assume there are no problems with Say's Law (e.g. corporations do not hoard their cash with share buybacks but decide to invest it in new consumer markets, or consumers are willing to work hard and spend their extra cash in consumer items as opposed to saving it or working less), workers hoping to gain power against employers are beaten back by innovation and automation, which in a private ownership economy tends to strengthen the power of the capitalists.

With the self-sustaining cycle of capitalism going through crisis and regeneration, we are- in the absence of sustained social movements to break that logic- unable to impose a universal basic income or other means of fundamentally decommodifying our life. A UBI that is high enough to sustain a basic lifestyle could be consolidating capitalism by providing a floor of consumption to the masses, but could also challenge it, because an integral part to capitalism has been the commodification of wage labor, which can only be guaranteed if the "whip of hunger" (as per Max Weber) hangs over the masses of the proletariat. This is a condition which the UBI would substantially undermine.

The regenerating cycle of capitalism can only be broken if the zero marginal cost society comes into fruition or if resource/ climate/ population constraints engender perennial stagnation. The capitalist economy can only persist if commodification and high exchange value (i.e. prices) get realized, but the point of automating production and making it nearly free to produce goods is that goods no longer fetch any exchange value even as use value goes through the roof. One of the greatest benefits of the modern information society is the free availability of information via Wikipedia, which is written by the collective commons, i.e. anyone who has any knowledge about any topic and can add his knowledge to it. But despite the immense use-value of Wikipedia, to the extent that knowledge is made available for free, there is no exchange value, and, thus, it can't be added to the GDP, which is the basis for economic calculations including those of profit. Some might argue that the contemporary rise of artificial intelligence means the proliferation and creation of new unheard of markets, i.e. another lease of life to capitalism. But who knows? Once technological systems are in place and produce things at the cost below subsistence wages to workers, why would it stop? Once the robots do all the work, it becomes questionable anyway why subsistence wages have to be high, which would only be the case if Zuckerberg, Bezos, Musk and Co. own the entire economy.

But maybe the capitalism defenders are right in that no internal contradiction of the capital valorization process will produce the downfall of capitalism. In that case, the only obstacles for capitalist expansion are quasi-external, which are related to population, resources and the climate. One important driver for the growth of capitalism is the "human resource", which government statisticians measure as the total size of the labor force available for the capitalists. Historically, capitalism has depended on a continuously growing population to realize economic growth because the population provides the base for both the labor force and the consumer market without which no economy can expand. It might be that a stagnant population furnishes continued sources of economic growth, but that only works if the existing population continuously refines its material tastes by continuing to work harder and find new ways to spend more money. In countries like the US, the absurd result of that thinking has resulted in the proliferation of super-size meals and an obesity epidemic, which has resulted in a decline in the quality of life for the chronically overweight/ obese population. Another element is the planned obsolescence of letting cell phones slow down or dysfunction after 2-3 years of use, thus forcing us to endlessly buy the newest cell phone, regardless of the huge waste that we produce with the discarded phones.

I would argue that capitalism has not gotten rid of population growth dependence, because countries in Europe have stemmed the much-feared demographic aging and decline only by allowing in more immigrants, which is somehow backfiring with increased xenophobia and right-wing populist support. Japan does not worry too much about multiculturalism, but they face structural economic stagnation with very low birth rates and almost no immigration. Abenomics has been sold as a promising bag to restore Japanese economic growth, but that is focused on doubling down on public debt-fueled investments and quantitative easing, but the real economy is still driven by the depopulation and subsequent dying of economic activity in the Japanese countryside.

From a global perspective, the world will not be suffering from a shortage in population, which is expected to peak at somewhere around 10 billion, perhaps by the end of the century, assuming that the secular decline in the fertility rate in the less developed countries continue. But once this peak has happened, capitalism can no longer be saved by the number alone.

A growing population with a rising standard of living has increased resource needs. And here we are talking about everything from food to fossil fuels, iron ore, cobalt, zinc, various other minerals and metals to something as basic as water. It could be argued that we are still decades away from running out of any natural resources, and even if some resources run out, humans have been smart enough to find new ways of generating new resources. The long-feared peak oil concerns had been muted since the US came up with fracking to get to new oil and gas. Human ingenuity, thus, works another lease on life to capitalism. But I expect resource struggles to increase, which could result in outright civil war and other means of armed conflict. There is generally no free-for-all as capitalism still relies on real growth of good consumption.

Lastly, climate change has produced an insurmountable externality to which world leaders have no real response other than vague, voluntary commitments to reduce CO_2 production (as in the Paris accords), which is undermined by Trump's decision to withdraw the US from that climate agreement. Essentially, the use of fossil fuels has resulted in the creation of modern civilization as we know it today, but has also produced the greenhouse effect, which traps the heat of the sun inside the earth atmosphere, thus contributing to global warming. Climate change is an externality in the economic sense, because the full cost (environmental and social) of climate change is not borne by the polluters but by later generations, including those people that are not even born yet.

The only way how capitalism defenders go about discussing climate change is that the energy transition to a low fossil-fuel economy (primarily nuclear power with its attendant flaws, and solar power) could decouple material economic growth with the deleterious effects of human-induced climate change. One really has to have strong faith to believe in that, and for the sake of humanity one has to pray that these people are right, but I suspect they are wrong. John Bellamy Foster and his co-authors (2011) claim that there is a contradiction in the simultaneous satisfaction of material growth needs and immaterial effects on the climate. In that case, environmental curbs on pollution could fatally hamper economic growth.

At this point, climate change is no longer an abstract academic discussion, but is reflected in the decision of individuals to pack up and leave their home territory in search for a better and safer life. A recent documentary I watched showed the great lengths that sub-Saharan African refugees go to climb the fence and reach the Spanish outposts on the north African coast bordering Morocco (Youtube, "Europe's most fortified border", 2018).[40] The EU responds by intensifying the building of external border walls and paying the Moroccan authorities to prevent these refugees from jumping the fence, which has become mortally dangerous. Remarkably, refugees are not deterred. Instead of continuing to languish in makeshift camps in Morocco, their strategy involves aggregating in large numbers and then attempt to storm the barricades and fences all at once. Moroccan and EU police will try to fend off as many refugees as possible, but some of them will inevitably slip through. Once they reach EU ground, they are entitled to apply for asylum.

The construction of border walls in the era of Trump might sound like a popular and viable option, but it isn't really. Even if the Europeans and Americans were to lose all common sense and humanity and create land mines and set up machine gun positions against desperate, unarmed refugees, that is not a reason for them to stop their trek if they see their choice between starving at home/ being jobless or risking their lives on the trek. What is even more disturbing is that the refugees that decide to take off tend to be the relatively better off, as it requires existing social networks and some money for the dangerous transportation to become a refugee in the first place. Most people, even those being desperate and

---

[40] https://www.youtube.com/watch?v=LY_Yiu2U2Ts

economically down and out, can at most move a few kilometers, not even really leaving their country, which may be marked by rampant official corruption, natural catastrophe and/or civil war. With the population pressure being the greatest in sub-Saharan Africa, I expect the push to Europe to increase. Any dreams about a fortress Europe fail.

In conclusion, the automated future might provide another lease of life to capitalism, or it could fatally undermine it along with other constraints related to population, resources and climate change.

Can Democracy be Combined with Capitalism?
Posted on June 23, 2018

The historic connection between democracy and capitalism is that democratic institutions have rarely existed outside of capitalism. The gradual expansion of the suffrage, which usually began with property-holding males, then all males and, lastly, women, happened over long stretches from the nineteenth century and the early twentieth century. Simultaneously, the effect of the industrial revolution was increasing urbanization, proletarianization, trade, technology, labor, consumer and financial markets, which happened around the same time.

This historic confluence of democracy and capitalism has given rise to the modernization theorists, who argue that modernization, which primarily involves the spread of markets and industrial growth, will result in increasing democratization. Modernization theory is not very neatly applicable across all contexts, because China's economic ascent has, thus far, not resulted in a movement toward increasing democratization. It could very well be that the rise of capitalism creates a rise of the middle class, and that middle class places higher demands on their governments and are no longer content with filling up their stomach, i.e. the demand for increasing political rights.

In the meantime, another vindication to modernization theory occurred with the collapse of the Soviet Union and other socialist economies. The Eastern European countries that became integrated into the European Union and NATO had adopted free elections and multi-party democracies. They have also adopted the economic institutions of markets, which replaced the centrally planned economy. But democratic institutions are not consolidated in Eastern Europe as the case of Hungary shows, where Viktor Orban has rigged the political institutions to ensure political dominance over the long term.

Let us first go back to history and examine briefly why democracies became associated with capitalist regimes out of which I develop the argument that *while the modern origin of democracy is linked to the rise of capitalism, over the long term democracies are undermined by capitalism*. In essence, there are two very different conceptions of what democracy is: firstly, it is about the formal institutions of free and fair elections to vote for representatives, who govern on behalf of the majority vote. We might call this *procedural democracy*. Secondly, it is-as with the Athenian leader Pericles (431 BC)- about the realization of policies to the benefit of the masses. We may call this *substantive democracy*. Capitalism can live with the first, but not with the second, and if we think that the benefit of the masses is an important element of a democratic system, then we should be worried about capitalism undermining democracies.

In a feudalist regime, there are no pretenses about democratic rule, because the feudal lords concentrate both economic and political power in their hands. Economic power involves the ownership of land, which produces all the economic goods that all people rely on for survival (primarily food). By laying ownership rights over that land landlords control the economic life of a community. This economic power usually originated from military conquest and the trust in a leader, who had been tasked with administering the grain storage facility. Over many generations, feudal ownership rights pass from one generation to the next, and subordinate peasants and serfs grow up to think that these ownership structures are the way how it is and should be.

Political power involves the exclusive right of the feudal lord to pass policies that pertain to the life of all subordinates living in that land. The ultimate right was with the king, who would draw on the landlords and peasants to draw tax revenues and soldiers to fight wars against neighboring kingdoms. But, practically, in the western European context, the collapse of the Roman empire resulted in the collapse of the central administration, and the rise of feudalism meant that the feudal lords would retain the majority of the political power. Economic and political authoritarianism became an integrated whole, and as long as the economic base of production remained in the countryside and the land, it was a stable political economy.

The undermining of the feudal system is only possible with the creation of an alternative economic base outside of the land. Cities proved to be the alternative. During the feudal era, cities tended to be very small and harbored clerics and scholars in the early universities. The first flourishing cities arose in Italy from the 1200s onward. Venice, Genoa, Padua and Florence picked up foreign trade, which their sea access to the Mediterranean provided. The traders were North Africans, Middle Easterners and East Asians, among others. The Italians developed double-entry bookkeeping, which became a useful tool for traders to document their trade, and that allowed for an increase in wealth in these cities. The increasing purchasing power that was concentrated in the cities resulted in an increase in the division of labor and services, which was the basis for the middle class and the bourgeoisie. The accruing economic wealth of the bourgeoisie did not come with the increase in political power of that class, which still rested with the feudal lords.

The rising self-confidence of the bourgeoisie resulted in an increase in political agitation for increased political rights for the bourgeoisie, which was reflected in the Magna Charter of 1215 in England. Barrington Moore (1966) argued that the rise of democracy was predicated on the strength of the bourgeoisie relative to the feudal lords. Feudal lords, whose rental economy was oriented toward subsistence as opposed to growth (which was the focus of the merchants, traders, financiers and later industrialists), had to make substantial concessions to the bourgeoisie and that included the respect for the limited political suffrage (for property-holders) and the capture of the ever-growing central state by an officialdom of the bourgeois class.

In Britain, the weakness of the landlords stemming from the industrial revolution and the rise of the industrial capitalist had culminated in the parliamentary passage of the repeal of the corn laws in 1846. The corn law had erected a high tariff barrier to the import of food stuffs, which provided economic protection to domestic landlords, who would otherwise not be able to compete with foreign food producers. The Whigs, the party of the bourgeoisie and the capitalists, were virulently opposed to the corn laws, because the high food prices forced capitalists to pay their workers high wages sufficient to purchase the food stuffs. By the mid-nineteenth century, the power of the capitalists was strong enough to repeal the corn laws, thus ushering in the era of free trade, at least from the British perspective.

In contrast, the relative strength of the feudal lords in Germany and Japan meant that the powerful, centralized state, which arose in the nineteenth century (primarily to ensure military dominance), was primarily dominated by the landlords. In Germany, the 1848 revolution had forced some political changes to accommodate the bourgeoisie, but they were not nearly as strong as in France or in Britain. The 1848 revolution resulted in the creation of a three-part suffrage, dividing voting rights into thirds of tax-paying classes. The few rich people that contributed one third of the taxes would have more voting rights than the many poor people that contributed relatively fewer taxes and would end up in the bottom third of the tax-paying class. Universal suffrage did not come until the Weimar Republic, after the devastating World War. To return to Moore's argument, the rise of fascism is intimately linked with the relative weakness of the bourgeoisie, which could not restrain the war-like ambitions of powerful landlords and land-hungry kings. Democratic consolidation in Japan and Germany occurred only with the external occupation of the US after World War II.

The third set of countries in Moore's model were countries with a powerful peasantry, which under the leadership of a communist party and their dedicated cadre, overthrew the landlord system in Russia and China. Land collectivization occurred in the 1930s in the Soviet Union and in the 1950s in China. For that reason alone, Marxism cannot be the same thing as Stalinism and Maoism, because the former was a statement on a capitalist system, which transitions into socialism (though Marx was notably silent in how that transition happens), while the latter two systems are about the communist takeover of a quasi-feudal system, which takes on industrialization and collectivization of farmland and private property at the same time.

If we buy Moore's argument that the bourgeoisie is the social basis for democracy, then democracy can only coexist with capitalism. It is quite a convincing argument, but we should zoom back into history one more time. The first preference of the bourgeoisie was not universal suffrage, which was imposed only after the end of World War I, which was even true for Britain. The bourgeoisie wanted to overthrow the landlords politically, not empower the workers or peasants. They were able to accumulate all this money, thus developing an independent economic base from the landlords, but they were not able to attain political power initially. The bourgeois discourse on democracy, free elections, freedom of speech/ press, civil rights, and a professional state bureaucracy never intended to accommodate the popular classes, which included peasants, and after they were removed from the land or lured into the city, the workers.

Only the World War provided the external shock to the equilibrium of the political economy, which was gradually shifting from the landlords to the bourgeoisie. The popular classes were drawn to fight the war, pay the taxes and create the ammunition, and after the war it was no longer possible for the ruling classes (whether landlord or bourgeoisie) to deny the suffrage to the popular classes. By the time universal suffrage was introduced the landlords were on the wane. In Germany, the Junkers (landlords) had organized in the German National Party and even held power in the Weimar era. The loss of Germany in World War II led to the territorial conquest of Prussia, which was incorporated into Poland and the Soviet Union. The remaining Prussian landlords were expropriated by the Soviet government. East Germany became communist and West Germany became capitalist. There no longer was any space for the landlords.

Marx' prediction that capitalism would simplify the class system to bourgeoisie and proletariat turned out to be true. (Well, actually, the contemporary advancement of technology, which is displacing more and more workers increases the ranks of the lumpenproletariat, a third floating class, which has no sense of job security and in some cases no job at all.) We no longer talk about landlords or peasants as being a meaningful political class, at least not in the most developed countries.

But where does it leave us with the prospects to democratic governance? The bourgeois capitalists had accepted universal suffrage, which had also resulted in the rise of social democratic parties, Keynesian government investment policy and the welfare state. The Polanyian double movement, i.e. the liberalization and deregulation of labor becoming re-regulated with state intervention, seemed to bear out the prediction that capitalism could be tamed with democratic institutions (Polanyi 1944).

But, strangely, we have witnessed the decline of this democratic consensus. While the liberal establishment still tries to convince us that our faith in the political and economic institutions (i.e. elections and capitalism/ private property) remain strong, we know that the political feedback of the electorate includes anti-establishment and anti-immigrant/ nativist sentiment. We see a gradual dismantling of the welfare state, the weakening of labor and collective bargaining rights, and the social democratic parties are decimated to oblivion.

In the absence of restoring the Keynesian consensus, which is built on huge economic growth and pro-popular redistributive policies and institutions, people will continue to be inclined to vote against the establishment, which we have observed with Trump, LePen, AfD, Five Star Movement and Brexit. We could be at the cusp of fascism. As heartbreaking as the Trump policy of separating families of undocumented immigrants arriving at the border (which has now apparently been reversed and replaced with extended family detention) may be, we are only seeing the early parts of ugly and human-demeaning policies. Inhumane policies become normalized, thus raising the bar for doing even uglier things. We should be happy that Trump lacks the long-term vision of a Hitler, but we should be equally disturbed that the anti-liberal and ultimately anti-democratic policies are only the beginning of a deteriorating trend in the national polity.

Democratic institutions in the US are already assailed by Supreme Court decisions that equate money (and their owners of big capital) with political speech, thus they can literally buy politicians to enact their agenda rather than the popular agenda. Martin Gilens and Benjamin Page (2014) find that the bottom 70% of the income distribution has virtually no influence over legislation in the US senate. The 2008 economic crash was followed by generous bank bailouts that were "systemically important" for the survival of the financial system, while the loss of houses and jobs among the working and middle classes were not deemed such. It is this neutered condition of substantive democracy (i.e. policies for the benefit of the masses, popular classes), which allows the capitalists to accept formal democracy. Until a populist dictator gets elected president, seize all the powers and neuter Congress and the Supreme Court, the capitalists can accept the continuation of formal democratic institutions as long as the politicians do their bidding in practice.

The undermining of substantive democracy while we maintain the formal democratic institutions should concern us to the extent that democratic institutions only make sense if they substantively deliver benefits for the popular classes. But political institutions do not exist in a vacuum, but are embedded in an economic context. The bourgeois capitalist owns the means of production in the economy, and they merely want the state and the political institutions to ensure private property and provide some public goods that help in capital accumulation. But as James O'Connor (1973) pointed out in *The Fiscal Crisis of the State*, the government has to additionally ensure that the losers of capital accumulation, especially unemployed workers, retired people and low-wage workers, are sufficiently compensated to retain political legitimacy under capitalism. But we are nibbling away at those social protections, thus undermining popular confidence in both the political and economic system.

Thus, the capitalist claim to private ownership (and economic inequality) is in direct contradiction to the democratic claim to one man, one vote (and political equality). It is unclear whether in the absence of substantive democracy, formal democracy is politically sustainable over the long term. The political events of the present make one quite pessimistic. But it seems to be that only when the formal democratic institutions are destroyed, that we can lay bare the corporate oligarchy controlling us and seriously contemplate alternatives to it. The rise of democracy may be linked to capitalism, but the continuation of democracy is a fragile construct in a capitalist economy.

The Limits of Liberalism
Posted on <u>June 27, 2018</u>

The often-cited End of History thesis of Francis Fukuyama (1989) became so popular, because the defeat of the Soviet Union and communism suggested that there are no more alternatives to the global liberal order, which contains an economic and a social/cultural component. In this article, I argue that both economic and social liberalism have their limits and could face complete rollback in the near future.

Economic liberalism is about the increased rights of global investors to dictate the policies of countries. In the words of Thomas Friedman (2007), the integration of different parts of the world into the global economy resulted in an "electronic herd", which reflects the reality that policies that restrain investor rights would be punished by capital outflow, which is controlled by big corporations and major investors.

But that is not the element that is emphasized when selling the idea of economic liberalism to the public. Economic liberalism is also about the creation of jobs with rising wage prospects, as workers are no longer restrained to sell their goods and services to the domestic market, but now have access to sell to the global economy. In the last 30 years, there was perhaps no country which took this lesson more to heart than China. China had been a dirt-poor country during the Mao Zedong era, but they had a giant workforce and functioning centralized state institutions to provide an environment friendly to development and foreign investments. Now it is only a matter of time until China will become the dominant superpower in the world.

Economic prosperity that comes along with the adoption of the most advanced technology, human capital training and functioning political institutions friendly to investors, is now spreading to more and more countries, especially those that are demographically quite young and dynamic. Max Roser (2018) shows that the proportion of children in the world that die in the first five years of life is continuously declining, which means that the blessings of technological progress and economic integration has worked to provide many more people even in disadvantaged sub-Saharan Africa with the basic goods to survive and perhaps to flourish.

The promises of the integration into the world economy means that non-western countries are expected to be quite supportive of economic globalization, even as poor countries continue to be held back by rich country export subsidies that suppress the development of domestic agriculture, rampant political corruption and foreign debt.

The story in the more developed western countries is altogether different. The abandonment of the Keynesian consensus, i.e. the general social contract between the working/ middle class with the capitalist class, meant that the working class faces downward economic mobility and economic instability with a gig economy becoming the major section of the labor market absorbing the surplus labor, while the owners of technology and capital get richer and richer.

As a result, the political center is collapsing while the forces of the extreme right and the left are rising, though the left is weakened by the lack of credibility in delivering a promising socialist solution (the last vestiges in North Korea and Venezuela are undesirably emulated elsewhere; Sanders and Corbyn merely want Scandinavian social democracy, which itself faces the limits and contradictions of its economic model). In the absence of a credible left-wing solution, the more likely alternative is the adoption of economic isolationism, which is exemplified by Trump's decision to dismantle the global liberal order with tariff wars against China, Canada, Mexico and the EU.

If the economically liberal agenda has hit its zenith, perhaps the socially liberal agenda can be salvaged. An Irish referendum removed restrictions to abortion; the Supreme Court decision legalized gay marriage; even in Wahhabist Saudi Arabia women are now allowed to drive cars (which had previously been prohibited); the MeToo and BlackLivesMatter movement is unraveling the sexist and racist regime, which has long plagued the US. I don't find it likely that many of these advances are about to be removed, but one cannot be so sure either.

A socially liberal agenda tends to be supported by the more urban, younger, female and ethnic minority populations. If you strip away these social characteristics you are left with the modal Trump voter: white men in the countryside, who are downwardly socially mobile, or who are still doing okay economically but fear for their future prospects. One might claim that in the US, they form a declining demographic, and even in Europe, demographic dynamism comes entirely from the immigrant population, primarily of Middle Eastern, North African heritage, but increasingly of Asian and sub-Saharan African descent.

But this demographic change is happening over the long term. In the meantime, there is a substantial political bloc that is generally socially conservative. Even among immigrants, one might find many social conservatives, who are unwilling to embrace socially liberal positions. The crude belief of most educated people (including many people, who read this blog, or the modal New York Times reader) that the country is getting ever more progressive, while the socially conservatives are a dying relic is not necessarily accurate. President Obama described the losers of social/ economic change as such,

*You go into these small towns in Pennsylvania and, like a lot of small towns in the Midwest, the jobs have been gone now for 25 years and nothing's replaced them. And they fell through the Clinton administration, and the Bush administration, and each successive administration has said that somehow these communities are gonna regenerate and they have not. **And it's not surprising then they get bitter, they cling to guns or religion or antipathy toward people who aren't like them** or anti-immigrant sentiment or anti-trade sentiment as a way to explain their frustrations.*

Smith (2008)

It tends to be more educated people that openly embrace a progressive social agenda, but among the common people, it is not entirely clear why they would be so supportive of such an agenda. But assuming that the social progressives win the day, the right-wing politicians can use a xenophobic, anti-immigrant and socially conservative agenda to get sufficient electoral support to win political office, while at the same time doubling down on a pro-corporate, liberal economic form of globalization or, on the contrary, turn abruptly to a protectionist agenda that is in line with "building walls" and getting the foreigners out of the country.

Interestingly, personal immigrant background does not inoculate one against opposition to more migration. Following the logic of "kicking away the ladder", one may have been successful in entering the country, working hard and getting citizenship, but there is no such enthusiasm to allow more immigrants to come in that are a serious source of labor competition. Austrians of Serbian and Turkish descent, for instance, are not very enthralled that Eastern European migrants flood the local labor market and do janitorial or health aide jobs they are accustomed to having.

The foundational premise of liberalism, whether in its economic or social variation, is the maximization or increase in liberty or freedom. Economically, one should be able to have the economic freedom to pursue jobs or own companies, and socially, one should be able to make family or personal decisions without the interference of the state. While this all sounds good, the devil is entirely in the details. Economically, the freedom of the capitalist to dispose of his capital (including the labor force) conflicts with the worker's desire to balance family/ personal life with work and enjoy a certain quality of life. Socially, the individual freedom to abort a fetus or marry a same-sex partner or to migrate to another country can be interpreted by some as violating social traditions, which value a fetus to the same extent as a human being, deem same-sex marriages as unnatural and not serving pro-creation, and argue that multiculturalism will lead to a decline in social trust and stability.

Historically, the economically liberal agenda tends to have a somewhat longer track record than social liberalism, because economic integration in the form of trade and the creation of markets tends to happen faster than the change in social values. The historical specificity of liberalism means that it can at some point be undermined (as opposed to prevail forever). The economic limits to neoliberalism can be found in the exhaustion of population and resource growth, the devastating consequences of climate change, and a technological revolution that could marginalize more and more workers. As for social liberalism, it is much harder to make a solid prognosis, in part, because once changes in social values are realized they are much harder to reverse. For instance, while one can still hear the voices of some anti-abortion activists, I have not heard anyone demanding the re-institution of slavery of blacks (in part, because the mass incarceration of blacks since the 1980s has recreated some of these oppressive conditions), or demanding women to return to the home and kitchen (though, female labor participation rate has stopped climbing around 2000).

The retrogression of social liberalism primarily takes the form of tougher immigration laws, which provide the domestic nationals with the false sense of security and domestic tranquility. Firstly, a substantial part of economic growth comes from immigrants, and secondly, the political instability that result in civil war means that the pressure to migrate to the rich countries can only be expected to increase in the near future. The awareness among people in poor countries of the higher standard of living in the rich countries means that the pressure to migrate will increase. Thus, a problematic situation arises, where more restrictive immigration laws and more pressure to migrate will expand the undocumented population, while continuing to fire up xenophobic and right-wing parties, who will ultimately destroy democracy for its incessant concern with minority rights and rule of law, i.e. the accommodation to the rights of the much-detested immigrants.

Subsequently, it is possible that the effects of both social and economic liberalism will create so much popular discontent that a charismatic dictator will rise up to remove both and engender a totalitarian regime that is economically autarkic and socially conservative. In the abstract, everyone will agree that the right and freedoms of the individual are worth preserving, though in practice it conflicts with other principles like the socialist desire for economic equality or the social conservative's desire for social stability. We better rethink what kind of liberalism is desirable before the changes ahead become too difficult to deal with. A universal basic income, for instance, can preserve individual economic freedom (both for the capitalists, who don't want anti-capitalist, protectionist sentiments to prevail and for the workers, who don't have to fear starvation without work), while potentially taking some wind out of the sail of social identity issues.

References:

Acemoglu, Daron, and Pascual Restrepo. 2017. "Robots and Jobs: Evidence from US Labor Markets." Working Paper 23285. National Bureau of Economic Research.

Ackerman, Spencer. 2017. "US Commando Dies in Yemen Raid as Trump Counter-Terror Plans Take Shape." *The Guardian*, January 29.

Aguiar, Mark, Mark Bils, Kerwin Kofi Charles, and Erik Hurst. 2017. "Leisure Luxuries and the Labor Supply of Young Men." Working Paper 23552. National Bureau of Economic Research.

Aristotle. 1988. *The Politics (Cambridge Texts in the History of Political Thought)*. Edited by Dr Stephen Everson. Cambridge, New York: Cambridge University Press.

Arnsdorf, Isaac. 2016. "Trump: 'The President Can't Have a Conflict of Interest.'" *Politico*, November 22.

Baumol, William J. 2013. *The Cost Disease: Why Computers Get Cheaper and Health Care Doesn't*. New Haven: Yale University Press.

Bentham, Jeremy. 1843. *The Works of Jeremy Bentham, Vol. 4 (Panopticon, Constitution, Colonies, Codification)*. Online Library of Liberty.

Berman, Eli, John Bound, and Stephen Machin. 1998. "Implications of Skill-Biased Technological Change: International Evidence." *The Quarterly Journal of Economics* 113 (4): 1245–79.

Bernays, Edward. 1928. *Propaganda*. London: Routledge.

Binderup, Charles. 1937. "Congressional Record- House." https://en.wikisource.org/wiki/Page:Congressional_Record_Volume_81_Part_3.djvu/154.

Bix, Amy Sue. 2001. *Inventing Ourselves Out of Jobs?: America's Debate over Technological Unemployment, 1929-1981*. Baltimore: Johns Hopkins University Press.

Black, Sandra, Jason Furman, Emma Rackstraw, and Nirupama Rao. 2016. "The Long-Term Decline in US Prime-Age Male Labour Force Participation." *VoxEU.Org (blog)*. July 6.

Borger, Julian, and Duncan Campbell. 2003. "Profile: Arnold Schwarzenegger" *The Guardian*, August 8.

Bostrom, Nick. 2016. *Superintelligence: Paths, Dangers, Strategies*. Oxford: Oxford University Press.

Botsman, Rachel. 2017. "Big Data Meets Big Brother as China Moves to Rate Its Citizens." Wired, October 21.

Bourdieu, Pierre. 1993. *The Field of Cultural Production: Essays on Art and Literature*. New York: Columbia University Press.

Brynjolfsson, Erik, Daniel Rock, and Chad Syverson. 2017. "Artificial Intelligence and the Modern Productivity Paradox: A Clash of Expectations and Statistics." Working Paper 24001. National Bureau of Economic Research.

Burke, Edmund. 1790. *Reflections on the Revolution in France*. London: James Dodsley, Pall Mall.

Calfas, Jennifer. 2016. "Trump's Cabinet Picks Have More Wealth than Third of American Households Combined." *TheHill*, December 15.

Carney, Jordain. 2017. "CBO: Senate Tax Bill Increases Deficit by $1.4 Trillion." *TheHill*, December 2.

Carroll, Lauren. 2017. "Trump Lawyer: Foreign Dignitaries Staying in a Trump Hotel Doesn't Violate Constitution." *PolitiFact*. January 13.

Case, Anne, and Angus Deaton. 2017. "Mortality and Morbidity in the 21st Century." Brookings Papers on Economic Activity.

Caulderwood, Kathleen. 2014. "Boko Haram And Nigeria's Economy: Why The Poorest Suffer Most." *International Business Times*, July 31.

Centeno, Miguel A., and Joseph N. Cohen. 2012. "The Arc of Neoliberalism." *Annual Review of Sociology* 38 (1): 317–40.

Centeno, Miguel Angel. 2002. *Blood and Debt: War and the Nation-State in Latin America*. State Park: Penn State University Press.

Chambers, Madeline. 2017. "Merkel Says Dutch Election Result Sends Pro-Europe Signal." *Reuters*, March 16.

Chambliss, Daniel F. 1989. "The Mundanity of Excellence: An Ethnographic Report on Stratification and Olympic Swimmers." *Sociological Theory* 7 (1): 70–86.

Chase, Jefferson. 2017. "Taxpayers Demand End to 'Soli' Tax to Boost Eastern German Economy." *DW.COM*, November 9.

Chomsky, Noam. 1967. "The Responsibility of Intellectuals." *The New York Review of Books*, February 23.

Chutel, Lynsey. 2017. "Post-Apartheid South Africa Is Failing the Very People It Liberated." *Quartz (blog)*. August 25.

Collins, Randall. 1979. *The Credential Society: A Historical Sociology of Education and Stratification*. Cambridge: Academic Press.

———. 1998. *The Sociology of Philosophies: A Global Theory of Intellectual Change*. Revised edition. Cambridge, Mass.: Belknap Press of Harvard University Press.

———. 2004. *Interaction Ritual Chains*. Princeton: Princeton University Press.

———. 2009. *Violence: A Micro-Sociological Theory*. Princeton: Princeton University Press.

———. 2016. "Trump and the Sopranos." *The Sociological Eye (blog)*. December 1.

———. 2017a. "Trump's Sad Face." The Sociological Eye (blog). March 23.

———. 2017b. "North Korea's ICBMs: A Cold War Solution." The Sociological Eye (blog). July 7.

Connelly, John. 2013. "Jester and Priest: On Leszek Kolakowski." *The Nation*. September 4.

Cotterill, Joseph, and David Pilling. 2017. "South Africa and Nigeria Limp out of Recession." *Financial Times*, September 5.

Crouch, Colin. 2015. *The Knowledge Corrupters: Hidden Consequences of the Financial Takeover of Public Life. 1 edition*. Cambridge, UK□; Malden, MA: Polity.

Crowley, Kevin. 2017. "#BlackMonday - Whites Own 73% of South Africa's Farming Land." *IOL Business Report*, October 30.

Das, Madhuparna. 2008. "Leather Complex Turns Threat to Environment." *Indian Express*. October 2.

DerStandard. 2017. "Das Regierungsprogramm von ÖVP Und FPÖ Im Überblick." *DerStandard.At*, December 16.

Die Zeit. 2017. "Arbeitsmarkt: Zahl der Aufstocker trotz Mindestlohn nur gering gesunken." *Die Zeit*, August 29.

Domhoff, G. William. 1967. "The Class-Domination Theory of Power." *Who Rules America?*.

Dou, Eva. 2017. "Jailed for a Text: China's Censors Are Spying on Mobile Chat Groups." *Wall Street Journal*, December 8.

Droit, R.P., and T. Ferenczi. 1992. "The Left Hand and the Right Hand of the State." Variant.

Dube, Arindrajit, Jeff Jacobs, Suresh Naidu, and Siddharth Suri. 2018. "Monopsony in Online Labor Markets." Working Paper 24416. National Bureau of Economic Research.

Duménil, Gérard, and Dominique Lévy. 2011. *The Crisis of Neoliberalism*. Cambridge: Harvard University Press.

Dunn, Bill. 2017. "Against Neoliberalism as a Concept." *Capital & Class* 41 (3): 435–54.

Economist. 2015. "Why so Many Dutch People Work Part Time - The Economist Explains." *Economist*, May 12.

Edwards, David. 2017 "Reuters Orders Reporters to Cover Trump like an Authoritarian Regime: Expect 'Physical Threats.'" *Raw Story*, February 1.

Elder-Vass, Dave. 2016. *Profit and Gift in the Digital Economy*. Cambridge: Cambridge University Press.

Estlund, Cynthia. 2017. *A New Deal for China's Workers?*. Cambridge: Harvard University Press.

Fernholz, Tim. 2016. "Bernie Sanders Is Leading the Democrats into Battle against Donald Trump on Jan. 15." *Quartz (blog)*, December 28.

Flaherty, Colleen. 2017. "'Running Out the Clock' on Grad Unions?" *Inside Higher Ed*, May 4.

Fleming, Sam, and Shawn Donnan. 2016. "Who Are the Team Trump Players Heading for Washington?" *Financial Times*, November 9.

Ford, Martin. 2016. *Rise of the Robots: Technology and the Threat of a Jobless Future*. New York: Basic Books.

Foster, John Bellamy, Richard York, and Brett Clark. 2011. *The Ecological Rift: Capitalism's War on the Earth*. New York: Monthly Review Press.

Frank, Thomas. 2005. *What's the Matter with Kansas?: How Conservatives Won the Heart of America*. New York: Holt & Co.

Frey, Carl Benedikt, and Michael A. Osborne. 2013. "The Future of Employment: How Susceptible Are Jobs to Computerisation?" Oxford University.

Friedman, Eli. 2014. *Insurgency Trap: Labor Politics in Postsocialist China. 1 edition*. Ithaca: Cornell University Press.

Friedman, Thomas L. 2007. *The World Is Flat: A Brief History of the Twenty-First Century*. London: Picador.

Fukuyama, Francis. 1989. "The End of History?" *The National Interest* 16: 3–18.

Fung, Brian. 2017. "The FCC's Net Neutrality Plan May Have Even Bigger Ramifications in Light of This Obscure Court Case." *Washington Post*, December 6.

Gebeloff, Robert, and Karl Russell. 2017. "How the Growth of E-Commerce Is Shifting Retail Jobs." *The New York Times*, July 6.

Gee, Oliver. 2017. "From Teacher to Lover to France's First Lady: Meet 'Madame Macron' ." *The Local*, May 7.

Georg Graetz, and Guy Michaels. 2015. "Robots at Work." Centre for Economic Performance.

Gilens, Martin, and Benjamin I. Page. 2014. "Testing Theories of American Politics: Elites, Interest Groups, and Average Citizens." *Perspectives on Politics* 12 (3): 564–81.

Gillespie, Patrick. 2017. "Mark Zuckerberg Supports Universal Basic Income. What Exactly Is It?" *CNN*, May 26.

Ginsberg, Benjamin. 2011. *The Fall of the Faculty: The Rise of the All-Administrative University and Why It Matters*. New York: Oxford University Press.

Gold, Matea. 2017. "Trump Lobbying Ban Strips out Language Requiring Public Reporting on Ethics Compliance." *Washington Post*, January 29.

Goldin, Ian. 2018. "Five Reasons Why Universal Basic Income Is a Bad Idea." *Financial Times*, February 11.

Goolsbee, Austan. 2018. "Public Policy in an AI Economy." Working Paper 24653. National Bureau of Economic Research.

Gordon, Robert J. 2014. "The Demise of U.S. Economic Growth: Restatement, Rebuttal, and Reflections." Working Paper 19895. National Bureau of Economic Research.

Graeber, David. 2013. "On the Phenomenon of Bullshit Jobs." Libcom.Org. 2013.

———. 2018. *Bullshit Jobs: A Theory*. New York: Simon & Schuster.

Harrison, Edward. 2017. "Did the Greek Bailout Money Go to 'Liquor and Women'?" *Credit Writedowns (blog)*. March 25.

Harvey, David. 2005. *A Brief History of Neoliberalism*. New York: Oxford University Press.

Hiltzik, Michael. 2017. "Sen. Rubio Tells a Secret: After Giving a Tax Cut to the Rich, GOP Will Cut Social Security and Medicare." *Los Angeles Times*, November 30, 2017.

Hochschild, Arlie Russell. 2016. "Special Report: I Spent 5 Years with Some of Trump's Biggest Fans. Here's What They Won't Tell You." *Mother Jones.*

Hosur, Suhas. 2004. *Consolation of Mind.* Bloomington: iUniverse, Inc.

Huang, Zheping. 2017. "What You Need to Know about Beijing's Crackdown on Its 'Low-End Population.'" *Quartz*, November 27.

Hung, Ho-fung. 2017. *The China Boom: Why China Will Not Rule the World.* New York: Columbia University Press.

IFR. 2017. "Robots: China Breaks Historic Records in Automation." *International Federation of Robotics (IFR).* August 16, 2017.

Jalili, Saeed. 2018. "Iran to Replace US Dollar with Euro in Financial Reports." *Al Jazeera*, April 18.

Jones, Robert. 2014. "Southern Evangelicals: Dwindling—and Taking the GOP Edge With Them." *The Atlantic*, October 17, 2014.

Kalecki, Michael. 1943. "Political Aspects of Full Employment." *Political Quarterly.*

Kalleberg, Arne. 2018. *Precarious Lives: Job Insecurity and Well-Being in Rich Democracies.* Cambridge: Polity Press.

Katz, Lawrence F., and Alan B. Krueger. 2016. "The Rise and Nature of Alternative Work Arrangements in the United States, 1995-2015." Working Paper 22667. National Bureau of Economic Research.

Killian, Linda. 2017. "Trump's Focus on Forgotten Men Masks Billionaire Agenda: Column." *USA Today*, January 20.

Korpi, Walter. 1985. "Power Resources Approach vs. Action and Conflict: On Causal and Intentional Explanations in the Study of Power." *Sociological Theory* 3 (2): 31–45.

Korpi, Walter, and Joakim Palme. 1998. "The Paradox of Redistribution and Strategies of Equality: Welfare State Institutions, Inequality, and Poverty in the Western Countries." *American Sociological Review* 63 (5): 661–87.

Kowalczyk, Michał. 2017. "Hungary's Unorthodox Economic Policies." *Central European Financial Observer*, May 18.

Lahiff, Edward. 2008. "Land Reform in South Africa: A Status Report 2008." Programme for Land and Agrarian Studies, Report No. 38.

Lanier, Jaron. 2014. *Who Owns the Future?* New York: Simon & Schuster.

Laughlin, Jason. 2016. "SEPTA Union Strikes as Contract Talks Fail." *Philadelphia Inquirer*, November 1, 2016.

Lazonick, William. 2014. "Profits Without Prosperity." *Harvard Business Review*, September 1.

Leswing, Kif. 2016. "5 Most Valuable Public Companies All Tech Companies." *Business Insider*, August 1, 2016.

Lie, John. 2004. *Multiethnic Japan*. Cambridge: Harvard University Press.

Lin, Ken-Hou, and Donald Tomaskovic-Devey. 2013. "Financialization and U.S. Income Inequality, 1970–2008." *American Journal of Sociology* 118 (5): 1284–1329.

Liu, Larry. 2014a. "Petrodollar Rule Needs to End." *Mr Liu's Opinions (blog)*. August 30.

———. 2014b. "Book Review of Wolfgang Streeck 'Buying Time: The Delayed Crisis of Democratic Capitalism' (London: Verso, 2014)." *Mr Liu's Opinions (blog)*. December 29.

———. 2015a. "Why Yanis Varoufakis Is the Best Finance Minister in Europe." *Mr Liu's Opinions (blog)*. May 4.

———. 2015b. "Book Review of Claus Offe, 'Contradictions of the Welfare State' (1984)." *Mr Liu's Opinions (blog)*. September 7.

———. 2016a. "Trump vs. Sanders: A Duel That the Establishment Denied." *Mr Liu's Opinions (blog)*, January 15.

———. 2016b. "The Discontents of Modern Academic Life." *Mr Liu's Opinions (blog)*. March 11.

———. 2016c. "I Endorse Abstention for the US General Elections." *Mr Liu's Opinions (blog)*. June 8.

———. 2016d. "Brexit: What Comes Next?" *Mr Liu's Opinions (blog)*. July 10.

———. 2016e. "US Elections: Vote However You Like." *Mr Liu's Opinions (blog)*. July 23.

Long, Heather. 2017. "The Senate GOP Tax Bill, Explained." *Washington Post*, November 30.

Malinowski, Bronislaw. 1922. *Argonauts of the Western Pacific*. London: Routledge.

Manne, Kate. 2015. "Why I Use Trigger Warnings." *The New York Times*, September 19.

Margonelli, Lisa. 2017. "You Never Get One Isolated Great Thinker at a Time." *Zócalo Public Square (blog)*. February 21.

McCurry, Justin. 2018. "North Korea Nuclear Test Site Has Collapsed and May Be out of Action – China Study." *The Guardian*, April 26.

McKenna, Megan L., Shannon McAtee, Patricia E. Bryan, Rebecca Jeun, Tabitha Ward, Jacob Kraus, Maria E. Bottazzi, Peter J. Hotez, Catherine C. Flowers, and Rojelio Mejia. 2017. "Human Intestinal Parasite Burden and Poor Sanitation in Rural Alabama." *The American Journal of Tropical Medicine and Hygiene* 97 (5): 1623–28.

Meltzer, Allan H., and Scott F. Richard. 1981. "A Rational Theory of the Size of Government." *Journal of Political Economy* 89 (5): 914–27.

Merton, Robert. 1968. "The Matthew Effect in Science." *Science* 159 (3810): 56–63.

Milanovic, Branko. 2016. *Global Inequality: A New Approach for the Age of Globalization*. Cambridge: Harvard University Press.

Mischel, Lawrence, and Heidi Shierholz. 2017. "Robots, or Automation, Are Not the Problem: Too Little Worker Power Is." *Economic Policy Institute (blog)*. February 21.

Moore, Barrington Jr. 1966. *Social Origins of Dictatorship and Democracy: Lord and Peasant in the Making of the Modern World*. Boston: Beacon Press.

NAACP. n.d. "Criminal Justice Fact Sheet." National Association for the Advancement for Colored People. Accessed July 9, 2018.

Nelson, Soraya Sarhaddi. 2018. "Hungary Reduces Number Of Asylum-Seekers It Will Admit To 2 Per Day." *NPR.Org*, February 3.

NOI-Polls. 2016. "Nigeria's Agricultural Sector Still Dominated by Subsistence Farming; as Farmers Call for More Support." November 1.

Nuyen, A. T. 2013. "The 'Mandate of Heaven': Mencius and the Divine Command Theory of Political Legitimacy." *Philosophy East and West* 63 (2): 113–26.

Nwagbara, Eucharia Nwabugo. 2011. "The Story of Structural Adjustment Program in Nigeria from the Perspective of Organized Labor." *Australian Journal of Business and Management Research* 1 (7): 30–41.

O'Connor, James. 1973. *The Fiscal Crisis of the State*. New Brunswick, N.J: Transaction Publishers.

Ogbimi, F.E. n.d. "Structural Adjustment Is the Wrong Policy." *African Technology Forum* 8 (1). Accessed July 9.

Olson, Mancur Jr. 1971. *The Logic of Collective Action.* Cambridge: Harvard University Press.

Orwell, George. 1949. *Nineteen Eighty-Four.* London: Seckar and Warburg.

Oxfam. 2013. "The True Cost of Austerity and Inequality: The Netherlands Case Study." Oxfam.

Oxfeld, Ellen. 1993. *Blood, Sweat, and Mahjong: Family and Enterprise in an Overseas Chinese Community.* Ithaca: Cornell Univ Press.

Painter, Richard W., and Norman L. Eisen. 2017. "Who Hasn't Trump Banned? People From Places Where He's Done Business." *The New York Times*, January 29.

Pericles. 431AD. "Funeral Speech of Pericles from Athens Democracy." http://www.rjgeib.com/thoughts/athens/athens.html.

Perkins, John. 2005. *Confessions of an Economic Hit Man.* New York: Plume.

Pettit, Becky, and Bruce Western. 2004. "Mass Imprisonment and the Life Course: Race and Class Inequality in U.S. Incarceration" *American Sociological Review* 69 (2): 151–69.

Piotrowski, Martin, Arne Kalleberg, and Ronald R. Rindfuss. 2015. "Contingent Work Rising: Implications for the Timing of Marriage in Japan" *Journal of Marriage and Family* 77 (5): 1039–56.

Polanyi, Karl. 1944. *The Great Transformation: The Political and Economic Origins of Our Time.* Boston: Beacon Press.

Polillo, Simone. 2013. *Conservatives Versus Wildcats: A Sociology of Financial Conflict.* Redwood City: Stanford University Press.

Popper, Karl R. 1963. "Science as Falsification." In *Conjectures and Refutations*, 33–39. London: Routledge and Keagan Paul.

Proshare. 2015. "Nigerian Manufacturing Sector Summary Report: 2010-2012." *Proshare Intelligent Investing*. January 22.

Reich, Robert. 2013. "The Irony of Republican Disapproval of Obamacare." *Christian Science Monitor*, October 28.

Roberts, Michael. 2016. "Basic Income – Too Basic, Not Radical Enough." *Michael Roberts Blog (blog)*. October 23.

Rodgers, Nile. 2011. *Le Freak: An Upside Down Story of Family, Disco, and Destiny.* New York: Random House Publishing Group.

Rodridguez-Franco, Diana. 2016. "Internal Wars, Taxation, and State Building - Diana Rodríguez-Franco, 2016." *American Sociological Review* 81 (1): 190–213.

Roser, Max. 2018. "Child Mortality." Our World in Data. 2018. https://ourworldindata.org/child-mortality.

Rubin, Richard. 2016. "Donald Trump's Win Gives GOP Fuel to Slash Taxes." *Wall Street Journal*, November 9.

Rudd, Rose A., Puja Seth, Felicita David, and Lawrence Scholl. 2016. "Increases in Drug and Opioid-Involved Overdose Deaths — United States, 2010–2015." *Morbidity and Mortality Weekly Report* 65 (50–51): 1445–52.

Saad-Filho, Alfredo, and Deborah Johnston, eds. 2005. *Neoliberalism: A Critical Reader.* London: Pluto Press.

Said-Moorhouse, Lauren, and Bryony Jones. 2017. "Dutch Elections: Wilders' Far-Right Party Beaten, Early Results Show." *CNN*, March 16.

Sandberg, Sheryl. 2013. *Lean In: Women, Work, and the Will to Lead.* New York: Knopf.

Sanders, Bernie. 2016. *Our Revolution: A Future to Believe In.* New York: Thomas Dunne Book.

———. n.d. "What Do the Koch Brothers Want?" *Sen. Bernie Sanders.* Accessed July 9, 2018.

Schaper, David. 2016. "University Of Chicago Tells Freshmen It Does Not Support 'Trigger Warnings.'" *NPR.Org.* August 26.

Scheidel, Walter. 2017. *The Great Leveler: Violence and the History of Inequality from the Stone Age to the Twenty-First Century.* Princeton: Princeton University Press.

Schmitt, John. 2009. "Unions and Upward Mobility for Service-Sector Workers." *Center for Economic and Policy Research.*

Scholz, Trebor. 2016. *Uberworked and Underpaid: How Workers Are Disrupting the Digital Economy.* Cambridge: Polity Press.

Schor, Elana, and Seung Min Kim. 2017. "Christian Groups Oppose Trump's Preference for Christian Refugees." *Politico*, January 29.

Schor, Juliet B., and William Attwood-Charles. 2017. "The 'Sharing' Economy: Labor, Inequality, and Social Connection on for-Profit Platforms." *Sociology Compass* 11 (8): e12493.

Schulmeister, Stephan. 2017. "Stephan Schulmeister über das Regierungsprogramm." *Kontrast.at*, December 21.

Schultheis, Emily. 2017. "President Trump Defends Travel Ban, Saying It's 'Not about Religion.'" *CBS News*. January 29.

Schumpeter, Joseph A. 1942. *Capitalism, Socialism and Democracy*. London: Routledge.

Schwarzenegger, Arnold. 2013. *Total Recall: My Unbelievably True Life Story*. London: Simon & Schuster.

Scott, Dylan. 2017. "House Republican: My Donors Told Me to Pass the Tax Bill 'or Don't Ever Call Me Again.'" *Vox*, November 7.

Shalev, Michael. 1980 "Industrial Relations Theory and the Comparative Study of Industrial Relations and Industrial Conflict." *British Journal of Industrial Relations* 18 (1): 26–43.

Shestakofsky, Benjamin. 2017. "Working Algorithms: Software Automation and the Future of Work." Work and Occupations 44 (4): 376–423.

Simmel, Georg. 1903. *Die Großstädte Und Das Geistesleben*. Dresden: Jahrbuch der Gehe-Stiftung Dresden.

Skocpol, Theda, and Alexander Hertel-Fernandez. 2016. "The Koch Network and Republican Party Extremism." *Perspectives on Politics* 14 (3): 681–99.

Skocpol, Theda, and Vanessa Williamson. 2016. *The Tea Party and the Remaking of Republican Conservatism*. Oxford, New York: Oxford University Press.

Smith, Ben. 2008. "Obama on Small-Town Pa.: Clinging to Religion, Guns, Xenophobia." *Politico*, April 11.

Smith, Gregory A., and Jessica Martinez. 2016. "How the Faithful Voted: A Preliminary 2016 Analysis." *Pew Research Center*. November 9.

Spiegel. 2017. "Griechenland-Gipfel: Athen Wirft Wolfgang Schäuble 'Provokation' Vor." *Spiegel*, June 14.

Stahl, Jeremy. 2016. "Trump: The President Can't Have a Conflict of Interest." *Slate*, November 22.

Storm, Servaas. 2017. "The New Normal." *Institute for New Economic Thinking*. May 19.

Streeck, Wolfgang. 2016. *How Will Capitalism End? Essays on a Failing System.* New York: Verso.

Summers, Dave. 2011. "What The Division Of North And South Sudan Means For Oil Production." *Business Insider*, February 13, 2011.

Tam, Pui-Wing, and Jose A. DelReal. 2018. "California Today: Facebook Under Fire, Yet Again." *New York Times*, March 21.

Tan, Kenneth. 2017. "After Fire Kills 19 in Beijing Shanty Town, Migrant Workers Flee Ahead of Forced Demolitions." *Shanghaiist (blog).* May 5.

Than, Nga. 2018. "'Ausländer Raus!'□: The Unleashing of Populism & Collateral Damage to All Ethnicities." *A Space for Productive Thinking (blog).* June 12.

TODAYonline. 2018. "China to Bar People with Bad 'social Credit' from Planes, Trains." March 16.

United Nations. 2014. "World Urbanization Prospects: The 2014 Revision."

Varoufakis, Yanis. 2013. *The Global Minotaur: America, Europe and the Future of the Global Economy.* New York: Zed Books.

Walkon, Thomas. 2016. "Justin Trudeau's Neo-Liberalism with a Human Face: Walkom." *The Star*, December 19.

WBIDC. 2009. "Industry Specific Review."

Weber, Max. 1978. *Economy and Society.* Edited by Guenther Roth and Claus Wittich. First Edition. Berkeley: University of California Press.

———. 1994. "The Nation State and Economic Policy." In *Weber's Political Writings*, edited by Peter Lassman and Ronald Speirs, 1–28. Cambridge: Cambridge University Press.

Wheeler, Lydia. 2017. "Senate Confirms Second Trump Nominee to Labor Board." *TheHill*, September 25.

Witte, Griff. 2018. "To Stop Viktor Orban, Hungary's Opposition Parties Need to Team up. But Can They?" *The Washington Post*, March 20.

Wittgenstein, Ludwig. 1961. *Tractatus Logico-Philosophicus.* London: Routledge & Kegan Paul.

Wolf, Martin. 2017. "A Republican Tax Plan Built for Plutocrats." *Financial Times*, November 21.

Worland, Justin. 2017. "Scott Pruitt's Mission to Remake the EPA." *Time*, October 26.

Yang, Yuan, and Xinning Liu. 2017. "Beijing Migrant 'Clean-out' Hits China Ecommerce Sector." *Financial Times*, December 2.

York, Geoffrey. 2012. "South Sudan's $4-Billion Query Answered: Oil Revenue Stolen by Corrupt Officials." *The Globe and Mail*, June 5.

Zakaria, Fareed. 1997. "The Rise of Illiberal Democracy." *Foreign Affairs*, November 1.

Zelizer, Viviana A. 1994. *The Social Meaning of Money*. Princeton: Princeton University Press.

Index